Edith Raim
Nazi Crimes against Jews and German Post-War Justice

New Perspectives on Modern Jewish History

Edited by Cornelia Wilhelm

Volume 3

Edith Raim

Nazi Crimes against Jews and German Post-War Justice

—

The West German Judicial System during
Allied Occupation (1945–1949)

ISBN 978-3-11-055401-4
e-ISBN (PDF) 978-3-11-030066-6
e-ISBN (EPUB) 978-3-11-039569-3
ISSN 2192-9645

The e-book of this title is freely available on www.degruyter.com.

Library of Congress Cataloging-in-Publication Data
A CIP catalog record for this book has been applied for at the Library of Congress.

Bibliographic information published by the Deutsche Nationalbibliothek
The Deutsche Nationalbibliothek lists this publication in the Deutsche Nationalbibliografie; detailed bibliographic data are available on the Internet at http://dnb.dnb.de.

© 2017 Walter de Gruyter GmbH, Berlin/Munich/Boston
This volume is text- and page-identical with the hardback published in 2013.
Typesetting: Michael Peschke, Berlin
Printing: CPI books GmbH, Leck

♾ Printed on acid free paper
Printed in Germany

www.degruyter.com

"The past is a foreign country: they do things differently there."
L.P. Hartley, *The Go-Between* (1953)

"The poetry of history lies in the quasi-miraculous fact that once, on this earth, once on this familiar spot of ground, walked other men and women, as actual as we are today, thinking their own thoughts, swayed by their own passions, but now all gone, one generation vanishing into another, gone as utterly as we ourselves shall shortly be gone, like ghosts at cockcrow."
G.M. Trevelyan, *Autobiography of an Historian* (1949)

Foreword

> Sometimes a man seeks what he hath lost; and from that place and time wherein he misses it his mind runs back, from place to place, and time to time, to find where and when he had it, that is to say, to find some certain and limited time and place in which to begin a method of seeking. Again, from thence his thoughts run over the same places and times to find what action or other occasion might make him lose it. This we call 'remembrance,' or calling to mind: the Latins call it reminiscentia, as it were a 're-conning' of our former actions.
>
> Thomas Hobbes, *Leviathan*

Writing in English proved (as expected) a sobering and yet (rather unexpectedly) an exhilarating experience for me. The former because of my admittedly limited linguistic competence, the latter because of the concise and succinct form German scholarship has not always relished. Richard Cobb, eminent British historian of French history, observed about his relationship with the French language: "To speak and to write in French is to acquire a second personality and to express oneself not only in another gear, but in a manner other than in one's first. I do not say the same things in French as I do in English, because I am not the same person."[1] I most wholeheartedly feel the same is true for me when writing in English.

Acquiring a foreign language is a long-winded, complicated and often frustrating process, thus thanks must go to many friends who have been talking with and writing to me in English literally for decades and whose tolerance I have stretched to the limits with my attempts at reciprocation. Nicola Deans and her family in Poole, Rita and Leslie Deans in St. Neots, Marjorie Smith and Audrey Smith in Chester-le-Street have been wonderful friends and fantastically supportive over many years and in many more respects than I can name. Thanks are also in order to the History Department at Princeton University in whose graduate school I spent the globally exciting (academic) year 1989/1990, to the German Department at Durham University in the years 1991 to 1995, and the History Department at Liverpool University 1994–1995, where I taught German and European History. Reminiscing (and even allowing for some nostalgia nearly 20 years later), I still feel tremendous gratitude to both students and colleagues who helped me in so many ways. As is true for many educators: one learns more from one's students than vice versa. It surely was so in my case: I learned English from my students and was introduced to British culture in manifold ways and even acquired a smattering of local dialects such as Geordie and Scouse. Special mention goes to my

---

[1] Richard Cobb, *A Second Identity: Essays on France and French History* (London: Oxford University Press, 1969), 18.

then colleagues Jo Catling, Waltraud Coles at Durham (who sadly died in 2005) and Liz Harvey and Charles Esdaile at Liverpool, whose advice in teaching helped turn my fledgling attempts into something – I hope – acceptable.

Moreover, the wonderful Trevelyan College Senior Common Room at Durham, where faculty from various countries and various disciplines met, added friendships to my life that outlasted my stay in Britain. The Reverend Stephen Ferns, Prof. Inés Sanmiguel, Jill Ramsay, Graham Geary, and Rhys Burriss (who taught me about the English legal system long before I started work on this book) all made my time there a most memorable one. Memories of sightseeing tours with my friends through Northumberland, Cumbria, Yorkshire, and Scotland gladden me to this day.

Research on this book began when I started my work as a researcher at the Institute for Contemporary History in Munich in 1999. While the project involved an enormous amount of travel to archives in Germany, Britain, France, and the USA, the support I received from my Institute has been crucial in every respect. The backing from my colleagues in Munich virtually carried me through all the highs and lows and made up for all the rigor of the archives. Input from archivists in Europe and the United States, but also help from clerical staff, cleaning staff, and security personnel at the archives and state attorneys' offices in Germany, who enabled me to pursue work beyond the regular access hours, turned my project into a labor of love. The first ideas for the book were conceived as part of a panel discussion at the 10th Lessons & Legacies Conference at Northwestern University, Evanston, Illinois, in 2008. There the kind interest of the audience – notably Christopher Browning, David Cesarani, Martin Dean, Jeffrey Herf, Susanna Schrafstetter, and Alan Steinweis – and input from the chair of the panel, Michael Marrus, and co-panelists Mark Roseman and Devin Pendas inspired me to pursue the topic further.

In 1985, as Germany prepared for the commemoration of the 40th anniversary of the end of World War II, I met two people who became very important to me: Col. (ret.) Irving Heymont (1918–2009), who as a young major had been a member of the American occupation forces and first head of the Landsberg Displaced Persons camp, and Toby Axelrod, a journalist who wrote an article on the Kaufering camps of Dachau in the surroundings of my hometown, Landsberg am Lech. Irving Heymont always thought that I ought to write a book in English and trusted that I could do it. So when Prof. Dr. Cornelia Wilhelm (Munich/Atlanta) suggested that I turn my German postdoctoral thesis into a shorter English version, I heartily agreed – relying once again on the kindness of my friend Toby Axelrod to bear the brunt of correcting my English and proofreading. Dr. Julia Brauch (De Gruyter) had been a most helpful and optimistic editor. Marcia Rothschild proved a fantastic copy editor – her thoughtful and sensitive editing significantly improved the final shape of the book. With her thoroughness and dedication, the book reached a clarity and lucidity that I could never have achieved. Finally, Tihomir Vrdoljak excelled at creating an index, proofreading and preparing the manuscript for print. My friends have, over many years, patiently watched the progress (and stagnation) of research on the book. Gerhard Zelger, with whom I had many discussions about the topic, did not live to see the final result as he tragically died in 2011 at age 51. Jürgen Wedemeyer's cheerfulness prodded me along when I bogged down. As always, one owes the greatest debt of gratitude to one's family: My parents, Elisabeth (1928–2012) and Ernst Raim, have supported me in every endeavor I have undertaken in my life. My younger sister Eleonore, attorney at law, explained the basics of German penal law to me when my knowledge on this topic bordered on the non-existent. Needless to say, all errors and mistakes are my own.

Not only in poetry, but also in history, the road one takes has great significance. And yes, Robert Frost got it right: "I took the one less traveled by /And that has made all the difference."

Table of Contents

Foreword —— vii
Introduction —— 1
    Sources and Method —— 7
    Scope and Aim —— 14
    A Note on Translations —— 15
    Notes on German Sources —— 16

Part I: The Reconstruction of the German Judicial System in the Western Zones

The Legal Divisions of the Western Allies —— 21
    The American Legal Division —— 21
    The British Legal Division —— 22
    The French Direction Générale de la Justice —— 22
    Western Allied Politics Concerning the German Judicial System —— 23
    German Courts Branch, German Courts Inspectorate,
    Contrôle de la Justice Allemande —— 26

The Re-opening of German Courts and the German Administration of Justice —— 29
    Re-opening of Courts in the American Zone of Occupation —— 30
    Re-opening of Courts in the British Zone —— 32
    Re-opening of Courts in the French Zone —— 33
    Re-opening of Courts in Berlin, Bremen, and the Saar —— 35
    Re-opening of the Courts of Appeal —— 38
    The Supreme Court in the British Zone —— 40
    The Renascent Ministries of Justice of the Länder —— 41
    The Central Legal Office —— 42

Physical Conditions for the Reconstruction of Courts —— 45
    The Search for Alternative Housing —— 46
    Attempts at Repair —— 48
    Files, Office Supplies, Communication, and Transport —— 51
    Excursus: Living Conditions of Members of the Judiciary —— 54

The German Administration of Justice at Work —— 55
    The Police Force and the Penal System —— 57
    Public Prosecutors and Courts —— 59
    Work Load —— 61
    Allied Criticism —— 62

Denazification and Personnel Politics —— 65
    Personnel Politics in the American Zone —— 66
    Denazification of the Judiciary in the American Zone —— 77
    Personnel Politics in the British Zone —— 85
    Denazification of the Judiciary in the British Zone —— 90
    Personnel Politics in the French Zone —— 100
    Denazification of the Judiciary in the French Zone —— 103
Criticism of the German Administration of Justice —— 108
Summary —— 110

Part II: Legal Foundations for the Prosecution of Nazi Crimes by the West German Judiciary

The Western Allies and the Prosecution of Nazi Crimes —— 115
    German Demands Concerning the Prosecution
    of "Crimes Against Germans" —— 117
    The Implementation of Control Council Law No. 10
    in the British Zone —— 120
    The Implementation of Control Council Law No. 10
    in the French Zone —— 126
    The Discussion Concerning Control Council Law No. 10
    in the American Zone —— 127
    German Jurists and Law No. 10 —— 135
The Phase-out of Allied Trials and Transfer to German Prosecution —— 143
    The American Point of View —— 143
    The British Stance —— 145
    The French Exception —— 149
    Allied Interventions in West German Trials —— 150
Summary —— 150

Part III: The Prosecution of Nazi Crimes Against Jews

The Reconstruction of Nazi Crimes Against Jews —— 157
    Early Excesses 1933 —— 158
    Racial Defilement —— 160
    Excesses 1934–1937 —— 164
    Excesses in 1938, Before November —— 166
    "Aryanization" —— 168

Excesses After November 1938 —— 169
Violent Acts After the Beginning of the War —— 171
Trapped in the "Judenhaus" —— 172
Denunciations —— 174
Bullying of Jewish Forced Laborers and Actions Against Jews in the Second Half of WW II —— 175
The Fate of Jewish Children in Foster Care —— 177
Desecration of Jewish Cemeteries —— 179

The Prosecution of the Pogrom —— 186
Local Peculiarities of the Pogrom —— 186
Property Offenses —— 188
The Ritual of Public Degradation —— 195
Deportations in the Course of the Pogrom —— 206
Perpetrators —— 208
Investigation of Pogrom Crimes During the Third Reich —— 221
First Post-War Trials —— 224
Problems of Investigation and Legal Problems —— 230
Semantics of Sentences —— 246
Adjudicating the Killings —— 249
Case Study: The Trial Concerning the Killing in Würzburg —— 250
Public Reaction to the Trials —— 253
The Balance and Remarks on the Investigation and Trials —— 262

The Prosecution of the Deportations —— 265
Deportation Trials in the French Zone —— 267
Deportation Trials in the American Zone —— 279
Deportation Trials in the British Zone —— 286

Summary and Outlook —— 290

Conclusion —— 302

Appendix —— 311
List of illustrations —— 311
Abbreviations —— 311
Archives —— 313
Bibliography —— 317

Index of Names —— 327

Index of Places —— 329

Introduction

> You are fond of history! –... At this rate, I shall not pity the writers of history any longer. If people like to read their books, it is all very well, but to be at so much trouble in filling great volumes, which, as I used to think, nobody would willingly ever look into, to be labouring only for the torment of little boys and girls, always struck me as a hard fate; and though I know it is all very right and necessary, I have often wondered at the person's courage that could sit down on purpose to do it.
>
> Jane Austen, *Northanger Abbey*, Chapter 14

More than 60 years after the Allied occupation of Germany (1945–1949), historians can safely assume that every stone has been turned and every detail has been scrutinized by decades of research on that period. Although interest in this period has withered somewhat in recent years, one can find scholarly editions of documents and monographs on a multitude of aspects.[1] Is it not the case then, that this span of time has been exhaustively (and thus terminally) explored?

In spite of that impression, there is indeed room for more. A closer look will reveal that there are still some uncharted territories on our mental map of the occupation years. One of them is the reconstruction of an administration of justice system in Western Germany; another is the nascent prosecution of Nazi crimes by West German authorities. While the budding legislature and the executive arm have been covered amply, and minutes of the regional assemblies (Landtage) and cabinet conferences of the *Länder* (provinces) have been elaborately edited, the judiciary has largely been ignored. How the third of Montesquieu's three columns of "checks and balances" could so completely escape historians' notice would probably merit a closer look at the degree to which topics in academic history are subject to fashion.

Even contemporaries stated that no other segment of society had more continually, quietly and unobtrusively performed its reconstruction in the post-war years, as the Freiburg prosecutor general and professor of history of law, Karl Siegfried Bader put it.[2] The Minister of Justice of Lower Saxony, Wilhelm Ellinghaus, knew that 99 percent of all matters of judicature are implemented in silence without anybody taking any notice.[3]

---

[1] For an overview see Wolfgang Benz, ed., *Deutschland unter alliierter Besatzung* 1945–1949/55: Ein Handbuch (Berlin: Akademie Verlag, 1999), 17.
[2] Karl S. Bader, "Rechtspflege und Verfassung: Zur Denkschrift des Zentral-Justizamts für die Britische Zone," in *Deutsche Rechts-Zeitschrift* 1 (1949), 1.
[3] Wilhelm Ellinghaus in the *Lower Saxon Diet*, November 10, 1949, column 4218.

The drawback of this genteel restraint was that historiography cold-shouldered the administration of justice, though Marc Bloch had already noted the affinity between the practices of historians and the examining magistrates. Hence, a look at diverse handbooks yields negative reports. Even in the above-mentioned handbook *Deutschland unter alliierter Besatzung*, edited by Wolfgang Benz (see footnote 1), the keywords *"Justiz"* and *"Justizverwaltung"* (administration of justice) are missing completely; the entry *"Strafrechtliche Verfolgung von NS-Verbrechen"* (prosecution of Nazi crimes) only briefly mentions the West German proceedings of this period, while the Allied trials – the Nuremberg International Military Tribunal, the subsequent American Nuremberg Military Trials, and other military tribunals by the Allies in their respective zones – are dealt with much more extensively. The *Lexikon der Vergangenheitsbewältigung* (*Dictionary of Coming to Terms with the Past*) yields a somewhat similar return, mentioning a high number of (West) German trials in the occupation years without going into further detail.[4] The most magisterial of German history's handbooks, the *Gebhardt*, which claims to be the most important handbook for German history, in which "each generation of historians sums up and reflects the state of German historical research and historiography,"[5] the entry *"Justiz* (Justice)" does not even appear in the subject index of the 9th edition; the resumption of Germany's judicial activities is mentioned in but one sentence;[6] and the 10th edition refers only to the trials against offenders of the pogrom of November 9, 1938,[7] although with a single glance into the – still not sufficiently well-known – first volumes of the edition *Justiz und NS-Verbrechen* (Justice and Nazi Crime),[8] one stands corrected.

Other handbooks bear witness to similarly sloppy and slapdash approaches referring to the legal system.[9] In a variety of accounts of the occupation period or

---

4 Torben Fischer and Matthias N. Lorenz, eds., *Lexikon der "Vergangenheitsbewältigung" in Deutschland: Debatten- und Diskursgeschichte des Nationalsozialismus nach 1945* (Bielefeld: transcript Verlag, 2007), 61-62.
5 Gebhardt, *Handbuch der deutschen Geschichte*, 10th edition, vol 1, x.
6 Karl Dietrich Erdmann, *Das Ende des Reiches und die Entstehung der Republik Österreich, der Bundesrepublik Deutschland und der Deutschen Demokratischen Republik*, 9th ed. (München: Deutscher Taschenbuch Verlag, 1999), 648.
7 Benz, *Deutschland unter alliierter Besatzung 1945–1949*, 110.
8 Christiaan F. Rüter and Adelheid L. Rüter-Ehlermann, *Justiz und NS-Verbrechen: Sammlung deutscher Strafurteile wegen nationalsozialistischer Tötungsverbrechen 1945-1966* (Amsterdam: University Press Amsterdam, 1968).
9 See Adolf M. Birke, *Nation ohne Haus: Deutschland 1945-1961* (Berlin: Siedler, 1989), 78 or Ernst Deuerlein, *Deutschland nach dem Zweiten Weltkrieg 1945–1955* (Konstanz: Akademische Verlagsgesellschaft Athenaion Dr. Albert Hachfeld, 1964), 75; Heinrich Potthoff and Rüdiger Wenzel, *Handbuch politischer Institutionen und Organisationen 1945–1949* (Düsseldorf: Droste Verlag, 1983); similarly fruitless: Walter Vogel, *Westdeutschland 1945–1950: Der Aufbau von Verfassungs-*

German history in the 20th century, a search for references to the issue of justice or the prosecution of Nazi crimes by Germans yields nothing.[10] The last nail in the coffin of preoccupation with the years 1945 to 1949 in West Germany was German unification. After 1990, interest in a scholarly approach to the *Trümmerzeit* (literally: time of debris) faded away as a new field of interest opened up with the access to archives in the former German Democratic Republic (East Germany).

Despite this desert of ignorance, we find small islands of knowledge as some undeterred authors boldly went where no historian had gone before. Hans Wrobel's book deals with justice and legal history in the years 1945 to 1949 in both German states, but relies mainly on published materials such as law gazettes and books.[11] Monographs are available for all Western Zones of occupation. Joachim Reinhold Wenzlau limits his scope to the British Zone, but presents a detailed picture by using a multitude of German sources.[12] The reconstruction of justice in the American Zone of Occupation was covered by Canadian and American

---

und Verwaltungseinrichtungen über den Ländern der drei westlichen Besatzungszonen (Boppard: Boldt, 1977*)*.

10 See Josef Becker, Theo Stammen and Peter Waldmann, *Vorgeschichte der Bundesrepublik Deutschland: Zwischen Kapitulation und Grundgesetz* (München: Fink, 1979); Christoph Klessmann, *Die doppelte Staatsgründung: Deutsche Geschichte 1945-1955* (Göttingen: Vandenhoeck & Ruprecht, 1982); Theodor Eschenburg, *Jahre der Besatzung 1945–1949* (Stuttgart: Deutsche Verlagsanstalt, 1983); Wolfgang Benz, *Von der Besatzungsherrschaft zur Bundesrepublik: Stationen einer Staatsgründung 1946-1949* (Frankfurt am Main: Fischer Taschenbuch Verlag, 1984); Wolfgang Benz., *Die Gründung der Bundesrepublik: Von der Bizone zum souveränen Staat* (München: Deutscher Taschenbuch Verlag, 1999); Heinrich August Winkler, *Der lange Weg nach Westen*, vol. 2 (München: C.H. Beck, 2000); Rolf Steininger, *Deutsche Geschichte: Darstellung und Dokumente in vier Bänden* (Frankfurt am Main: Fischer Taschenbuch Verlag, 2002); Hans-Ulrich Wehler, *Deutsche Gesellschaftsgeschichte*, vol. 4 (München: C.H. Beck, 2003), XVII-XVIII, although Wehler explicitly excludes legal history; Wolfgang Benz, *Potsdam 1945: Besatzungsherrschaft und Neuaufbau im Vier-Zonen-Deutschland* (München: Deutscher Taschenbuch Verlag, 2005); Wolfgang Benz, *Auftrag Demokratie: Die Gründungsgeschichte der Bundesrepublik und die Entstehung der DDR 1945-1949* (Berlin: Metropol Verlag, 2009); also unsatisfactory are the recently published Dierk Hoffmann, *Nachkriegszeit: Deutschland 1945-1949* (Darmstadt: Wissenschaftliche Buchgesellschaft, 2012) and Martin Löhnig, ed., *Zwischenzeit: Rechtsgeschichte der Besatzungsjahre* (Regenstauf: Gietl Verlag, 2011).
11 Hans Wrobel, *Verurteilt zur Demokratie: Justiz und Justizpolitik in Deutschland 1945-1949* (Heidelberg: Decker & Müller, 1989).
12 Joachim Reinhold Wenzlau, *Der Wiederaufbau der Justiz in Nordwestdeutschland 1945 bis 1949* (Königstein: Athenäum, 1979).

authors Andrew Szanajda[13] and Jeffrey Gaab,[14] respectively, both of whom made use of the large body of sources produced by the Office of Military Government, United States (OMGUS) and especially its legal division. The dissertation by Joachim Gross concerns itself – for the first time – with the French lore of sources referring to the German administration of justice and makes extensive use of both German archives and the relevant French archive, the *Archives de l'Occupation Française en Allemagne et en Autriche* (Archives of the French Occupation of Germany and Austria or AOFAA).[15] Michael Stolleis and Bernhard Diestelkamp have written solid overviews.[16]

A study has been published for the Bremen Enclave – the part of the American Zone situated within the British Zone of Occupation.[17] Smaller regional studies covering the administration of justice in the *Land* (province/state) of North Rhine-Westphalia[18] and Rhineland-Palatinate[19] were published for 50-year anniversaries of the creation of these lands. The design of the German three-ti-

---

[13] Andrew Szanajda, *The Restoration of Justice in Hesse, 1945–1949* (PhD diss., McGill University Montreal, 1997); Andrew Szanajda., *The Restoration of Justice in Postwar Hesse, 1945–1949* (Lanham: Lexington Books, 2007).

[14] Jeffery Scott Gaab, *"Zusammenbruch und Wiederaufbau":The Restoration of Justice in Bavaria, 1945-1949* (Stony Brook: State University of New York at Stony Brook, 1992); Jeffery Gaab, *Justice Delayed: The Restoration of Justice in Bavaria under American Occupation 1945-1949* (New York: Peter Lang, 1999).

[15] Joachim Gross, *Die deutsche Justiz unter französischer Besatzung 1945–1949: Der Einfluss der französischen Militärregierung auf die Wiedererrichtung der deutschen Justiz in der französischen Besatzungszone* (Baden-Baden: Nomos, 2007).

[16] Michael Stolleis, "Rechtsordnung und Justizpolitik 1945–1949," in *Europäisches Rechtsdenken in Geschichte und Gegenwart: Festschrift für Helmut Coing zum 70. Geburtstag*, ed. Norbert Horn (München: C.H. Beck, 1982); Bernhard Diestelkamp/Susanne Jung, "Die Justiz in den Westzonen und der frühen Bundesrepublik," *Aus Politik und Zeitgeschichte 13* (1989); Bernhard Diestelkamp, "Die Justiz nach 1945 und ihr Umgang mit der eigenen Vergangenheit," *Justizalltag im Dritten Reich*, ed. Bernhard Diestelkamp and Michael Stolleis (Frankfurt am Main: Fischer Taschenbuch Verlag, 1988).

[17] Walther Richter, *Die Organisation der ordentlichen Gerichte in der Enklave Bremen 1945–1947* (Bremen: Senator für Justiz und Verfassung, 1990).

[18] Wolfgang Heilbronn, "Der Aufbau der nordrhein-westfälischen Justiz in der Zeit von 1945 bis 1948/9," in *50 Jahre Justiz in Nordrhein-Westfalen*, ed. Justizministerium des Landes NRW (Düsseldorf: Justizministerium des Landes NRW, 1996); see also Christiane Hottes, *Zum Aufbau der Justiz in den Oberlandesgerichtsbezirken Düsseldorf, Hamm und Köln in der frühen Nachkriegszeit*, ed. Justizakademie des Landes Nordrhein-Westalen (Recklinghausen: Justizministerium des Landes NRW, 1995).

[19] Paul Warmbrunn, "Wiederaufbau der Justiz nach Kriegsende," in *Beiträge zu 50 Jahren Geschichte des Landes Rheinland-Pfalz*, ed. Heinz-Günther Borck (Koblenz: Verlag der Landesarchivverwaltung Rheinland, 1997); see also Korden, "Wiederaufbau der Justiz im Landgerichtsbezirk Koblenz," *Jahrbuch für westdeutsche Landesgeschichte* 31 (2005).

er-legal system (high courts, district courts, local courts) results in most studies concentrating on the topmost level of courts, i.e. the high courts or courts of appeal. Again, no comprehensive works exist. For Berlin, Friedrich Scholz compiled the history of the Berlin court of appeal (traditionally named Kammergericht).[20] The dissertation of Ernst Reuss covers the legal history of Berlin with special attention given to the local court Berlin-Mitte, penal justice and the legal administration of justice in East Berlin after the split.[21] The former president of the high court of Bamberg grapples with the reconstruction of justice in the local district of the high court.[22] So-called Festschrifts – here publications celebrating the anniversary of the installation of a high court – were brought out by several courts of appeal, most notably Celle, which is bedecked with no less than three books honoring the work of centuries of judicial dealings, in particular the new start after 1945.[23] Other courts also published their own festschrifts.[24] However, some high courts, such as Munich and Nürnberg, sadly lack any festschrift; others content themselves with historical accounts published decades ago. For

---

20 Friedrich Scholz, *Berlin und seine Justiz: Geschichte des Kammergerichtsbezirks 1945-1980* (Berlin: de Gruyter, 1982).
21 Ernst Reuss, *Berliner Justizgeschichte: Eine rechtstatsächliche Untersuchung zum strafrechtlichen Justizalltag in Berlin von 1945-1952, dargestellt anhand der Strafgerichtsbarkeit des Amtsgerichts Berlin-Mitte* (Berlin: Berliner Wissenschaftsverlag, 2000); Ernst Reuss, *Vier Sektoren – eine Justiz: Berliner Justiz in der Nachkriegszeit* (Berliner Wissenschaftsverlag, 2003).
22 Hans Schütz, *Justitia kehrt zurück: Der Aufbau einer rechtsstaatlichen Justiz nach dem Zusammenbruch 1945* (Bamberg: Fränkischer Tag, 1987).
23 *250 Jahre Oberlandesgericht Celle 1711-1961* (Celle: Pohl, 1961); *Festschrift zum 275jährigen Bestehen des Oberlandesgerichts Celle* (Celle: Eigenverlag, 1986); Peter Götz von Olenhusen, ed., *300 Jahre Oberlandesgericht Celle* (Göttingen: Vandenhoeck & Ruprecht, 2011).
24 Michael Meisenberg, ed., *200 Jahre Appellationsgericht/Oberlandesgericht Bamberg: Festschrift* (München: C.H. Beck, 2009); Rudolf Wassermann, ed., *Justiz im Wandel der Zeit: Festschrift des Oberlandesgerichts Braunschweig* (Braunschweig: Joh. Heinr. Meyer, 1989); Edgar Isermann and Michael Schlüter, *Justiz und Anwaltschaft in Braunschweig 1879-2004: 125 Jahre Oberlandesgericht und Rechtsanwaltskammer Braunschweig* (Braunschweig: Joh. Heinr. Meyer, 2004); Heinrich Wiesen, ed., *75 Jahre Oberlandesgericht Düsseldorf: Festschrift* (Köln: Heymanns, 1981); *Rechtspflege zwischen Rhein und Weser: Festschrift zum 150-jährigen Bestehen des Oberlandesgerichts Hamm* (Hamm: Verein für Rechtsgeschichte im Gebiet des Oberlandesgerichts Hamm e.V. in Hamm, 1970), *100 Jahre Oberlandesgericht Frankfurt am Main 1879-1979* (Frankfurt am Main: Eigenverlag, 1979); *175 Jahre Oberlandesgericht Oldenburg. 1814 Oberappellationsgericht; Oberlandesgericht 1989*, Werner Münchbach, *Festschrift 200 Jahre Badisches Oberhofgericht Oberlandesgericht Karlsruhe*; *50 Jahre Oberlandesgericht und Generalstaatsanwaltschaft Koblenz 1996*; *1945–1998. 50 Jahre Schleswig-Holsteinisches Oberlandesgericht in Schleswig*; Eberhard Stilz, ed., *Das Oberlandesgericht Stuttgart: 125 Jahre, 1879-2004* (Villingen-Schwenningen: Neckar-Verlag, 2004); Erhard Zimmer, *Die Geschichte des Oberlandesgerichts in Frankfurt am Main* (Frankfurt am Main: Waldemar Kramer, 1976); Josef Wolffram and Adolf Klein, *Recht und Rechtspflege in den Rheinlanden* (Köln: Wienand, 1969).

example, Hamburg is covered in a – fortunately completely outdated – Festschrift originating in 1939 and edited by the rather notorious Nazi secretary of state in the ministry of justice, Curt Rothenberger.[25]

The personal side of reconstruction and the return of tainted prosecutors and judges to the ranks of the judiciary have attracted the interest of historians to a much greater degree, although methodologically, the theme is highly difficult to grasp because of lack of sources and obfuscation by prejudice. The last *Handbuch der Justizverwaltung* (*Handbook of the Administration of Justice*) – listing no fewer than 14,048 judges and 2,596 prosecutors in the Reich – appeared in 1942, and the first post-war edition of the *Handbuch der Justiz* was published as late as 1953, thus leaving the period in which we are interested completely unexplored. For this reason, historians dealing with the biographies of jurists have often limited themselves to case studies.[26] A more systematic approach can be found in the recently published book by Hubert Rottleuthner, whose guiding interest is in the continuities of the careers of legal personnel. He used an unprecedented plethora of personal data on about 34,000 jurists employed in the judiciary civil service from 1933 to 1964.[27] Biographies[28] and autobiographies[29] of important legal personnel have also been published.

---

25 Curt Rothenberger, ed., *Das Hanseatische Oberlandesgericht: Gedenkschrift zu seinem 60jährigen Bestehen* (Hamburg: Hanseatische Verlagsanstalt, 1939)..

26 See Ingo Müller, *Furchtbare Juristen: Die unbewältigte Vergangenheit unserer Justiz* (München: Kindler Verlag, 1987); Klaus-Detlev Godau-Schüttke, *Ich habe nur dem Recht gedient: Die "Renazifizierung" der schleswig-holsteinischen Justiz nach 1945* (Baden-Baden: Nomos, 1993); Wolfgang Benz, "Die Entnazifizierung der Richter: Justizalltag im Dritten Reich," in *Justizalltag im Dritten Reich*, ed. Bernhard Diestelkamp and Michael Stolleis (Frankfurt am Main: Fischer Taschenbuch Verlag, 1988); Hans-Eckhard Niermann, "Zwischen Amnestie und Anpassung: Die Entnazifizierung der Richter und Staatsanwälte des Oberlandesgerichtsbezirks Hamm 1945 bis 1950," in *50 Jahre Schleswig-Holsteinisches Oberlandesgericht in Schleswig. Aufsätze und Erinnerungen* (Schleswig: Schleswiger Gesellschaft Justiz + Kultur e.V., 1998); Denazification of the judiciary in the Celle high court district is covered by Hinrich Rüping, *Staatsanwälte und Parteigenossen: Haltungen der Justiz zur nationalsozialistischen Vergangenheit zwischen 1945 und 1949 im Bezirk Celle* (Baden-Baden: Nomos, 1994); Björn Carsten Frenzel, *Das Selbstverständnis der Justiz nach 1945: Analyse der Rolle der Justiz unter Berücksichtigung der Reden zur Wiedereröffnung der Bundes- und Oberlandesgerichte* (Frankfurt am Main: Peter Lang, 2003) deals with inauguration ceremonies of high courts to analyze the self-concept of the Administration of Justice.

27 Hubert Rottleuthner, *Karrieren und Kontinuitäten deutscher Justizjuristen vor und nach 1945* (Berlin: Berliner Wissenschafts-Verlag, 2010).

28 Volker Tausch, *Max Güde (1902-1984): Generalbundesanwalt und Rechtspolitiker* (Baden-Baden: Nomos, 2002), Daniel Ihonor, *Herbert Ruscheweyh: Verantwortung in schwierigen Zeiten* (Baden-Baden: Nomos, 2006).

29 Heinz Düx, *Die Beschützer der willigen Vollstrecker: Persönliche Innenansichten der bundesdeutschen Justiz* (Bonn: Pahl-Rugenstein, 2004); Theodor Spitta, *Neuanfang auf Trümmern: Die*

Sources and Method

A monograph based on sources taking into account the full history of the reconstruction of justice in the Western zones is still lacking. There could be manifold reasons for this absence of a central theme in early German post-war history. Among them, the sources themselves may be the most important. The first obvious source for historians interested in this field is the ministries of justice, specifically the archival holdings on these ministries in the relevant state and city archives. Apart from the fact that, due to the federal structure of Germany, one has to deal with about a dozen separate institutions, spot-checks show that records on this period are scarce, bordering on non-existent. Perhaps existing records were lost over time; or perhaps the lack of paper was due to a "clever limitation of written materials"[30] allowing the first minister of justice in North Rhine-Westphalia, Eduard Kremer, to quip that he could stuff his whole ministry into one briefcase.[31] Whatever the reason, historians will not find sufficient material in German archives or with the relevant ministries of justice of the Länder. The problem is further aggravated by the fact that the reconstruction of the German administration of justice began from the bottom, i.e., before the ministries of justice came into being. In the British Zone, the state ministries of justice were not created before the end of 1946, thus a considerable span of time cannot be accounted for altogether. Even the records of the Central Legal Office,[32] which functioned as a veritable ministry of justice for the entire British Zone, have not been used much by historians. Also of interest are the records of the Supreme Court in the British Zone.[33] Although not all of them have been published – protocols from Bremen and Hamburg are missing – minutes of the regional diets also proved to be of little value. While denazification matters and amnesties were amply discussed, men-

---

Tagebücher des Bremer Bürgermeisters Theodor Spitta 1945-1947: Biographische Quellen zu deutschen Geschichte nach 1945, ed. Ursula Büttner and Angelika Voss-Louis (München: Oldenbourg Wissenschaftsverlag, 1992); Karl S. Bader, "Der Wiederaufbau: Tagebuch Juli 1945 bis Juni 1946," in *Gelb-rot-gelbe Regierungsjahre: Badische Politik nach 1945*, ed. Paul Ludwig Weinacht (Sigmaringendorf: Regio, 1988).

30 L. Kewer, "Aus der Geschichte des Oberlandesgerichts Hamm," in *Rechtspflege zwischen Rhein und Weser: Festschrift zum 150-jährigen Bestehen des Oberlandesgerichts Hamm*, ed. Verein für Rechtsgeschichte im Gebiet des Oberlandesgerichts Hamm (Hamm: Verein für Rechtsgeschichte im Gebiet des Oberlandesgerichts Hamm, 1970), 110.

31 Wenzlau, *Wiederaufbau der Justiz*, 257; also cited in Heinrich Wiesen, "Das Oberlandesgericht von 1945 bis zur Gegenwart," in *Fünfundsiebzig Jahres Oberlandesgericht Düsseldorf: Festschrift*, ed. Heinrich Wiesen. (Köln: Heymanns, 1981), 93-94.

32 Bundesarchiv Koblenz (BAK), Z 21; selection of copies also in archives of the IfZ, Fg 17/1-22.

33 BAK, Z 38.

tions of legal cases are few and far between. Since it is a parliamentary principle not to interfere with open court cases, only a few spectacular ones were recorded.

When it was clear that a reconstruction of the German judicial service would be impossible using records issued by the original authorities, this author decided to turn to the far more complete record of the Western Allies. To her utter amazement it was easier to follow the paper trail of the Western Allies in their descriptions of the German administration of justice in Aix-la-Chapelle, Brunswick, Cologne, Mayence, Neuville, Deux-Ponts, or Trèves, than the output of German judicial services in Aachen, Braunschweig, Köln, Mainz, Neustadt, Zweibrücken, or Trier. The American, British, French and German voices that can be heard in these sources add up to a complex choir of perspectives reflecting the international atmosphere of the occupation period. For the American Zone I used both the central files of Legal Division, OMGUS[34] and Legal Division, and in particular the German courts branch in the states of Bremen, Bayern, Hesse and Württemberg-Baden (OMGBR, OMGBY, OMGH, and OMGWB).[35]

A large collection of records concerning the legal system in the British Zone, the Legal Division, and the German Courts Inspectorate was available in the record group "Foreign Office" (FO) in the National Archives (TNA)[36] in Kew.

Analogous to the Legal Division in the American and British Zones was a *Division de la Justice* in the *Archives de l'Occupation Française en Allemagne et en Autriche*.[37] Like the American Legal Division, it is divided into a central level for the zone (direction) and a separate level for each of the four states (provinces): (southern) Baden, the Palatinate, (southern) Rhineland and Württemberg. Most of the American, British and French sources on the German legal system were barely used by previous researchers.

Is there not a danger in relying more or less solely on the records of the Western Allies? Does one not fall into the trap of perpetuating history as the propaganda

---

34 Legal Division, OMGUS, Record Group (RG) 260, Box 1-152, National Archives and Records Administration, College Park, Maryland, USA (NARA).

35 For further guidance see the excellent *OMGUS-Handbuch*, Christoph Weisz, ed., *OMGUS-Handbuch: Die amerikanische Militärregierung in Deutschland 1945-1949* (München: Oldenbourg Wissenschaftsverlag, 1994).

36 Mainly Foreign Office (FO) 1049; 1050; 1060, National Archives (TNA), formerly Public Record Office, Kew, United Kingdom. For further information see the excellent inventory in 11 volumes, here in particular vol. 6: Adolf M. Birke, Almut Bues and Ulrike Jordan, eds., *Akten der britischen Militärregierung in Deutschland: Sachinventar 1945-1955* (München: K.G. Saur, 1993).

37 Record Group Affaires Judiciaires, "Division de la Justice: Contrôle de la Justice Allemande – Direction" and Record Group "Division de la Justice: Contrôle de la Justice Allemande – Provinces" (for Baden, Palatinate, Rhineland and Württemberg), Archives de l'Occupation Française en Allemagne et en Autriche (AOFAA), Colmar, France.

of the victors? Unfortunately, here historians are caught between a rock and a hard place because the fund of available primary sources is so small. However, in all of the Western Allies' records concerning the German administration of justice, we also find the German records, letters by petitioners, correspondence between German institutions and the Western Allies' military governments, statistics and reports of German courts and prosecutors addressed to the Allied legal divisions that are sorely missed in the nascent German administrations of justice. In any case, the records of the Allies also hold original German materials that no longer exist in German archives. For the perspective of German legal personnel I used the relevant articles of legal gazettes.[38] Historians often rely on newspapers as sources. I have refrained from doing so for a multitude of reasons. A complete analysis of press would entail looking at no fewer than 169 licensed newspapers (20 in West Berlin, 71 in the British Zone, 58 in the American Zone and 20 in the French Zone)[39] published from 1945 to 1949, and the complete number of periodicals is not even known.[40] Even if one limited oneself to only delving into a representative part of press production (or broadcasting services!), the number would go far beyond the scope of this study. Thus, I opted for using the selected clippings contained in the records of trials (collected by the press staff at the state prosecutors' offices). It can be safely assumed from a cursory look at some newspapers, that only a few spectacular cases received comment in the media and that the vast majority of all early trials concerning Nazi crimes went more or less unremarked on by journalists, or were only briefly noted in local newspapers.

A further epistemic value of newspapers would, in my eyes, be narrow. As is known, the licensed press was controlled by the occupation authorities; permission to publish a newspaper could be withdrawn so that one can assume there was either a deliberate or an inadvertent disciplining of journalists.[41] The licensed publishers and editors enjoyed the trust and confidence of the Military Government and were more likely to share the same opinions than were the majority of

---

38 The main gazettes were *Süddeutsche Juristen-Zeitung* (SJZ; published from April 1946 on), *Deutsche Rechts-Zeitschrift* (DRZ; since July 1946), *Monatsschrift für deutsches Recht* (MDR; since April 1947), *Juristische Rundschau* (JR; since July 1947) and *Neue juristische Wochenschrift* (NJW; since October 1947). The *Deutsche Richterzeitung* was re-founded in 1950 and was thus not consulted; ditto *Neue Justiz* (NJ), which was published in the Soviet Zone. The *Zeitschrift für die gesamte Strafrechtswissenschaft* (ZStW) appeared in a last issue of 1942/1944 and not again until 1951, and is thus also not included this study.
39 Harold Hurwitz, "Die Pressepolitik der Alliierten," in *Deutsche Presse seit 1945*, ed. Harry Pross (Bern: Scherz, 1965), 35.
40 Ingrid Laurien, *Politisch-kulturelle Zeitschriften in den Westzonen 1945–1949: Ein Beitrag zur politischen Kultur der Nachkriegszeit* (Frankfurt am Main: Peter Lang, 1991), 5.
41 Ibid., 36-41.

German editors in the Western Zones. Pre- and post-censorship differed from zone to zone and became more relaxed during the occupation, making it cumbersome to reconstruct.[42] Several newspapers and magazines of record today did not yet exist. The *Spiegel* came into being in January 1947 and the *Frankfurter Allgemeine Zeitung* issued its first edition in November 1949. The shortage of paper limited print runs and newspapers were prevented from gaining a supra-regional sphere of influence. Due to licensing, they could only be distributed within a narrowly defined territory and importation of press products from abroad (and even other zones) was forbidden.

While the prosecution of National Socialist crimes in West Germany in the 1950s and 1960s has been researched in detail,[43] the years of 1945 to 1949 have not been re-scrutinized since the trailblazing article by Martin Broszat.[44] Henry Friedlander refers to the early efforts as does Devin Pendas (who is mainly concerned with the British Zone).[45] Annette Weinke's study has the advantage of comparing the parallel developments in both German states, but does not cover the occupation period.[46] Kerstin Freudiger's book only refers to some verdicts of the years 1945 to 1949.[47]

---

[42] Dieter Felbick, *Schlagwörter der Nachkriegszeit 1945–1949* (Berlin: de Gruyter, 2003), 77.

[43] Michael Greve, *Der justitielle und rechtspolitische Umgang mit den NS-Gewaltverbrechen in den sechziger Jahren* (Frankfurt am Main: Peter Lang, 2001); Marc von Miquel, *Ahnden oder amnestieren?: Westdeutsche Justiz und Vergangenheitspolitik in den sechziger Jahren* (Göttingen: Wallstein Verlag, 2004); Norbert Frei, *Vergangenheitspolitik: Die Anfänge der Bundesrepublik und die NS-Vergangenheit* (München: C.H. Beck, 1996); Andreas Eichmüller, *Keine Generalamnestie: Die strafrechtliche Verfolgung von NS-Verbrechen in der frühen Bundesrepublik* (München: Oldenbourg Wissenschaftsverlag, 2012).

[44] Martin Broszat, "Siegerjustiz oder strafrechtliche 'Selbstreinigung': Aspekte der Vergangenheitsbewältigung der deutschen Justiz während der Besatzungszeit 1945-1949," *Vierteljahrshefte für Zeitgeschichte* 29 (1981).

[45] Henry Friedlander, "The Judiciary and Nazi Crimes in Postwar Germany," *Simon Wiesenthal Center Annual* 1 (1984); Devin Pendas, "Retroactive Law and Proactive Justice: Debating Crimes against Humanity in Germany, 1945-1950," *Central European History* 43 (2010).

[46] Annette Weinke, *Die Verfolgung von NS-Tätern im geteilten Deutschland: Vergangenheitsbewältigung 1949-1969 oder: Eine deutsch-deutsche Beziehungsgeschichte im Kalten Krieg* (Paderborn: Ferdinand Schöningh Verlag, 2002).

[47] Kerstin Freudiger, *Die juristische Aufarbeitung von NS-Verbrechen* (Tübingen: Mohr Siebeck, 2002).

On a regional level, the endeavors of several prosecuting agencies such as Hamburg;[48] courts such as Düsseldorf[49] and Aurich;[50] high court districts such as Oldenburg;[51] or federal Länder such as Hesse,[52] North Rhine-Westphalia[53] and Schleswig-Holstein[54] have been discussed. Their perception is clearly based on a territorial organizing principle, while I opt for a chronological and thematical approach. The prosecution of certain crimes, especially after the creation of the Central Agency Ludwigsburg (responsible for the investigation of Nazi crimes before handing them over to the responsible prosecutors at the district courts in various *Länder)* fell to specific agencies based on an organizing principle that remains relevant in the German legal system today: The public prosecutor responsible for the investigation is determined by the jurisdiction in which the deed was committed – the *Tatortprinzip* (scene of the crime principle) – or by the jurisdiction where the main defendant lives – the *Wohnortprinzip* (residence principle). Because the majority of Nazi crimes investigated in the last 50 years concern atrocities committed outside the German Reich, one falls back on the *Wohnortprinzip* – which, in a way, was quite arbitrary. Thus certain prosecutors' offices dealt with certain crimes more or less because certain alleged Nazi perpetrators had chosen to live in a particular district.

The decentralized investigation of National Socialist crimes before 1958 (the creation of the Central Agency Ludwigsburg) added to the impediments to research on prosecutions prior to the founding of the Federal Republic of Germany. During

---

48 Helge Grabitz, *Täter und Gehilfen des Endlösungswahns: Hamburger Verfahren wegen NS-Gewaltverbrechen 1946-1996*, ed. Justizbehörde Hamburg (Hamburg: Ereignisse Verlag, 2011).
49 Volker Zimmermann, *NS-Täter vor Gericht*: Düsseldorf und die Strafprozesse wegen nationalsozialistischer Gewaltverbrechen (Frankfurt am Main: Waldemar Kramer, 1976).
50 Peter Bahlmann, *Verbrechen gegen die Menschlichkeit?* (PhD diss.: University of Oldenburg, 2008). The dissertation deals with 42 trials of Aurich district court in the years 1945–1955.
51 Walter Müller, "Die Verfolgung von NS-Strafsachen im OLG-Bezirk Oldenburg," in *175 Jahre Oberlandesgericht Oldenburg: 1814 Oberappelationsgericht, Oberlandesgericht 1989: Festschrift* (Köln: Heymanns, 1989).
52 Friedrich Hoffmann, *Die Verfolgung der nationalsozialistischen Gewaltverbrechen in Hessen* (Baden-Baden: Nomos, 2001); Regina Maier, *NS-Kriminalität vor Gericht: Strafverfahren vor den Landgerichten Marburg und Kassel 1945-1955* (Darmstadt: Hessische Historische Kommission Darmstadt, 2009).
53 Heinz Boberach, "Die Verfolgung von Verbrechen gegen die Menschlichkeit durch deutsche Gerichte in Nordrhein-Westfalen 1946 bis 1949," in *Themen juristischer Zeitgeschichte: Schwerpunktthema: Recht und Nationalsozialismus*, ed. Franz Josef Düwell and Thomas Vormbaum (Baden-Baden: Nomos, 1998).
54 Mandy Jakobczyk, "'Das Verfahren ist einzustellen': Staatsanwaltschaftliche Ermittlungsverfahren wegen nationalsozialistischer Gewaltverbrechen in Schleswig-Holstein bis 1965: Überblick auf der Bases eines empirisch-quantifizierenden Ansatzes," in *Demokratische Geschichte* 15 (2003).

the occupation period, all existing state prosecutors and courts in the Western zones – the number runs up to about 100 – were concerned with investigation of Nazi crimes. Those files are now located in more than 30 state archives, but isolated cases are still with the state attorneys. Quite frequently, files became so voluminous or were transferred so often between various authorities – police agencies, state prosecutors, coroners, courts, courts of appeal, etc. – that they got out of control, as official jargon would euphemistically put it. In plain language, parts of trial records, or even records of entire trials, were lost to the point that they are no longer discernable. Still, the volume of files is well beyond the work capacities of most historians (and, as the author is happy to admit, her own as well). In 1960, various administrations of justice of the Länder had been asked to compile lists of all criminal proceedings they had held against Nazi criminals. The nearly unanimous response was that this enterprise was doomed and completely inexecutable.

However, thanks to the insistence of the newly founded Ludwigsburg Central Agency of the Länder (regional) Administrations of Justice for the Investigation of National Socialist Crimes, lists of criminal proceedings were compiled. These lists (transferred into a database) formed the basic body of information for further research in the archives of state prosecutors and courts. The database developed at the Institute for Contemporary History not only lists all relevant criminal proceedings, but also provides a plethora of additional information.[55] A statistical overview of the database has already been published by Andreas Eichmüller.[56]

The well-proven strategy of *de l'audace, et encore de l'audace, et toujours de l'audace* (literally, audacity, and again audacity, and always audacity) in the face of overwhelming odds and adverse conditions kept me going. Fortunately, I had no idea at the outset just how much audacity I would need to master the mountains of files. Many of the records I would review had not been viewed since they were deposited in the archives; others had been lying untouched for decades in the cellars and attics of state prosecutors' offices. While it is true that there are overwhelming numbers of sources, it is also true that a huge number of files have been lost. If investigations were inconclusive (e.g., the defendant had died or could not be traced, or the evidence was not sufficient), the case would not have gone to trial. In those instances, disregard by state attorneys who could not have cared less about a case that had been closed, and archivists who saw the case as

---

55 *Die Verfolgung von NS-Verbrechen durch deutsche Justizbehörden seit 1945. Datenbank aller Strafverfahren und Inventar der Verfahrensakten*, comp. Andreas Eichmüller and Edith Raim on behalf of the Institute for Contemporary History Munich – Berlin.
56 Andreas Eichmüller, "Die Strafverfolgung von NS-Verbrechen durch westdeutsche Justizbehörden seit 1945 – Eine Zahlenbilanz" *Vierteljahrshefte für Zeitgeschichte* 56 (2008).

insignificant because evidently it had not been important enough to end in a trial, combined with practical constraints (lack of space, etc.) led to various house cleanings over the years. The result was a great and irretrievable loss of records for the fields of law and history. These gaps particularly occur during the years of occupation, first because of the considerable span of time that has since passed – which inevitably brings about a loss of written records – but also because of a certain disdain for the period of the Allied occupation itself, which was viewed as a time of deprivation and lack of freedom.

Completeness cannot be achieved as in many cases files both of abandoned investigations and of trials were destroyed after a certain amount of time had passed.[57] Fortunately, other state prosecutors had a more sensible approach to preserving files, so that the documentation for some agencies is, in fact, nearly complete, enabling an almost full reconstruction of the investigation effort.

It should be noted that the initial conditions on site varied, and thereby substantially influenced the outcome. If Gestapo (the Nazi secret police) files or court registers and records of special courts had survived eradication at the end of the war, the search for informers was much easier and more often successful than in locations where these files had been completely destroyed – either deliberately or by air-raids. Thus in many cases historians have to create order out of chaos.

As this book concentrates on penal justice, I will not deal with the reconstruction of labor, financial, social, or administrative courts, nor will I get into the Federal Supreme Court or Federal Constitutional Court. For reasons of simplicity I use current terms rather than historical names: Greater Hesse is always referred to as Hesse, and I do not differentiate (unless specifically necessary) between Rhineland-Hesse-Nassau, Middlerhine-Saar, Hesse-Palatinate, but rather refer to them as Rhineland-Palatinate; the provinces of Hannover, North Rhine, Westphalia, and the Länder Braunschweig (Brunswick), Lippe-Detmold, Schaumburg-Lippe, and Oldenburg are subsumed under their current territorial names of Lower Saxony and North Rhine-Westphalia.

The state attorney at the high court is referred to as prosecutor general even though the legal term is *Staatsanwaltschaft beim Oberlandesgericht* (state prosecutor at the court of appeal); the heads of the high courts are not referred to by their former name, *Chefpräsidenten* (Chief Presidents), but simply as presidents of high courts. I distinguish simply between *Beschuldigten* (suspects) and

---

57 Andreas Eichmüller, "Die Datenbank des Instituts für Zeitgeschichte München – Berlin zu allen westdeutschen Strafverfahren wegen NS-Verbrechen," in *Vom Recht zur Geschichte: Akten aus NS-Prozessen als Quellen der Zeitgeschichte*, ed. Jürgen Finger, Sven Keller and Andreas Wirsching (Göttingen: Vandenhoeck & Ruprecht, 2009), 234, with examples of bad practice referring to the destruction of files in Duisburg, Hamburg and Bochum.

Angeklagten (defendants) but don't go into further differentiation with the *Angeschuldigter*, i.e., a suspect who is being investigated by a coroner after the initiation of the coroner's inquest. For regional allocations I use the then current high court and district court territories. In general, I have not indicated the frequent changes of names for the legal divisions of the Western Allies (e.g., from "Legal Division" to "zonal officer of the legal adviser"), although when quoting from correspondence, I give the current name of the institution. I have not adjusted location names (written sometimes in German, sometimes in English, both using English characters, e.g., Nuremberg, Brunswick, etc.), but have left them as given in the original letter. For a better distinction I refer to the Bavarian Military Government as OMGBY, although the abbreviation OMGB is more common in the files. References to literature are always given in an abbreviated version; the full information is found in the bibliography.

Scope and Aim

The book is divided into three sections. The first is an account of the reconstruction of the German system for the administration of justice in the Western Zones. Due to the collapse of the Reich with its breakdown of political, social, economic, and cultural structures this is, in some respect, also a social history of the renascent judicial system.

The second part deals with the general conditions of the prosecution of Nazi crimes by the judiciary of the Western zones in the years 1945–1949. The term "Western zones" specifically rules out the inclusion of those parts that would later belong to the Federal Republic of Germany, but were not part of the Western zones, namely Berlin and the Saar region. Berlin had been split into four sectors and was governed directly by the four Allies. Even the German administration of justice was directly subordinated to the Allied Command.[58] Nevertheless, all West German investigations and trials that took place in this period, including those from West Berlin and the Saar, are included in the statistics. To give an idea of the dimension of investigations and trials we are dealing with, let me mention that more than 13,000 proceedings were initiated in this period (though, as has been explained above, by no means are all of them extant). Seventy percent of all con-

---

[58] See Andreas Eichmüller, "'Es ist ganz unmöglich, diese Milde zu vertreten': Die strafrechtliche Verfolgung von NS-Verbrechen im Saarland 1945-1955," in *Last aus tausend Jahren: NS-Vergangenheit und demokratischer Aufbruch im Saarstaat*, ed. Ludwig Linsmayer (Saarbrücken: Saarland Landesarchiv, 2013).

victions concerning National Socialist crimes in West Germany took place during this span of time.

The third segment concerns one of the most salient questions: How did the German judiciary deal with crimes committed against (German) Jews? In this section I show how the German judiciary investigated crimes (most of which are completely forgotten nowadays, but will assuredly further our research into the Third Reich), how crimes that occurred during the pogrom were dealt with, and how deportation crimes were treated by the German courts.

A Note on Translations

In the occupation period, the West German legal system consisted of three tiers: *Amtsgerichte* (which I have translated as local courts), *Landgerichte* (district courts) and *Oberlandesgerichte* (high courts). Only in the British Zone did a Supreme Court exist. A court is usually headed by a president (*Amtsgerichtspräsident, Landgerichtspräsident,* or *Oberlandesgerichtspräsident*); the chambers of the court are headed by directors (*Amtsgerichtsdirektor* or *Landgerichtsdirektor*) or presidents (*Senatspräsident* – president of the senate at the high court). The organization of the state attorneys is similar: An *Amtsanwalt* worked at the *Amtsgericht* (prosecutor at a local court), a *Staatsanwalt* at a district court. The *Generalstaatsanwalt* (prosecutor general) is affiliated with the high courts. *Erster Staatsanwalt* and Oberstaatsanwalt are titles for state prosecutors.

Titles of Nazi organizations and party ranks are mindboggling affairs for translators. Wherever possible, English equivalents have been used. I have tried to keep things simple because sometimes the exact rank of a suspect in the Nazi Party hierarchy either could not be established beyond doubt (perpetrators used to deny their position and often claimed to have been appointed provisionally) or proved to be of little consequence for the judicial treatment of the case. Among the *Ortsgruppenleiter* (local Nazi Party chiefs), *Kreisleiter* supervised those at a *Kreis* (county) level, and *Gauleiters* headed entire regions. For storm troopers or SS men I give the closest equivalents to German ranks in order to maintain American English. Penal affairs in this book fall mainly into one of two categories: investigations that end with a closing of the proceedings usually for lack of proof or death of the suspect and trials with the usual sequence of indictment, main hearing and verdict, plus possibly an appeal to a higher court and a renewed trial at a lower court. In some cases, preliminary hearings were held, which meant that after initial investigations and a possible subsequent indictment, inquiries were conducted by a coroner rather than by a prosecutor. The advantage here was that testimonies of suspects or witnesses could be more easily introduced at a subsequent main hearing before the court, since evidence had already been given before a judge. As far as penalties are concerned, a custodial sentence was either confinement in a prison, or in a penitentiary (*Zuchthaus* – a harsher form of imprisonment reserved for graver crimes). With the reform of German criminal law in the 1960s and 1970s, *Zuchthaus* sentences were abolished. Even at the risk of slight inaccuracy, I have tried to keep things simple, which might disappoint readers with a legal background but will hopefully entice those who are less familiar with legalese. For reasons of uniformity I use the German place names for the state prosecutors (i.e. Nürnberg-Fürth rather than Nuremberg, Regensburg rather than Ratisbon, Braunschweig rather than Brunswick). Quotes from American or English sources are unaffected by this.

Notes on German Sources

Investigations generated by German prosecutors received file references consisting of a number (signifying the responsible department within the prosecution authority), the letters *Js* (signifying inquiry), a consecutive number, a slash, and the year in which they were generated. For example, the reference *Hamburg 14 Js 573/47 (formerly Hamburg 14 Js 85/46)* provides the reader with information on both the place (Hamburg) and the year(s) in which the investigation had been initiated (/47), and points to the fact that an earlier investigation had existed (/46). Sometimes investigations were transferred from one state attorney to another (for competent jurisdiction) or received new file references (this can also be gleaned from the files themselves and from my footnotes). As soon as prosecutors turned an investigation over to the courts, new file references are used, once again pointing to the cognizant chamber at the court and the year legal proceedings were instituted (*Ds, Ls, Ms*, etc., at local courts; *KLs, KMs, Ks* at district courts). Again, this is mentioned in the footnotes. Most of the files are now with the corresponding state archives; in this case I give the archival call number as well. A reference given as "AG Lichtenfels Ds 82/46; Ds 216/46; later Coburg 2 Js 546/47 = KMs 5/47 a,b, KMs 5ab/47, StA Coburg, StAnw Coburg Nr. 142" informs the reader that in 1946 there were two trials initiated at local court Lichtenfels (or at least two proceedings with different reference numbers that might have merged into one main hearing), and that the trials – due to an appeal – were transferred to the cognizant district court in Coburg, where investigations and trial(s) were initiated in 1947. The files are now to be found with the Coburg state archive under the archival call slip "Staatsanwaltschaften Nr. 142." References to the district court or the public prosecutor give some indication as to the vicinity in which the crime took place – which in the vast majority of cases was within the district of the particular court where the crime was tried.

Where I relied on the database alone and have not consulted the original files in the archives, I simply use the record tokens given by the courts and/or state attorneys. For newspapers, I usually give the title of an article and the date on which it was published. As newspapers of that time were not voluminous affairs, readers wishing to consult the original source should be able to locate articles fairly quickly. For the minutes of the regional diets, the name of the member of parliament and the date will suffice as a finding aid.

Office of Military Government files are quoted by shipment, box and folder and are separated by a slash (e.g. OMGUS 17/201-2/2), British Foreign Office material by division and folder (e.g. FO 1060/1033), and records from the French Occupation Archive by division (Affaires Judiciaires), file bundle (paquet) and folder (dossier) (e.g. AJ 805, p. 605, dossier 17).

Part I: The Reconstruction of the German Judicial System in the Western Zones

The Legal Divisions of the Western Allies

> History is that certainty produced at the point
> where the imperfections of memory
> meet the inadequacies of documentation.
>
> Julian Barnes, *The Sense of an Ending*

It had become obvious to the three Western Allies during the war that following the surrender, the military governments would have to take care not only of the occupation as such, but of the existing German legal system, with its courts and prisons, as well. Existing German institutions – such as the Reich Ministry of Justice – were considered improper tools.[1]

The American Legal Division

Beginning in September 1945, the United States Group Control Council was known as the Office of Military Government, US (OMGUS). In 1944/1945, the American legal division comprised five offices: Director, Legal Advice Branch, Justice Ministry Branch, Judicial Branch, and Prisons Branch. The directors of the Legal Division were Charles Fahy in 1945/1946, Alvin J. Rockwell from 1946 to 1948, and finally John M. Raymond.

Very broadly defined, the American Legal Division initially had four tasks:
1. To completely eliminate Nazi ideology in the German administration of justice and the legal system
2. To reorganize and denazify the former Reich Ministry of Justice, the patent office and all subordinated institutions of the Reich Ministry of Justice
3. To punish war criminals as well as delinquents transgressing against occupation rules
4. To create and implement military government laws.[2]

By 1949, its tasks read as follows:
1. "The establishment and perpetuation of a German system of justice which accords with the principles of democracy, due process of law, justice under

---

[1] Handbook for Military Government in Germany Prior to Defeat or Surrender, NARA, OMGUS 11/3 – 1/24.
[2] Organization of Legal Division, OMGUS, NARA, OMGUS 17/251 – 1/15; see also NARA, OMGUS 17/199 – 1/20.

law, and equal rights for all persons without distinction by reason of race, nationality, political belief or religion"[3]
2. The prevention of any revival of Nazi ideology
3. The implementation of principles stemming from Control Council (CC) Law No. 10 and military government laws
4. "To educate the legal profession, the public, and governmental officials as to the fundamentals of the legal systems of democratic countries as contrasted with the systems of totalitarian countries."[4]

The Legal Division (OMGUS) had its counterparts on the regional level. Military governments in Bavaria (OMGBY), Hesse (OMGH), Württemberg-Baden (OMGWB) and Bremen (OMGBR) had legal branches that dealt with the German legal system in the American Zone.

The British Legal Division

Scholars have characterized the structure of British Military Government in Germany as highly complex. The Control Commission for Germany (British Element) (CCG/BE) was set up in November 1943. In August 1945, the responsibilities were transferred from the war and foreign offices to a separate ministry responsible for Germany and Austria (Ministry for the Affairs for the Control of Germany and Austria). The advanced headquarters (the central headquarters) was located in Berlin, with the main headquarters and smaller offices (Zonal Executive Control Offices) located in several small towns in Eastern Westphalia. The Legal Division, headed by Colonel John Frances Warre Rathbone (1909–1995), had its headquarters in Herford, a small town in Westphalia.[5] The size of the British Control Commission was impressive. In October 1946, the British contingent employed about 26,000 people,[6] prompting calls for cuts in staffing and improvements in efficiency.

Similar to those of its American counterpart, the British legal division's tasks included control of the military government courts (Control Commission Courts); the German justice administration, prisons and internment camps; drafting of laws and decrees; and advising their respective military governments.

---

[3] This refers directly to the Agreement of Potsdam.
[4] Policy statements, [undated, after January 10, 1949], NARA, OMGUS 17/215 – 2/20.
[5] Information on John Rathbone courtesy of his niece, Ms. Marilyn Crawford, London.
[6] Benz, *Deutschland unter alliierter Besatzung 1945–1949/55*, 239.

The French Direction Générale de la Justice

The French had been latecomers among the occupying powers of Germany; furthermore, they had not been present at the conference in Potsdam. They would compensate for this by establishing a formidable administration. The military government for the French Zone (Gouvernement Militaire de la Zone Française d'Occupation) was located in Baden-Baden. Its General Directorate for Justice (Direction Générale de la Justice) was headed by Charles Furby until the end of 1947, and then by Henri Lebègue. Its sphere of influence comprised four provinces of the French Zone of Occupation: southern Baden, Württemberg-Hohenzollern, Palatinate, and the southern Rhineland. Each regional directorate had a German justice section responsible for the functioning of the German courts, the supervision of the German higher judicial officials (state attorneys, judges, solicitors, and notaries), questions of German law and the protection of Allied interests.[7]

Western Allied Politics Concerning the German Judicial System

Military Government Law No. 2 gave the occupiers wide-ranging authority over the German administration of justice. Supervision and control over trials, unlimited access to files and registers; review and cassation or alteration of sentences and decisions; removal of higher judicial officials from office; and general supervision of staff, budget and administration, including the possibility of transferring trials to military courts if the interests of the occupying powers were involved.

Control over the German judicial system was an ambivalent task for the Western Allies. After the disastrous German judiciary of the Third Reich, only continuous supervision could smooth the path back to a state governed by the rule of law. On the other hand, the goal – to foster a functioning legal system in German hands – entailed that the Allies respect the independence of justice, thus intervening as little as possible. The Americans boiled it down to the brief formula of maximum surveillance with minimal intervention.[8]

The British called it a "policy of indirect control," under which supervision would only affect the level of the courts of appeal.[9] They were also fully aware of

---

[7] Letter Section de la Justice to Délégué Supérieur, Wurtemberg, December 27, 1945, AOFAA, AJ 805, p. 605, Dossier 17.
[8] Military Government (US) Directive [undated], see under TNA, FO 1060/977.
[9] Letter of J.F.W. Rathbone, Legal Division, CCG (BE), Lübbecke to Chief, Legal Division, Advanced HQ, Berlin, April 4, 1946, TNA, FO 1060/1033; letter also in NARA, OMGBR 6/62 – 1/26.

the historic dimensions of this task, noting that "any form of control of a modern legal system by foreigners is unprecedented."[10]

All Western legal divisions altered their initially rigid control to a softer system of supervision, guidance and regular inspections. From early on, the Americans intended to gradually grant the German legal administration more responsibility and subsequently to reduce control. Any interventions were limited to a sensible degree.[11] This objective was also clearly expressed in the policy statements of the German justice administration: "The independence of the judicial and legal administration will be fostered by allowing the courts freedom in their interpretation and application of the law and by limiting the regulatory measures of military government to the minimum consistent with the accomplishment of the objectives of the occupation."[12] Similarly, it read,

> It is the policy of Military Government to establish and maintain the independence of the German judiciary. In conformity with that policy, supervision by Military Government will be confined to the minimum consistent with the protection of the occupying force and the accomplishment of the aims of the occupation.[13]

The tasks were clearly defined: "Hold Germans responsible to administer justice between themselves, provided there is no interference with Military Government objectives."[14]

Nevertheless, the American occupying power felt it necessary to check all appointments or re-appointments within the German justice administration to ensure that each staff member had the necessary qualifications as well as a positive attitude towards democracy, were loyal to the Military Government and respected the reserved areas of law of the occupying powers. As the American Legal Division would soon discover, supervision of all courts was a tall order. In the American Zone alone, there were a staggering 285 local courts and 38 district courts for which "continuous supervision ... [would] continue to be exercised through systematic field trips and by analysis of reports."[15] The British Legal Division was facing a similarly overwhelming volume of 229 local courts, 29 district courts, five re-opened courts of appeal (which would soon swell to the original

---

[10] Planning Instruction "Control of German Ordinary Courts," February 13, 1945, TNA, FO 1060/951.
[11] Letter of Ltn. Col. G.H. Garde, Legal Division, OMGUS to OMGBY, OMGH, OMGWB, OMGBR and Berlin Sector, November 27, 1946, NARA, OMGBR 6/62 – 1/49.
[12] Policy statements [undated, after January 10, 1949], NARA, OMGUS 17/215 – 2/20.
[13] Plan for the Supervision of German ordinary courts [undated], NARA, OMGUS 17/217 – 3/3.
[14] Legal Division General Procedure [undated], NARA, OMGBR 6/63 – 1/34.
[15] Administration of Justice Branch [undated report of activities], NARA, OMGUS 17/199-1/20.

pre-occupation number of eight, 35 district courts, and 371 local courts).[16] The French had to deal with a more modest number of courts, but had to establish new high courts.

The American Military Government called for moderate control. Their aim was to encourage the self-government of the German people, thus endeavoring to find a means to, on the one hand, do justice to the interests of the Military Government and the occupying powers, while on the other hand allowing for the reconstruction of an independent German judicial system. In short:

> The success of our occupation depends, in part, upon a feeling of mutual cooperation between the German judicial officials and Military Government. Any attempt on the part of US personnel to interfere with the independence of the German judiciary only tends to destroy much of what has already been accomplished in the democratization of the German judicial system.[17]

British occupation authorities agreed with this view stating: "Our intention is not to run the German courts ourselves, but merely to prevent the Germans, in running their courts from doing certain things to which we object."[18] Unlike in a colonial empire, any supervision was to be discreet:

> Any method of control must, therefore, be such as to leave the German courts functioning independently under their own judges, prosecutors, etc. Plans should not be prepared of a kind which really assume that British lawyers will be going into Germany to supervise the German courts, either directly or in the same way that in the past, native courts, e.g., in Egypt and elsewhere, have been supervised under a system of paternal despotism. Our control in Germany must be indirect and limited.[19]

This approach would involve a certain number of liaison officers who would be in touch with the chief officials of the German courts of appeal, who in turn were responsible for the control of personnel in the lower courts. Direct interventions were repudiated. British legal officers understood their task to be a quest for the pre-Nazi status quo in the German administration of justice. As the president of the Court of Appeals of Düsseldorf once put it: "The English wanted everything to be as it had been."[20] The British Legal Division remained true to this policy of

---

[16] Letter Legal Division, Lübbecke, to HQ Mil Gov Hannover, Westphalia, Schleswig-Holstein, North Rhine, Hansestadt Hamburg, December 31, 1945, TNA, FO 1060/1005; see also statistics, October 15, 1945, TNA, FO 1060/977.
[17] Memorandum of OMGBY, October 1948, NARA, OMGBY 17/186 – 3/28.
[18] Planning Instruction "Control of German Ordinary Courts," February 13, 1945, TNA, FO 1060/951.
[19] Ibid.
[20] Werner Baerns quoted in Wiesen, *Das Oberlandesgericht von 1945 bis zur Gegenwart*, 91.

distant surveillance: "Control of the German courts will be exercised direct by Mil Gov through the Oberlandesgerichte."[21]

Thus the re-opening of the courts of appeal was vital. Presidents of the courts of appeal and the prosecutors general were responsible to the Military Government; given the shortage of legal officers, a more ambitious control was not to be put into effect. Analysis of statistics, short visits at courts, discussions with judges, or spot checks of complaint files would replace a more encompassing scheme. "Any interference with the German Legal Administration must be exercised very sparingly and this principle has been carefully observed since the beginning of the occupation."[22] Indeed, even the possibility of control would keep the German judiciary in check.[23]

German Courts Branch, German Courts Inspectorate, Contrôle de la Justice Allemande

Because the professional requirements were quite rigid, the control instances of the Legal Divisions of the Western Allies – the American German Courts Branch, the British German Courts Inspectorate and the French Contrôle de la Justice Allemande – were rather small and chronically understaffed. In addition to a good working knowledge of the German language, the members had to be acquainted with German law and its procedures.[24]

American affiliates of the German Courts Branch were equipped with the *Handbook for Military Government in Germany* as well as the *Technical Manual for Legal and Prison Officers*, which contained directions for the re-opening of German courts as well as criteria for checking trials and excerpts from the German penal code. Similar demands on linguistic and legal qualifications were made by the British Legal Division.[25] The French also expected language skills, as well as elementary awareness in law and legal procedural techniques.[26]

---

[21] Legal Division to Administration HQ, First Cdn. Army (Mil Gov), June 9, 1945, TNA, FO 1060/977; also TNA, FO 1060/1024.
[22] Letter of Rathbone, Ministry of Justice Control Branch to HQ Legal Division, Berlin, June 26, 1948, TNA, FO 1060/88.
[23] Ibid.
[24] Letter of Leonard J. Ganse, Legal Affairs Division, Land Commissioner for Bavaria, to Kenneth J. van Buskirk, Assistant Land Commissioner, January 4, 1950, NARA, OMGBY 17/188 – 3/1.
[25] Planning Instruction "Control of German Ordinary Courts," February 13, 1945, TNA, FO 1060/951.
[26] Monthly Report for the French Zone (and Saar), December 1947, AOFAA, AJ 3680, p. 21, Dossier 1.

As in the American zone of occupation, members of the German Justice Administration in the British Zone were often flabbergasted that the German Courts Inspectorate had excellent knowledge of German judicial affairs. The British Legal Division invested in special training for their German Courts Inspectorate and its three lawyers. In a two-week crash course at the local and district courts of Oldenburg they were acquainted with the finesses of the German court system. For purposes of revision, an 11-page memorandum had been compiled with which the legal officials could bone up on such subtleties as the German abbreviations of criminal law: "Ks: case tried by Schwurgericht, KLs: felonies tried by the Large Strafkammer, KMs: misdemeanours [sic] tried by the Large Strafkammer, Ls: felonies tried by the Schöffengericht, Ms: misdemeanours tried by the Schöffengericht."[27] Reports on the inspection tours produced "an overall picture on the working of the German Courts in each Mil. Gov. Region or Oberlandesgericht district . . ."[28] Interventions – even in cases of malpractice – were not encouraged. Instead, the Inspectorate was to report to the Legal Division, which would then inform the relevant regional Military Governments, which would in turn take the presidents of the courts of appeal or prosecutors general to task. "The Inspectorate is, however, empowered to remove court records revealing irregularities in order to prevent destruction thereof or alterations therein."[29] The journeys through the German countryside to small and removed courts were often hampered by several factors, e.g., the German drivers were given wrong instructions or misunderstood them; cars or food rationing stamps were not available.[30] Problems of transport led to delays, thus causing complaints. The British Inspectorate was not the only one to face the forbidding living conditions in post-war Germany – lack of transport and personnel hampered the French in their areas as well.

In all three Western Zones the control instances for the German judicial system rarely amounted to more than five or six individuals responsible for several dozen German courts in each zone. They were entrusted with a formidable number of tasks concerning the German courts, briefly summarized as "close, purge, later re-open and use under supervision."[31] This was easier said

---

[27] Memorandum on the Office Procedure, Filing System and Registers of the Amtsgerichte and Landgerichte [undated, 1946], TNA, FO 1060/1005.
[28] General Instructions to German Courts Inspectorate by Legal Division, CCG (BE), March 18, 1946, TNA, FO 1060/1005; also FO 1060/247.
[29] Ibid.
[30] Report A. Brock, Ministry of Justice Control Branch, Legal Division, ZECO, CCG (BE), Herford, to Director General, Ministry of Justice Control Branch, December 12, 1946, TNA, FO 1060/1005.
[31] Operational Plan, Legal Branch [1945], NARA, OMGBR 6/62 – 1/2; Legal Division General Procedure [undated], NARA, OMGBR 6/63 – 1/34.

than done. Their working days consisted of "(a) unannounced, periodic visits to courts for the purpose of observing proceedings; (b) regular inspections of court registers and case files; c) examinations of civil and criminal cases selected at random; and (d) periodic examinations of cases investigated by the *Staatsanwaltschaft* (state's attorney) but not brought to trial."[32] Furthermore, the tasks had a nasty habit of multiplying, as the following description implies: "to observe and review, as required, the trial of Germans accused of crimes against humanity where such crimes were offenses against local law; to consider further extension of the jurisdiction of German courts over persons, offenses and actions, and the advisability of transferring the prosecution of certain violations of Military Government laws and ordinances to German courts."[33] As denazification procedures were set in motion, staff lists submitted by the presidents of the courts of appeal and Länder ministries of justice had to be checked and new personnel appointments coordinated with the proper agencies.

The British Legal Division briefed its inspectors for their contact with the German justice administration. The inspections were designed to ensure that: (1) members of the German courts understood the policies and orders of the Control Commission and implemented them; (2) that the German courts worked in accordance with Allied politics in an efficient manner; (3) Problems that cropped up were handled by the German judicial service in accord with the British Inspectorate; and (4) the British Inspectorate eased communication between the legal officers of the regional Military Governments and the Zonal Legal Division (CCG/BE).

As the occupation period drew to a close, the control of the German courts grew more erratic. The American Legal Division stated that "after a brief transitional period the German courts have completely outgrown AMG [American Military Government] control."[34] It was debatable just how influential the control had been. A former member of the Legal Division thought that the Military Government helped the Germans along on a route they would have taken anyway:

> Whether these achievements ... were brought about by American planning and direction or by German efforts, the answer will vary with the viewpoint of the observer. It may seem certain that the Germans, if left to themselves, would have returned sooner or later to where their institutions and techniques had been before perversion by Hitler. AMG [American Military Government] officials not given to self-admiration would add that the best that could be said of AMG's activities in the legal field was that they did not unduly hamper or obstruct

---

32 Policy statements [undated, after January 10, 1949], NARA, OMGUS 17/215 – 2/20.
33 Functional Program, Legal Division, 1.3.1948-30.9.1948, NARA, OMGUS 17/217 – 3/33.
34 Karl Loewenstein, "Reconstruction of the Administration of Justice in American-Occupied Germany," *Harvard Law Review* 61 (1948), 440.

the Germans in retracing their steps towards Weimar ... If credit should be given to any specific group, it goes to the Ministers of Justice and their capable ministerial bureaucracy, who made the most conspicuous single contribution to what has been achieved.[35]

The founding of the Federal Republic of Germany and the creation of a Federal Ministry of Justice finally brought Allied instances of control to an end.

For German legal history of the occupation period, the control instances of the Western Allies were a godsend. The sources they created provided a bonanza of information, giving a rare insight into the courts in the early days of post-war Germany. The Allied observers wrote literally hundreds of reports describing the German judicial system and its staff. While it was a disadvantage that they caught a particular situation only on the spur of a moment, it was much to their advantage that they could view the system as outsiders, without having to take superiors or subordinates into account. The accounts and memoranda of the Western Allied observers could be written without diplomatic respect. Most of the reports went unseen by German courts; since they were directed only to the Legal Divisions and a few German high officials.[36] Reports of both German and Allied origins give us an impressive insight into far more than the judicial system. As a contemporary French observer put it: "Justice touches upon private as well as public questions, work, property, economy, a general outlook, and morals – it mirrors the aspirations, hopes and mentality of a people."[37]

To get an impression of the intensity of the report activity, it is well worth noting that the head of the British German Courts Inspectorate visited all the district courts in the British Zone in 1946. By the middle of 1947, the German Courts Branch in Bavaria had conducted 400 inspections of local courts, plus an additional 92 inspections of district courts. In Hesse, about 145 inspections of Hessian courts took place in 1947. The particularly industrious American inspector in Hesse, Edward H. Littman, covered no less than 12,000 miles in the course of duty. Despite the impressive number of inspections, it is obvious that during the four years of occupation most German courts were inspected only a handful of times – maybe once or twice yearly. Furthermore, courts in far-flung areas might have escaped the attention of the Allied observers altogether.

---

35 Ibid., 466.
36 Letter Legal Division, ZECO, CCG (BE), Herford to Chief Legal Officer in Lower Saxony, North Rhine/Westphalia, Schleswig-Holstein, Hamburg, December 31, 1946, TNA, FO 1060/1005.
37 Inspection OLG and LG Freiburg, April 15, 1946, AOFAA, AJ 372, p. 23.

The Re-opening of German Courts and the German Administration of Justice

The Allies first action was to order the closing of all German courts, resulting in a standstill in the course of justice. The SHAEF Proclamation No. 1 declared all National Socialist laws invalid; a return to the penal code as it was before Hitler's rise to power (January 30, 1933) was proclaimed. Allied laws formed the framework for the German administration of justice. Military Government Law No. 1 barred the punishment of deeds according to "analogy" or a reference to the so-called "*gesundes Volksempfinden*" (popular instinct). Military Government Law No. 2 abolished the Reichsgericht, the Volksgerichtshof (People's Court), special courts, and party courts. Members of these courts were immediately arrested because of their membership in the Nazi Party and affiliation with these bodies of jurisdiction. Members of the regular courts (local, district, and courts of appeal), however, were instructed to remain in their offices without remuneration or effective work. Due to the circumstances, sensible employment of members of the judiciary was often impossible. Courts had sometimes been completely deserted by their staffs.

With Proclamation No. 3 of the Control Council, basic principles were re-introduced into German life: equality before the law; the sanctity of life, liberty and property (inviolability of the home) were proclaimed. The right of the indicted to an immediate and public trial, notification of the indictment, confrontation with witnesses of the prosecution, and the provision of defense counsel were guaranteed. Sentences based on political, racial, or religious prejudices were forbidden; unjust or cruel punishments were banished; the independence of judges was proclaimed. Control Council Law No. 4 fixed the reconstruction of the system of administration of justice in the frame of the so-called law of the constitution of the courts *(Gerichtsverfassungsgesetz)* of 1877 – with the three-tier system of local, district and appeal courts.

Re-opening of Courts in the American Zone of Occupation

The earliest re-openings of courts took place in the American Zone of Occupation. German courts began to function here in the summer of 1945. Local courts were even re-admitted before district courts (thus without superior German control or review). At the end of June 1945, local courts in the Stuttgart area reopened their doors for legal business, receiving members of the public seeking legal advice. The competent district court of Stuttgart would not resume its activities until September of that year. The American occupiers admitted, however, that this course of action was unusual and dictated by circumstances.[38] The renaissance of the German Justice Administration was often characterized by minimal and modest beginnings. In Bamberg, supervision by German superiors and payment of salaries were interrupted. Some courthouses in Upper and Lower Franconia had been severely damaged by aerial bombings or as collateral damage; the whereabouts of members of the judiciary were unknown. The zonal borders affected the administration of justice when they cut through the territory of the German legal districts, which was the case in some courts in Württemberg-Baden. Previously, the courts of Nürtingen and Leonberg (both in the American Zone) had been subordinated to the Tübingen district court, now located in the French Zone – thus they were to change their allegiance and become attached to Stuttgart. Conversely, Münsingen, Ehingen and Riedlingen (French Zone) had been part of the Ulm District Court territory, now in the American Zone.

Chaos surely characterized the first months. The Landesdirektor für die Justiz (later the Minister of Justice) in Württemberg-Baden, Dr. Beyerle, despaired of the situation. Activity in the previously opened courts was slack; clerical staff and attorneys not encumbered by a Nazi past were few and far between. Since the American Military Government had ordered the suspension of all civil servants who had joined the Nazi Party before 1937, a large percentage of the judiciary was forcibly withdrawn and required to quit the service. To find replacements for these positions was like looking for needles in haystacks.[39]

The American Military Government, however, reminded the judiciary and the German population that the re-opening of courts meant – despite the nagging headaches the post-war penury produced – a return to the rule of law and justice.[40] The Military Government would not create impediments for German courts. Controls were to be seen as a safety net to ensure that all remnants of the dictatorship were eradicated in the judicial system. American privileges of dismissal and suspension of judges, American inspections and visitations on main hearings and the checking of each sentence (with an eventual right to annul, suspend or modify a sentence) were to be seen in this light alone. A democratic concept of the law and the independence of the judiciary were essential to the success of both the legal division's mission and the German administration of justice.[41] However,

---

38 Memorandum for the re-opening of LG Stuttgart, July 21, 1945, NARA, OMGWB 12/136 – 3/36.
39 Landesdirektor für Justiz, Dr. Beyerle, in a letter to the American Military Government, Stuttgart, August 23, 1945, NARA, OMGWB 12/137 – 1/4.
40 Speech of Colonel Dawson at the inauguration ceremony of the district court Stuttgart, September 10, 1945, NARA, OMGWB 12/136 – 3/42.
41 Ibid.

the German officials also had their duty to fulfill: "It is your own judicial house that must be cleaned, put in order and made to operate. You have the task to perform."⁴² The Minister of Justice in Württemberg-Baden, Dr. Beyerle stressed that everybody had to abide by the law in an effort to return to an orderly society. A democratic consciousness of right and wrong was to be the motivation and at the same time limitation of all aspirations and actions. "Law and order, cleanliness and respectability" were the keys to this state of affairs.⁴³

Re-opening of Courts in the British Zone

Like the Americans, the British were also keen on helping the courts get their act together – at a minimum in order to reduce work for the Military Government Court (or Control Commission Courts).⁴⁴ The master plan already existed: "Find, denazify and make the best possible use of sufficient judges, prosecutors and other officials to deal temporarily with urgent business. Secure all records, registers, names and addresses of all local judges and prosecutors and legal personnel; vet all local judges and prosecutors and select those suitable for emergency duty. Serve the judge with directions."⁴⁵

Further measures for the re-opening of German courts were a sufficiently large, trained and equipped German police force to make investigations and arrests of suspects, and a functioning prison system for custody.⁴⁶ Local courts were to re-establish their criminal and civil divisions at the earliest possible moment; district courts were to put special diligence into the re-emergence of their criminal chambers (*Strafkammern*). The Military Government was to control the district courts, which in turn would supervise the local courts. As in the American Zone, it was expected that in some cases local courts would be inaugurated before district courts, thwarting an efficient control.⁴⁷ Spot checks of files and forms, spontaneous visits and talks with German personnel, and follow-up of complaints were to afford some rudimentary control. District courts would have

---

42 Ibid.
43 Speech of Dr. Beyerle at inauguration ceremony of the Stuttgart District Court, September 10, 1945, NARA, OMGWB 12/136 – 3/42.
44 Planning Instruction "Control of German Ordinary Courts," February 13, 1945, TNA, FO 1060/951.
45 Memorandum [undated, 1945], TNA, FO 1060/977.
46 Letter Legal Division, Norfolk House, London to Director, Control Branch, June 15, 1945, TNA, FO 1060/977.
47 Letter Brigadier J.A. Carter, Mil Gov to Adm HQ, First Cdn Army (Mil Gov), June 9, 1945, TNA, FO 1060/1024.

to function for a time without the super-ordinate courts of appeal.[48] The idea was that once the judicial personnel were vetted, the courts of appeal could start their work again, but administrative tasks were to be performed sooner. Deliberations concerning the reconstruction of the German administration of justice took place as early as May 1945. In Hamburg, German lawyers met with the British Military Government on May 5 in an effort to discuss legal questions in this field. Several courts also had an early start: Although records are hazy – giving dates either in April, May or June 1945 – the local and district court of Aachen re-opened its doors even before Germany's unconditional surrender.[49] Hannover had a functioning local and district court by June 1, 1945. Even at this early stage, personnel, i.e., the president of the court, 13 judges and clerical staff, had to address 113 criminal cases.[50] Several local and district courts in Westphalia were inaugurated in July and August 1945, and by the end of November 1945, all ten district courts in Westphalia and the adjacent province of Lippe-Detmold had been re-initiated, and more than 70 local courts were again doing business. The North Rhine province followed suit with several district courts re-opening as early as October and November 1945. By August 1945, 15 district courts in the British Z.one had re-established their functions. Westphalia led with seven courts, Lower Saxony followed closely with six courts, and the North Rhine province (Aachen) and Hamburg with one each.[51] Many courts had re-established only part of their departments. The only functioning court of appeal in the British Zone at this time was located in Hamm and did administrative, but not yet judicial, work. While the plight of the badly damaged industrial areas of the British Zone can hardly be exaggerated, the post-war judicial service at least kept up appearances to some degree. The conditions, however, were frequently pathetic at the outset: Personnel were in dire need of food and housing; there were no files or legal libraries; registers had been confiscated; and there were no telephones or even paper, so that the calendars and printed stationery of former Nazi organizations had to remain in use.

---

48 Letter A.E. Grasett, Lieutenant-General, Supreme Headquarters Allied Expeditionary Force to ACOS, Sixth Army Group, ACOS, Twelfth Army group, November 25, 1944, TNA, FO 1060/1024.
49 List of re-opened courts subordinated to the court of appeal in Cologne [undated, October 1945], TNA, FO 1060/1029, List dated November 25, 1946, TNA, FO 1060/1036.
50 Report MG Legal, June 9-14, 1945, TNA, FO 1060/977.
51 Letter Legal Division, Lübbecke, to Chief, Legal Division, August 25, 1945, TNA, FO 1060/1024. Information on Schleswig-Holstein was missing from the letter.

Re-opening of Courts in the French Zone

The process of re-initiating court business was slightly delayed in the French Zone because of the zone's formation. The historic Länder of Baden and Württemberg were both split into southern (French) and northern (American) areas of responsibility. The French Legal Division did not hesitate to contact members of the higher judicial service by appointing the aforementioned Josef Beyerle to be head of the administration of German justice in Stuttgart, Württemberg in June 1945.[52] This early start was rendered null and void shortly afterwards when it became clear that the division of Württemberg into two different zones would also call for the creation of a judicial authority for southern Württemberg. Thus in August 1945, a French judicial department was created in Tübingen, headed by the *Directeur Régional de la Justice* (Regional Director of Justice), which would subsequently also supervise the renascent German judicial service.

In southern Baden, courts were closed from April 1945 to October 1945. The chief of the German judicial service for Baden, Dr. Paul Zürcher, was appointed by the French Legal Division to prepare local, district and high courts in the region for the resumption of their intended purpose.

Judicial personnel had to pledge allegiance to their official duties in front of representatives of the French Military Government. On October 4, 1945, Freiburg district court resumed its activities after a standstill in legal affairs of more than five months. Zürcher announced further re-openings of courts and praised the legal culture of Baden, which, after the foundation of the grand duchy of Baden by Napoleon, had been profoundly influenced by French law. Legal traditions in Baden were – in his opinion – still firmly rooted in law and order and the German civil code (Bürgerliches Gesetzbuch), despite Prussian dominance in the Reich legal sphere.[53] The French regional Legal Director for Baden reminded the Germans of the French suffering caused by German aggression, but stressed that the agenda of the French was not revenge, but punishment of wrong-doers.[54] Additional courts – Offenburg, Baden-Baden, Konstanz and Waldshut – resumed their work in October. In Württemberg, four district courts – Tübingen, Hechingen, Rottweil and Ravensburg – were re-opened in October and November 1945. The newly created district court of Lindau, Bavaria was an anomaly. This part of

---

[52] Report "Organisation Judiciaire de la Province du Wurtemberg-Hohenzollern" [undated, written after June 1, 1949], AOFAA, AJ 806, p. 615, Dossier 2.
[53] Speech of Dr. Zürcher at the inauguration of the Freiburg district court, October 4, 1945, AOFAA, AJ 372, p. 19.
[54] Speech of Directeur Régional de la Justice du Pays de Bade, Lieutenant-colonel Robert, October 4, 1945, AOFAA, AJ 372, p. 19.

Bavaria had been split off of the American Zone to give the French better access to the Austrian part of their occupation zone. The Lindau region had previously had only local courts that were subordinated to the Kempten district court (now in the American Zone). It was thus neither part of the justice administration in Württemberg nor in Bavaria, but eked out a somewhat strange extra-territorial existence for several years.[55]

Analogous situations dominated in the southern Rhineland and the Palatinate. Historically, the southern Rhineland had been a subordinate of the high court in Cologne, while the Palatinate (with its own court of appeal at Zweibrücken) had been part of Bavaria. At the end of August 1946, the two provinces were merged into a new Land, Rhineland-Palatinate. Developments in the administration of justice pre-dated this change. One district court in Trier resumed business as early as October 1945. Again, at the inauguration ceremony, the French authorities spoke not of revenge but of encouraging the Germans to strive for independent adjudication.[56]

Re-opening of Courts in Berlin, Bremen, and the Saar

While we have discussed developments in the three zones of occupation, we have not yet mentioned the legal developments in three regions that – while they formed part of Western Germany – either did not belong to the zones of occupation (the Saar region and Berlin) or were subject to alternating (and conflicting) American and British occupation interests e.g., Bremen. Berlin, because of its four-power status, was another thing entirely. The high court of Berlin – the Kammergericht – was initially located in the Soviet Sector (it was moved in February 1949 when the split between West and East became blatant); the district court was in the British Sector; and more than a dozen local courts were dispersed in the American, British and French sectors. (In the Soviet Sector, the Administration of Justice had been ordered by the Soviet commander in Berlin to switch to a two-tier system with 21 *Bezirksgerichte* (borough courts) subordinated to one *Stadtgericht* (city court) as court of appeal.) Unlike in the western zones, courts and the department of public prosecution in West and East Berlin were all directly mandated to the Allied command.

In the Saar, the district court of Saarbrücken re-opened in September 1945. Because the French had cut the Saar from their Zone of Occupation in February

---

55 Report "Organisation Judiciaire de la Province du Wurtemberg-Hohenzollern" [undated, written after June 1, 1949], AOFAA, AJ 806, p. 615, Dossier 2.
56 Monthly Report for the Rhineland, October 1945, AOFAA, AJ 3679, p. 12.

1946 and had attributed to it the special status of protectorate (Protectorat de la Sarre), with the intention of incorporating the area into French territory, it also needed a superior court, which was established in October 1946.

Bremen was a special case; political borders and borders of courts collided there. Bremen was now an American enclave, but had traditionally been subordinated to the Hamburg High Court in the British Zone. Even before zones of occupation increased the confusion regarding areas of competency, the region around Bremen had been a highly debated entity among such high court administrative territories as Oldenburg, Hamburg, and Celle.

Bremen territory was occupied by the British until mid-May 1945, then by American troops. The Bremen District Court was opened by an American legal officer at the end of June 1945, but problems remained. There was no high court for Bremen in the American Zone, and it was against occupation principles to subordinate a district court in one zone to a high court in another, even if the zones were adjacent or nearby. Furthermore, responsibilities continued to remain unclear as the American enclave of Bremen was diminished in size due to a December 10, 1945, agreement between the British and American occupiers.[57] This gravely affected the administration of justice in Bremen because certain local courts were restituted to other district courts. The transfer from American to British authority did not function smoothly. The justice administration at one of the local German courts still accepted orders from the American side, despite the fact that the British were now in charge. To spare the German Justice Administration the awkward and unfortunate position of being servant to two masters, the British intended to interrupt relations with the Americans altogether, as J. F. W. Rathbone, head of the British Legal Division, wrote in a letter to the chief of the legal division in Berlin: "I instructed the Landgerichtspräsident and Oberstaatsanwalt that they will on no account have any direct contact with the Americans."[58] Bremen had to address its requests first to the court of appeals or the department of the public prosecutor in Hamburg; from there, requests went to the Legal Branch, HQ Mil Gov Hamburg.

When a celebratory ceremony for the re-integration of Bremen into the Hamburg legal realm took place on April 2, 1946, Bremen Senator of Justice (the equivalent of a minister of justice) Dr. Theodor Spitta pointed out his peculiar position as senator without a domain – the official control over the Bremen District Court (and the local courts) being exercised by the Hamburg High Court,

---

[57] Agreement, December 10, 1945, NARA, OMGBR 6/62 – 2/13; Terms of completion for the American and British Agreement, March 19, 1946, NARA, OMGBR 6/62 – 1/26.
[58] Letter of J.F.W. Rathbone, Legal Division, Main HQ, CCG (BE), Lübbecke to Chief, Legal Division, Advanced HQ, Berlin, May 28, 1946, TNA, FO 1060/1057.

while control of administration, budget, and staff was conducted by British Legal officers. His activities were thus reduced to participation in legal committees of the Bremische Bürgerschaft (regional diet), filing, and administration. It may have been some consolation that the legal duties remained in the family, as the president of the Hamburg Court of Appeal was his cousin, Wilhelm Kiesselbach. The Americans asked the British to send a legal officer to Bremen to take care of the German courts and prisons, as they no longer fell under American responsibility. This, however, put the British in a quandary because they lacked suitable personnel to fulfill the request. Instead, a legal officer was designated to travel from Hamburg to Bremen once a week to look after Bremen's legal affairs. Still, the British were anxious that "[their] administration and control of the German legal system ... not compare unfavorably with that of the Americans."[59]

The attachment of the Bremen court system to the Hamburg legal realm drew mixed reactions. On one hand there was the tradition of a joint court of appeal in Hamburg; on the other hand, the presence of a high court in Bremen had a special appeal to the city and its legal dignitaries.[60] Rathbone noted that "all the speeches of the Bremen authorities contained a significant and wistful longing for the good old days of US control when it was anticipated that they would have their own Oberlandesgericht and their own independent legal system, and they all asked for a British Legal Officer in Bremen to help them through this difficult transitional period."[61] He foresaw that the Bremen Administration of Justice would reject control from Hamburg. A German memorandum noted that the reconstruction of the German judicial system had prospered under the aegis of American legal officer, but was flagging now under British authority following the British-American Agreement of December 10, 1945.[62] Supervision of the Bremen Judicial Administration by Hamburg (German and British authorities) was considered too complicated – especially geographically, since Bremen still belonged to the American administration. Legal discrepancies between Bremen and the British Zone of Occupation cropped up and were considered unbridgeable.[63]

---

59 Letter of J.F.W. Rathbone, Legal Division, CCG (BE), Lübbecke to Chief, Legal Division, Advanced HQ, Berlin, April 4, 1946, TNA, FO 1060/1033; letter also under NARA, OMGBR 6/62 – 1/26.
60 See Walther Richter, „Die Errichtung des Hanseatischen Oberlandesgerichts in Bremen," *Zeitschrift für Sozialreform: Festschrift für Harry Rohwer-Kahlmann* 29 (1983), 582.
61 Letter of J.F.W. Rathbone, Legal Division, CCG (BE), Lübbecke to Chief, Legal Division, Advanced HQ, Berlin, April 4, 1946, TNA, FO 1060/1033; see also NARA, OMGBR 6/62 – 1/26.
62 Memorandum "Bremen under the Military Government as seen from the point of view of the Juridical Administration" [undated, 1946/1947], NARA, OMGBR 6/62 – 1/3. The document is written from a German perspective and contains several rather German-inspired vocabularies.
63 Letter Legal Division, ZECO, CCG (BE), Herford, to Chief Legal Officer, HQ Mil Gov Hamburg, April 8, 1947, TNA, FO 1060/1234.

Disillusioned and annoyed, the British stated that parochialism and hunger for power dominated,[64] and considered looking for a replacement for the recalcitrant head of the Bremen District Court.[65]

As the confusing situation became untenable, the American and British military governments concluded a new agreement. Bremen's court system was once again put under American legal control, with the German judicial personnel supervised by the Americans. The Hamburg High Court was no longer responsible for the administration of justice in Bremen. A certain relief was felt on the German side.[66] Even the British thought it was good riddance.[67] Bremen became a federal state on January 1, 1947, and the rights reserved to Hamburg were returned to it on April 1. The Hamburg Court of Appeal handed over the administration of justice in Bremen to the Landesjustizverwaltung in Bremen; the epitome of Bremen's rise to legal altitude was the foundation of its court of appeal on July 15, 1947. Now that Bremen had broken loose from Hamburg's dominance, opinions were once again divided. Hamburg's Administration of Justice still hoped for the transient nature of the arrangement; a joint court of appeal was to be accomplished as soon as political circumstances would permit. This, however, contradicted the declared aims of the Americans, whose view was that "a system which would entail final decision of judgments in Land Bremen, which is under United States control, by a court subject to the authority of another zone, would be inadvisable." Therefore, they continued, "a separate Oberlandesgericht (Court of Appeals) for Land Bremen should be established."[68] When the Bremen High Court was finally established, things were kept very quiet.[69] Even celebrations were somewhat subdued. Acute shortage of staff and lack of experience among recruited personnel dimmed any emerging enthusiasm.

---

64 Letter of W.W. Boulton, Legal Division, Lübbecke, to Controller General, MOJ Control Branch, May 24, 1946, TNA, FO 1060/1035.
65 Ibid.
66 Memorandum "Bremen under the Military Government as seen from the point of view of the Juridical Administration" [undated, 1946/1947], NARA, OMGBR 6/62 – 1/3.
67 Letter Legal Division, ZECO, CCG (BE), Herford, to HQ Legal Division, CCG (BE) Berlin, November 17, 1946, TNA, FO 1060/1057.
68 Letter of Lt. Col. G.H. Garde, OMGUS, to Chief Legal Officer, Bremen, April 16, 1947, NARA, OMGBR 6/62 – 2/57.
69 Memorandum of Hans W. Weigert, Legal Division, OMGUS, July 4, 1947 about Field Trip of June 23-27, 1947 to Bremen, Bremerhaven and Hamburg, NARA, OMGBR 6/62 – 2/60.

Re-opening of the Courts of Appeal

While some local and district courts had started their work by the spring and summer of 1945, it took longer to re-establish the high courts that, for the time being, formed the last unit of the German court system. In the British Zone, legal officers urged an early start at the high court level, which they saw as the proper exercise of their own control. In autumn 1945, three courts of appeal (reduced from eight) were working again in the British Zone of Occupation: Hamm (in Westphalia), Hamburg and Kiel (Schleswig-Holstein). Preparations for the high court in Celle (Lower Saxony) were under way; appointments of the president of the court of appeal and the prosecutor general had been made and announced. In November 1945, Braunschweig re-opened its Oberlandesgericht, Düsseldorf followed in December 1945, and by early 1946, all eight courts of appeal (Braunschweig, Celle, Cologne, Düsseldorf, Hamburg, Hamm, Kiel and Oldenburg) had been re-established. Whether it was the British pragmatic approach (not adding to the existing confusion by dismantling historic structures) or a simple reluctance to meddle too much in German legal affairs, all high courts were re-established at their old sites and, as far as possible, within their former borders (Braunschweig lost some of its local courts, which became part of the Soviet Zone of Occupation, while Cologne, as mentioned, lost the courts of Koblenz and Trier to the French Zone). In 1947, following a contentious decision in the regional diet of Schleswig-Holstein, the high court of Kiel was transferred to Schleswig, where it remains to this day.

As in the British Zone of Occupation, the federal Länder (and their respective judicial portfolios) were late to emerge. Therefore, the British legal officers transferred significant number of responsibilities to the presidents of the high courts. They could – subject to British permission – issue orders, provisions, and regulations for the courts; and make suggestions for laws to the Military Government, thus rising to the status of "local ministers of justice," as a historian once described it.[70] While this model was opposed to Montesquieu's idea of checks and balances (in which the legislation makes the law while the judiciary only applies it), the legal profession's initiatives in the British Zone were nevertheless modest. They included regulations concerning the statute of limitations in civil law; reversals of Nazi penal justice such as the abrogation of the punitive rights of the police, which were once again transferred to the hands of the judiciary and courts; the settlement of appeals to the no longer extant Reichsgericht; or the re-insertion of complaints into civil law. Fundamental or radical reform was not their aim. Material and formal law remained as they had been – minus the changes made by the Nazis.

---

70 Wenzlau, *Der Wiederaufbau der Justiz in Nordwestdeutschland*, 169.

In the American Zone, there were fewer high courts. Stuttgart was the court of appeal for Württemberg-Baden (with a senate in Karlsruhe), Frankfurt for Hesse (with senates in Darmstadt and Kassel), and three courts of appeal in Munich, Bamberg and Nuremberg were to settle legal affairs in Bavaria. To coordinate the activities of these three high courts, a Bavarian department, the Oberstes Landesgericht (Most Superior Court), was re-created in 1948, having been dissolved by the Nazis in 1935. The origins of the Bremen High Court have already been described.

The biggest upheavals in the domain of the high courts took place in the French Zone, which, as is known, had been cut out from the American and British spheres of influence. The Palatinate (part of the Land Bavaria until 1945) had its own high court at Zweibrücken. However, as the building had been severely damaged, the French decided to transfer the court to Neustadt an der Haardt, where it opened in August 1946.[71] For the southern parts of Württemberg and Baden, two completely new high courts were established: Freiburg (effective from March 1946) and Tübingen (which opened at the end of June 1946). Both had previously been administered by, respectively, Karlsruhe and Stuttgart, both in the American Zone, a situation of considerable inconvenience.[72]

The southern Rhinelands also needed a superior instance (at Koblenz), since its territory combined the former jurisdictions of Cologne and Hamm (British Zone), Frankfurt and Darmstadt (American Zone) and parts of Zweibrücken.[73]

The Supreme Court in the British Zone

For both the American and French zones, the courts of appeal formed the highest instance of German justice. The British, however, were planning the creation of an Oberster Gerichtshof (Supreme Court) in order to replace the abolished Reichsgericht. Their reasoning was that for the purposes of coordination of jurisdiction and the preservation of the unity of German law "it may eventually be desirable to set up a Supreme Court for the British and American Zones, or for the whole of Germany."[74] But the Britons were not able to convince even their closest ally to join them in this undertaking, thus rendering the initiative ineffectual and

---

71 Warmbrunn, "Wiederaufbau der Justiz nach Kriegsende," 207.
72 Report "Organisation Judiciaire de la Province du Wurtemberg-Hohenzollern" [undated, written after June 1, 1949], AOFAA, AJ 806, p. 615, Dossier 2.
73 Heinz Georg Bamberger and Johannes Kempf, "Zur Geschichte und Vorgeschichte des Oberlandesgerichts Koblenz," in *50 Jahre Oberlandesgericht und Generalstaatsanwaltschaft Koblenz 1996* (Frankfurt am Main: Peter Lang 1996), 21.
74 Letter Legal Division, Herford, to Legal Division, Berlin, May 8, 1947, TNA, FO 1060/783.

leaving the Supreme Court in the British Zone with authority solely over the eight high courts in Braunschweig, Celle, Cologne, Düsseldorf, Hamburg, Hamm, Oldenburg and Schleswig. The British Legal Division feared problems in jurisdiction if there were no highest instance. "Where the Oberlandesgerichte in the various parts of the British Zone reach different decisions on the same point of law which may arise before two or more of those Courts, there is no single Supreme Court to reconcile the conflicting decisions. The situation has in fact already occurred on a number of occasions."[75]

In order to give the Americans the chance to join in on the project of a Supreme Court, Cologne (the southernmost high court district) was chosen as a location. The Supreme Court for the British Zone came into being on September 1, 1947, but inauguration ceremonies did not take place until May 1948.[76] The Legal Division saw the creation of the court as a milestone in legal developments in Germany.[77]

The Renascent Ministries of Justice of the Länder

The Länder came into being at different times, with the Americans opting for a federal structure from very early on, while the French and British military governments took longer to constitute the regional structures. Not until late 1946 and early 1947 were Länder ministers of justice appointed in Schleswig-Holstein, Lower Saxony, and North Rhine-Westphalia. For some time, the portfolio of the ministries of justice in the British Zone of Occupation was severely limited, since they had to share their authority with the powerful presidents of the courts of appeal, as well as with the Central Legal Office (which will be described shortly). When the first North Rhine-Westphalian minister of justice, Dr. Kremer, demanded 30 members of the higher service for his ministry, the Director of the British Legal Division was taken aback by the request, "which in view of the present demands on legal civil service (to be aggravated by the impending trials of members of criminal organisations [sic]) I consider to be most extravagant."[78] In January 1947, the military government in North Rhine-Westphalia expressed the opinion that the whole German legal pro-

---

75 Ibid.
76 Walter Vogel, "Organisatorische Bemühungen um die Rechtseinheit in den westlichen Besatzungszonen 1945-1948," in *Aus der Arbeit des Bundesarchivs: Beiträge zum Archivwesen, zur Quellenkunde und Zeitgeschichte*, ed. Heinz Boberach and Hans Booms (Boppard: Boldt, 1977), 463.
77 Letter Legal Division, Berlin, to Military Governor and Commander-in-Chief, Berlin, November 19, 1947, TNA, FO 1060/782.
78 Letter of Rathbone, Director, MOJ Control Branch, Legal Division, Zonal Executive Office, CCG (BE), Herford to HQ Legal Division, December 1, 1946, TNA, FO 1060/1036.

fession would view the idea of a Landesjustizministerium (Land Ministry of Justice) with dread and mistrust.[79] The role of the ministers of justice as newcomers was particularly complicated in the British Zone, as tasks had already been allocated. Jurisdiction was in the hands of the courts; legislation was the job of the regional parliament and administration; preparatory work on laws and questions of staff were in the hands of the Central Legal Office. Routinely bashing the state ministries of justice was by no means limited to North Rhine-Westphalia. The conference of presidents of the courts of appeal thought that an installation of a ministry with functions beyond an office of corporate counsel (Justitiariat) was utterly unnecessary.[80] In the Lower Saxon regional diet, the budget of the new ministry of justice was excoriated as "nearly grotesque in its expenses."[81]

In the beginning, the ministries of justice comprised a handful of members. The ministry in North Rhine-Westphalia consisted of the minister himself, one additional member of the higher judicial service, a secretary, an office worker, and a driver.[82] Eduard Kremer once quipped that he could fit his whole administration into a briefcase.[83] By the end of 1947, the ministry in North Rhine-Westphalia – which was, after all, the most densely populated of the Länder – numbered 51 members; however, only five typewriters were available, severely hampering the production of typed texts.[84] Furthermore, ministers were frequently replaced. In some Länder during the relevant period, up to four incumbents were dealing with legal affairs.

The Central Legal Office

Unlike the American and French military governments, the British legal officers were not content with the federal structure of the Administration of Justice, but created their own central institutions for their zone. Apart from the above-mentioned Supreme Court (Oberster Gerichtshof für die Britische Zone), on October 1, 1946, they also formed the Central Legal Office on in Hamburg. Their intention was to fill the vacuum that the abolition of the Reich Ministry of Justice had left

---

[79] Letter Military Government Northrhine-Westphalia to Ministry of Justice, Northrhine-Westphalia, January 14, 1947, BAK, Z 21/95.
[80] Resolution of president of courts of appeal, October 29, 1946, BAK, Z 21/1310.
[81] Liberal Party MP Dr. Otto Heinrich Greve in the Lower Saxon Diet on July 10, 1947, column 257.
[82] Minutes of the conference of ministers of justice, April 29-30, 1948, HStA Düsseldorf, Gerichte Rep. 255/187.
[83] Eduard Kremer quoted in Wenzlau, *Wiederaufbau der Justiz*, 257; see also Wiesen, "Das Oberlandesgericht von 1945 bis zur Gegenwart", 93.
[84] Heilbronn, "Der Aufbau der nordrhein-westfälischen Justiz in der Zeit von 1945 bis 1948/9", 22.

behind. They wanted a "highest German legal authority in the Zone" as a "temporary measure [to] exercise for the British Zone certain of the functions previously exercised by the Reich Ministry of Justice."[85] More or less since the beginning of their occupation, they saw a dire need for the centralization of the administration of justice. A joint supreme Justice Administration of all occupiers in Berlin was contemplated in autumn 1945. This idea was shattered, so in April 1946 the British Military Government commissioned the president of the Oldenburg high court, Dr. Ekhard Koch, and the vice president of the Hamburg High Court, Dr. Herbert Ruscheweyh, to draw up an organizational chart for a central authority for the administration of justice in the British Zone. A first draft was handed over in May 1946. As neither Koch nor Ruscheweyh had experience with the actual administration of justice – both had been advocates – Ruscheweyh consulted with the legal department of the Hamburg High Court. The choice of people admitted into Ruscheweyh's confidence was far from wise. One was Dr. Wolfgang Mettgenberg (who was later sentenced to five years' imprisonment in the Nuremberg Trials), and another was Dr. Friedrich Priess, personnel specialist under the Nazi president of the Hamburg High Court, Curt Rothenberger.[86] Still, the plans for nothing less than a ministry of justice for the complete British Zone were proceeding smoothly. Koch suggested that the president of the Hamburg high court, Dr. Wilhelm Kiesselbach, should lead the Central Legal Office. Though Dr. Kiesselbach was not seen as the perfect candidate, there was no other option. According to Rathbone, "Dr. Kiesselbach may not be the ideal man for this appointment, but there is no suitable alternative at present available ... Lingemann of Düsseldorf was considered as a possibility, but he is disliked in the legal profession and has not shone as the legal representative on the ZAC [Zonal Advisory Council]."[87]

The main personnel choices were made in September 1946. The principal duties lay in the preparation of legislative proposals for the British Legal Division; the co-ordination of the activities of the courts of appeal, each of which published its own papers announcing their decisions in a *Justizblatt* (justice journal); and in matters of clemency, which was the responsibility of the British Legal Division. All commands and writs passed by the Central Legal Office had to be approved by the British Legal Division. The Central Legal Office also arranged appointments of staff at the courts. Initially, about 12 people of the higher civil service were working in the Central Legal Office. In May 1947 there were 76 employees, many

---

85 Report Legal Division, August 24, 1946, TNA, FO 937/15.
86 Ihonor, *Herbert Ruscheweyh*, 187.
87 Letter of J.F.W. Rathbone, Legal Division, Herford to HQ Legal Division, Berlin, August 6, 1946, TNA, FO 1060/1071.

in clerical positions; in September 1947 there were 84;[88] in the beginning of 1949 the total was 98, with 34 of them higher civil servants.[89]

Besides the appointment of the 79-year-old Kiesselbach (characterized by the British Legal Division as demonstrating "astonishing vitality, both mental and physical."[90]) as president, and the 44-year-old Ekhard Koch, head of the Oldenburg high court, as vice president, Dr. Curt Staff, prosecutor general at Braunschweig, was to become head of the criminal department of the Central Legal Office. Staff, who had been imprisoned in Dachau Concentration Camp from 1933 to 1936, was highly regarded by the British Division, where he was considered a "staunch upholder of democracy and an opponent of the Nazi regime."[91] Elsewhere, Staff was praised for his "outstanding qualities."[92] Staff had been reluctant when offered the position of "Head of the Criminal Department in the new Central Legal Office for the British Zone" in June 1946, in Rathbone's words, "partly because he feels he is not a good administrator or legislator (which I doubt) and partly because he does not want to leave his present house in the country in order to go to Hamburg."[93]

Directions and briefings were produced regularly and the amount of correspondence also grew. Grand legislation initiatives were not produced in the Central Legal Office, which itself stated that these were not in order because the reform or revision of laws was to be reserved for a less provisional institution. In general, cautious adaptations rather than dashing reforms, preservation of the unity of the German law rather than unilateralist leanings were preferred.

Of all Western allies, the British had drawn the most problematic card. Damage in their zone was the most daunting, thus also making reconstruction the most difficult. This also holds true for the administration of justice in the zone, where the living and working conditions were bad for all concerned.[94] After four years of occupation, "the legal civil service is still convalescent and working under appalling conditions."[95] Apart from the low salaries of judges, the profes-

---

[88] Staffing of Central Legal Office, September 30, 1947, TNA, FO 937/15.
[89] Activity Report Central Legal Office, April 1, 1948 to March 31, 1949, TNA, FO 1060/108.
[90] Report Legal Division, August 24, 1946, TNA, FO 937/15.
[91] Ibid.
[92] Letter of J.F.W. Rathbone, Legal Division, Lübbecke to Chief, Legal Division, Advanced HQ, Berlin, January 27, 1946, TNA, FO 1060/1028.
[93] Letter of J.F.W. Rathbone, Legal Division, Lübbecke, to Chief, Legal Division, Advanced HQ, Berlin, June 25, 1946, TNA, FO 1060/1033.
[94] Christmas Message, J.F.W. Rathbone, December 10, 1947, TNA, FO 1060/777; German text "Glückwunsch der Legal Division CCG (BE)," *Zentral-Justizblatt für die Britische Zone*, January 1948, 12.
[95] Memorandum, J.F.W. Rathbone, March 8, 1948, TNA, FO 1060/740.

sional self-esteem was also low, indicating that "the German legal profession, therefore, [continues to require] constant assistance and encouragement and an enhancement of its status and self-confidence."[96] Instead of brandishing the stick, the British had opted to wave the carrot saying,

> It is not the policy forcibly to superimpose British jurisprudential concepts upon the Germans, but much is being done to inject our ideas into them and every effort is being made to improve the conditions of the legal civil service. It is thought that [the] Legal Division has gained the confidence of the German legal profession in the British Zone and that a reasonably good start has been made in the rebuilding of the German legal administration upon a sound basis and in the maintenance of the rule of law in the British Zone.[97]

Physical Conditions for the Reconstruction of Courts

The devastation of court buildings often beggared all description. When the president of the district court of Mönchengladbach visited the local court in Rheydt in March 1946, the courthouse roof was still missing. Rain penetrated the whole building so that rooms on the first floor and the ground floor were regularly flooded. Roofs and walls were permeated by water, causing the paint to peel away, thus revealing the bare brickwork underneath. None of the rooms had windows with intact glazing. In most cases, the glass was missing altogether, replacements being difficult to get. A glazier had started, but then abandoned the task. Tidying up and cleaning the building was considered useless as plaster continued to come off the walls. Certain rooms were completely "open air" and full of rubbish. In one room, partly burned Land registry records were discovered under the rubble.[98] Many courts in the British Zone of Occupation were similarly affected. Several local courts showed analogous deficiencies: leaking roofs, mold on the walls, windows without glass and covered by cardboard, a foul and musty smell emanating from the rooms.

While the British Zone was worst afflicted, destruction also encumbered courts in other zones. The Koblenz courthouse, which housed the local and high court plus the treasurer's office, lacked a roof as late as 1948. Building materials needed to remedy the situation were not available, which was also the case for

---

96 Ibid.
97 Ibid.
98 Inspection AG Rheydt by LG President Mönchengladbach, March 28, 1946, TNA, FO 1060/1007.

court buildings in the Palatinate such as Landau, Frankenthal and Zweibrücken. In Hesse, the district court of Wiesbaden had suffered from aerial bombing, rendering the east wing of the building unusable.

The Search for Alternative Housing

Towards the end of the Nazi dictatorship, some court buildings had already been converted into military hospitals or quarters for troops. With the advent of Allied troops and with the German Justice Administration defunct, courthouses were once again used for billeting. Southern Baden was especially affected by the confiscation of court buildings by French troops. In Waldshut, the court shared the building with French troops, which considerably affected the dignity associated with court buildings. Furthermore, the Germans felt rather chagrined due to the fact that the tricolor decorated the courtroom thus giving the impression that German judges were not independent, but were agents of the French authorities.[99] The French Legal Service acknowledged the truth of damages caused by soldiers saying that the soldiers used the court archives and the last wills stored in the courthouse for lighting fires, thus causing destruction in the whole building and especially the restrooms.[100] Troops were often reluctant to leave the courthouses. Similar conditions prevailed in southern Württemberg. Troops occupied parts of some court buildings, thus displacing the German courts into rooms that did not allow for proper work and were not befitting the dignity of the court.[101] Other court buildings housed German prisoners of war. In Bavaria, the court of Bayreuth had to share its abode with American troops, just as American military police had taken up quarters in the courthouse in Bamberg.

Replacement quarters for courts were often pathetic. The local court of Coesfeld (district of Münster) was housed in a shed.[102] The local court of Burgsteinfurt had found refuge in the local teachers' seminary, but squalidness and dispersion over a large area dampened the joy over the interim quarters.[103] If court buildings were left intact and unclaimed by Allied authorities, the Justice Administration still had to cede rooms to other agencies or refugee families. The Cologne court

---

99 Letter Dr. Zürcher to Direction Régionale de la Justice, Baden, December 12, 1945, AOFAA, AJ 372, p. 22/2.
100 Letter Directeur Régional de la Justice, Baden, to Section Justice, Délégué du District de Constance, January 21, 1946, AOFAA, AJ 372, p. 22/2.
101 Monthly Report Württemberg, October 1946, AOFAA, AJ 806, p. 616.
102 Inspection OLG district Hamm and Düsseldorf, April 8-19, 1947, TNA, FO 1060/1006.
103 Inspection AG Burgsteinfurt by LG-Präsident Münster, July 3, 1948, TNA, FO 1060/985.

housed several homeless people, as the British poet Stephen Spender witnessed when he encountered families using old legal files to fuel an open fire intended for cooking.[104]

The local court of Lampertheim (district of Darmstadt) was described as follows:

> This court still has considerable difficulties concerning space for its operations. 6 courtrooms and 7 rooms of the judges' apartment are still occupied by a Jewish committee operating under the supervision of IRO Frankfurt. Part of these rooms are used as club rooms. At least one additional room is needed for the court to permit storage of files which presently have been dumped into the large court room [sic] so that the judges have to try cases in their offices.[105]

When the previous occupants left, the buildings looked pretty run down. In Nuremberg, the court building was ransacked by former foreign workers, former prisoners, and German civilians. Nearly 250 typewriters from the buildings had disappeared without trace.[106] Though years had passed since the unconditional surrender, some buildings still gave a dire impression, as in the case described by the public prosecutor in Osnabrück: "All the rooms are small, personnel are cramped for space, most of the furniture is borrowed, many files and books, because of lack of shelves lie on the floor, and there is general atmosphere of gloom."[107]

The room situation was further aggravated by the creation of denazification tribunals (*Spruchkammern*). Several courts had to relinquish space to these newly constituted tribunals. Cologne lost 35 painstakingly restored rooms when the Supreme Court moved into the building. Though the edifice was far from tempting, the need for space was acute, "the 35 restored rooms having been put at the disposal of the Zonal Supreme Court," overcrowding was severe, with "8 judges using one office." Add to this the fact that "the roof of the building [was] still not weatherproof."[108]

The variety of housing appropriated as ersatz courtrooms was vast. Tax and revenue offices, apartment blocks, schools, barracks, firms, inns, breweries, and shops were all conscripted as provisional courthouses. Tübingen District Court was

---

104 Stephen Spender, *Deutschland in Ruinen: Ein Bericht* (Frankfurt am Main: Suhrkamp, 1998), 184.
105 Inspection AG Lampertheim, November 7, 1947, NARA, OMGH 17/209 – 1/2.
106 "Bericht über die Verhältnisse der Rechtspflege in Nürnberg," June 19, 1945, StA Bamberg, Rep. K 100/V, Nr. 2549.
107 Inspection LG Osnabrück, June 22, 1949, TNA, FO 1060/1237.
108 Inspection LG Düsseldorf, Kleve, Krefeld, Duisburg, Wuppertal, Köln, Aachen, Bonn, Bielefeld, Detmold, Hagen, Paderborn, Essen, Bochum, Dortmund and Arnsberg, March 30, to May 14, 1948, TNA, FO 1060/247.

housed in the local university, which was considered a favorable solution. The Heidelberg District Court building was requisitioned by an American military unit and the Kammergericht building in Berlin was occupied by the Allied Control Council.[109] Others were in prohibited areas and thus forced to move. Apart from all other problems implied by constant moves and insecurity as to the next whereabouts, the function of the courts was severely endangered. Others had to give up even their traditional locations. The district court of Heilbronn, after having been heavily bombed, had taken refuge at the local court of Öhringen during the war and stayed on there for the time being, while the public prosecutor of Heilbronn was situated in Schwäbisch Hall.[110] As the courthouse in Nuremberg first housed the International Military Tribunal and then the American military tribunals, the district court of Nürnberg-Fürth moved to the building of the local court of Erlangen. In 1948, the legal administration of Nürnberg-Fürth was dispersed in not less than 11 venues.[111]

For larger meetings, most courthouses were either unsuitable or unavailable. Therefore, the second inter-zonal conference of the heads of the German Justice Administration took place in the auditorium of the Wiesbaden rheumatism hospital. The atmosphere left a lot to be desired, as we know from a report of the Legal Division, OMGUS:

> The meeting was held in the auditorium of the so-called Rheuma Clinic in Wiesbaden, a dismal and ramshackle building facing the bombed-out city hall on Palace Square. While the meeting was underway, speakers would frequently be interrupted by the shrill whistle and the rattling noise of the narrow-gauged trains that crisscross the city hauling loads of rubble from the ruined houses to dumping places outside the city limits; and its symbolic significance was not lost upon the members of this gathering whose task likewise consisted in cleaning away the heaps of debris left upon the German legal system by the total destruction of Hitler's edifice.[112]

Attempts at Repair

Attempts to repair the dilapidated court buildings were all but futile. Building materials were difficult to come by and it was hard to find artisans willing to do

---

109 Matthias Etzel, *Die Aufhebung von nationalsozialistischen Gesetzen durch den Alliierten Kontrollrat (1945–1948)* (Tübingen: Mohr Siebeck, 1992), 48.
110 Description LG district Heilbronn [undated; 1945], NARA, OMGWB 12/136 – 3/36; Letter LG-Präsident Heilbronn, Dr. Richard Kautter, to American Mil Gov Heilbronn, June 27, 1945, NARA, OMGWB 12/140 – 2/28.
111 Conferences with Bavarian Ministry of Justice, November 29, 1948, NARA, OMGBY 17/187 – 3/1.
112 Report Legal Division, OMGUS, December 16, 1946 about Second Interzonal Jurists' Meeting in Wiesbaden, December 3-6, 1946, NARA, OMGBR 6/62 – 1/50.

the work because public service jobs were not lucrative. In Cologne the president of the high court considered using impounded cigars and cigarettes to bribe artisans.[113] Progress was often slow when state building authorities (*Staatsbauämter*) were involved. Sometimes a hands-on approach was the sole solution: "A great deal has been accomplished in the rebuilding of Landgericht Dortmund. This was achieved with the help of Court personnel including judges who were performing all the unskilled labour."[114] At other times the Allied aim of reconstruction got into conflict with the Allied aim of denazification. The owner of the firm contracted to do repairs at the Bremen courthouse had been dismissed because of his former Nazi Party membership. As the courthouse was in a desperate state the Legal Division hoped the Denazification Branch would temper justice with mercy.[115] Housekeepers had been as difficult to obtain for employment as artisans; only currency reform would eventually remedy that situation so that buildings were once again presentable.[116]

Lack of Room, Heating, and Lighting

Scarcity of rooms posed a serious challenge to the German administration of justice in all three Western zones. "[In Darmstadt] it was found that one room is shared by 7 judges. Conditions are even worse in Giessen where the whole prosecutor's office works in the cellar of the court building."[117] In Göttingen in the British Zone, three prosecutors and three interns had to share an office, making it impossible to question witnesses in the room.[118] At Rottweil District Court, 11 civil servants were sharing four rooms, forcing even the president of the district court to share his office with two other judges.[119] Even the French occupying authorities admitted that the rooms were unsuitable.[120] In Cologne, the district court president himself had a room that could not be heated, while conditions in other

---

113 Conference of OLG Presidents in Bad Pyrmont, February 16/17, 1948, HStA Düsseldorf, Gerichte Rep. 255/186.
114 Inspection OLG-district Hamm (and LG Essen, Bochum, Dortmund and Hagen), January 12-22, 1947, TNA, FO 1060/1006.
115 Letter Legal Division, OMGBR to Denazification Branch, November 13, 1945, NARA, OMGBR 6/62 – 1/12.
116 Inspection LG Frankfurt, July 27, 1948, NARA, OMGH 17/209 – 1/2.
117 Inspection of courts in Hesse, November 18, 1946, NARA, OMGUS 17/199 – 2/22.
118 Inspection LG and StA Göttingen, March 2, 1949, TNA, FO 1060/1237.
119 Monthly Report Württemberg, November 1946, AOFAA, AJ 806, p. 616.
120 Monthly Report Württemberg, December 1946, AOFAA, AJ 806, p. 616.

rooms were characterized as "appalling."[121] Involuntary office communities dominated courts in virtually every district court and several local courts.

This shortage of room (and even furniture) also curbed any further expansion or improvement of judicial services. In Hamburg it was stated that "even if additional judges could be found there would be no room for them."[122] This was true for other jurisdictions, too. Rathbone noted in a letter to the headquarters of the Legal Division: "Landgericht Essen is now 20 judges short and even if these judges are available it will be difficult to employ them owing to shortage of accommodation as a result of bomb damage."[123]

Besides of the lack of buildings and rooms therein, the cold post-war winters posed further problems. Many courts in the American Zone were closed for weeks. The work of the German court dockets in Bremen was nearly a month behind schedule because the lack of coal and any heating facilities had forced the buildings to be closed.[124] The courthouse in Ulm was considered unusable in the winter – even after the roof had been repaired, forestalling any further deterioration – "because the building [could not] be heated."[125] Ellwangen in Württemberg-Baden had central heating but lacked fuel, forcing the building to be closed over the winter.[126] Other judges reduced their office hours, some introducing a "four-hour shift schedule."[127] The preference to work in one well-heated room rather than in several unheated or badly heated rooms forced still others to share offices. The lack of fuel also affected ministries of justice, as Haven Parker – head of the Administration of Justice branch, Legal Division (OMGUS) – noted in describing a meeting in the Bavarian ministry:

> I also conferred with Dr. Hoegner [Wilhelm Hoegner, Bavarian Minister of Justice], Dr. Konrad and Dr. Rosner [high officials in the Bavarian Ministry of Justice] in the office of Dr. Hoegner in the Ministry of Justice Building. This building has had no heat in it for at least fifteen days and I can state from my personal experience that I have seldom been more uncomfortable or colder. During the conference we sat with all our outer coverings. Dr. Hoegner was in his heaviest coat and we wore gloves. Dr. Hoegner's hands were swollen as a

---

121 Letter of J.F.W. Rathbone, Legal Division, Lübbecke to Chief, Legal Division, Advanced HQ, Berlin, January 4, 1946, TNA, FO 1060/1029.
122 Inspection OLG-district Hamburg, December 2-6, 1947, TNA, FO 1060/1006.
123 Letter of Rathbone, Controller General, MOJ Control Branch, Legal Division, Main HQ, CCG (BE), Lübbecke, to Chief, Legal Division, Advanced HQ, Berlin, May 20, 1946, TNA, FO 1060/1034.
124 Letter of Haven Parker to Colonel John Raymond, January 22, 1947, NARA, OMGUS 17/199 – 2/21.
125 Weekly report, October 19, 1945, NARA, OMGWB 12/135 – 2/1.
126 Weekly report Ministry of Justice, Württemberg-Baden, October 13, 1945, NARA, OMGWB 12/137 – 1/4.
127 Inspection AG Reichelsheim, February 26, 1948, NARA, OMGH 17/209 – 1/2.

result of the constant cold. Dr. Konrad's hands were actually blue and looked as if they were the hands of a corpse.[128]

In the winter of 1945/1946, legal activities at the courts had nearly ceased. The following winter – 1946/1947 – was a little better, but the Central Legal Office could not heat its quarters for several weeks due to lack of coal.[129] Bremen closed its courts altogether that winter.

Furthermore, a curious lack of light bulbs left many court buildings in the dark. In September 1946, the president of the Kammergericht in Berlin ordered that all light bulbs were to be removed from their sockets and locked away at the end of the workday; each and every staffer was held responsible for the light bulb at his work station and would be forced to pay for replacements if bulbs were stolen or lost.[130] In Braunschweig a similar dearth was observed.[131] The shortage led to a strange way of economizing at the local court of Gelsenkirchen: Corridors were lit by light bulbs but "practically all offices are without electric light."[132]

Files, Office Supplies, Communication, and Transport

Files had often already been destroyed, either accidentally during the war or on purpose at the end of the war. Other records had been stored for safekeeping in other locations. With the arrival of the Allies, remaining files were seized. Courts and state prosecutors had to devote a lot of time to either searching for or reconstructing missing files. If surviving files were located in different zones, a return was either considered impossible (as from the Soviet Zone) or delicate and demanding. Due to the pathetic conditions in many courts, even new files got lost. At the public prosecutor's offices in Bonn, "30 files of cases from 1947 could not be traced."[133] Conditions were similar for the prosecutor in Arnsberg, who

---

[128] Letter of Haven Parker to Alan J. Rockwell, Director, Legal Division, OMGUS, February 17, 1947, NARA, OMGUS 17/199 – 2/22.
[129] Activity Report of President Central Legal Office, October 1946 to April 1947, TNA, FO 937/15.
[130] Reuss, *Berliner Justizgeschichte*, 101.
[131] Letter of J.F.W. Rathbone, Legal Division, Lübbecke to Chief, Legal Division, Advanced HQ, Berlin, January 27, 1946, TNA, FO 1060/1028.
[132] Inspection AG Gelsenkirchen by OLG-President Hamm, November 5, 1946, TNA, FO 1060/1009.
[133] Inspection LG Düsseldorf, Kleve, Krefeld, Duisburg, Wuppertal, Köln, Aachen, Bonn, Bielefeld, Detmold, Hagen, Paderborn, Essen, Bochum, Dortmund and Arnsberg, March 30, to May 14, 1948, TNA, FO 1060/247.

noted that "the whereabouts of a number of files could not be traced and a few files requested by the Inspectorate could not be found."[134]

Even though members of the judiciary had complained about the *"Papierkrieg"* (red tape, i.e., the amount of paperwork they were forced to do), occupied Germany was blissfully short of paper. In August 1946 the British Zone required 77 tons of paper per month, but only 19 tons materialized.[135] The judiciary was frustrated: How to write up letters, memos, and sentences? Others felt downright pleased: No files, no phone, no commentaries or works of reference to consult – a true liberation from old-fashioned law, minute statistics and tiresome dossiers that befogged the mind.[136]

Necessity being the mother of invention, clerical personnel in Berlin wrote judgments even on the backs of maps or on applications for leave dating from the 19th century.[137] The scarcity of typewriters and typewriter ribbons increased the delay in producing written decisions.[138] Talented tinkering developed in Schleswig-Holstein where "some court offices improvised typewriter ribbons from strips of carbon paper. These strips break frequently making the typing a very slow and nerve-[w]racking process indeed."[139] And even if the material had been readily available, personnel were difficult to summon. In Wiesbaden, all potential secretaries offered their services to the American occupation authorities first due to the obvious economic advantages employment there offered.[140] In Baden-Baden, the head of the job center always met with refusal if he tried to send workers to German employers because the French paid better and handed out extra food ration cards.[141] Material needs were considered worst in North Rhine-Westphalia, which had sustained the greatest war damage.[142]

Libraries were also few and far between. Books at the public prosecutor in Kiel had been damaged by water and bookshelves could not be constructed

---

134 Ibid.
135 Memorandum of Legal Division, July 22, 1946, TNA, FO 1060/247.
136 Wilhelm Gilsdorf, "Franzosenzeit eines Justizministers," in *Das Land Württemberg-Hohenzollern 1945-1952: Darstellungen und Erinnerungen*, ed. Max Gögler and Gregor Richter (Sigmaringen: Thorbecke, 1982), 276.
137 Reuss, *Berliner Justizgeschichte*, 97.
138 Inspection LG Düsseldorf, Kleve, Krefeld, Duisburg, Wuppertal, Köln, Aachen, Bonn, Bielefeld, Detmold, Hagen, Paderborn, Essen, Bochum, Dortmund und Arnsberg, March 30, to May 14, 1948, TNA, FO 1060/247.
139 Inspection OLG-Bezirk Schleswig, November 24, to December 7, 1946, TNA, FO 1060/1005.
140 Inspection LG Wiesbaden, April 15, 1948, NARA, OMGH 17/209 – 1/2.
141 Letter of Dr. Zürcher to Direction Régionale du contrôle de la Justice Allemande, Baden, July 10, 1946, AOFAA, AJ 372, p. 20.
142 Report Legal Division, ZECO, CCG (BE), July 25, 1947, TNA, FO 1060/247.

because no ration cards for wood had been allotted.¹⁴³ In Munich, 25 judges shared two copies of a commentary of the German Civil Code (BGB) that each of them needed every day – and this was not in the early days, but towards the end of the occupation period, in 1949.¹⁴⁴ Assembling new libraries was easier said than done. The budget for new purchases of books was small; Allied so-called local documentation teams and research units carried out further raids of court libraries in order to impound suspicious materials such as commentaries, documents, headed notepaper or other stationery. The former minister of justice in Lower Saxony moaned that a jurist without his collection of statutes, commentaries, and law gazettes is as helpless as a cobbler without leather.¹⁴⁵ This disorientation attracted the attention of American inspectors.¹⁴⁶ Because of the lack of paper, new military laws published in law gazettes were not widely distributed. Therefore, the average lawyer was no longer certain as to which laws were valid or what new legal decrees had been issued.

Broken lines of communication added to the confusion. Initially all use of mail services by Germans had been forbidden, causing military government orders to be transmitted slowly. Summons to court hearings were handled by the local bailiff personally; military government laws and decrees were posted on walls; and a collection of previously issued laws and decrees was in the hands of the legal officers, but not those of the German courts. In Württemberg, it took six to eight weeks for a military government order to reach the courts via the German Ministry of Justice or the court of appeal. Postal services, if available, were also slow. The prosecutor in Fulda "mentioned that letters from Fulda to Kassel ordinarily take 3 days and that he has to wait usually a full day for completing a telephone call to Kassel."¹⁴⁷ Conditions were, if anything, worse in the north, where it took a week for a letter to go from Kiel to Flensburg.¹⁴⁸ All this hampered investigations to the point of rendering them wholly impossible. Among the German judiciary, contacts were also limited. Members of the courts initially knew little about their colleagues – not only beyond the zonal borders, but also within the legal districts of the high courts.

Cars were rare amenities, drawing covetous looks. An American legal officer summed up the sad situation in Bremen:

---

143 Inspection public prosecutor Kiel by prosecutor general Kiel, August 17, 1946, TNA, FO 1060/1008.
144 Minister of Justice, Dr. Josef Müller, in the Bavarian Diet, December 1, 1949, p. 251.
145 Wilhelm Ellinghaus in the Lower Saxon Diet, November 10, 1949, column 4215.
146 Letter Ernst Anspach, Chief, German Administration of Justice, Legislation & Legal Advice Branch to Edward H. Littman, April 23, 1948, NARA, OMGH 17/209 – 1/2.
147 Inspection AG Fulda, August 4, 1947, NARA, OMGH 17/209 – 1/2.
148 Inspection LG Bremen, Hamburg, Kiel, May 20-22, 1946, TNA, FO 1060/1035.

> Through denazification, lack of coal, failure to provide proper protection in the way of housing for judges and other court officials, and just plain, pure cussedness on the part of several people I know, the administration of justice in the Bremen Enclave is rapidly "going to pot", and now, on top of all that, the Staatsanwaltschaft has been denied the use of its one and only automobile, which belongs to Dr. Bollinger, the Staatsanwalt.[149]

In Ellwangen, in the south, the problem was not so much the lack of cars but of gasoline. For example: "The Landgericht and the Chief Prosecutor's Office, Ellwangen, are especially hampered in their functions by the lack of gasoline for judicial circuits. Only an insignificant amount could be placed at the disposal of the two offices through the Aalen Fahrbereitschaft [motor pool]."[150] Getting around and doing the work posed enormous challenges to the German presidents of district courts when checking on their subordinate local courts. Public prosecutors could not carry out investigations, primarily because of the "lack of transport for securing the attendance of material witnesses living in widely scattered areas."[151] And as late as 1948, British legal inspectors admitted that "the transport situation at certain Landgerichte is deplorable."[152] As of mid-1949, the president of the Osnabrück district court was still unable to procure a car. His farthest Amtsgericht being 150 km away, "he … [felt] the lack of transport acutely."[153]

Excursus: Living Conditions of Members of the Judiciary

The plight of the early post-war years obviously also affected the German judiciary, many of whose members lived in abject poverty. French observers stated that the most pressing question was food.[154] The lack of nutrition caused sickness and had a detrimental effect on motivation and the ability to work. "In Hamburg alone, for example, 147 out of approximately 800 judicial officials and 25 out of approximately 249 prosecuting officials are either in hospital or incapable of working as a result of hunger, edema, or malnutrition."[155]

---

149 Letter Robert W. Johnson to Transportation Division, OMGBR, January 21, 1947, NARA, OMGBR 6/62 – 2/61.
150 Weekly Report, January 19, 1946, NARA, OMGWB 12/135 – 1/8.
151 Letter Legal Division to HQ Mil Gov North Rhine Region, May 30, 1946, TNA, FO 1060/1005.
152 Letter Legal Division, ZECO, CCG (BE), Herford to Chief Legal officer HQ Land North Rhine/Westphalia, May 25, 1948, TNA, FO 1060/247.
153 Inspection LG Osnabrück, June 22, 1949, TNA, FO 1060/1237; see also BAK, Z 21/1359.
154 Inspection LG Konstanz, September 17, 1946, AOFAA, AJ 372, p. 23.
155 Memorandum of Legal Division, July 22, 1946, TNA, FO 1060/247.

To make things worse, "judges and prosecutors [were] affected more adversely than any other section of the population, because whilst the overwhelming majority lives by supplementing rations from black-market sources, judges and prosecution, who are at present largely concerned with sentencing persons to various punishments for black-market activities, are expected to set an example to the community of scrupulous honesty."[156] The Western Allies were intent on relief, but things took time and the distribution of extra rations began slowly.

Judges or advocates who resided in representative villas often lost these to requisitioning. The British Legal Division complained that if judges and prosecutors had no "reasonable sense of security" concerning their lodgings, they would not be able to do their jobs properly.[157] Thus members of the judiciary appointed to leadership positions made it a condition of their appointment that appropriate accommodations be put at their disposal. But even high-flying jurists lived in rather appalling digs or commuted daily because they could not find housing at their places of work. The search for a prosecutor general in Bamberg had proven futile with "Several candidates [having] turned down the job because the housing situation is prohibiting."[158] In Württemberg-Hohenzollern several senior judges refused promotion to the high court of Tübingen because no housing was available.

The German Administration of Justice at Work

It is a well-known fact that the crime rate in the immediate post-war years was enormous. The devastations of the war were not only visible in a ruined country but also in the behavior of its people. Regardless of whether this "anarchy" was a reaction to the Nazi dictatorship's draconian punishments and oppression (as was felt in Offenburg),[159] or to the Allied bombings and the loss of German authority (as was stated in Freiburg)[160] or the belated re-opening of German courts, law and order were clearly at stake.

An uprooted and morally shattered population showed little respect for the rule of law. Even formerly law-abiding circles were now involved in criminal activities. In North Rhine-Westphalia the situation was described as follows: "The whole economy of Land North Rhine-Westphalia, from the biggest producer to the

---
156 Memorandum of Legal Division, HQ, July 28, 1947, TNA, FO 1060/777.
157 Inspection LG Kiel and Hamburg, August 19-21, 1946, TNA, FO 1060/1035.
158 Letter of Hans W. Weigert to Haven Parker, July 8, 1947, NARA, OMGUS 17/200 – 1/11.
159 Inspection LG Offenburg, May 1946 [no day given], AOFAA, AJ 372, p. 23.
160 Inspection OLG and LG Freiburg, April 15, 1946, AOFAA, AJ 372, p. 23.

humblest worker, is based practically entirely on barter transactions for which the expression 'Kompensation' has been universally coined by the Germans."[161] And no remedy was at hand. Even the president of the high court in Düsseldorf stated that harsher punishments would not change anything because individual consumers were forced to transgress against by-laws in order to survive. How was a criminal judge to determine the guilt of a defendant if food rationing was so meager that everybody was virtually forced to obtain groceries on the black-market in order to maintain a modicum of health?[162] In many German cities and rural areas, crime was abundant. Judges blamed the materialist notions as a byproduct of National Socialist "ethics". With their fathers detained as POWs and their mothers busy earning a living, youngsters were running wild. Even in small-town Constance, there was out-and-out juvenile gangsterism.[163]

The judiciary also enjoyed little respect. The French authorities saw a true crisis of confidence resulting from the people's experiences during the Third Reich. As the Nazi Party or party dignitaries frequently interfered with judicial matters, the population lost any trust in the free reign of independent justice.[164] For some time the public continued to address the occupying authorities with complaints about the judges and their political pasts in the hope that sentences would be altered.[165]

In particular, sexual morals came under close scrutiny. Procuring, which was defined in the broadest of senses, was a frequent offense. If a mother allowed her daughter the mere acquaintance with Allied soldiers or to sleep in the same room with one of them, she could be accused of procuring. Even conservative politicians agreed that the criminalization of sexual relationships between consenting adults was passé.[166]

The presence of Allied soldiers added to the supposed immorality of the age. In Kitzingen (Lower Franconia) the local prison was hounded by American soldiers protesting the arrest of two dozen prostitutes. Other American troops demanded the release of German women who were behind bars because of

---

161 Letter Legal Division, Herford, to Legal Division, HQ, Berlin, November 30, 1947, TNA, FO 1060/1027.
162 Letter OLG-President Düsseldorf to President Central Legal Office, January 25, 1947, BAK, Z 21/426.
163 Inspection LG Konstanz, September 17, 1946, AOFAA, AJ 372, p. 23.
164 Inspection LG Offenburg, May 1946 [no day given], AOFAA, AJ 372, p. 23.
165 Report Capitaine Hoffstetter, Chef du Service du Controle de la Justice Allemande, Baden, June 20, 1946, AOFAA, AJ 372, p. 23.
166 Minutes of the meeting of Bavarian Ministry of Justice, Legal Division, OLG Presidents and Prosecutors Generals, November 29, 1948, NARA, OMGUS 17/201 – 2/2.

abortion or vagrancy – and they did not flinch from trying to bribe or intimidate members of the judiciary to accomplish their aim.[167]

Divorces were very much in vogue as well, and continued to occupy the civil courts. At some of them, nearly 90 percent of all civil affairs were divorces.[168] Between mid-1947 and mid-1948 Bavaria alone saw 13,668 divorce cases.[169] Other problems included the frequency of abortions and applications for inquests into alleged paternity.

The Police Force and the Penal System

Apart from the problems hampering the legal system, police forces and prisons were not in good shape either. Many of the newly recruited police officers had no or little training, various members of the Nazi police force having been either put under automatic arrest or dismissed due to their SS membership.[170] In Württemberg-Hohenzollern, denazification tore huge gaps in the ranks.[171] In the British and the French Zones, nowhere near all members of the police were armed. In Schleswig-Holstein, not even half the police were equipped with handguns, and in Rhineland-Palatinate, the police force – which numbered about 4,000 men – had about 1,000 arms at their disposal.[172] The insufficient staff, equipment, and means of transport all affected the quality and speed of police work and criminal investigations. Some officers lacked the intellectual preconditions or personal disposition. Some had previous criminal records, while others were easily bribed. American observers rendered harsh judgments on police in the area of the local court Gross-Gerau (near Darmstadt), describing them as "eager, but helpless."[173]

The Ministry of Justice in Rhineland-Palatinate summed up the problems of investigations. It took a long time to search for witnesses, especially if they lived in different zones of occupation. Delays were also caused by the fact that state attorneys and coroners had to conduct their interrogations in internment camps. The difficult transport situation added to the general aggravation of investiga-

---

167 Interference with German courts [undated], NARA, OMGBY 17/186 – 3/28.
168 Inspection LG Giessen, May 29, 1947, NARA, OMGH 17/209 – 1/2; Inspection OLG and LG Freiburg, April 15, 1946, AOFAA, AJ 372, p. 23; Inspection LG Aachen by OLG-President Cologne, March 13, 1946, TNA, FO 1060/1007.
169 Memorandum of Bavarian Ministry of Justice, July 19, 1948, HStA München, MJu 22692.
170 Falco Werkentin, *Die Restauration der deutschen Polizei: Innere Rüstung von 1945 bis zur Notstandsgesetzgebung* (Frankfurt am Main: Campus Verlag, 1984), 35.
171 Weekly report Württemberg-Hohenzollern, March 1947, AOFAA, AJ 806, p. 616.
172 Werkentin, *Die Restauration der deutschen Polizei*, 41, 47.
173 Inspection AG Gross-Gerau, July 22, 1947, NARA, OMGH 17/209 – 1/2.

tions.¹⁷⁴ Gumming up the works even further, sometimes the police handed over their findings to both the German state attorneys and the military government authorities, both of which then initiated action on the files.

Some prisons had suffered bomb damage; others had been sequestered by the occupiers. Control Council Directive No. 19 (November 1945) stated that the enforcement of sentences was to be humane. Rehabilitation and reform, not revenge, should govern the regime of prisons. Beatings were forbidden, prison administrations were urged to provide work and educational facilities such as prison libraries. Due to the lack of suitable buildings, monasteries and old fortresses, which were of only limited value as prisons, were often used. The guards were trained and psychologists were employed.

While prisons and penitentiaries had been nearly empty in the immediate post-war period, as soon as courts began their work, prisoners filled them once again. As early as July 1946, prisons in the American Zone were filled beyond their capacity.¹⁷⁵ Nearly half of the prisoners were remanded because German courts were slow in processing penal cases. In November 1946, the population in German prisons in the American Zone numbered 28,000 inmates.¹⁷⁶ Conditions were often unsatisfactory, as in Heidenheim prison, which received the following report: "Unclean cells, beds are not in usable condition, bottles in cells, personal effects in cells, prisoners not clean and tidy, in general no orderliness. Shortage of fuel, therefore, several cells unused, while others are crowded. Women's cell was cold."¹⁷⁷ In winter "in several prisons there was absolutely no heat for weeks at a time. A number of prisoners suffered frostbite right in their cells. In many cases work programs were interrupted and prisoners were allowed to remain in bed to keep warm."¹⁷⁸ Personnel heading the prisons – again, often freshly recruited – did not always live up to expectations. Sometimes the fox was put in charge of the henhouse. The penitentiary in Ebrach was put under the direction of a man who turned out to have several convictions.¹⁷⁹ Similar conditions prevailed in the British and the French Zones. In the British Zone it was noted that professional

---

174 Report Ministry of Justice in Rhineland-Palatinate to Legal Division in Koblenz, January 9, 1948, AOFAA, AJ 3680, p. 21.
175 Report on Legal and Judicial Affairs, October 7, 1947, NARA, OMGUS 11/5 – 21/1.
176 Ibid.
177 Inspection Heidenheim prison, January 18, 1947, NARA, OMGWB 12/133 – 2/4.
178 History of the Administration of German Prisons, January 1, 1947 -June 30, 1948, NARA, OMGUS 11/5 – 3/2/38.
179 Letter OLG-President Bamberg to Bavarian Ministry of Justice, October 22, 1945, StA Bamberg, Rep. K 100/V, Nr. 2549.

black marketeers had no trouble making bail and were thus not as frequently jailed as one might have expected.[180]

In the French Zone prisons were sometimes so overcrowded that detainees had to sleep on the floor. Many of them had been caught when trying to cross the border illegally to get to the Saar region, France or Luxemburg in order to look for work.[181]

While conditions in the prisons were often pathetic, so were security measures. The makeshift set-up of improvised prisons facilitated attempted breakouts while the guards could only look on helplessly. One inspection report read: "The Wachtmeister in charge of this jail is in dire need of a weapon. He was assaulted two weeks ago by nine prisoners, strangled and badly bruised, but could escape and hold the situation in hand."[182] To make matters worse, windows were often not barred and guards had no telephones with which to summon help. The Americans also found it difficult to understand the mentality of the guards regarding the high rate of escape: "One of the problems encountered by Military Government prisons officers in combatting the high escape rates of the German prisons was the German notion that every prisoner has the right to attempt to escape."[183]

Public Prosecutors and Courts

As has been already described, many cases had accumulated by the time the courts re-opened to the public. Judicial personnel as well as Allied Legal Divisions despaired over the number of cases piling up. One can only give a brief sketch of what was in store for the courts. They had to deal with cases that had been pending with the now-defunct Reichsgericht (Reich court) or the infamous People's Court. Convictions for specific Nazi notions of crimes (e.g., racial defilement) were to be erased from the rap sheet. Nazi impoundments of property had to be reverted. Restitution chambers were established to deal with the claims of Nazi victims or their heirs. Even seemingly uncomplicated matters as the Land registers proved tricky. In Leer (Lower Saxony) many Jews had lost their property prior to emigration or deportation; as many as 90 percent were estimated not to

---

180 Inspection LG Lüneburg, Braunschweig, Göttingen, Hildesheim, Hannover, September 23 – October 8, 1947, TNA, FO 1060/247.
181 Report Ministry of Justice Rhineland-Palatinate to French Legal Division, April 9, 1948, AOFAA, AJ 3680, p. 21, Dossier 4.
182 Inspection AG Nidda, January 14, 1948, NARA, OMGH 17/209 – 1/2.
183 History of the Administration of German Prisons, January 1, 1947-June 30, 1948, NARA, OMGUS 11/5 – 3/2/38.

have survived. "The question now at issue [was] what to do with their properties and how the Grundbuch [property registry] should be altered or amended."[184] On the other hand, new breaches of law had to be adjudicated. Falsification of denazification questionnaires or forged new identities or contravention of Allied military laws came up in the courts. The former head of the district authority of Giessen was discovered to have falsified his denazification papers and was sentenced to a severe term of imprisonment, after which the American side noted with satisfaction: "Thus ends the story of a racketeer who believed that by the assumption of another name and by the fraudulent representation of an education and civil service experience he could fool American and German authorities because he was not aware of the Berlin Document Center records and relied upon the fact that he had come to the Western zones from the new Polish zone of Germany."[185] Jurists who were convicted of similar crimes were considered anathema by the Americans. "In our opinion, such a conviction indicates moral turpitude in the character of the offender and should bar him from any permanent appointment or reinstatement as judge or prosecutor."[186]

Even though the Americans criticized the apparent leniency of German courts with respect to falsified denazification questionnaires, the number of cases was still impressive. In Bavaria alone, 10,909 cases had been finalized within one year (1947/1948) and a further 2,869 were pending.[187]

The jurists found it difficult to define what constituted a Nazi law. During Hitler's dictatorship not less than 9,573 laws had been issued.[188] A complete list of unacceptable Nazi laws was never compiled. Even more complicated was the code of practice. Which sentences were explicitly contaminated by Nazi spirit? Not every sentencing of a common thief during the Third Reich was blatant Nazi injustice. The French authorities made it clear that they did not want to give precise directives to purge the law of Nazi influence, since some of the laws were even considered useful.[189] An inter-zonal meeting of jurists came to the conclusion that the penal code had suffered from Nazi abuse, but in its actual core was not to be viewed as based in Nazi ideology. Observers from the American Military Government were disappointed. "The failure of the meeting to come to a clear understanding as to what elements make a law Nazi in character must be consid-

---

184 Inspection OLG Oldenburg, October 2-26, 1946, TNA, FO 1060/1003.
185 Activity Report, November 24, 1948, NARA, OMGH 17/209 – 1/2.
186 Letter of Ralph E. Brown, Chief, German Justice Branch to Director Legal Division, OMGUS, July 7, 1947, NARA, OMGWB 12/140 – 1/1-20.
187 Memorandum of Bavarian Ministry of Justice, July 19, 1948, HStA München, MJu 22692.
188 Etzel, *Die Aufhebung von nationalsozialistischen Gesetzen durch den Alliierten Kontrollrat*, 51.
189 Monthly Report Württemberg, February 1946, AOFAA, AJ 3679, p. 12.

ered one of the most serious shortcomings of the discussions."[190] While the Allied Control Council suggested purging the German penal code of National Socialist and militaristic influences, most speakers at the inter-zonal conference opted for a reform of the penal code under a democratically elected German parliament – in other words, "not now." Initiatives for new laws were to be avoided altogether in order not to endanger the German unity of the law (Rechtseinheit). Unclear competencies (Allied Control Council, zonal military governments, and individual military governments of the Länder) and German authorities (ministries of justice in the Länder, Central Legal Office in the British Zone, and presidents of high courts) only added to the general confusion.

Work Load

Due to the high demands on the courts, judges and prosecutors were often overworked. Besides fulfilling their normal tasks, some also had to serve in denazification chambers. Others, however, had a more relaxed attitude towards work. Allied inspectors were infuriated when they performed spot checks and found empty offices. Many German courts habitually closed their offices to the public after midday or for the afternoon, which was a rather unusual practice in the eyes of the Allied inspectors. In winter, even more lenient rules seemed to apply, as a court staffer carelessly admitted: "In the afternoon we are usually here unless it gets too cold, then we just take off."[191] Observers had hoped for more diligence and motivation in the performance of work, since the German judicial personnel seemed to handle cases "during limited office hours."[192] The Legal Division found it to be "true that occasionally some judges do not work as hard as it is necessary at the present time of emergency and that they pursue their work in the old established manner they have used for many decades."[193] The British described the situation acidly at the local court in Cologne: "It will be seen that the Amtsgericht [local court] is a most inefficient organization ... When convictions are obtained sentences are noticeably low. The prosecutors are poor. The judges claim to be overworked, but in fact appear to do little work."[194]

---

[190] Report Legal Division, OMGUS, December 16, 1946 about Second Interzonal Jurists' Meeting in Wiesbaden, December 3-6, 1946, NARA, OMGBR 6/62 – 1/50.
[191] Letter of Ralph E. Brown to Ministry of Justice Württemberg-Baden, April 1, 1947, NARA, OMGWB 12/140 – 1/1-20.
[192] LSO Kassel, Weekly Intelligence Report, December 23, 1946, NARA, OMGUS 17/217 – 3/3.
[193] Letter Henry H. Urman to Alvin J. Rockwell, January 9, 1947, NARA, OMGUS 17/217 – 3/3.
[194] Letter Summary Court Officer to Legal Division, August 29, 1945, TNA, FO 1060/977.

Curfews imposed by the occupation authorities also hampered judicial work. In the French Zone, personnel in higher courts had to be issued with *laissez-passer* (permits to pass) to conduct their work, when necessary, at night.[195] Due to the rural nature of certain legal districts, judicial work was not distributed evenly throughout the year. At the local court of Hilders (a small branch of the local court of Fulda in the legal district of Kassel) it was determined that in summer the population was so occupied with tilling the land that hardly any (civil) trials were initiated; a similar observation was made in Gersfeld.[196] The frequency of trials also depended on the makeup of the population. In Gelsenkirchen, a working-class mining community, courts were not tested as frequently as in Gelsenkirchen-Buer, a middle-class neighborhood.[197] The population of Laasphe (Siegen district) had risen substantially due to the influx of refugees from the east, but this had no influence on the rate of trials as the refugees were penniless and generated very little work in the area of penal justice, litigation affairs and guardianships.[198]

While Allied legal officers did not try to tell German judges how to do their jobs, a little politeness on behalf of the German legal staff towards the German public was considered helpful and surely increased "customer satisfaction." When a local judge well known for giving short shrift to petitioners of lawsuits was transferred, contentment was noted: "Due to the fact that the population of this district which had been scared away by Amtsgerichtsrat [name omitted] who treated the public like concentration camp inmates is regaining confidence into the Administration of Justice, operations have considerably increased."[199]

Allied Criticism

A source of permanent sorrow for American, British, and French legal divisions was the seemingly lackadaisical approach of German courts. Nearly every report lists "backlog," "arrears of business," "*arrière*" (behind) or "*affaire en souffrance*" (case pending) and discord among Allied and German authorities. In Bremen, the head of the American Military Government confronted Mayor Wilhelm Kaisen with

---

[195] Sûreté, Délégation Supérieure pour le Gouvernement Militaire du Pays de Bade to Directeur Régional du Contrôle de la Justice, May 9, 1946, AOFAA, AJ 372, p. 19.
[196] Inspection AG Hilders, August 5, 1947, NARA, OMGH 17/209 – 1/2; Inspection AG Gersfeld, August 5, 1947.
[197] Inspection AG Gelsenkirchen by LG President Essen, May 22, 1946, TNA, FO 1060/1007.
[198] Inspection AG Laasphe by LG President Siegen, July 19, 1946, TNA, FO 1060/1008.
[199] Inspection AG Oberaula, September 28, 1948, NARA, OMGH 17/209 – 1/2.

the "extremely slow" functioning of German courts: "Operation of the German judicial system is the task of the German authorities, and to the extent of prompt trials of persons accused of crime, they are failing in this task."[200] If things did not speed up, the Military Government would be forced to intervene. The senator of justice (i.e. the Bremen minister of justice) countered by referring to the lack of staff caused by denazification and the rise in criminality in the harbor cities of Bremen and Bremerhaven. In other parts of the American Zone another reason for the slow processing of cases surfaced: "A tendency on the part of German legal officials to avoid the responsibility for independent action where possible has been making itself increasingly evident."[201]

The British agonized over the bottleneck in the German courts.[202] With winter looming, the rate of case processing seemed especially endangered. One memorandum read: "The present position is critical, but the coming winter may well bring about a crisis."[203] The British Legal Division was convinced that there was no ill will on behalf of the German judicial apparatus – the Germans were intent on handling cases quickly. But the work seemed to be increasing at an exponential rate. A steady flow of refugees into the British Zone and the pathetic economic situation as well as denazification cases were bound to create more work for the courts.[204]

While the causes were easily named, it was obviously much more difficult to produce relief. Again, the British Legal Division was willing to honor the attempts made by the German justice administration, reporting that "the German Ordinary Courts [had] played a very considerable part during the past 18 months in the maintenance of law and order in the British Zone, under highly abnormal conditions."[205] The British were adamant about continuing to transfer more tasks to the Germans mandated by "the generally adopted principle of devolution of responsibility to the Germans." Despite all the problems, "it [was] surprising but nevertheless a fact that the courts in the British Zone [were] disposing of a far greater volume of business than before the war."[206] While occasional setbacks were discovered – such as in Aachen where no fewer than 12,525 pending cases were unearthed in April 1947, eliciting a cry of horror from the British Legal Divi-

---

200 Letter Thomas F. Dunn, Director, OMGBR to Mayor Wilhelm Kaisen, July 21, 1948, NARA, OMGBR 6/63 – 1/4.
201 Weekly report, June 28, 1946, NARA, OMGWB 12/135 – 1/9.
202 Memorandum of Legal Division, July 22, 1946, TNA, FO 1060/247.
203 Ibid.
204 Letter Legal Division, ZECO, CCG (BE), Herford to Legal Division, CCG (BE), Berlin, March 18, 1947, TNA, FO 1060/247.
205 Report Legal Division, July 25, 1947, TNA, FO 1060/247.
206 Ibid.

sion[207] – on the whole the German judiciary seemed to be set on a track back to the regular disposal of work.

The French Legal Division also deplored the slow disposal of work.[208] To be fair, all the Western Allies took the facts into consideration. It was not laziness or inertia on the part of prosecutors and judges, but the war itself that was responsible for the backlog with which the justice administration in Germany was still wrestling. During the war, many higher court officials had been recruited into the army so that only the bare necessities had been pursued. Furthermore, the Allies also found fault with their own policy. "It was clear that justice would have to take a low priority as compared with other more essential fields of German life, for example, economics, agriculture and building reconstruction."[209]

The American Legal Division pointed to the fact that judges were old and undernourished, with scant provision against the cold; courthouses and flats were badly heated, leading to frequent illness. Thus "it [was] very hard to make them responsible for not reducing the backlog."[210] In the French zone, a similar vicious circle existed: The backlog would lead to long working hours and overtime; overwork and malnutrition would cause illness; the lack of personnel and the high crime rate would again produce more work for the courts.[211] Due to extraordinary circumstances, a few courts had no backlogs. For example, the district court of Würzburg had been bombed in March 1945, resulting in a nearly complete loss of records.[212] Others lost their records in fires and to Allied troops housed in court buildings.

The Allies also found fault with the mild sentences meted out by German judges. After a visit to a summary court in Giessen, the American Legal Division complained that judges often sympathized too much with defendants, crediting them with extenuating circumstances too frequently. On the whole, they showed "too much human understanding."[213] Sentences in black market crimes were "exceedingly mild and in many cases ridiculously low."[214] One reason was that even the state prosecutors asked for lenient sentences. The British Legal Division advised prosecutors general to demand that prosecutors seek harsher punish-

---

207 Inspection OLG district Düsseldorf and Cologne, May 12-21, 1947, TNA, FO 1060/1006.
208 Monthly Report Württemberg, November 1946, AOFAA, AJ 806, p. 616.
209 Memorandum of Legal Division, July 22, 1946, TNA, FO 1060/247; also in TNA, FO 1060/1005.
210 Letter Henry H. Urman to Alvin J. Rockwell, 9.1.1947, NARA, OMGUS 17/217 – 3/3.
211 Inspection LG Offenburg, May 1946 [without exact date], AOFAA, AJ 372, p. 23.
212 Inspection LG Würzburg, June 16, 1947, NARA, OMGBY 17/183 – 2/13; see also under NARA, OMGUS 17/217 – 3/3.
213 Inspection Schnellgericht Giessen, June 24, 1948, NARA, OMGH 17/209 – 1/2.
214 Weekly Report, September 6, 1946, NARA, OMGWB 12/135 – 2/1.

ments and appeal to a higher court if the punishment was not satisfactory.[215] The French agreed with this opinion.[216] German justice showed *une trop grande indulgence* (too much indulgence) towards crime.[217] And because they were so mild, the sentences obviously encouraged new breaches of law, as the delinquents had not had sense knocked into them. Because the tribunals did not yield to the pleadings of the state prosecutors, the fault was not with the state attorneys, but with the courts.[218] The French observers had an explanation ready: "Under the Nazis, the German judges had been too repressive, now they are being too indulgent."[219] Previously, the state attorneys had received instructions from the Reich Ministry of Justice as to how they were to plead and the judges then decided accordingly. Nowadays, public prosecutors addressed themselves to the judges at the military tribunals or to members of the Legal Division to inquire as to which degree of penalty would be considered appropriate. In 1948, the French came to similar conclusions.[220]

Denazification and Personnel Politics

The biggest problem the Allies faced in their reconstruction of the German judicial system was one of personnel. It is difficult to research the personnel situation methodically because sources are nearly nonexistent. The last relevant handbook (*Handbuch der Justizverwaltung*) of the Third Reich was published in 1942 and the first post-war edition of the *Handbuch der Justiz* (Handbook of Justice) came out in 1953. Changes in personnel for the period in question are thus extremely difficult to trace.

The Control Council Law No. 4 (October 30, 1945) declared that all former active NSDAP members and all those involved in penal justice of the Third Reich would no longer be admitted to practice as judges or prosecutors. The devil, however, was in the details: What was the definition of "active support of the Nazi Party"? How was "participation in the Nazi penal system" to be measured? The Western Allies agreed that the following were unacceptable:
– membership in the Nazi Party before April 1933

---

[215] Letter Legal Division, CCG (BE) to HQ Mil Gov. Hannover, Schleswig-Holstein, Westphalia, Northrhine and Hansestadt Hamburg, June 30, 1946, TNA, FO 1060/247.
[216] Monthly Report Württemberg, December 1946, AOFAA, AJ 806, p. 616.
[217] Monthly Report Rhineland, February 1946, AOFAA, AJ 3679, p. 12.
[218] Monthly Report Baden, October 31, 1946, AOFAA, AJ 3679, p. 13, Dossier 7.
[219] Monthly Report Württemberg, October 1946, AOFAA, AJ 806, p. 616.
[220] Monthly Report Württemberg, May 1948, AOFAA, AJ 806, p. 618.

- activity and membership in a party court
- membership in the SS
- lasting membership in both NSDAP and SA (from 1933 to 1945)
- lasting membership in the Party and SA since 1937 if an officer's rank had been attained.

Curiously, affiliation with the notorious special courts (*Sondergerichte*) was not branded.

In any case, denazification criteria were general, i.e., not directed at the small circle of legal personnel at the courts and prosecutors' offices.

Although Americans, British, and French legal officers all faced the same problem in reference to the German judicial personnel, each would handle the problem differently.

Personnel Politics in the American Zone

The Americans were initially very rigorous in their denazification efforts. By the end of July 1945, 70,000 people in the American Zone had been dismissed from their posts because of their Nazi affiliations; by the end of March 1946, a total of 140,000 members of the public service had lost their jobs. This obviously affected the administration of justice as well. In some places, the higher judicial personnel had been reduced to as little as half of its previous number. In Northern Baden, a breakdown was looming. As noted in the February 1946 monthly report for the area, "German justice officials fear a collapse in the judicial system as a result of the lack of personnel to handle the constant accumulation of business."[221] While in 1939, 789 higher judicial staff members had been employed in the territory that was later to become Baden-Württemberg, by 1948 the number was down to 458.[222] A similar situation was found in Bavaria. In 1933 there had been 1,393 judges in Bavaria (including the territory on the left bank of the Rhine). By 1946 there were 1,222 positions for judges in the (slightly reduced) Bavarian territory. Of these, only 526 were filled. For the prosecutors, 212 positions were occupied by only 87 incumbents.[223]

---

221 Monthly Report Baden, February 1946, NARA, OMGWB 12/135 – 1/9.
222 Monthly Report, October 30, 1948, NARA, OMGWB 12/136 – 1/2; Monthly Report, November 1, 1948, NARA, OMGWB 12/137 – 2/7.
223 Conference of the heads of the highest judicial authorities in the British and American Zone in Bad Godesberg, July 16-17, 1946, BAK, Z 21/1309.

Due to the de-centralized denazification strategies, each location appeared to apply different rules. Some personnel were dismissed in one place but re-employed in another. Guiding principles were not discernible for outsiders.[224]

Examples of Personnel

At the outset, the Americans appointed small teams of German staff. In the early days, military government local detachments dismissed and appointed personnel as they saw fit, but this created several problems. In some cases, the Americans chose totally unqualified people or charlatans. In Landshut, the local Military Government appointed a trainee to the highest position at the district court.[225] In Hassfurt (Lower Franconia), the German authorities noted with horror that a member of the clerical staff, a mere judiciary inspector (*Justizinspektor*), was offered the position of a judge or notary.[226] At the local court of Kötzting, a man called Baron of Maydell officiated as a local judge even though he had not completed the necessary German state exams to enter the civil service. By the time he was found out and dismissed, he had already collected nearly 3000 RM (*Reichsmarks*) in earnings.[227] The local court of Forchheim was headed by a man who was not a professional judge at all, but a publisher. For the details of the sentences, he would contact the local military government office and ask how they would handle the case.[228] Shortly afterwards, he was removed from office and arrested for deception. This met with some schadenfreude on behalf of the Justice Administration, which warned against blue-eyed admissions of "Northern Germans" according to their "white" (i.e., false) questionnaires.[229] The high court in Bamberg warned against letting the American Military Government fill the positions at the local courts at will. Judges whose affiliations with the Nazi Party were well known locally would be driven out of office, to be replaced by unknown judges or lawyers who claimed not to have been members of the Nazi

---

[224] Letter of high court president of Bamberg, Dr. Lorenz Krapp, to Bavarian Ministry of Justice, October 22, 1945, StA Bamberg, Rep. K 100/V, Nr. 2549.
[225] Letter Juan Sedillo, Director, Legal Division, OMGBY to German Courts Branch, Legal Division, OMGUS, November 18, 1947, NARA, OMGUS 17/217 – 1/15.
[226] Report "Some reasons for the resumption of activity of the high court," June 2, 1945, StA Bamberg, Rep. K 100/V, Nr. 2549.
[227] Weekly Report, September 21, 1946, NARA, OMGBY 17/183 – 3/13.
[228] Memorandum "Situation at the local court Forchheim" [undated, 1945], StA Bamberg, Rep. K 100/V, Nr. 2549.
[229] Report of President local court of Würzburg, Dr. Lobmiller, September 18, 1945, StA Bamberg, Rep K 100/V, Nr. 3649/I.

Party. The overly credulous American Military Government would create a situation in which Bavarians would be outcasts, while courts would be staffed with alien, adroitly camouflaged Nazi elements whose personal files, criminal records, or other papers were "missing" or "lost."[230] After yet another case of falsely assumed identity – a former teacher, previously convicted for fraudulent bankruptcy, posing as a judge at the local court in Kronach was exposed[231] – it was decided that all appointments were to be made by the Bavarian Ministry of Justice in accordance with the Military Government. Differing denazification guidelines and arbitrariness didn't help. There was an

> almost unbelievable chaos of denazification management in the early period after unconditional surrender, when the criteria changed from Land to Land, district to district, and even locality to locality, according to the whim of the AMG [American Military Government] legal officer involved. These officers were not always immune to personal influence, particularly when communicated by an attractive female, and a judge who found readmission difficult in one locality could sometimes obtain a 'discretionary, no adverse recommendation' elsewhere."[232]

A member of military government mused retrospectively that an earlier establishment of a state Ministry of Justice might have helped coordinate the selection and appointment of judges and state prosecutors.[233]

On the other hand, impostors turn up even in long-established democracies where candidates are checked and interviewed by expert panels, so it's no surprise that pretenders were able to slip past local Military Government officials not too familiar with German procedures, and make their way into a fledgling, chronically overworked and understaffed bureaucracy in the early post-war period! Furthermore, the activity of a local judge resembles – at least superficially – that of an Anglo-American Justice of the Peace, with the important exception that a German local judge must be a professional jurist.

Toward the end of 1945, the Americans withdrew from the appointment of German judges and prosecutors, leaving the task to the Länder ministries of

---

230 Letter of OLG-President Dr. Lorenz Krapp to Prime Minister of Bavaria, Bavarian Ministry of Justice, President of the district government for Upper Franconia in Ansbach and President of the district government for Lower Franconia in Würzburg, August 18, 1945, StA Bamberg, Rep. K 100/V, Nr. 2549.
231 Letter of OLG-President Dr. Lorenz Krapp to Ministry of Justice, January 24, 1946, StA Bamberg, Rep. K 100/V, Nr. 2550.
232 Loewenstein, "Reconstruction of the Administration of Justice", 447.
233 Eli E. Nobleman, "The Administration of Justice in the United States Zone of Germany," *Federal Bar Journal* 8 (1946), 91.

justice. They nevertheless insisted on the fulfillment of certain criteria according to a list of preferences:
1. Preferential treatment was to be given to legal personnel who had been persecuted or had been avowed opponents of the Nazi regime.
2. The second category of preferred employees was personnel with positive political qualities for the re-building of a German democracy.
3. The designation as less-tainted, fellow-traveler, or non-tainted would not guarantee re-admission to office.
4. Persons marked as major offenders or tainted after denazification were not to be re-appointed, except to menial jobs.
5. Persons suspected as major offenders or tainted whose *Spruchkammer* (denazification) proceedings were not yet concluded would not be appointed or employed.

Lack of the personal qualities needed for the re-building of democracy; continuation in a position that ran contrary to the aims of the military government; filibustering or ignoring an order from the Military Government; or earlier sentencing by a military government court, would result in loss of the previously held office.[234] The Americans looked on warily as the legal personnel they had appointed were successively replaced. "In this connection it ought to be said that former party members who had been denazified recently are trying to use their political party connections to get key positions held for the last 2½ years by non-party members appointed by Military Government in the early stages of the occupation."[235]

Among the first legal personnel appointed to their jobs were the new president of the high court in Bamberg, Dr. Lorenz Krapp (who had retired in 1933) and the new prosecutor general, Dr. Thomas Dehler (whose wife was Jewish).[236] Though both were clearly anti-Nazi, they were far from enthusiastic about the new tasks. Both had been told that if they continued refusing, the Military Government would send completely unknown people from Frankfurt to take up office in Bamberg.[237] In Nuremberg, the new president of the high court, Dr. Hans Heinrich, had even recognized a Jew's right to a pension in a civil case as late as

---
234 Policy statements [undated, after January 10, 1949], NARA, OMGUS 17/215 – 2/20.
235 Monthly report, January 24, 1948, NARA, OMGBY 17/183 – 3/15.
236 Udo Wengst, *Thomas Dehler, 1897-1967: Eine politische Biographie* (München: Oldenbourg Wissenschaftsverlag, 1997), 43, 66.
237 Letter of OLG-President Dr. Lorenz Krapp to Prime Minister of Bavaria, Bavarian Ministry of Justice, President of the district government for Upper Franconia in Ansbach and President of the district government for Lower Franconia in Würzburg, August 18, 1945, StA Bamberg, Rep. K 100/V, Nr. 2549.

1941.[238] Richard Schmid, prosecutor general in Stuttgart (later to become president of the high court in Stuttgart in 1953), had been sentenced to three years in prison in 1940 for planning high treason – he had tried to re-create the forbidden SAP (Sozialistische Arbeiterpartei Deutschlands), a left socialist split-off of the Social Democratic Party dating from 1931) in Württemberg. After serving the sentence he was banned from the profession. Other jurists included the president at the district court of Nürnberg-Fürth, Camille Sachs, whose Jewish origins led to his dismissal during the Third Reich; or Dr. Max Silberstein who – after having been imprisoned in Buchenwald in 1938 – emigrated to France, returning in 1946 to become a judge at the district court of Mannheim.[239]

While the German Land ministries of Justice (in Bremen, Hesse, Bavaria and Württemberg-Baden) could appoint judges and state prosecutors, they were still supposed to calibrate their procedures with the Americans. The Americans noted shortages of suitable people[240] and reaffirmed their intention of employing only politically cleared personnel. This would, however, drive them to despair when higher positions – as in Bavaria for the three high courts in Munich, Nuremberg and Bamberg – were in question.[241] Because of this shortage of suitable judges, the Americans were willing to compromise.

Obsolescence

One way of circumventing the shortage of judges and prosecutors was to draw on the reserve staff that had been pensioned off at the beginning of the Third Reich. At local and district courts in Hesse, quite a few septuagenarians and even some octogenarians were officiating. The senior prosecutor in Wiesbaden was discounted as "pleasant, but apparently overaged";[242] in Bad Orb (district of Hanau) one judge was "beyond retirement age";[243] AG Melsungen (district of Kassel) was

---

238 Letter of Gaurechtsberater Oeschey to vice NSDAP-Gauleiter Holz, December 18, 1942, Nuremberg Documents NG 2167; see also personal file of Dr. Hans Heinrich, HStA Munich, MJu 25217.
239 Letter of Ralph E. Brown, German Justice Branch, OMGWB to Director Legal Division, OMGUS, July 23, 1947, NARA, OMGWB 12/137 – 1/2; see also under NARA, OMGWB 12/140 – 1/1-20; also: Reiner Haehling von Lanzenauer, "Das Oberlandesgericht Karlsruhe und sein Präsident Max Silberstein," *Zeitschrift für die Geschichte des Oberrheins* 151 (2003).
240 Report, August 28, 1947, NARA, OMGWB 12/140 – 1/1-20.
241 Monthly Report, January 24, 1948, NARA, OMGBY 17/183 – 3/15.
242 Inspection LG Wiesbaden, April 15, 1948, NARA, OMGH 17/209 – 1/2.
243 Inspection AG Bad Orb, February 12, 1948, NARA, OMGH 17/209 – 1/2.

headed by a 73 year old;[244] AG Witzenhausen (also district of Kassel) by a 77 year old.[245] And he was by no means the oldest. At AG Biedenkopf (district Limburg) a 78-year-old judge still worked,[246] as was the case at AG Kirchhain (district Marburg).[247] A senior judge at Kassel District Court was born in 1866 and thus was 81 years old in 1947.[248]

Obviously, age and the dire living and working circumstances took their toll and not everyone was still fit to conduct the work the job demanded. One judge in Marburg was nearly blind due to old age;[249] at Reichelsheim local court the 73-year-old judge – who had clocked a stunning 49 years of service – was now "completely senile and very hard of hearing."[250]

On average, judges and prosecutors in Hesse were 55 to 60 years old.[251] Because such a large stratum of the German Justice Administration seemed to resemble a retirement home, younger practitioners of the legal craft stood out, such as the Hessian Minister of Justice, Dr. Zinn, a "fortunate choice, as he does not appear to be over 50 years old and has considerable vigor of mind, without the bias frequently found among German lawyers."[252] Dr. Beyerle, on the other hand, was born in 1881 and was well over 60 when he began his position as minister of justice in Württemberg-Baden, belonged to the older generation.

In some cases, even the American legal officers suggested sending some of the judges and prosecutors into retirement.[253] In Bremen and Bremerhaven it was the members of the prosecutor's office who were considered too old and tired: "The offices are understaffed and some of the prosecutors now in office so overaged [sic] and physically exhausted that, in the case of Bremerhaven, I feel that they are absolutely incapable of handling their affairs properly."[254]

Younger judges and prosecutors were also suffering from various ailments, which slowed down work considerably. Some had been invalids since World War

---

244 Inspection AG Melsungen, November 12, 1947, NARA, OMGH 17/209 – 1/2.
245 Inspection AG Witzenhausen, November 12, 1947, NARA, OMGH 17/209 – 1/2.
246 Inspection AG Biedenkopf, September 25, 1947, NARA, OMGH 17/209 – 1/2.
247 Inspection AG Kirchhain, November 18, 1947 and September 28, 1948, NARA, OMGH 17/209 – 1/2.
248 Inspection LG Kassel, March 20, 1947, NARA OMGH 17/209 – 1/2.
249 Inspection AG Marburg, April 28, 1948, NARA, OMGH 17/209 – 1/2.
250 Inspection AG Reichelsheim, February 26, 1948, NARA, OMGH 17/209 – 1/2.
251 Letter of Henry H. Urman to Alvin J. Rockwell, January 9, 1947, NARA, OMGUS 17/217 – 3/3.
252 Memorandum by Norman C. Shepard, Administration of Justice Branch, to Charles Fahy, Director, Legal Division, December 27, 1949, NARA, OMGUS 17/53 – 1/6.
253 Letter of Henry Urman to Charles H. Kraus, March 13, 1947, NARA, OMGUS 17/199 – 2/22.
254 Report Hans W. Weigert, Legal Division, OMGUS about Field Trip to Bremen, Bremerhaven and Hamburg, July 4, 1947, NARA, OMGBR 6/62 – 2/60.

I.²⁵⁵ As has been pointed out before, hunger was a constant companion. While the population in the American Zone was supplementing the allocated daily 1,550 calories with black-market purchases, higher members of the Justice Administration had to refrain from resorting to similar means. The death rate, unsurprisingly, was high among the over-aged, overworked and poorly nourished jurists.

Those in office did not look impressive, as can be inferred from a report about judges in Bavaria:

> As to the physical condition of the judges, they are mostly older men ranging from 45 to 60 and over. Many of them are above retirement ages. At the present time about 130 of the former judges in Bavaria are held as prisoners of war mostly in the Russian Zone. The rural judge is in much better physical shape than those of the city for obvious reasons. Many judges have lost their homes and are living under inadequate conditions. Dr. Hoegner stated that it is very difficult to make transfer of judges from one district to another because of the difficulty of finding places for them to live. Some judges who are politically cleared, especially those who get promotions, are unable to draw their full salary because their property is still blocked.²⁵⁶

Judges and prosecutors in Hesse did not look much better:

> Legal and judicial qualities of personnel are not always too good. Personalities like the newly appointed General Prosecutor for Greater Hesse, Dr. Quabbe, are rare. The reasons are obvious: personnel are either over-age [sic], or have been out of practice for years as a consequence of the war. Most of them are hampered in their efforts by strong although unavoidable inconveniences on their personal life."²⁵⁷

Personnel met with snide remarks, but the whole system was considered awry:

> The German reaction to its own legal system is apathetic. Judges and court personnel are few and untrained; innumerable cases are pending and undisposed of; lawyers do not voluntarily come to the aid of their own judicial system to help in the trial of cases because of poor pay; judicial service is not regarded as highly as in the States; and certain lawyers have stated openly that they would be deprived of a lucrative livelihood if they were required to do judicial service instead of practicing before the MG courts. The foregoing are some reasons why it is felt among the general public that trials in German courts, with their long delays, are not justice at all and Germans could prefer to be tried by MG courts and be assured of a fair and impartial trial and hearing without delay.²⁵⁸

---

255 Inspection AG Witzenhausen, July 9, 1947, NARA, OMGH 17/209 – 1/2.
256 Report of Haven Parker to Alvin J. Rockwell, February 17, 1947, NARA, OMGUS 17/199 – 2/22.
257 Letter of Henry M. Rosenwald to Chief, Administration of Justice Branch, Legal Division, OMGUS, November 18, 1946, NARA, OMGUS 17/199 – 2/22.
258 LSO Kassel, Weekly Intelligence Report, December 23, 1946, NARA, OMGUS 17/217 – 3/3.

The choice of judge was crucial: "Everything depends upon the personality of the judge (or judges), whether he is independent, impartial, competent, experienced." Due to the lack of unimpeachable personnel, the whole system was not working; the public spread rumors about bribes and biased judges, especially in denazification affairs. "A legal system cannot be isolated from the rest of the social structure. A hungry judge is a tempted judge."[259]

Obstacles

Although the search for new staff was under way, certain obstacles did indeed slow its progress.

One such problem was common to virtually all ministries of justice in West German Länder: the insistence on employing *"Landeskinder,"* i.e., native jurists, born and bred Bavarians, Württemberger, Westphalians, Hannoverians, etc. This insistence was partly due to the traditional federal structure of Germany dating back decades and even centuries, and the post-war vilification of the centralization of the legal system (*Verreichlichung*) under the Nazis. The return to small units such as the province was supposed to promise better control and reliable, honest personnel. Sources galore deplored the flooding of the professional market with legal staff from other corners of Germany.

The Bavarian minister of justice, Dr. Josef Müller, declared that one could admit lawyers from Berlin or East Germany only if this meant a gain (left unspecified) for the German Ministry of Justice.[260] "Foreigners," i.e., from other parts of the former Reich, were suspect on principle. The Nuremberg prosecutor general complained that lawyers from the *Sudeten* territories lacked professional qualities maintaining that, "Astonishing bad legal training of [these] personnel has been noticed. Careful control will be necessary."[261] A report from Bamberg exemplifies the ominous tone with which people from other regions were described:

> Given the <u>contribution of Germans of other tribes</u> [emphasis in original] or even of foreigners in the Bavarian judicial service, the members of the Bamberg High Court pronounced that in general they had nothing against southern Germans, but that when it came to northern and central Germans, who up to that point already occasionally had been taken in, there had been generally bad experiences. The worst were those from Saxony. In addition,

---

259 Ibid.
260 Minutes Conference in the Bavarian Ministry of Justice, November 29, 1948, NARA, OMGUS 17/201 – 2/2.
261 Quoted in Weekly Report, April 5, 1947, NARA, OMGBY 17/183 – 3/14.

most of those from the Rhineland and other Prussians failed; only once in a while were there also useful and good candidates among them.²⁶²

Furthermore, experiences with lawyers in private practice who wanted to become civil servants were bad; in addition, the records for legal personnel employed in administration (*Verwaltungsjuristen*) wanting to join the Justice Administration were not good. The court system was not to become a dumping ground for all those who were searching for new fields of employment. Equipped with such pieces of advice from the high court in Bamberg, the head of the Würzburg local court must have been hard-pressed to find any acceptable judges whatsoever.

The American lack of regional bias in choosing German personnel met with criticism from the local Justice Administrations, particularly in Bavaria. Fear of foreign infiltration, the unfamiliarity of northern German lawyers with local tradition and habits – let alone Bavarian federal state law (*Landesrecht*) – fueled alienation both of the courts and of the local populations and foretold a pessimistic road ahead if Americans continued on their misguided path of appointments.²⁶³ Not only did those applicants from beyond Bavarian borders lack the "high magisterial ethos" Bavarian judges supposedly had managed to safeguard throughout and despite the Nazi dictatorship, some did not even speak German sufficiently well.²⁶⁴ Krapp, the president of the high court in Bamberg, took offense with all those who, in his eyes, were trying to infiltrate the Bavarian Justice Administration in search of Bavarian state salaries and pensions.

The American Legal Division was not content with this development, as the Bavarian Ministry of Justice also tried to replace non-Bavarian judges with indigenous personnel, stating, "This does not seem to be fair to those non-Bavarians who had tried their best to build up the courts in 1945 and 1946."²⁶⁵ Fortunately, even within Bavaria there were prejudices among those from its northern and southern regions. Bamberg Prosecutor General Steffen complained that the highly desirable positions in Munich were preferentially filled with applicants from Munich.²⁶⁶ The president of the Bamberg high court, Dr. Thomas Dehler, found fault with the universities that were flooding the legal profession with ill-qualified trainee lawyers due to the fact that exams no longer served as a selec-

---

262 Report of Dr. Lobmiller, June 15, 1945, StA Bamberg, Rep. K 100/V, Nr. 3649/I.
263 "Bericht über die Verhältnisse der Rechtspflege im OLG-Bezirk Bamberg," July 5, 1945, StA Bamberg, Rep. K 100/V, Nr. 2549.
264 Letter of OLG President Bamberg, Krapp, to Ministry of Justice, December 12, 1945, StA Bamberg, Rep. K 100/V, Nr. 2550.
265 Annual Historical Report, June 30, 1947, NARA, OMGBY 17/184 – 2/6.
266 Minutes Conference Ministry of Justice, November 29, 1948, NARA, OMGUS 17/201 – 2/2.

tive principle. He especially took the University of Würzburg[267] – ironically, his own alma mater – to task.

The second obstacle was the so-called established post (*Planstelle*), which affected more or less all positions in the higher judicial service (judges and prosecutors). A *Planstelle* guaranteed its incumbent lifelong employment; only if grave malfeasance was proven (in a disciplinary action) could the post be forcibly vacated – obviously a complicated process in which the defendant could prolong proceedings considerably with appeals. Such positions had to be kept open for the incumbent regardless of whether he was missing, was a POW, or had been dismissed for embroilment with Nazi organizations or Nazi penal justice.[268]

Personnel politics thus reached a stalemate: Either fill positions by taking on applicants from other territories and get the work done (a tactic that Land and local Justice Administrations resented because of the employment of "foreigners" and thus tried their uttermost to prevent) or keep the already established posts (*Planstellen*) free until their rightful owners either returned or were cleared by denazification (a tactic that the American Legal Division resented because it slowed things down).

Furthermore, suitable personnel were scarce. To some extent, an advocate trained to represent one side as best as possible could stand in for a judge or prosecutor, but obviously lacked experience as advocate of the state. As the legal profession (particularly judges and prosecutors) during the Weimar Republic had been a small one, applicants from this pool were not ubiquitous. While the situation at local courts was not too bad, the situation at district or high courts was unimpressive.[269] At the Bavarian high courts, only 40 of 81 positions had been filled thus far.[270]

Recruitments were not always auspicious. In Aschaffenburg a former advocate now turned state attorney released a murder suspect to attend mass. He continued to view cases with the eyes of a criminal defense lawyer rather than a state prosecutor or judge.[271] To tempt a lawyer away from his lucrative chambers to join the (badly paid) civil service was not easy. And to lure younger ones into the thankless task of state prosecutor or judge in some backwater was not much easier, "since salaries [were] frozen at pre-war levels, and private practice

---

[267] Ibid.
[268] Letter of Franklin J. Potter, Director, Legal Division, OMGH, to Administration of Justice, Legal Division, OMGUS, 27 February 27, 1948, NARA, OMGUS 17/197 – 1/6.
[269] Weekly Activities Report, December 3, 1948, NARA, OMGUS 17/214 – 1/3.
[270] Ibid.
[271] Monthly report, April 23, 1948, NARA, OMGBY 17/183 – 2/14.

[offered] greater financial security."[272] The American Legal Division even went so far as to encourage the German Administration of Justice to pay their members better.[273] "It [was] believed that the salaries must be raised to an approximate level of that of the incomes of attorneys with substantial practices developed through years of training and experience."[274] At some courts, judges resigned because of the low salaries.[275]

The lack of suitable personnel was partially caused by Allied politics. Many jurists were attracted by the higher remuneration to be got at Spruchkammern. "The fees for lawyers and attorneys pleading cases before Spruchkammern are so high that a high judge's salary for a month is earned by a defense counsel in a forenoon sometimes."[276] In Bavaria, Minister of Justice Hoegner considered excluding attorneys (classified by denazification as followers) from the lucrative appointments to be had at Spruchkammern:

> Dr. Hoegner deplores that, unlike civil servants on whom some disabilities can be imposed, lawyers in the 'follower' category once they are re-admitted to the bar have the full financial advantage of the prestige they built up in Nazi days. A plan, presently under consideration by Special Branch, this headquarters, to exclude such lawyers [in the 'follower' category] from the lucrative practice before denazification tribunals might be a step in the right direction."[277]

From Amberg district courts, the few lawyers were in such demand that they were being fetched from main hearings at the district court to participate in sessions of the American Summary Court, thus interrupting the German proceedings for indeterminate spans of time.[278]

The American Legal Division relished in bringing new wind to the sails. "A former lawyer as president of the OLG meant a novelty in the Bavarian judiciary which was without precedent."[279] It had been easier for the advocates to remain aloof under the Nazis. On the whole, the practicing lawyers had stood the moral test of the Nazi period much better than the judicial class. As members of a free

---

272 Report on Legal and Judicial Affairs, OMGUS, October 7, 1947, NARA, OMGUS 11/5 – 21/1.
273 Letter of Ralph E. Brown to Ministry of Justice Württemberg-Baden, February 24, 1947, NARA, OMGWB 12/1 33 –2 /5.
274 Ibid.; see also Weekly Report, March 14, 1947, NARA, OMGWB 12/135 – 2/2.
275 Weekly Report, September 21, 1946, NARA, OMGBY 17/183 – 3/13.
276 Weekly Report, April 26, 1947, NARA, OMGBY 17/183 – 3/14.
277 Letter of Ralph E. Brown to Ministry of Justice Württemberg-Baden, February 18, 1947, quoting from a report from Wilhelm Hoegner, Bavarian Minister of Justice, NARA, OMGWB 12/133 – 2/5.
278 Weekly report, February 15, 1947, NARA, OMGBY 17/183 – 3/13.
279 Report, July 9, 1947, NARA, OMGBY 17/183 – 2/13.

profession, lawyers were exposed to little pressure, and those who had not acted as counsel for enemies of the régime, or make themselves otherwise courageously obnoxious, could easily steer clear of any embroilment.[280]

No notable number of female jurists entered the civil service. During the Third Reich, the enrollment of women at universities had been discouraged (though not forbidden) and under the Nazis, women could not per se become judges or state prosecutors. Dr. Beyerle, minister of justice in Württemberg-Baden, was not so sure whether they should find employment in post-war Germany. He knew "from experience that the population was not willing to accept a female judge."[281]

Denazification of the Judiciary in the American Zone

As is well known, the Americans were most relentless in their attempts at denazifying the German population, a fact that is also reflected in their handling of the German jurists. They would have preferred to have no party members at all in the legal system. Only reluctantly did they accept "nominal" Nazis. The first standards for the purge were fixed by the Directive of July 7, 1945. With the Law of Liberation from National Socialism and Militarism (March 5, 1946), denazification was put into German hands. One of the most dominant features of denazification was a questionnaire (*Fragebogen*) with 131 questions concerning curriculum vitae, and past political and personal views. This lead to classification into five categories. Early on – in the summer of 1945 – it became obvious to the Americans that they would have to staff the courts with tainted individuals, or wait indefinitely while searching for others. What held true for a small local court also applied to many higher courts.[282] Initially, Americans were optimistic.[283] The American purge led to heavy personnel shortfalls.

Jurists, like any other strata of society, were not always honest when it came to filling in the questionnaire. They were shocked to learn that the Americans were in possession of the index of party members and intended to cross-check all information supplied in the questionnaires. The Legal Division mused: "The wrath of the Berlin Document Center is continuing to hit right and left in the

---

[280] Loewenstein, "Reconstruction of the Administration of Justice", 456.
[281] Conferences with Minister of Justice Dr. Beyerle, August 20, 1945, NARA, OMGWB 12/136 – 3/37.
[282] Detachment I 4 C 3 to Commanding Officer, July 21, 1945, NARA, OMGWB 12/139 – 2/6.
[283] Letter William W. Fearnside, Captain and Henry H. Urman, Civilian, to Director, Legal Division, OMGUS, August 30, 1945, NARA, OMGUS 17/229 – 2/17.

Administration of Justice."²⁸⁴ Even these documents, however, tell only part of the story. Proper documentation lagged behind as the war dragged on. Some information was not included, as the following case shows: Richard J. Jackson, Chief Legal Officer of OMG for Bavaria, agreed to the appointment of a state prosecutor named Dr. Karl Seither in Regensburg on April 1, 1946.²⁸⁵ Seither's biography seemed respectable enough. Although he had been a member of the storm troopers from July 1933 to the beginning of 1935, he had not been a party member and had left the storm troopers when his wife proved to have a non-Aryan grandmother. Apart from this, Seither referred to a short spell as member of a military court at the end of the war (June 1944 to January 1945). Fortunately, the Americans did not have to witness how the Germans initiated several investigations against Seither (by then senior prosecutor in Munich), who admitted to having been prosecutor and a member of a drumhead court-martial that imposed death sentences and executions on several deserters in the last days of the war.²⁸⁶

Even the ministers of justice in the provinces were not above critique. "Dr. Josef Müller … has not always been a guarantee for democratic justice."²⁸⁷ "There is a growing aversion [among] Bavarian judges against Minister Müller's attempts to make a political machine out of the Ministry of Justice."²⁸⁸ Müller, who had been accused in a newspaper of having taken part in a 1933 extortionate robbery involving a Jew,²⁸⁹ was now in the line of fire. "The fact remains that the frequent criminal cases involving the minister of justice do not help build up the confidence of the population in the Administration of Justice which was shaken so badly during the Nazi regime."²⁹⁰

The German judiciary felt early on that denazification rendered the courts unworkable. Ministries of justice themselves checked the personal records. Due to the lack of personnel, standards were constantly watered down. In Württemberg-Baden, the head of the German Courts Branch complained that the Ministry of Justice consequently sought out implicated former members of the judiciary or kept positions free while politically reliable and competent jurists such as advo-

---

284 Activity Report, October 8, 1948, NARA, OMGH 17/209 – 1/2.
285 HStA, MJu 26889; See also Weekly Report, September 21, 1946, NARA, OMGBY 17/183 – 3/13.
286 Augsburg 7 Js 1063/53, StA Augsburg (hanging of three deserters on April 20, 1945 in Münding near Kaisheim); Ansbach 1 Js 681/54, StA Nürnberg, StAnw Ansbach 1 Js 681/54 (shooting of two deserted soldiers on April 13 or 14, 1945 in Leutershausen near Ansbach); Ansbach 1 Js 312 ab/54, StA Nürnberg, StAnw Ansbach 1 Js 312 ab/54 (shooting of a deserted soldier in Kössen, Tyrol, May 6, 1945).
287 Report "The Administration of Justice in Bavaria," July 1, 1949, NARA, OMGBY 17/188 – 3/1.
288 Monthly Report, March 3, 1949, NARA, OMGBY 17/184 – 2/4.
289 München I 1 Js 1946/48, NARA, OMGUS 17/215 – 2/21.
290 Monthly Report, February 1, 1949, NARA, OMGBY 17/184 – 2/4.

cates or members of the administration were excluded from admission. All the while, they cheekily stated that

> politically acceptable applicants for German justice positions are almost unavailable ... It has been noted that since the start of operations by the denazification tribunals, persons classified as lesser offenders, followers, or exonerated persons have been rather consistently reinstated in their former or other positions in the German justice system in Württemberg-Baden. This includes judges, prosecutors, lawyers, notaries, and lower justice personnel. In various instances it has been alleged that vacancies are intentionally being kept open for former judges of whom it was anticipated that they might be "cleared" by Denazification Tribunals. This way, politically unimplicated and professionally well-suited applicants for such positions have been rejected.[291]

But a short time afterwards, the Americans agreed to the German policy of "forgive and forget" when it came to the personal history of members of the judiciary. The head of the American Military Government in Württemberg-Baden agreed to the appointment of former members of the special courts of Stuttgart and Mannheim, provided they had been denazified and had not taken part in blatant miscarriages of justice.[292] The results of this lackadaisical approach soon became obvious. "It was pointed out that through the lenient procedures of the German denazification authorities and a consequent liberal employment policy by the Minister of Justice, a large part of formerly removed Nazis had been reinstated within the Württemberg-Baden justice system."[293]

And Württemberg-Baden was by no means the only province within the American Zone where this development occurred. The ambivalent situation of the Justice Administration in Bremen (falling first under American, then British, then again American authority) meant that denazification succumbed either to the disputes of competence among the Western Allies or to procrastination by the German Justice Administration.

The British Legal Division noticed that the American denazification board made such strict use of Control Council Directive No. 24 that almost nobody who had joined the Nazi Party before 1937 would stand a chance of re-admission.[294]

---

[291] Letter of Ralph E. Brown, Chief, German Justice Branch, to Ministry of Justice Württemberg-Baden, November 25, 1946, NARA, OMGWB 12/131 – 2/5; see also NARA, OMGWB 17/144 – 1/18.
[292] Letter of Charles H. Kraus, Administration of Justice Branch, Legal Division, OMGUS to Chief Legal Officer, OMGWB, August 6, 1947, NARA, OMGUS 17/216 – 3/10.
[293] Monthly Report, August 28, 1948, NARA, OMGWB 12/135 – 3/15; see also NARA, OMGWB 12/137 – 2/7.
[294] Letter of Major Romberg, Ministry of Justice Control Branch, to Legal Division, Mil Gov Hamburg, June 20, 1946, TNA, FO 1060/1033.

The British found the denazification approach in Bremen wanting and feared a complete breakdown in the German legal system within the Bremen enclave.

> The American denazification policy in Bremen appears to be completely arbitrary and unrealistic. They have German denazification Panels and Review Boards but do not rely on their findings. The ultimate decision rests with an American Review Board, who follow our Zone Policy Instruction No. E and literally interpret Control Council Directive No. 24 ... Judges, prosecutors and junior Court officials are being kept in office on a day to day basis and I urged the American Special Branch officers to clear up a state of affairs which is now chaotic.[295]

By the end of 1946, the British Legal Division had concluded that the American interpretation of Control Council Directive No. 24 had been "so literally and so ruthlessly" applied that the German Justice Administration in Bremen was on the verge of a breakdown.[296] For Bremen, in 1946 and 1947 the American Legal Division ordered the purge of certain members of the judiciary – a command that was simply ignored by the Justice Administration. This strategy enraged the Americans, who called it "favoritism, subterfuge, and possibly even downright dishonesty."[297] In 1948, the American denazification unit at the Military Government accused the Legal Division of obstructing. The Bremen senator of justice, Dr. Spitta, claimed that 42 jurists had been dismissed due to denazification, though all of them were re-admitted on temporary work contracts and later cleared in denazification procedures. A juicy detail in this denazification affair was that one of the 42 jurists whose dismissal had been ordered (and then so conveniently circumvented by re-admission on a contract basis) was a young lawyer whom the Americans had treated to a research scholarship at the Yale Law School in 1948. His considerable charm led to a letter of grateful thanks from the dean of the Yale Law School as everybody was "very favorably impressed" by the young man who was later to embark on a political career and ultimately become Federal President of Germany: Dr. Karl Carstens.[298] The American Legal Division claimed

---

[295] Letter of J.F.W. Rathbone, Legal Division, Lübbecke to Chief, Legal Division, Advanced HQ, Berlin, June 25, 1946, TNA, FO 1060/1033.
[296] Letter of Legal Division, ZECO, CCG (BE), Herford, to HQ Legal Division, CCG (BE) Berlin, November 17, 1946, TNA, FO 1060/1057.
[297] Letter of Thomas F. Dunn, Director, OMGBR, to the mayor of Bremen, Wilhelm Kaisen, September 2, 1948, NARA, OMGBR 6/63 – 1/5.
[298] Letter from Office of the Dean, Law School, Yale University to Robert W. Johnson, Chief, Legal Division, OMGBR, November 5, 1948, NARA, OMGBR 6/63 – 1/5.

that denazification in Bremen had not been sabotaged, but that the mistake had probably been made during the British tenure of affairs in Bremen.[299]

The Legal Division OMGUS as such was aware that "the percentage of nominal Nazis in the German courts is continuously increasing."[300] More supervision was called for, as well as additional reports from German courts with special reference to cases with a political or financial dimension. Legal divisions of military governments ought to give notification if a nominal member of the NSDAP was found to be employed at ministries of justice, at high courts, or as president or senior prosecutor; they also should give notification if a judge or prosecutor who was a former member of the NSDAP was involved in penal justice concerning the adjudication of Nazi crimes in the post-war era.

Meanwhile, the American occupying powers had lost faith in the raison d'être of denazification. The Legal Division OMGUS understood that the mere fact that somebody had not been a NSDAP member did not necessarily point to a democratic disposition. "Some people were too old or too insignificant to be forced to join the party but nevertheless still have Nazi ideology, whereas others who had to join the party to hold their jobs never shared that ideology."[301] The shortage of personnel and the lack of faith in one's own criteria led even American legal officers to give recommendations for former NSDAP members and give competence in legal matters precedence over political integrity.[302]

The absurdity of the denazification criteria struck the American Legal Division anew with each case. "The whole silliness of the denazification program is demonstrated in [the case of a long-standing Nazi Party member and active storm trooper] by the fact that he was placed in Class V, as he explains because he refused to carry out an order during the last few weeks of the war to use Hitler Youth for a military action."[303]

The Americans were also annoyed by the use of former members of the special courts in political cases in the post-war period.[304] The American Legal Division had already sent a list naming former members of the special courts who had been simply classified as "fellow travelers" by denazification and re-ad-

---

299 Letter of Robert W. Johnson, Chief Legal Officer, OMGBR, to Director, OMGBR, August 18, 1948, NARA, OMGBR 6/63 – 1/5.
300 Letter of Lt. Col. G.H. Garde, Legal Division, OMGUS to OMG Länder and American Sector Berlin, July 22, 1947, NARA, OMGBR 6/63 – 2/47.
301 Memorandum of John M. Raymond, Director, Legal Division, OMGUS, August 30, 1948, NARA, OMGUS 11/5 – 3/20/11.
302 Inspection LG Giessen, March 23, 1948, NARA, OMGH 17/209 – 1/2.
303 Inspection AG Melsungen, June 2, 1948, NARA, OMGH 17/209 – 1/2.
304 Monthly report, February 3, 1948, NARA, OMGWB 12/139 – 3/22.

mitted to the legal profession.³⁰⁵ All protests were in vain as the German Justice Administration campaigned for this group of jurists early on, employing them as auxiliary personnel in simple tasks. If these judges and prosecutors could not even be employed in menial and auxiliary positions, then the whole work flow of courts and prosecution agencies would slow down because the others could not get all their work done and replacements were not easily found, not to mention provided housing.³⁰⁶ Because of their rights as civil servants, even those labeled as dismissed were not considered ejected from the German Justice Administration. Instead, the Ministry of Justice differentiated between dismissal and the current "non-occupation" of office. A true dismissal would destroy rights linked to employment as a civil servant; "non-occupation" meant that these rights were simply in abeyance.³⁰⁷

Early on, the American Legal Division began battling rearguard action. The head of the Administration of Justice branch announced that "the whole policy concerning nominal Nazis participating in such trials [political cases, E.R.] and holding key positions in the administration of justice may undergo a change in the near future."³⁰⁸ Legal Division members complained that it was difficult to ensure that only non-Nazis were given key positions. On the one hand the weakening of standards was welcomed, since the readmission of nominal Nazis to office would lead to a standardization of procedures among the Western Allies as British and French authorities. On the other hand the experiences in the British and French zones had been so bad that it would be more reasonable if British and French authorities adopted the standard prevalent in the American Zone.³⁰⁹ When they discovered that now even key positions (i.e., at high courts or high-ranking positions at district courts) were staffed with judges categorized as hangers-on by denazification authorities, the Americans maintained once again that as per previous agreements, "this constituted an extreme and deplorable violation of our mutual understanding to the effect that the Oberlandesgericht [High Court] is to be staffed only with judges not incriminated under Law 104 and as well as a breach of your assurances given to OMGUS legal representatives in this connec-

---

305 Letter of Richard J. Jackson, Director, Legal Division to Legal Division, OMGUS, June 23, 1947, NARA, OMGWB 17/140 – 2/26.
306 Letter of Minister of Justice Württemberg-Baden to Legal Division, OMGWB, October 14, 1946, NARA, OMGWB 17/142 – 2/5.
307 Letter of Minister of Justice Württemberg-Baden to Denazification Section, OMGWB, April 19, 1947, NARA, OMGWB 17/142 – 2/6.
308 Letter of Ernst Anspach, Administration of Justice Branch, to Edward H. Littman, March 29, 1948, NARA, OMGH 17/209 – 1/2.
309 Letter of Franklin J. Potter, Director, Legal Division, OMGH to German Administration of Justice Branch, Legal Division, OMGUS, February 27, 1948, NARA, OMGUS 17/197 – 1/6.

tion."[310] The ministry in Württemberg-Baden replied pointing out that personnel had been chosen with the greatest possible care, the decisive points being competence and qualification. Insistence on the American criteria of politically irreproachability would lead to a collapse of the dispensation of justice.[311] In Bavaria, "the percentage of politically incriminated judges and prosecutors [was] increasing alarmingly and [was] cause for serious concern. The effect [was] evident in court decisions and actions of prosecutors which reflect[ed] a growing sympathy for Nazis and Nazi and militaristic ideologies."[312] In mid-1948, 75 percent of judges and 81 percent of state prosecutors were affected by the law of liberation (i.e., had been affiliated with the Nazi Party in one way or another); previously (July 1947) only 60 percent of judges and 73 percent of state prosecutors in Bavaria had been thus afflicted. Now, as the American Legal Division lamented, former Nazis were even admitted to the highest positions in the Justice Administration. Numbers originating from the Bavarian Ministry of Justice for the three high court districts Munich, Nuremberg and Bamberg confirm this tendency. Overall, 1,336 judges and state attorneys were employed. Of those, 798 (59.7 percent) had been party members and 207 had benefitted from several amnesties (youth, Christmas, repatriation or Berlin-Kommandatura amnesty); 1,005 (75.2 percent) had been members of the NSDAP or their organizations.[313]

An analogous situation was to be found in other parts of the American Zone: In Württemberg-Baden, Minister of Justice Dr. Josef Beyerle stated that more than 50 percent of all judges had formerly belonged to the Nazi Party; among notaries and the upper echelons of the civil service the number ran to about 70 percent.[314] In Hesse, 55 percent of judges and prosecutors were former Nazi Party members;[315] in Bremen the figure was 65 percent according to American estimates of the higher echelons of the judiciary.[316]

---

310 Letter of Ralph E. Brown, Chief, German Justice Branch, Legal Division, OMGWB to Minister of Justice Württemberg-Baden, September 24, 1948, NARA, OMGWB 17/142 – 2/12-15.
311 Letter of Minister of Justice Württemberg-Baden to Legal Division, OMGWB, September 28, 1948, NARA, OMGWB 17/142 – 2/12-15.
312 Report for the year 1947/1948 (July 1, 1947 to June, 30 1948), German Courts Branch, OMGBY, NARA, OMGUS 17/197 – 1/28.
313 Lists of judge and state prosecutor, compiled by the Bavarian Ministry of Justice, April 1, 1949, NARA, OMGUS 17/200 – 2/9.
314 Dr. Josef Beyerle in the Diet of Württemberg-Baden, February 23, 1949, p. 2661.
315 Walter L. Dorn, *Inspektionsreisen in der US-Zone: Notizen, Denkschriften und Erinnerungen aus dem Nachlass*, ed. Lutz Niethammer (Stuttgart: Deutsche Verlags-Anstalt), 159.
316 Joseph F. Napoli, "Denazification from an American's Viewpoint," *Annals of the American Academy of Political and Social Science* 264 (1950), 118.

The Americans were particularly concerned that no former Nazi members among the judiciary were involved in the adjudication of Nazi crimes.[317] This, however, meant preaching to the converted: "Former PGs are anxious to avoid political cases because they are afraid that they would be under attack no matter what they do: if their sentences appear lenient one would say they have remained Nazis; if their sentences appear harsh the charge would be that now they try to redeem themselves at the expense of other Nazis."[318] Again the shortage of personnel forced the Allies' hands, as in the prosecutor's office in Nuremberg where of five prosecutors only one had not belonged to the party.[319] Land Director Murray D. Van Wagoner thus addressed a strict note to the Bavarian prime minister:

> It is my considered opinion that any judge who was a member of the Nazi party or its formation or an officer of any of its affiliated organizations is incompetent to try such cases by reason of his previous affiliation with the Party. Such judges are regarded as being automatically disqualified from sitting in judgment of any and all crimes or atrocities committed under the sponsorship or sanction of the Nazi Party or in furtherance of its militaristic or tyrannical ideologies or policies.[320]

The Bavarian prime minister should, it was argued, request the minister of justice to refrain from using former party members as judges in penal cases involving the prosecution of Nazi crimes.

Thomas Dehler, president of the Bamberg High Court, begged to differ. If a judge or prosecutor had been denazified according to the law of liberation and was in office with the agreement of the Military Government, then he was also to be entitled to conduct each and every trial – including politically sensitive cases.[321] A branch of the American Legal Division thought differently and had their eye particularly on the German public:

> There is no doubt about the fact that, in the eyes of the German population, such judgements of German courts in Nazi crime cases which were passed by judges who themselves were in the past closely affiliated with the criminal system indirectly on trial in these cases would be suspected of being "controlled by bias."[322]

---

317 Letter of Ralph E. Brown to Minister of Justice Württemberg-Baden, April 21, 1947, NARA, OMGWB 12/140 – 1/1-20; see also Report, October 30, 1947, NARA, OMGBY 17/184 – 2/4.
318 Inspection LG Kempten, February 28, 1949, NARA, OMGBY 17/186-3/20.
319 Activity Report, August 23, 1947, NARA, OMGBY 17/183 – 3/15.
320 Letter of Murray D. Van Wagoner, Land Director, to Bavarian Prime Minister Dr. Hans Ehard, June 29, 1948, NARA, OMGUS 11/5 – 3/20/11; See also NARA, OMGUS 17/217 – 2/26, NARA, OMGBR 6/63 – 1/5 and NARA, OMGBY 17/187 – 1/6.
321 Wengst, *Thomas Dehler*, 95.
322 Letter of Charles H. Kraus, Chief, Administration of Justice Branch to Colonel John M. Raymond, July 28, 1948, NARA, OMGUS 17/217 – 3/4.

With the foundation of the Federal Republic of Germany on May 23, 1949, any attempt by the Western Allies to influence the Ministry of Justice met with cool reactions; the "instructions" given were no longer considered mandatory.[323]

The American Legal Division feared in particular that the appointment of former Nazis in the German judiciary loomed.[324] Thus the assessment by the chief of the Legal Affairs Division was quite ambivalent:

> In the initial phases of the occupation our work was hampered by crowds of sycophants who thronged into our offices, and, protesting their difference from the German pattern, tried to curry favor with us, and obtain advantages for themselves, by applauding and praising each and every one of our ideas and decisions. These opportunists have often prevented us from a proper assessment of the situation and from meeting those people who were genuinely and for altruistic reasons interested in making a new start.
>
> More recently, with the resurgence of nationalistic sentiment, we are meeting in many instances with an obstinacy which precludes true cooperation and integration, and resistance which have the sole purpose of winning the acclaim of a chauvinistic populace which, faced with the shame, guilt and destruction of the Nazi era, once more prefers the psychological escape hatches of xenophobia and self-pity to the difficult way of salvation through candid self-analysis, self-criticism and proper self-assertion.[325]

Personnel Politics in the British Zone

Lack of suitable staff characterized the situation in the British Zone, too. In the whole high court district of Düsseldorf, which in 1939 had been home to 550 judges, 158 judges were still employed in 1946.[326] In the high court district of Hamm (Westphalia) before the war, 755 judges had been sitting in court; at the beginning of 1946, there were 323 and of these only 174 had never joined the Nazi Party. Of 161 state attorneys, only 68 remained.[327]

Though the judges employed battled bravely against the mounting files – "Col. [Nils] Moller said that he was most impressed with the manner in which 30 judges were disposing of as great a volume of business as formerly employed 92

---

323 Letter of General Gross, Land Commissioner Württemberg-Baden to Ministry of Justice Württemberg-Baden, January 15, 1951, NARA, OMGWB 17/144 – 1/18.
324 Memorandum of Hans Weigert, March 2, 1950, NARA, OMGWB 17/144 – 1/18.
325 Letter of Ernst Anspach, Chief, Legal Affairs Division, to Dr. Georg August Zinn, November 3, 1949, NARA, OMGUS 17/215 – 2/25.
326 Wiesen, "Das Oberlandesgericht von 1945 bis zur Gegenwart," 95.
327 Letter Legal Division, Lübbecke, to Chief, Legal Division, Adv. HQ, Berlin, February 2, 1946, TNA, FO 1060/1034. At the end of February 1946, Military Government for Westphalia counted 356 judges and 73 state attorneys. TNA, FO 1060/1034.

judges in LG Cologne"[328] – in the long run, the situation was untenable. It was suggested that all work be concentrated on penal justice and that all civil chambers be closed.[329] But it soon became obvious that more personnel was needed, and that meant employing former Nazis.

In their planning before the occupation, the British Legal Division assumed that control of German justice via personnel was elementary: "This is by far the easiest method of imposing control, since if the personnel are in fact reliable, no other control is necessary."[330] Categories of German personnel were developed: those to be permanently dismissed, those to be temporarily suspended, and those who could be further employed.[331] Those permanently dismissed were Nazi Party members who had joined the party before 1933, members of the People's Court (*Volksgerichtshof*), special courts, NSDAP, SS and police courts; drumhead court martials; functionaries of the Nazi association of professional jurists (*NS-Rechtswahrerbund*); general counsel of the Nazi Party (*Reichsrechtsamt der NSDAP*); the Nazi Academy of German Law; the leading functionaries of the Reich Ministry of Justice, members of the Reich court and patent offices; as well as all presidents, vice-presidents and prosecutors general of all high courts, and all presidents, vice-presidents and senior prosecutors at the district courts.

The British Legal Division was particularly concerned about the state prosecutors:

> The Staatsanwaltschaften are more understaffed than the Courts. Generally speaking a greater percentage of prosecutors have been removed or excluded than is the case with the judiciary. Furthermore, volunteers for the Staatsanwaltschaften are scarce because they feel insecure from a political point of view vis-à-vis any government which may arise in Germany in the future.[332]

The greatest care was called for when so-called key positions were filled: "As these officials hold key appointments, they should not be re-instated without most careful consideration."[333] The Western Allies in their respective zones were

---

[328] Minutes of the Conference of the British Military Government with members of the German Administration of Justice, June 5, 1946, TNA, FO 1060/1029.
[329] Minutes of the Conference of the British Military Government with members of the German Administration of Justice, August 1, 1946, TNA, FO 1060/1029.
[330] Planning Instruction "Control of German Ordinary Courts," February 13, 1945, TNA, FO 1060/951.
[331] Memorandum of CCG, Legal Division, Norfolk House, London, March 28, 1945, TNA, FO 1060/951.
[332] Letter Legal Division, ZECO to Division Chief, Legal Division, May 2, 1947, TNA, FO 1060/1020.
[333] Legal Division, Norfolk House, London to Coordination Section, June 19, 1945, TNA, FO 1060/977.

in a catch-22 situation: On the one hand there was the pressing need to reconstruct the German Administration of Justice as smoothly as possible; on the other hand there was the wish to admit only impeccable, carefully vetted personnel, which meant extensive and time-consuming correspondence with various authorities and the checking of personnel files, thus obstructing the rebuilding of the judicial system.

When the fields of duties of general administration and the Justice Administration were divided, the high court presidents were the only ones entitled to name staff for the courts – in accord with the Military Government. For the key positions – high court presidents, vice-presidents, and presidents of the senates therein, as well as prosecutors general – the consent of the Legal Division of the Military Government was necessary.[334] The final authority, previously held by the Reich Ministry of Justice, lay now with the Military Government. The presidents of the courts were responsible for the inner administration of the courts and the training of trainee jurists (*Referendare* and *Assessoren*) and for the control of district courts. Only with the creation of the provinces in the British Zone were the ministries of justice allotted their competence as the highest authority in the German Justice Administration.

Unsurprisingly, advice from British and German legal experts was quite similar: Disqualify judges who had joined the Nazi Party before 1933 and anybody who was a functionary in the Nazi Party or held an officer's rank with the storm troopers; and exclude any members of the SS or the SD (security service), as well as persons actively promoting the Nazi Party or its policy. Mere "nominal" membership in the Nazi Party or the storm troopers, however, would not indicate a deep-rooted identification with Nazi policies, especially if the person concerned had refrained from any leading activity. Exclusion of purely nominal members would render the reconstruction of the judicial system impossible.[335]

For applicants in key positions, the required paperwork was considerable. There were questionnaires, followed by an evaluation of these questionnaires by a denazification commission, as well as a report by the president of the high court and the opinion of the Legal Division officer. The Legal Division soon found out that it was by no means an easy task to find staff for these positions.[336] In some cases, appointment meant re-appointments. Both Dr. Kiesselbach (President of

---

[334] Military Government to HQ, 1 Corps District, Mil Gov, July 20, 1945, TNA, FO 1060/977; see also Legal Instruction No. 100 of September 18, 1946, TNA, FO 1060/1025.
[335] Questionnaires POW Study Group in Camp 13 [undated, before June 28, 1945], TNA, FO 1060/977.
[336] Letter of J.F.W. Rathbone, Legal Division, Lübbecke, to Finance Division, November 15, 1945, TNA, FO 1060/1028.

the High Court Hamburg from 1928 to 1933) and Dr. Kuhnt (President of the High Court in Kiel) had lost their offices due to the National Socialist dictatorship. Kiesselbach was 78 years old when he once again became head of the High Court in Hamburg. Dr. Kuhnt moved into his old office when the Kiel High Court was reopened.[337] Others were driven to resign: Heinrich Lingemann, post-war head of the Düsseldorf High Court, had relinquished his position in 1938 as he came under increasing pressure because of his Jewish wife. Wilhelm Mansfeld, 70 years old in 1945, became head of the Brunswick Court of Appeal after being pensioned in 1939 because of his partly Jewish descent. The Social Democratic jurist Dr. Curt Staff had already been considered for the post of a prosecutor general during the Weimar Republic, and had been dismissed under the Nazis according to the *Gesetz zur Wiederherstellung des Berufsbeamtentums* (law for the restoration of the professional civil service).

As in the American Zone, quite a few of the newly recruited staff were quite old indeed. It was obvious that they could stand in only temporarily. Thus once again the search began for personnel outside the pool of former court members.

Emigrants returning to Germany were few and far between.[338] The reluctance of the German judiciary to invite emigrants back was marked. Even the president of the high court in Düsseldorf, Dr. Lingemann (whose wife was Jewish), stated that, in the interest of the applicants, he would not encourage return as anti-Semitism in Germany was still virulent.[339]

Displeasure over the newly staffed courts and prosecutors' offices was prevalent among the British.[340] The Legal Division found out that applicants from other regions, in particular refugees, were actively being deterred from applying while local applicants and former members of the judiciary enjoyed preferential treatment. This was true for the district of the high court of Hamm but also for Kiel: "Dr. Kuhnt had refrained from recommending lawyers from the East of Germany for practice at Flensburg. He thought that the political situation on the border was a special one and that only former residents of Schleswig-Holstein should be employed there."[341]

Apart from the regional aspects, the political past loomed heavy over many applications. Field Security rejected some candidates point-blank as they fell

---

337 Re-opening OLG Kiel, November 26, 1945, TNA, FO 1060/1035.
338 Rottleuthner, *Karrieren und Kontinuitäten*, 276.
339 Chief Legal Officer, Mil Gov North Rhine/Westphalia to Legal Division, Herford, December 2, 1946, TNA, FO 1060/1029.
340 Letter of A. Brock, German Courts Inspectorate, to Director, MOJ Control Branch, December 16, 1946, TNA, FO 1060/1025.
341 Letter of W.W. Boulton, Legal Division, Lübbecke, to Controller General, MOJ Control Branch, May 24, 1946, TNA, FO 1060/1035.

into the "automatic arrest" category; others were simply so objectionable as to be undesirable for employment.[342] Even people in key positions were not to the liking of the British Legal Division, as in the case of the high court president and prosecutor general in Kiel, for which it was noted: "Neither Dr. Kuhnt nor Dr. Dörmann inspire confidence."[343] Dörmann was simply too right-wing for an uninhibited relationship, having been described as one who was "politically very much to the right wing who could never reconcile fully his national ideas to those of the Nazi regime."[344] In Berlin, Prosecutor General Dr. Wilhelm Kühnast met with outright disapproval: "Ever since Dr. Kühnast was inherited in October 1945 from the Soviet-sponsored Stadtgericht [city court] we have shared the view that he was probably a rogue but that he was at least an efficient and co-operative rogue and the most capable Generalstaatsanwalt [attorney general] who was available."[345]

Although the lack of personnel caused a pressing need for new judges, idiosyncratic attitudes prevailed. In Celle, High Court President Hodo von Hodenberg declared he would reject those judges who had left the civil service some time ago as well as those who were not resident in the British or American zones. Applicants from the Soviet Zone would have to prove their qualifications, but war invalids would be specifically considered.[346] Dr. Kiesselbach rejected refugees "as it [was] in fact impossible to check up on their Nazi activities and difficult to assess their professional qualifications."[347] At Celle, 40 refugee judges were refused employment on the basis that "some of these were of bad character and unsuitable."[348] The widespread provincial sentiments and parochial feelings boggled the mind. Refugees from the East were rejected as long as there was hope that the previous incumbents could be successfully denazified or would return from POW camps. The usual excuse was that the background of refugees was unknown and the risk in employing them too high.[349] The number of refugees among the judi-

---

342 Letter HQ Military Government North Rhine Province 714 (F) Det to HQ Legal Division, Lübbecke, October 8, 1945, TNA, FO 1060/1029.
343 Letter of Rathbone, Legal Division, Main HQ, CCG (BE), Lübbecke to Chief, Legal Division, February 17, 1946, TNA, FO 1060/1035.
344 Letter of Major J. Nicholson, Legal Division, MCC Kassel to Mil Gov HQ 21 Army Group, BLA, July 30, 1945, TNA, FO 1060/1035.
345 Monthly Report Chief Legal Officer, Berlin Sector, May 1947, TNA, FO 1060/1165.
346 Minutes Conference of presidents of high courts Hamburg, Celle, Braunschweig, Oldenburg, September 27, 1945, TNA, FO 1060/977.
347 Letter of J.F.W. Rathbone, Legal Division, Lübbecke to Chief, Legal Division, Advanced HQ, Berlin, December 16, 1945, TNA, FO 1060/1032.
348 Minutes Meeting Legal Division, Military Government Hannover and OLG-President of Celle, November 16, 1945, TNA, FO 1060/1028.
349 Letter Legal Division, ZECO to Division Chief, Legal Division, May 2, 1947, TNA, FO 1060/1020.

cial staff differed. In North Rhine-Westphalia, between 13 percent and 30 percent of judges and between 23 percent and 30 percent of prosecutors were refugees; in Lower Saxony, between 33 percent and 50 percent of judges and between 39 percent and 62 percent of prosecutors came from the east.[350]

As in the American Zone, the staff was on the older side. The average age of judges in the British Zone was 58 years.[351] Age and malnutrition limited efficiency of work. The few members of the Justice Administration were overburdened with work and prone to sickness.[352] This situation always impacted recruitment. The desire to join the judicial service with its lack of even minimal benefits concerning food or housing and its hardly competitive salaries must have been preciously tiny, as the service offered pleasures only to those who enjoyed roughing it. The difficulties in checking on information supplied by applicants created further problems. A lawyer in Hattingen proved to be an imposter;[353] another in Schleswig-Holstein claimed to have been imprisoned for political reasons under Hitler when in reality he had been punished for a sexual felony.[354] Not only wrong information about political memberships, but also falsified exam results and ill-gotten qualifications were discovered.

Denazification of the Judiciary in the British Zone

The vetting of the judiciary was first in the hands of the British Military Government, which made its decisions on readmission based on questionnaires and personal files. In the summer of 1947 and with the denazification law, the Germans were commissioned to take denazification into their hands. The British Military Government handled cases of major culprits and others. As did the Americans, the British immediately understood how handy the files of the former Reich Ministry of Justice came: "The Legal Division now has access to records of the Reich Ministry of Justice, which will enable final vetting to be carried out centrally in

---

350 Inspection OLG Hamm, Düsseldorf and Cologne, October 21-22 and 25-28, 1948, TNA, FO 1060/1237; Inspection OLG Braunschweig, Celle, Oldenburg, September 23-29, 1948, TNA, FO 1060/1237.
351 Letter Legal Division, ZECO to Division Chief, Legal Division, May 2, 1947, TNA, FO 1060/1020.
352 Inspection LG Lüneburg, Braunschweig, Göttingen, Hildesheim, Hannover, September 23, to October 8, 1947, TNA, FO 1060/247.
353 Inspection AG Hattingen by LG-President Essen, August 10, 1946, TNA, FO 1060/1008.
354 Letter of Ritchie, Legal Branch, HQ Military Government Schleswig-Holstein to Legal Division, Main HQ, Lübbecke, May 9, 1946, TNA, FO 1060/1035.

respect of nearly all German legal personnel."³⁵⁵ It was considered particularly fortunate that not only political affiliations, but also professional qualifications could be gleaned from the records. In July 1945, the Military Government ordered the dismissal of all members of courts who had belonged to the NSDAP before April 1, 1933. Later, German personnel commissions came about, which gave recommendations to the British Military Government. Appeals against decisions were possible and usually led to a reversal, as candidates could attach character references from unimpeached parties.

To show the limits of denazification, I refer to the case of the first president of the Hamm Court of Appeal, Dr. Ernst Hermsen, who had been appointed president of a penal senate at the Hamm Court of Appeal in 1933, a position he held until 1937. Hermsen, born in 1883 in Essen, had been a stout supporter of the Catholic Center Party until 1933, thus rendering any allegations of Nazi sympathies absurd. And yet his downfall did not take long.

At Hermsen's inauguration as president, the Chief of the Legal Division felt "confident that under his presidency the Administration of Justice will be restored to the high and independent level, which guarantees the right of all men in every civilised [sic] community."³⁵⁶ When his personal file was unearthed, it turned out that he had been praised by the Nazis for quashing communists and sentencing political opponents (Communist Party and Social Democratic Party members) for high treason during his tenure as president of the penal senate at Hamm. Still, the British were willing to give him the benefit of the doubt. They argued that in these personnel reviews, the candidate's reasons for not joining the party were particularly important, and that "it [was] therefore not improbable that the statement about Dr. Hermsen's activities in connection with the communists was merely inserted in order to justify his retention as a judge, contains a great deal of exaggeration and need not be taken seriously."³⁵⁷ Hermsen pointed out that he himself had not been a party member and that the trials for high treason were conducted in accordance with valid German penal law in regular courts with public main hearings. However, criticism of Hermsen did not cease. Telegrams, even from the United States, accused Hermsen of having sentenced hundreds of socialists to long imprisonment for their anti-Nazi activities. Although no death sentence could be attributed to him, Hermsen was considered bloodthirsty.³⁵⁸ The head

---

355 Re-opening and control of German Courts, Legal Div Instruction No. 1, [undated, after July 16, 1945], TNA, FO 1060/977.
356 Speech at opening of OLG Hamm, December 1, 1945, TNA, FO 1060/1034.
357 Ibid.
358 Letter from Major at No. 8 ASO Arnsberg to GSI HQ 1 Corps Dist., January 1946, TNA, FO 1060/1034.

of the Legal Division stressed that none of this had been found in his personal record or the questionnaire. Since Hermsen had already been appointed, the British felt obliged to support him, unless he should turn out to have been a Nazi or completely incapable.[359]

Unwelcome publicity appeared in the form of articles, even in the New York emigrants' paper *Aufbau*.[360] A communist paper criticized Hermsen as an opprobrium to the German judiciary, rendering ample proof that the judges were morally corrupt and reactionary, thus not deserving of any trust.[361] The British clearly disliked this open criticism, but felt unable to censor or to suppress it altogether.[362]

By December 1945 the Military Government had already hinted at the possibility of dropping Hermsen, while the Legal Division believed for some time they could save him.[363] A public board of enquiry was formed with the high court president of Düsseldorf, Dr. Heinrich Lingemann; the prosecutor general of Hamburg, Dr. Walter Klaas; and the prosecutor general in Brunswick, Dr. Curt Staff as members.[364] The board of enquiry had to resolve two questions: first, was Hermsen an opponent of the Nazis, and second, was he identified in the public with Nazi ideology? The investigating committee convened in public sessions from February 20, 1946, to April 15, 1946, in Düsseldorf, Hamm, and Hannover, interviewing 110 witnesses, including 70 testifying against Hermsen. The committee concluded that Hermsen should be considered an opponent of the Nazi regime, but because of his activity as president of the penal senate from 1933 to 1937 in Hamm, he was associated in the eyes of the public with the Nazi dictatorship. Hermsen was pensioned off quickly for "health reasons", entitling him to a full retirement beginning on May 31, 1946.[365] This decision was met with great acclaim in the region.[366]

---

359 Letter of J.F.W. Rathbone to Col. D.S. Dunbar, Norfolk House, London, December 10, 1945, TNA, FO 1060/1034.
360 "The Hangman of the Ruhr – Justice in the British Zone," *Aufbau*, June 7, 1946; see also TNA, FO 1060/1034.
361 "Fehlurteil," *Neuer Weg: Mitteilungsblatt der KPD in der Region Hannover*, June 7, 1946; see also TNA, FO 1060/1034.
362 Letter of Lt. Col. Noel Annan, German Political Branch, Political Division CCG (BE), Lübbecke to J.F.W. Rathbone, Legal Division, June 19, 1946, TNA, FO 1060/1034.
363 Letter of Major R.V. Hemblys-Seales, Counter Intelligence Bureau to Legal Division, Main HQ, Lübbecke, January 16, 1946, TNA, FO 1060/1034.
364 Letter Legal Division, Main HQ, CCG (BE) to HQ Mil Gov Hannover Region, Westfalen Region, North Rhine Region, Hansestadt Hamburg, January 31, 1946, TNA, FO 1060/1034.
365 Letter of Rathbone to W.W. Boulton [undated, after April 15, 1946], TNA, FO 1060/1034.
366 Letter British Special Legal Research Unit, Office of the Legal Advisor to the Control Office for Germany and Austria, London to J.F.W. Rathbone, MOJ Branch, Legal Division, Main HQ, Herford, December 3, 1946, TNA, FO 1060/1001.

A possibly even bigger disaster than the appointment of Hermsen was the choice of a member of the prosecutor general's department in Hamm. This particular member would find himself on trial for Nazi crimes a few years later. Senior Prosecutor Friedrich Wilhelm Meyer joined the prosecutor general's office in Hamm in 1946 after having been cleared by the Public Safety Branch on September 12, 1945.[367] But two years earlier (until August 1944), he had belonged to Department IV (penal justice and legislation) in the Reich Ministry of Justice, and in 1942 had participated in a conference with most serious consequences: On October 9, 1942, after Reich Minister of Justice Otto Thierack and Propaganda Minister Joseph Goebbels had agreed to the transfer of so-called "asocial" prison inmates to concentration camps according to the Nazi program of "extermination through work", a conference took place in the Reich Ministry of Justice where the conditions of the transfer from prisons to concentration camps were discussed. Not only did Meyer participate in the meeting, but he was also given the task of reviewing about 4,000 cases of German and Czech prisoners who had been given minimum jail sentences of eight years. He even traveled to penitentiaries to check on prisoners and get the personal opinions of prison staff and local prosecutors. Based on the files, but also on inspection, Meyer cast his vote. The review of about 2,000 prisoners led to the categorization of "asocial" in about 1,400 cases, thus resulting in transfer to concentration camps. At least 600 prisoners were in fact transferred because of Meyer's vote, particularly to Mauthausen. Of these, more than one third died; it was assumed that at least 60 of them were actually murdered.[368] The Military Government initiated investigations against Meyer and handed the case over to the German Justice Administration. At the end of 1949, Meyer was charged in Wiesbaden for accessory to at least 300 murders and to attempted murder in at least another 300 cases.[369]

Even at the beginning of the purge, tainted personnel were kept on whenever members of high standing among the judiciary interceded on their behalf. Von Hodenberg acquired quite a reputation in suggesting former party members as presidents of district courts.[370]

Denazification posed greater problems in some regions than in others. Rathbone wrote:

---

[367] Letter of Rathbone, Legal Division, ZECO, Herford to Chief Legal Officer, North Rhine/Westphalia, December 22, 1947, TNA, FO 1060/924; see also BAK, Z 21/1356.
[368] The numbers follow the judgement Wiesbaden 2 Ks 2/51, which – due to the lack of files – used rounded minimum numbers. The sentence is printed in Rüter, vol. IX, No. 310.
[369] Wiesbaden 2 Js 600/48 = Wiesbaden 2 Ks 2/51, HStA Wiesbaden, Abt. 468, Nr. 426/1-31.
[370] Letter of J.F.W. Rathbone, Legal Division, Lübbecke to HQ Mil Gov Hannover Region, January 14, 1946, TNA, FO 1060/1028.

The main object of my visit was to deal with the de-nazification of the Schleswig-Holstein legal administration, which presents a more serious problem than in any other part of the British Zone. The trouble goes back before the date when any of the present officers were there. But the figures are alarming. Out of 120 judges 85 are so-called nominal Nazis (69 percent); out of 38 prosecutors 26 are nominal Nazis and barely 50 percent of the attorneys admitted to courts in the *Oberlandesgericht* district of Kiel are similarly nominal party members.[371]

The British were aware from early on that denazification was a Sisyphean task that would satisfy no one. One judge, who had belonged to the Nazi Party beginning in 1933 and had been part of a penal chamber, was clearly a case for dismissal. Nevertheless, colleagues and defendants campaigned for him, supplying documents stating that he had used his position in either the penal chamber or the Party to achieve a milder sentence for a defendant who otherwise would have had to face severe punishment. An advocate similarly tainted by membership in the party had had a Jewish law partner who perished in a concentration camp – but he paid the shares on his revenue to the widow as if the partner were still practicing. The British concluded it was best if the Germans were to decide the denazification cases themselves.[372]

The German Administration of Justice criticized the decisions of Field Security as inconsistent, arbitrary and incomprehensible. If explanations were requested, the Military Government replied that this information was confidential. The following statement, coming from the head of the high court in Celle, von Hodenberg, was somewhat far-fetched but points to the disappointment and frustration denazification had caused for large parts of the German jurists: "A Jewish and avowed anti-nazi Landgerichtsrat at Hannover ... refused this job [Oberlandesgerichtsrat] and said he was perfectly ready to act as a judge at a subordinate court, but could not bear to be mixed up with the injustices of de-nazification which were far worse now than under the Nazis."[373]

Denazification procedures as such were long-winded and appointments by the Military Government were sometimes preliminary, sometimes final, sometimes conditional, and sometimes temporary. Results produced by Field Security were often schematic. In Brunswick, 20 percent of former judges (and NSDAP

---

[371] Letter of J.F.W. Rathbone, Legal Division, Main HQ, CCG (BE), Lübbecke to Chief, Legal Division, February 17, 1946, TNA, FO 1060/1035.
[372] Letter of Colonel Carton, S/Ldr 609/LEG/401 to Commander 609 (L/R) Det Mil Gov, December 11, 1945, TNA, FO 1060/1032.
[373] Letter of J.F.W. Rathbone, Legal Division, Lübbecke to Chief, Legal Division, Advanced HQ, Berlin, January 27, 1946, TNA, FO 1060/1028.

members) were simply re-admitted.[374] Some candidates had to hand in their questionnaires several times, causing considerable delay.[375]

Vetting and re-vetting impacted the lawyers and the British feared this would also influence adjudication.[376] The German Courts Inspectorate advised re-vetting judges only if substantial evidence of a changed state of affairs were evident. Dismissal of judges should be made more complicated; temporary and conditional appointments should be turned into permanent positions. In fact, the Legal Division of the Military Government in Hamburg had already assured the high court president there that there would be no further voluminous re-vetting of already admitted higher judicial personnel.[377] However, personnel admitted under directives other than Control Council Directive No. 24 would have to be re-vetted. German jurists insisted that a renewed checking of jurists by denazification commissions was diametrically opposed to the principle of the independence of the judicature.[378] Since their approaches differed so extremely, the British Military Government responded in a friendly yet determined manner by insisting on re-vetting and ascertaining information on how individual German denazification commissions worked. German objections focused on the independence and motivation of the judiciary, which was obstructed by re-denazification measures. The Legal Division at Herford sympathized with the German jurists:

> This old fear of political interference still haunts the legal civil service and the present threat of rescreening is now undermining the independence of the judiciary in the British Zone ... There is little doubt that the status of the German judiciary in the British Zone is now generally in far worse a condition than it was under the Nazis ... German judges and prosecutors now feel that they have no protection against the somewhat arbitrary and discriminatory treatment of the German denazification authorities ... It is clear also that unless the legal civil service is given some security and the denazification of the German legal profession is brought to a speedy and just conclusion, the Administration of Justice in the British Zone is likely to break down entirely. The serious consequences of this are incalculable.[379]

Insecurity was already causing a strain on the actual adjudication of cases.[380]

---

374 Minutes conference OLG-Presidents Hamburg, Celle, Braunschweig, Oldenburg on September 27, 1945 in Lüneburg, TNA, FO 1060/977.
375 Inspection OLG districts Düsseldorf and Köln, May 12-21, 1947, TNA, FO 1060/1006.
376 Letter of A. Brock, German Courts Inspectorate, to Director, MOJ Control Branch, December 16, 1946, TNA, FO 1060/1025.
377 Letter Legal Division, Military Government Hamburg to High Court President Hamburg, August 15, 1946, BAK, Z 21/268.
378 Letter of Dr. Koch, Central Legal Office, to high court presidents and prosecutors general in the British Zone, October 2, 1946, BAK, Z21/268.
379 Letter of Rathbone, Legal Division, Herford to HQ ZECO, December 11, 1946, BAK, Z 21/268.
380 Ibid.

In any event, denazification led to a further shortage of personnel. It took time for the Public Safety Special Branch units of the Military Government to give the green light, delaying appointments of judges and prosecutors. The Legal Division complained that questionnaires from the North Rhine province that had been submitted in September 1945 had yet to be reviewed as of May 1946; questionnaires from Schleswig-Holstein submitted in December 1945 had not been attended to as late as April 1946.

All this hampered the restart of the German judicial system. Other impeding factors were also noted:

> It is clear, however, that this shortage is being deliberately aggravated in some districts, particularly those of Köln, Düsseldorf, and Celle, by the refusal of Oberlandesgerichtspräsidenten [high court presidents] and Generalstaatsanwälte [prosecutors general] to appoint to the legal civil service refugees from the East or from England or other persons who are not natives of the British Zone or who are unknown to the senior German legal officials concerned.[381]

Members of the German Administration of Justice were to be told to appoint personnel promptly because "an extremely serious view [would be] taken of any action ... which will prevent the immediate filling of their legal establishments."[382]

To alleviate the personnel shortage, a piggy-back arrangement took hold in the German Administration of Justice in the British Zone in October 1945, allowing the high court presidents to appoint one former Nazi Party member for each non-party member admitted to the German judiciary, thus aiming at a 50 percent quota, but the regulation was abandoned in spring 1946. Originally, the British had hoped to denazify the jurists more thoroughly, aiming at the exclusion of even just "nominal" party members. "As a very great concession it had been decided that up to 50 percent of the personnel appointed could be ex-members of the NSDAP. No senior officials would be ex-members of the NSDAP and the figure should be kept as far as possible below 50 percent and must at no time exceed 50 percent."[383]

To arrive at the 50 percent quota, either new non-Nazis had to be appointed, or nominal Nazis had to be dismissed. One hoped to rely on POWs, lawyers, expatriates in exile in England and refugees from the East for the recruitment of non-party members.

---

381 Letter Legal Division, ZECO, CCG (BE) to Chief Legal Officers, Northrhine-Westphalia, Hannover, Schleswig-Holstein, Hamburg, November 21, 1946, TNA, FO 1060/247.
382 Ibid.
383 Minutes Conference Legal Division, Military Government Hannover and OLG-President Celle, November 16, 1945, TNA, FO 1060/1028.

However, it turned out that the 50 percent quota was utopian. Alarming reports arrived from Celle and Brunswick that the vast majority of appointed judges and state attorneys were former Nazi Party members. The president of the high court in Celle refused to dismiss former Nazi Party members or refrain from appointing new "tainted" staff; the president of the high court in Brunswick repeatedly pleaded with the British to reverse dismissals or refute rejected promotions of former Nazi Party members. Hodenberg, himself a former advocate, refused to appoint the available stock of advocates as prosecutors because "(a) good lawyers would not take on the job of prosecutors and (b) bad lawyers could not do the job."[384]

The prosecutor general in Brunswick, Dr. Curt Staff, was pessimistic regarding the lack of non-tainted members for the higher legal service, especially the prosecutor's office, noting that "his is the most unpopular branch of the legal civil service and members of the Bar will not look at it."[385] The higher legal civil service was not considered attractive enough, new members of the Justice Administration appointed by the Allies were viewed with distrust. Furthermore, there was insecurity as to what would happen with these members of the legal profession at the end of the British occupation.

Again, statistics could be manipulated. Neither former members who had been expelled by the NSDAP (though dismissal from the NSDAP might have been for other than political reasons) nor those who had let their membership drop voluntarily and left the NSDAP of their own accord were counted as members. Applicants to the party, however, were counted as members. Combatants and minors who were transferred from Hitler Youth membership directly into the party were also – according to von Hodenberg – to be considered exempt, the first because the melting pot of the war burned off all slag and the second because they hadn't had much of a say in the matter.[386] Rumor had it that higher legal personnel fulfilling purely administrative tasks (i.e. not functioning in the public as judge or prosecutor) were not counted in the 50 percent Nazi quota.[387] In January 1946, the British Legal Division asked the presidents of the high courts to terminate these contracts because even purely administrative employment was subject to admis-

---

[384] Minutes Conference, November 16, 1945, TNA, FO 1060/1028.
[385] Letter of J.F.W. Rathbone, Legal Division, Lübbecke to Chief, Legal Division, Advanced HQ, Berlin, January 27, 1946, TNA, FO 1060/1028.
[386] Letter of OLG-Präsident Celle, Hodenberg, to Legal Division Main HQ, Hannover Region, January 15, 1946, TNA, FO 1060/1028.
[387] Minutes Conference Legal Division Hannover Region and OLG-President Celle, December 13, 1945, TNA, FO 1060/1028.

sion by the British.[388] On the other hand, the British saw that former advocate von Hodenberg, to whose court they particularly referred, needed experienced personnel in the running of the court.

Criticism also came from the high court president of Cologne, who claimed that the application of the 50 percent rule inhibited the course of law and pleaded for a less strict interpretation.[389]

The special denazification commissions for jurists came into being according to a decision made by the high court presidents of the British Zone on May 13–14, 1946. War criminals, NSDAP employees, anyone with membership in the party dating from before 1937; members of the general SS, as well as officers and non-commissioned officers of the Waffen-SS; storm troopers who had held posts as functionaries and SA memberships dating from before 1933; functionaries of the Nazi legal professional association (*NS-Rechtswahrerbund*); chairmen of tribunals and co-chairs, presidents, and vice-presidents of high and district courts; personnel officers of courts and heads of local courts were considered unacceptable. Members of the *Waffen-SS*, applicants to the SS, storm troopers who joined after April 1933, "nominal" Nazi members (who joined after May 1937) and party aspirants were closely scrutinized. The German denazification commission compiled advisory opinions for the British legal officers and suggested the further course of action: obligatory dismissal, mandatory dismissal or recommendation for or against employment without qualms about re-employment, positive recommendation for employment. The final decision lay with the British legal officers. Classification usually amounted to either a rating in the category of hangers-on or a discharge (*entlastet*). When denazification passed into the responsibility of the *Länder*, Control Council directive No. 38 (with its categorizations) remained important. The return of those who had been dismissed as intolerable was made possible only with the Basic Law and its Article 131, and a closer definition of this article in a bill passed on 10 April 1951 by the West German parliament.

Though the British were generous in their 50 percent rule, the Germans by no means stuck to it. June 1946 saw the termination of the 50 percent rule. The Military Government admonished the German Administration of Justice that although more than 50 percent of former party members could be admitted, "the interpretation of nominal membership must be strictly regarded being persons

---

388 Letter of J.F.W. Rathbone, Legal Division, Lübbecke to Chief, Legal Division, Advanced HQ, Berlin, January 27, 1946, TNA, FO 1060/1028.
389 Minutes weekly meeting presidents of high courts and prosecutors general with members of the Legal Division, March 27, 1946, TNA, FO 1060/1025.

who signed their names on the party membership lists but did little else."[390] Personnel from the special courts were still persona non grata; even if they could explain their previous participation in those courts, an appointment to a new position would have deplorable public consequences for the courts.

In the autumn of 1946, it was announced that the quota of 50 percent of former NSDAP-members in each high court district could be exceeded, provided a German denazification or appeal commission had cleared the candidates in question. Consequently, the number of members of the higher judicial service increased. In the British Zone there were 3,359 positions for judges and state attorneys in 1948.[391] In fact, more people were employed than there were positions. In 1948, 2,871 people filled 2,849 positions for judges; the following year there were 3,051 judges in 2,851 positions. For the state attorneys there were 510 positions in 1948 filled by 653 and in 1949 by 692 persons.[392] Still, the output left much to be desired.[393] Thus the re-nazification of the judicial system became obvious as early as 1948.[394]

The British complained that denazification committees were "exceedingly liberal"; nearly everybody ended up being in Category V (*Entlastete*, i.e., persons exonerated), although many of those thus denazified were "totally unsuitable for re-employment." The independence of justice would be at stake if all these old Nazis were to re-enter the judicial service. Rathbone wrote: "We consider the maintenance of a sound and independent judiciary in the British Zone to be a question of fundamental importance, but do not think that the Germans can at present attain this objective without our assistance. The appointment of judges and prosecutors thus requires special treatment."[395]

Disappointment and disenchantment with the whole process of denazification led to strange advice. As the head of the British Legal Division told the North Rhine-Wesphalian Minister of Justice Dr. Sträter, "I ... urged him not to sacrifice the legal administration in the Land North Rhine/Westphalia to denazification,

---

[390] Minutes of the Conference of Military Government with members of the Administration of Justice, June 21, 1946, TNA, FO 1060/1029.
[391] Jess, "Die Berufsaussichten des akademischen juristischen Nachwuchses unter besonderer Berücksichtigung der Verhältnisse in der Justiz der britischen Zone," *Zentral-Justizblatt für die Britische Zone*, May 1949, 82.
[392] Justizstatistik, Beilage zum *Zentral-Justizblatt für die Britische Zone*, July 1949, 131.
[393] Inspection LG Düsseldorf, Kleve, Krefeld, Duisburg, Wuppertal, Köln, Aachen, Bonn, Bielefeld, Detmold, Hagen, Paderborn, Essen, Bochum, Dortmund and Arnsberg, March 30 – May 14, 1948, TNA, FO 1060/247.
[394] Letter of Rathbone, Legal Office of the Legal Adviser, Herford, to Political Division, Berlin, October, 21 1948, BAK, Z 21/268.
[395] Ibid.

which was only a temporary and evil necessity and now rapidly approaching its conclusion."³⁹⁶

Personnel Politics in the French Zone

Not surprisingly, the French faced similar problems to those plaguing the American and British military governments. At the beginning of their occupation, they found a dearth of suitable judicial personnel. The French were adamant that the numbers were insufficient.³⁹⁷ But finding new candidates was difficult. Much to the chagrin of the French, very few jurists were available to be nominated who had not been party members. For the whole French Zone, 500 jurists were deemed necessary. In February 1946, only 346 jurists were working in the French Zone (Baden, Württemberg, Palatinate, and southern Rhineland) plus the Saar. Just two months previously, in December 1945, there had been 401.³⁹⁸ New controls had reduced those already admitted. The difficulties become clear in light of the fact that purges were occurring at different times. In Baden, the purge of the justices was declared terminated by December 1945, while in other regions of the French Zone, denazification of the legal profession continued. As the supply of candidates dwindled, the French Legal Division became interested in the experiences of the neighboring American Legal Division and inquired as to what policies they had followed. ³⁹⁹

Personnel politics and denazification were intrinsically linked. In southern Rhineland, recruitment slowed as officials awaited results of denazification.⁴⁰⁰ By the end of 1946, denazification seemed to have come to a complete standstill. Of 202 candidates applying to positions as judges or state prosecutors, only 39 had successfully completed the denazification process; of 140 applicants for the advocacy, only 16 had been vetted; of 53 notaries, only nine were cleared. The French Legal Division got quite worked up about these numbers.⁴⁰¹ It turned out that German judicial personnel counted all cases of denazification that had been dealt with, while the French were only interested in those individuals who had

---

396 Letter of J.F.W. Rathbone, Legal Division, ZECO, to HQ Legal Division, Berlin, January 21, 1947, TNA, FO 1060/1030.
397 Monthly Report Württemberg, November 1945, AOFAA, AJ 806, p. 615, Dossier 3.
398 Monthly Reports for the French Zone (and Saar), December 1945, January 1946 and February 1946, AOFAA, AJ 3679, p. 12.
399 Monthly Report for the French Zone (and Saar), February 1946, AOFAA, AJ 3679, p. 12.
400 Monthly Report Rhineland, November 1946, AOFAA, AJ 3679, p. 14.
401 Letter of Georges Veper, Chef du Contrôle de la Justice, Bad Ems, to Directeur Général de la Justice, January 28, 1947, AOFAA, AJ 3679, p. 14, Dossier 2.

been denazified *and* subsequently deemed suitable for readmission. In the Palatinate, for instance, it was discovered that several higher members of the German legal administration who had been marked for dismissal were still working at the courts.[402]

In Württemberg-Hohenzollern, 125 judges and 22 state prosecutors had been employed; by the end of 1945, there were only 52 judges and 10 state prosecutors in office.[403] It would take until 1950 to bring the Ministry of Justice in Württemberg-Hohenzollern back to its former numbers. The lack of personnel was similar in the Palatinate. In 1939, 179 judges and 56 prosecutors were employed at courts in the province, plus 91 advocates and 51 notaries. In 1944 there were only 75 judges, 21 prosecutors, 42 advocates, and 24 notaries. After the war, it was estimated that at least 100 judges, 24 prosecutors, 90 advocates, and 50 notaries were necessary to get the courts working again.

The first (French) reports from Baden hint at the satisfaction among the German legal profession as Nazis and Prussian jurists were dismissed, particularism revived and the "old Baden school of thought" returned to the bar and bench.[404] The French Legal Division was pleased at how neatly their idea of strengthening particularism (which was one of the French aims of occupation) fit into the inherent plans of the German Ministry of Justice. Nominations of personnel would take into account the regional bias.[405]

Also, newly formed territories posed more problems than did historic lands. In the Palatinate (formerly part of Bavaria, now governed from Koblenz) members of the German courts felt at a disadvantage; the Ministry of Justice in Koblenz would systematically appoint Protestant jurists whereas the Catholics would not stand a chance. In Neustadt (Palatinate), Protestant groups were protesting against too many Catholics at the high court and the prosecutor general's office.[406]

The higher judicial personnel numbered 110 persons in Baden by December 1946.[407] In 1939, there had been 124 judges and 28 prosecutors in southern Baden, but there was already more staff than in 1944 when there were 91 higher jurists.

---

[402] Monthly Report for the French Zone (and Saar), September 1947, AOFAA, AJ 3680, p. 27, Dossier 2.
[403] Report "Der Neuaufbau des Justizwesens in Württemberg-Hohenzollern seit 1945" (compiled by the Ministry of Justice Württemberg-Hohenzollern for the Chef du Contrôle de la Justice en Wurtemberg), July 11, 1949, AOFAA, AJ 805, p. 605, Dossier 7.
[404] Monthly Report Baden, January 1946, AJ 3679, p. 13, Dossier 2.
[405] Letter Directeur Général de la Justice to Section Justice at Délégué Supérieur, Baden, November 8, 1945, AOFAA, AJ 373, p. 25/1.
[406] Monthly Report Palatinate, November 1949, AOFAA, AJ 3680, p. 26, Dossier 3.
[407] Letter Directeur Régional du Contrôle de la Justice, Baden, to Directeur Général de la Justice, Military Government, French Zone, February 25, 1947, AOFAA, AJ 373, p. 25/1.

And numbers were still rising. In 1948 there were 180 members of the higher judicial service.

As in the American Zone of Occupation, the French re-activated jurists who had been pensioned off before the Third Reich or had been active throughout National Socialism, as long as they had no party taint and involvement in penal justice. The Minister of Justice for southern Baden, Dr. Hermann Fecht, was 65 when the war ended – French reports characterize him uncharmingly as "worn out mentally and physically diminished, he does not seem to be a very constructive part of the Germany of tomorrow."[408] Prof. Dr. Emil Niethammer, born in 1869, headed the high court in Tübingen beginning in mid-1947, when he was a strapping septuagenarian – and by no means the oldest lawyer around.[409] Among the still active solicitors, two had been born in 1863 and 1868 respectively.[410]

The refugee problem among jurists, so prominent in both the American and British zones, played no role here as the French Military Government admitted few refugees, and these only relatively late. Most of them – according to the documents – apparently did not try to enter the judicial service or did not try to do so in large enough numbers to merit notice.

Notable are a few examples of persecutees returning from exile. Dr. Emil Odenheimer (born in 1872) had been a judge at the local court in Pforzheim and was pensioned for "racial reasons" in 1935. He became judge at the district court in Baden-Baden.[411] Dr. Julius Ellenbogen, born in 1878 and judge at the High Court Freiburg beginning in 1946, named "deportation" as the reason for the end of his last employment during the Third Reich. (He had not been working at a court at this stage, but was employed by the Jewish Congregation in Baden.) A former attorney-at-law, Albert Levi, a victim of the November pogrom and subsequently prisoner at the Dachau Concentration Camp, had fled when deportation loomed in February 1945; he became judge at Offenburg District Court.[412] In Kaiserslautern, the former lawyer Dr. Paul Tuteur became a judge at the district court and, in 1949, president of a senate at the high court of Neustadt. He had been imprisoned as a Social Democrat and Jew in 1933 and during the pogrom.[413]

---

408 Appraisal by Délégué de Cercle [undated], Dossier Hermann Fecht, AOFAA, AJ 3681, p. 36.
409 CV Niethammer, September 4, 1947, Dossier Emil Niethammer, AOFAA, AJ 3683, p. 55.
410 List of personnel for Baden, AOFAA, AJ 372, p. 23/1.
411 Questionnaire Odenheimer, August 25, 1947, Dossier Emil Odenheimer, AOFAA, AJ 3683, p. 55.
412 Questionnaire Levi, October 15, 1947, Dossier Albert Levi, AOFAA, AJ 3682, p. 50.
413 Several post-war investigations and trials are concerned with the arrest of Dr. Tuteur on March 17, 1933 in Kaiserslautern, see Kaiserslautern 7 Js 40/48, Kaiserslautern 7 Js 7/49 and Kaiserslautern 7 Js 110/49. For the excesses during the pogrom see Zweibrücken 7 Js 61/49 = KLs 62/49 and Zweibrücken 7 Js 62/49 = KLs 59/49.

Denazification of the Judiciary in the French Zone

While the Americans had the most rigorous approach to denazification, the French attitude most resembled the British, which was far more pragmatic. Like the other Western Allies, the French were intent on looking for German personnel who would guarantee the development of democratic justice, i.e., personnel who had been dismissed under the Nazis and were willing to cooperate with the French without being resentful.[414]

For the sake of expediency, the French were willing to accept jurists tainted with a Nazi past. The Director General of Justice in Germany in the French Zone of Occupation, Charles Furby, knew it would take four to five years to educate a teacher but ten years to train a judge – in his eyes an argument for a prolonged occupation of Germany.[415] But time would cut short many good intentions. In some cases the French "collected" personnel rejected by the Americans. For example, the first president of the newly created high court of Tübingen was Eugen Boeckmann, who, while not a party member, had been dismissed by the Americans in September 1945 at the high court of Stuttgart due to the fact that he had been promoted during the Nazi regime (in 1941) to president of a senate at that court. Because the new district court of Lindau considered jurists from the neighboring district court of Kempten in the American Zone, candidates rejected there applied to the French Zone as rumors of its more liberal denazification policies spread.[416]

The French considered the personnel politics of the Americans most honorable but doomed to failure. In a consultation, the Americans had declared their intention of purging all Nazi Party members from the higher judicial service and stressed the need for enforcement of this policy from a psychological point of view. The French appraisal was succinct, theoretically a nice idea, but practically impossible.[417]

The French complained that the Americans had dismissed all former Nazi Party members at Kempten at the price of letting the court go to pot. And even the American officer in charge of this measure admitted that soon the Americans would have to abandon this policy in order to keep the courts working.[418] The French Legal Division thought it better to rely on compromised, but competent,

---

414 Report "Organisation Judiciaire de la Province du Wurtemberg-Hohenzollern" [undated, after June 1, 1949], AOFAA, AJ 806, p. 615, Dossier 2.
415 Statement for the press by Charles Furby, March 4, 1947, AOFAA, AJ 805, p. 605, Dossier 17.
416 Monthly Report Württemberg, October 1945, AOFAA, AJ 3679, p. 12.
417 Monthly Report Württemberg, August 1945, AOFAA, AJ 806, p. 615, Dossier 3.
418 Ibid.

personnel than to have amateurs dabbling at justice, which could result in a cure worse than the disease.[419]

While the French had to swallow the bitter pill of re-admitting old Nazis, they tried putting on a happy face. Somebody who had joined the Nazi Party because of opportunism might serve the occupation authorities with exactly this same zeal, loyalty, and conscientiousness again fed by opportunism. To merit the trust placed in him, a former party member would most likely follow all instructions closely.[420]

In the past, it had often been the persons not previously affiliated with the NSDAP who had caused the greatest trouble to the Allied authorities. Positive vibes were coming from Baden, where "a visible satisfaction" was noticed within the Justice Administration; former NSDAP members in particular were thoroughly impressed by French tolerance and were purported to be particularly docile.[421] A similar report was received from Württemberg.[422]

The Americans were not particularly pleased by the liberal French approach to denazification. Distrustful, they observed the nonchalant handling of denazification standards in the French Zone, which had been noticed by others, too. "It became more and more obvious in the eyes of the population that the French are not denazifying along the same lines as the US Forces."[423] The awkward situation led to a migration of dismissed German staff from the American Zone to the neighboring French Zone to once again assume important positions in public life. Worse, "in many cases it [appeared] that officials of the Land government in the US Zone [were] actively conniving or assisting in placing undesirables where they are spared further denazification."[424] While the population on the whole would prefer the American Zone, the upper echelons of the civil service had nurtured a certain weakness for the lackadaisical French denazification mentality. This had even led to the development of Nazi nests in the French Zone, such as at the University of Tübingen, which is considered "a hotbed of Nazi activity even today."[425]

The American Legal Division criticized the French side in a memorandum stating that the

---

[419] Letter of Commandant Renard, Legal Officer at Military Court Lindau to Directeur Général de Justice at Military Government of the French Zone in Baden-Baden, November 7, 1945, AOFAA, AJ 806, p. 620, Dossier 2.
[420] Ibid.
[421] Monthly Report Baden, October 1945, AOFAA, AJ 3679, p. 12.
[422] Monthly Report Württemberg, November 1945, AOFAA, AJ 3679, p. 12.
[423] Weekly Report, December 19, 1945, NARA, OMGWB 12/135 – 2/1.
[424] Ibid.
[425] Ibid.

French authorities have frequently appointed to office individuals who would be considered to come within the mandatory removal category and who could not be admitted at the present time under the German Law for the Liberation from National Socialism and Militarism. This went so far that individuals who originally resided and held office in our zone 'emigrated' [sic] to the French Zone and were promptly given even key positions in the Administration of Justice. We should make sure that no lawyers who would be disqualified to practice law in our zone gain access to the Landgericht Kempten (US Zone) by having been admitted to practice in Lindau (French Zone)."[426]

When the Ministry of Justice of Württemberg-Baden proposed to the German Justice Branch the admission of advocates from the French Zone to courts of the American Zone, the idea was met with strident refusal because it would contradict the American's objectives of occupation.[427] In a draft for a letter, things were put even more blatantly: "Denazification in French Zone is different from ours and practically nonexistent. It is known that numerous Nazi lawyers, who had not been admitted here, are practicing in French Zone … No disciplinary power or supervision over such lawyers in our zone would be available."[428]

Only when American standards of denazification had slackened considerably did cooperation become conceivable. However, the French Legal Division was not naive when it came to the relocation of jurists, always checking into why legal personnel had left the American Zone.[429]

Denazification met with criticism from both the German and French sides. Germans complained about the injustice of the procedure as the purge would affect the really guilty as well as the passive hangers on and thus cause embitterment. Even opponents of the Nazis would be irked by harsh measures. Dissatisfaction was growing day by day.[430]

The French Legal Division, on the other hand, found that amnesties and great leniency on behalf of the denazification commissions had caused the return of higher judicial personnel who had been dismissed in the early phases of the purge. The French means of control were limited. While some control could be exerted in the civil service, the free professions and the advocates were beyond control. A huge number of former Nazis had applied for admission to the advocacy as they could not resume their former positions as *Landräte* (province adminis-

---

426 Memorandum of Walter H. Menke to Colonel E. McLendon, September 3, 1946, NARA, OMGUS 17/198 – 1/1.
427 Report, October 18, 1946, NARA, OMGWB 12/135 – 2/4.
428 Draft for Major Brown, Chief, German Justice Branch, OMGWB for an answer to the bar association of Karlsruhe, October 7, 1946, NARA, OMGWB 17/142 – 2/9.
429 Letter of Directeur Général de la Justice to Délégué Supérieur du Gouvernement Militaire du pays de Bade à Fribourg, August 19, 1947, Dossier Kurt Ritter, AOFAA, AJ 3683, p. 59.
430 Monthly Report Baden, May 1946, AOFAA, AJ 3679, p. 13, Dossier 2.

trators), mayors, judges, or prosecutors because of their involvement during the Third Reich. The free professions would provide a niche and there were no regulations to exclude them, though these former Nazis were beyond the pale.

As in the other zones, the French Legal Division was caught between the wish to denazify and the need to re-open the courts and resume the normal functioning of civil society. The French Military Government ordered its divisions to supervise the denazification of German personnel in all spheres. But the results were meager.[431] One outcome was a drop in the quality of the staff.[432] The head of the French Legal Division considered denazification a thankless task.[433]

As in other parts of Germany, jurists in the French Zone were obliged to hand in their questionnaires and apply for re-admission to the bar and the bench. Like other Germans, lawyers did not always stick closely to the truth. One's own membership in the Nazi Party was either suppressed altogether or dated as beginning at a later point. This attempt at obfuscation was particularly enticing as it was known that personnel files had disappeared or fallen victim to war action. To the horror and great discomfort of many jurists, files of the Reich Ministry of Justice had been found, which enabled Allied legal officers to check the information given in the questionnaires. Furthermore, the Nazi Party membership index (to be housed in the Berlin Document Center) was also available for reference. The zonal French Legal Division encouraged the Legal Divisions in the provinces to refer to the collection of the Berlin Document Center, the *Wehrmachtauskunftsstelle* (German Army Information Point), as well as the Central Registry of War Criminals and Security Suspects (CROWCASS).[434] As a consequence, the Military Government or German courts sentenced jurists for falsification of questionnaires. For misdemeanors, sanctions tended to be harmless. Some advocates were excluded from accepting certain mandates for a limited period of time. But those who had denied membership altogether and had been caught via the party index were subject to harsher measures and were banned from the profession; civil servants were punished by a freeze on promotions.

While falsifications did draw consequences, not all of them were discovered right away. A young solicitor admitted to having been a navy judge but denied all involvement in special courts or drumhead courts martial in order not to endanger his admission to the bar. His entanglement with Nazi military courts would

---

[431] Letter of Administrateur Général to Directors General, October 16, 1946, AOFAA, AJ 373, p. 25/1.
[432] Three-monthly Report Württemberg, May to July 1946, AOFAA, AJ 806, p. 616.
[433] Press statement Furby, March 4, 1947, AOFAA, AJ 805, p. 605, Dossier 17.
[434] Letter Directeur Général de la justice to Divisions de la Justice at regional Military Government and French Military Tribunals, July 2, 1947, AOFAA, AJ 373, p. 25/1.

catch up with him exactly 30 years later, when – as then governor of Baden-Württemberg – he was forced to acknowledge his involvement in death sentences in the years 1943 and 1945, thus leading to a swift resignation.[435]

Criticism of denazification was never hard to find. The first director of justice in the Palatinate was considered entangled in Nazi law himself and was accused of having promoted Nazi legal interpretation during the Third Reich. At the end of 1945, he was asked to resign.[436] His successor, Ludwig Ritterspacher, was considered too lenient by the French, though they thought it was his age and pleasant nature rather than ill will that produced this disposition.[437]

As in the other zones, the purge in the French Zone of Occupation was a complicated affair caught between the functioning of the courts and the effort to eradicate Nazi attitudes.

The French occupation authority pleaded for more strictness and stringency saying that appointments should take place only after the denazification commission had issued its ruling, thus avoiding having to suspend civil servants because of their Nazi involvement or participation in martial courts.[438]

Denazification as such meant very little in many cases, since even some who had been heavily ensnared in Nazi activities were declared "cleared." As more and more former Nazi Party members (re-)entered the legal service, the French occupation authority saw the aims of denazification in danger. A true "*invasion d'anciens éléments nazis*" (invasion of former Nazis)[439] seemed to overrun the civil service. According to French reports, in Württemberg-Hohenzollern 45–70 percent of personnel in the different branches of the civil service and the ministries were former NSDAP members. The Ministry of Justice was worst off. Of a total of 180 members of the higher judicial service, only 31 percent had not been party members; the rest had belonged to the Nazi movement. Of those, the denazification officials had imposed only mild punishments on 63.3 percent, 4.4 percent received fines and enforced retirement; and 32 percent went scot-free without any sanction at all. On the whole, the French were not pleased with this outcome. Conflicting orders from the Military Government, as well as the means of appeal, had allowed even heavily implicated Nazis to return to gainful employment in the legal service.[440]

---

435 Questionnaire Filbinger, January 9, 1948 and supplementary questionnaire [undated], Dossier Hans Filbinger, AOFAA, AJ 3681, p. 37.
436 Monthly Report for the French Zone (and Saar), December 1945, AOFAA, AJ 3679, p. 12.
437 Monthly Report for the French Zone (and Saar), March 1948, AOFAA, AJ 3680, p. 21, Dossier 4.
438 Monthly Report Baden, September 1947, AOFAA, AJ 3679, p. 20, Dossier 1.
439 Monthly Report Württemberg, April 1949, AOFAA, AJ 3680, p. 24, Dossier 3.
440 Ibid.

Although most historians agree that denazification was a failure, the procedure per se brought considerable hardship to some of those subjected to it. Some were acutely affected by the withholding of salaries and the freezing of accounts. The long duration of denazification delayed re-admission and forced jurists to look – at least for some time – for other employment, often menial work.

Criticism of the German Administration of Justice

Because of the typically less than appealing image of lawyers – regardless of which legal system prevails – there is a long tradition of criticizing members of the legal profession, individual sentences, and penal justice in general. As in Shakespeare's *Henry VI*, a planned change in government typically began with the charge: "The first thing we do, let's kill all the lawyers."

Not only did the German jurists receive a lot of negative comments from Allied legal divisions, but from the German press, too. Articles from different papers attacking sentences were numerous. In Bremen, the minister for justice, Theodor Spitta, complained about permanent agitation.[441] In Schleswig-Holstein, judges on temporary contracts, afraid of being criticized in the press and then dismissed at the behest of important pressure groups, refused to get involved in penal justice.[442]

Many articles commented on the corruption of the judiciary during the Third Reich, comparing the judgments of the post-war years with those of the National Socialist era. Nazi law and practice had led to an estrangement between courts and the German people. Members of the legal profession recognized that the Nazi guidance of judicature and the Nazi crimes, recast as "legal" judgments had completely shattered the faith of the people in a just system of law. In Hamburg, Wilhelm Kiesselbach declared that the judiciary had injured the people's sensitivities to law and justice.[443] The Member of Parliament in Württemberg-Baden, the communist Antonie Langendorf, put it succinctly: "The administration of justice is probably the public institution which finds least sympathy with the peo-

---

441 Spitta, *Neuanfang auf Trümmern*, 314.
442 Report about courts in Schleswig-Holstein, August 30 – September 4, 1948, BAK, Z 21/1357.
443 Speech Kiesselbach (on the occasion of the dissolution of the Central Legal Office), October, 27, 1949, BAK, Z 21/1302; published as Wilhelm Kiesselbach: "Rechenschaftsbericht des Zentral-Justizamts anlässlich des Abschiedsfestaktes des Zentral-Justizamts für die Britische Zone am 27. Oktober 1949," *Zentral-Justizblatt für die Britische Zone*, November/December 1949, 212.

ple."⁴⁴⁴ Furthermore, the Allies did not welcome criticism of Allied judgments. All displeasure and resentment was directed towards the German judiciary.

Due to the limits of space and the plethora of newspapers and broadcasts published and spread in the early post-war years, a thorough analysis is not yet possible. It seems likely that criticism usually focused on a small selection of trials that – for one reason or another – attracted the attention of the press. Not all of the journalists writing about the German trials were familiar with the law; sometimes they simply voiced a fuzzy discomfort or used the opportunity to blast populist appeals and criticize a caste that had few sympathizers among the population.

Members of the German judiciary were often enraged by the comments published in the press. Fair sentences never found mention in the press; only scandals hit the newspapers. The overwork; the difficult legal situation; the overlapping of occupation, German law, administrative, and penal law; the difficulties of obtaining documents and evidence – life-blood to the judges and prosecutors in the post-war period – were never mentioned.

To some extent, criticism in the press has to be seen as a war by proxy: The pent-up resentments about Nazi blatant injustice, the state attorneys pleading death sentences, the high-handed and autocratic judges, and the wrongful sentences had all been common legal fare during the Third Reich, but without a safety valve for expressing public opinion. In a way, voicing criticism after 1945 might have been a means of catching up on the suppressed dissent of the Third Reich.

Jurists reacted testily, suing members of the press for libel and defamation. Their reactions hinted at great insecurity exacerbated by the general circumstances of occupation.⁴⁴⁵ The Western Allies cautioned patience and circumspection. Acknowledging that "An Oberstaatsanwalt is, by the nature of his position, not meant to be popular,"⁴⁴⁶ they were nevertheless concerned about the antagonism between the legal profession and the population.⁴⁴⁷ At the same time, criticism was a sign of the process of normalization. Public opinion was to accept law and justice, but a public prosecutor had to be able to withstand criticism.⁴⁴⁸

---

444 Speech KPD Member of Parliament Antonie Langendorf in the regional diet of Württemberg-Baden, May 24, 1949, 3003.
445 Letter of A. Brock (German Courts Inspectorate) to Director, MOJ Control Branch, December 16, 1946, TNA, FO 1060/1025.
446 Inspection district court Marburg, March 9, 1948, NARA, OMGH 17/209 – 1/2.
447 The Cultural Exchange Program of Legal Division [undated typescript], NARA, OMGUS 17/213 – 3/40.
448 Ibid.

Summary

The Western Allies came into a country devastated by warfare with a doubly demoralized populace. Not only the dozen-year experience of the Third Reich with its shady National Socialist ethics, but also the disappointment over the lost war and subsequent occupation had shaken Germans to the core.

Within a short span of time, the Western Allied Legal Division managed to find a handful of reliable German jurists who took it on themselves to re-organize the judicial system and enable society to return to law and order. All three Western occupation authorities were shrewd enough to refrain from major interventions in the German legal system; to a greater or lesser degree, they all aimed for a return to the status quo prior to 1933. The organization and number of courts, districts of courts, and tasks of the German judiciary all were geared toward what had existed (and on the whole functioned reasonably well) before 1933. The centralization of the judicial system (*Verreichlichung der Justiz*) introduced by the Nazis was abolished and the state ministries of justice were returned to their former important function of hub between periphery and center. The necessary abolishment of the Reich Ministry of Justice led to a vacuum that the Western Allies filled in their individual ways. The British Legal Division first relied on the high court presidents in their zone (who inherited some of the Reich ministry's tasks) and later created the Central Legal Office, which functioned as a ministry of justice for the British Zone. Furthermore, they brought into being the Supreme Court for the British Zone to act as arbiter in legal issues resulting from the different judicature of eight separate high courts in their zone.

For the Americans, immersed in the tradition of the United States, where federal and state laws happily co-exist, the parallel existence of many states with different legislation mattered little. Unlike the British, they promoted the early creation of German *Länder* and then encouraged the exchange between the ministers of justice of the *Länder* in the American Zone, who could settle many tasks on the individual *Länder* level (rather than the zone level). The French Legal Division welcomed the small size of their zone – no province within it contained more than six court districts – which was comparatively easy to control. (By contrast, the Americans and British had to cover huge distances when checking on the German courts in territorial states such as Lower Saxony or Bavaria.) The French reckoned that the occupation would last a long time and thus were not intent on creating unified authorities that could serve as precursors for federal German institutions. Of all the Western Allies, they had the greatest affinity to German law due to the common roots of Roman (codified) law. Much German penal law and procedure was influenced by French Law in the first place, dating back to the Napoleonic Penal Code. Procedure in penal trials – with the monopoly of indictment by the state, the binding of the prosecutor by instructions of his superiors, the public form of trials – and the general separation of administration and jurisdiction all stem from the French model. This might have been one reason why the French interfered most with the German courts, as we will see in the next section.

While the Western Allies found little fault with the structure and organization of the German legal system per se, they often despaired over the German personnel with whom they had to deal. Even if the most exposed Nazis were removed from the judicial body, the personnel question remained the most pressing. Very few of the German judges and prosecutors found favor with the Allies. They often came across as too conservative, too distant from the people to adjudicate cases requiring common sense. The biggest effort to influence the minds of the jurists came from the American occupation authority, which offered re-education and re-orientation in manifold ways.

Perhaps the most curious outcome is that, despite the rather inauspicious beginnings – following a lost war, in an occupied country, with a majority of more or less unreformed Nazis among the legal service and the general population – the reconstruction of a democratic legal system flourished.

The concept of the Western Allies worked: Return to the structures of the pre-1933 legal system; leave bigger reforms to the Germans; rely on a small staff of untainted jurists in key positions, who would control the rank and file of former opportunist Nazis who, it was hoped, would not create major turmoil and would in due time become reasoned supporters of democracy. The much criticized denazification played an important role in this, as a signal that, as the writer George Eliot put it a century earlier, "Our deeds still travel with us from afar/and what we have been makes us what we are," thus forcing us to face the consequences. Jurists were called to account for their political affiliations in the process of denazification and were held responsible for any falsifications they perpetrated. Even if after a certain time tainted jurists returned to the bar and bench, they often had experienced months and years of insecurity and abasement as they had been suspended or dismissed and forced to scrape out a living in auxiliary or menial tasks, suffering under property control (the freezing of assets) and loss of income, not to mention the general privations of the post-war years. The aplomb of a self-assured and sometimes high-handed professional guild was thoroughly unsettled because jurists had to report to the Western Allied Legal Divisions, consult and accept orders from foreign authorities. In the next section we will try to show how difficult it was to cope with the Nazi crimes.

Part II: Legal Foundations for the Prosecution of Nazi Crimes by the West German Judiciary

The Western Allies and the Prosecution of Nazi Crimes

> The whole German population had turned into a criminal affair.
>
> Friedrich Dürrenmatt, *Suspicion*

As soon as news of the first massacres became known to the Allies, proclamations for a future prosecution of these crimes were made. By far the best-known wartime proclamation is the Moscow declaration of October 1943 in which Britain, the United States, and the Soviet Union announced their intention of bringing to trial any German officer, soldier, or Nazi Party member involved in atrocities and executions in occupied territories. The main culprits whose crimes were not limited to a fixed territory would be tried as well. During several Allied conferences, the need for investigation and trial of these crimes was repeated. Apart from the International Military Tribunal in Nuremberg against the highest representatives of the Third Reich – where American legal concepts played a dominant role – the Americans undertook 12 subsequent trials in Nuremberg against medical doctors, jurists, army, industry, SS, and ministries, as well as the six main Dachau trials against the concentration camp personnel of Dachau, Flossenbürg, Buchenwald, Mittelbau-Dora, Mauthausen, and the satellite camp Mühldorf. In addition, they held several trials concerning the murder of Allied POWs. Concentration camp trials were also conducted by the British, mainly concerning Neuengamme, Bergen-Belsen and Ravensbrück. The French also carried out several trials, involving staff of the outer camps of Natzweiler concentration camp and the SS special camp Hinzert, as well as smaller trials dealing with assorted staff from several camps and crimes against French and Soviet POWs. Furthermore, there were trials before permanent military courts in France dealing mainly with the crimes committed during the German occupation of France. The Soviet trial program was also extensive, the Sachsenhausen trial being probably the most notable.

The Allies understood that their own systems would prosecute most of the main Nazi crimes – predominantly those involving atrocities committed during the war (and in the occupied territories) involving Allied victims. Prosecution of the criminal deeds the Nazis perpetrated against German victims (or stateless persons) in Germany would be left to the German courts. Early on, the Western Allies – to varying degrees – intended to involve the German judiciary in the adjudication of these crimes ("particularly individual offenses of German against German, which will remain for trial in the German criminal courts as they are re-established").[1] The American Military Government emphasized that this task would be one of the occupation aims.[2] As soon as the German courts were functioning again, work on this task could begin.[3] The Americans emphasized the (assumed) cathartic element of these trials for the Germans.[4]

It quickly became clear that even though the German courts were to deal only with a section of the crimes perpetrated, the task would be enormous because this concerned "other atrocities and offenses, including atrocities and persecutions on racial, religious or political grounds, committed since January 30, 1933."[5] The demarcation line – Allied victims, thus Allied court responsibilities; German (or stateless) victims, thus German court responsibilities – was clear-cut, but turned out to be tricky, as we will see.

The Dachau concentration camp, opened in March 1933, concerned mostly Allied, but also German victims. Therefore, two sorts of trials were initiated. The Americans undertook the effort of trying atrocities committed especially during the war, while the German state prosecutor for the region of Munich (responsible for crimes committed in Munich county and surroundings) was charged with the investigation of crimes committed in the camp before the war. Murder in Hadamar fell under the responsibility of the German prosecutor at Limburg and Frankfurt (as the gassing of so-called feeble-minded Germans was adjudicated), but it also fell under the jurisdiction of the American tribunal as during the final year of the war Polish and Soviet foreign workers had also been murdered by injections there. In a way, this already challenged boundaries since "it appeared that the Hadamar trial and the concentration camp trials were very close to the borderline between the traditional conception of war crimes and a departure from it."[6]

The American Military Government entrusted the prosecution of these "petty criminals" to the German courts as early as 1945 and charged the ministers of justice in the *Länder* of the American zone with the task.[7]

---

[1] Memorandum for the Theater Judge Advocate, compiled by Colonel Charles Fairman, Chief, International Law Section, October16, 1945, NARA, OMGUS 17/53 – 1/5.
[2] Plan for the Prosecution of War Criminals and other Nazi Offenders [undated, end of 1945], NARA, OMGUS 17/53 – 1/5
[3] Memorandum for the Theater Judge Advocate, compiled by Colonel Charles Fairman, Chief, International Law Section, October 16, 1945, NARA, OMGUS 17/53 – 1/5.
[4] Ibid.
[5] Ibid.
[6] Maximilian Koessler, "American War Crimes Trials in Europe," *The Georgetown Law Journal* 39 (1950/1951), 80.
[7] Minutes Conference of Ministers of Justice of Bavaria, Württemberg-Baden and Hesse, in Stuttgart, December 18, 1945, NARA, OMGWB 12/137 – 1/4.

For the British Military Government (and the French), the nationality of victims would determine the responsibility of the court. Perpetrators involved in camps where both Allied and German nationals had been imprisoned had to face two trials. The work camp (*Arbeitserziehungslager*) Nordmark-Hassee near Kiel was handled by a British military tribunal in Hamburg and was also a topic of investigation by the state attorney at Kiel.[8] In the case of a widow of Kerzenheim who had entertained "forbidden relations" with a Polish foreign worker, which led to his hanging and her suicide, consequences against the informers were instigated at both the Tribunal Général in Rastatt (prosecuting the execution of the Pole) and the state attorney at Kaiserslautern (investigating the death of the widow).[9]

Confusion over responsibilities and the zonal borders often prevented effective work. The murder of a group of Soviet POWs in Neustift near Vilshofen, Lower Bavaria, in April 1945 was first investigated by a German state prosecutor, but the case had to be abandoned in October 1948 as military government courts took over. Apparently, no trial followed; German investigations resumed later, the case having been transferred to the German state prosecutor for the city of Munich and for the greater Munich region where it was finally terminated due to lack of proof of murder and the statute of limitations applying to manslaughter.[10]

German authorities were often uncertain as to how to proceed. In February 1945, Soviet foreign workers had burglarized the gingerbread factory Häberlein & Metzger in Nuremberg and the factory security guard had shot two of the burglars. "Oberstaatsanwalt Nuremberg, Dr. Meuschel, informed this office of the foregoing but stated that he did not arrest K. [the suspect] because he doubted whether he has jurisdiction to do so, United Nations members being involved ... The judge ... failed to arrest the man, ordered his release when brought before him and failed to decide upon the demand of the prosecutor's office to have the man arrested. His excuse was that he was not the proper judge but only [the] duty official on that Sunday."[11]

The French Military Government aimed at an ambitious prosecution, but did not accomplish much: The French Sûreté (security force) conducted many investigations that were later passed on to German authorities.

---

8 Kiel 2 Js 487/48, LA Schleswig-Holstein, Abt. 352 Kiel; Nr. 908.
9 Kaiserslautern 7 Js 207/49, AOFAA, AJ 3676, p. 36.
10 Passau 5a Js 86-90/48, 3 Js 268/54 = München II 13 Js 33/68 = München I 116 Js 2/71.
11 Activity report, July 26, 1948, NARA, OMGBY 17/183 – 3/15.

German Demands Concerning the Prosecution of "Crimes Against Germans"

Before and throughout the war, German anti-Nazis (in exile) had stressed the importance of the prosecution of Nazi crimes. After the war, it was the courts' task to put this into effect. Higher court officials approached the Military Government in their efforts to instigate proceedings of previously unpunished crimes.[12]

The heads of government of the *Länder* in the American and British zones sent a letter to the Control Council affirming that the majority of Germans supported the prosecution of Nazi crimes and welcomed the punishment of the culprits, but also requesting "with all insistence that the leaders of National Socialism and their accomplices be brought to account for the vast crimes they have committed against the German people in its entirety and against countless individual Germans." They complained that Hitler's crimes against the German people had played no role at the International Military Tribunal, despite their being of gigantic proportions. In fact, in their eyes, the "German people ... had to suffer under the criminal activity of the National Socialists sooner than other peoples and thereby longer." They clamored for a German court whose effect on the German people would easily surpass the influence of the International Military Tribunal, asserting that

> a sentence imposed by a German court would have a political effect on the German people which could never be accomplished with equal effectiveness by a sentence imposed by an International Military Tribunal. With respect to the development of a sound German democracy within the coming years, the political importance of such a procedure which would have the greatest influence upon the final purgation from National Socialism of the German people, cannot be overestimated.[13]

When meeting again in October 1946 in Bremen, the prime ministers of the American and British zones renewed their quest in a trial centering on crimes against the Germans that had so far not been fathomed, stating:

> The question of guilt toward the German people, on the basis of existing German law, has not been solved by virtue of this decision. This question of guilt must be examined and decided before long by German courts of law.[14]

---

12 Letter Control Branch, Legal Division to Chief, Legal Division, July 28, 1945, TNA, FO 1060/977.
13 Letter of Prime ministers to Control Council, March 26, 1946, NARA, OMGUS 17/143 – 3/9; mentioned also under BAK, Z 21/800.
14 Resolution No. 7 "Trial of War Criminals by a German Court" by the Bremen Conference of Prime Ministers, October 4-5, 1946, NARA, OMGUS 17/143 – 3/9; Discussions about resolution con-

The Legal directorate at the Control Council flatly rejected the prime ministers' plan of establishing a central German court for the adjudication of National Socialist crimes.[15] Wilhelm Kiesselbach, doyen of German jurists in the British Zone, also opposed the plan, maintaining that while National Socialist atrocities in their totality had been abominable and outrageous, they had not been committed against the German people as a whole, but rather against German individuals and thus did not qualify as crimes against the German people.[16] In addition, the prime ministers' declaration would not be directed at holding individual perpetrators to account, but would summarily reject National Socialism as such. This, however, was a political aim to be achieved by political means.

Dr. Curt Staff, the prosecutor general of Brunswick, was also at a loss as to what the prime ministers of the *Länder* actually wanted. The Nuremberg sentence relied on international law, thus not touching crimes against the entirety of the German people. The idea of a crime against the totality of the German people was alien to German penal law. Once again the prime ministers had succumbed to the popular fallacy of the conflation of political wrong and criminal injustice.[17] Obviously, the heads of the Länder were interested in outlawing political wrongdoing rather than criminal wrongdoing.

Irrespective of whether this attempt at a German "Nuremberg Tribunal" was utopian from the beginning or simply an ill-conceived idea, judges lamented for quite some time what could have been if only Germans had been allowed to have a say in the adjudication of Nazi criminals of the highest echelon. An article published by a judge in 1949 stated that it still pained the German judges that they had not been able to install a tribunal to judge the spoilers of Germany and Europe.[18]

Last but not least, demands from the Soviet Zone stressed the need for a German court, claiming that the crimes against Germans "must be atoned for in a German Court which will pass judgment on all war and Nazi criminals including those who were sentenced [in Nuremberg] and those acquitted."[19]

---

cerning the Nuremberg International Military Tribunal in: *Akten zur Vorgeschichte der Bundesrepublik Deutschland 1945–1949*, vol. 2, 925-940.
15 See NARA, OMGBR 6/62 – 2/60.
16 Statement Wilhelm Kiesselbach, BAK, Z 21/800.
17 Letter Prosecutor General Braunschweig to Kiesselbach, December 28, 1946, BAK, Z 21/800.
18 Alexander Micha, "Richter und Politik," *Die Rheinpfalz*, December 3, 1949.
19 Letter "Verbindungsbüros der Einheitsfront" to Allied Kommandatura, October 4, 1946, NARA, RG 260, Box 190, Folder ACA (Allied Control Authority), DLEG (Records of the Legal Directorate) V 2000-4/4.

The Implementation of Control Council Law No. 10 in the British Zone

In December 1945, the Allied Control Council issued Law No. 10 aiming at the "punishment of persons guilty of war crimes, crimes against peace and against humanity." After reference to the Moscow Declaration of October 30, 1943, and the London Agreement of August 8, 1945, Article II (1) defined four acts as crimes: (a) Crimes against Peace, (b) War Crimes, (c) Crimes against Humanity and (d) Membership in categories of a criminal group or organization declared criminal by the International Military Tribunal. While (a), (b), and (d) were rather clear-cut and unambiguous, (c) would pose graver considerations as it encompassed a plethora of crimes:

> (c) Crimes against Humanity. Atrocities and offenses, including but not limited to murder, extermination, enslavement, deportation, imprisonment, torture, rape, or other inhumane acts committed against any civilian population, or persecutions on political, racial or religious grounds whether or not in violation of the domestic laws of the country where perpetrated...[20]

Article II (2) defined perpetrators and accessories, article II (3) the degrees of penalty. In Article III 1 (d) it was specified that

> each occupying authority, within its Zone of Occupation ... shall have the right to cause all persons so arrested and charged, and not delivered to another authority as herein provided, or released, to be brought to trial before an appropriate tribunal. Such tribunal may, in the case of crimes committed by persons of German citizenship or nationality against other persons of German citizenship or nationality, or stateless persons, be a German Court, if authorized by the occupying authorities.

Although the preamble of Control Council (CC) Law No. 10 stated the wish "to establish a uniform legal basis in Germany for the prosecution of war criminals and other similar offenders, other than those dealt with by the International Military Tribunal," the outcome would be very different. Not all of the Allied trials were conducted according to CC Law No. 10, nor was the law applied in all (West) German courts. Rarely did a law find so many different interpretations as did CC Law No. 10.

In the British Zone, Ordinance (*Anordnung*) No. 47 would entitle German regular courts to apply CC Law No. 10, provided the victims were German (or stateless) nationals. Political deliberations convinced the British Legal Division that before a general permission could be issued to German courts, a few prototypical trials needed to be conducted, since German courts had no experience in dealing with

---

[20] *Amtsblatt des Kontrollrats in Deutschland*, No. 3, January 31, 1946, 50.

crimes against humanity.²¹ This practice of exemplary trials clearly stemmed from the English tradition of Common Law in which the adjudication of a single case has an exemplary, i.e., model, character for others. In these cases, the demarcation line (German victims – German trials, Allied victims – allied trials) did not apply.

The German prosecutors were definitely keen on getting down to business concerning National Socialist crimes. At a conference of the prosecutors general of the British Zone a unanimous decision was made urging the Military Government to give them an immediate opportunity to apply CC Law No. 10, in part because proceedings were already under way in the American Zone.²² The prosecutor general of Hamburg stated that for months jurists had been waiting for the authorization to apply Control Council law, either as a blanket right or in singular cases.²³

But the British Legal Division kept the German jurists waiting. The presidents of the high courts bemoaned the fact that they could not get started on these cases, fearing that the delay would bring further criticism from the public about the tardiness and dilatory practice of both the military government and the German administration of justice. The British Legal Division tried to smooth the waters, explaining that "as soon as a small number of these crimes had been dealt with by Military Government Courts, a Carrying-Out Ordinance to Law No. 10 would be promulgated handing jurisdiction over these cases to the German ordinary courts."²⁴

The British Legal Division was not oblivious of the demands of the public:

> For months past there has been clamour by the German public for punishment under Control Council Law No. 10 of Nazis who committed atrocities during the Hitler regime. It was, however, the policy of the Control Office that a number of these cases should first be tried by Mil Gov [sic] Courts in order that precedent could be established.²⁵

---

21 Letter Legal Division, Zonal Executive Office CCG (BE), Herford to HQ Mil Gov Hanover Region, HQ Mil Gov North Rhine-Westphalia Region, HQ Mil Gov Schleswig-Holstein Region, HQ Mil Gov Hansestadt Hamburg, HQ Mil Gov Westfalen Region (Rear Party), September 10, 1946, HStA Düsseldorf, NW 928, Nr. 474; Decree Legal Division, Mil Gov – Legal/MOJ/52 343/1 of September 10, 1946, Justizministerialblatt für das Land Nordrhein-Westfalen, September 1947, Nr. 5, 50.
22 Conference of prosecutors general in the British Zone, July 11, 1946, here quoted in a letter of the prosecutor general Hamburg to Ralph and Egon Giordano, August 9, 1946, quoted in Hans Konrad Stein-Stegemann, "Das Problem der 'Nazi-Juristen' in der Hamburger Nachkriegsjustiz 1945-1965," in *Karrieren und Kontinuitäten deutscher Justizjuristen vor und nach 1945*, ed. Hubert Rottleuthner (Berlin: Berliner Wissenschafts-Verlag, 2010), 355.
23 Ibid.
24 Letter of J.F.W. Rathbone, Legal Division, ZECO, to HQ North Rhine, Westphalia, Hannover, Schleswig-Holstein and Hamburg, August 16, 1946, TNA, FO 937/15.
25 Letter Legal Division, ZECO, CCG (BE) to Secretary I.A&C. Division, ZECO, Bünde, December 20, 1946, TNA, FO 1060/247.

A 1947 memorandum reinforced this strategy, stating that "it was decided as a matter of policy in the summer of 1946 that certain specially selected cases of crimes against humanity should be tried by Control Commission courts in order that a precedent with regard to sentences might be established for the assistance of German Courts."[26]

The first case tried in the British General Military Court of Oldenburg involved crimes committed in a prison camp for delinquent Wehrmacht members in the Emsland (northwest Germany) towards the end of the war. A 19-year-old Wehrmacht private named Willi Herold deserted, got hold of a captain's uniform, gathered a group of other soldiers and together they ransacked the Emsland. The regional commander of the NSDAP for the Weser-Ems territory punished him by having him kill prisoners in the Aschendorfermoor camp. More than 100 prisoners, many of whom had themselves been sentenced for desertion from the Wehrmacht, were executed using automatic weapons.[27] Herold and six members of the staff of the penal camp were sentenced to death on August 29, 1946, by the General Military Court of Oldenburg; Herold and five others were executed on November 14, 1946, at Wolfenbüttel prison.

After the termination of this trial, German courts were entitled to apply CC Law No. 10 and Ordinance No. 47 to all crimes committed by staff of camps (such as SS, Gestapo, police) on prisoners of concentration and forced labor camps or prisons. Furthermore, in conjunction with CC Law No. 10, German penal law could be applied if the crime also constituted an offense according to German law.[28]

The second case the British tried was the so-called Hinselmann trial or "Gypsy Sterilization Case," concerning forced sterilizations of Sinti and Roma carried out in a Hamburg hospital. The trial took place December 2–7, 1946, at Special High Court Hamburg. In all, six doctors and policemen were tried and sentenced to several years of imprisonment.[29]

---

26 Memorandum "Crimes Against Humanity," August 14, 1947, TNA, FO 1060/1075.
27 The sentence of the General Military Court of Oldenburg Nr. 10436, (copy in StA Osnabrück, Rep. 945 Akz. 2001/054 Nr. 210) assumed 350 victims, more probable are about 160 dead, see Paul Meyer, "'Die Gleichschaltung kann weitergehen!:' Das Kriegsende in den nördlichen Emslandlagern und der falsche Hauptmann Willi Herold im Spiegel britischer und deutscher Gerichts- und Ermittlungsakten," in *Die frühen Nachkriegsprozesse: Beiträge zur Geschichte der nationalsozialistischen Verfolgung in Norddeutschland*, ed. Kurt Buck, vol. 3 (Bremen: Edition Temmen, 1997), 210.
28 Letter Legal Division, ZECO, CCG (BE) to Secretary, I.A.&C. Division, ZECO, CCG, Bünde, December 20, 1946, TNA, FO 1060/247.
29 See Gipsy Sterilisation Case, TNA, FO 1060/1061; for German investigations in this and associated matters see also Hamburg 14 Js 573/47 (formerly Hamburg 14 Js 85/46), StA Hamburg, Best. 213-11, Nr. 19075/64.

The third British precedence trial was a pogrom trial that took place in June 1947 at Aachen High Court.[30] As early as July 1946 the legal officer of the British military government had announced to German state prosecutors that the November 1938 riots against Jews would be attended to before a court.

The German prosecutors and judges had been so eager (or confusion about the relevant legal provisions had been so great) that several German trials (according to German penal law) had already been carried out by June 1947 (e.g., in Aurich and Bielefeld). Others were put on hold until the British trial of the pogrom of Aachen had been finished.

The British trial focused on the mayor of Aachen, the NSDAP district head, the police president, and members of police and fire brigade. A large number of Germans attended the trial;[31] the mayor and two members of the fire brigade were acquitted, while the head of the NSDAP of the district and the chief of police were each sentenced to a fine of 5,000 RM and five years in prison. Three policemen were sentenced to two years each. Once this trial had finished, German courts were authorized to try crimes against humanity.[32]

Why the British picked these three cases from the plethora of Nazi crimes committed in Germany is not quite clear. The criteria were probably dictated by several considerations: The trials were exemplary of typical crimes (i.e., crimes committed toward the end of the war, sterilizations, pogroms) and reasonably spread across different courts of the British Zone (Oldenburg in Lower Saxony, Aachen in North Rhine-Westphalia, and Hamburg), thus covering three of four *Länder* of the British Zone. There are indications that further trials were planned, as noted in a letter from the headquarters of the Military Government of North Rhine-Westphalia: "It is hoped by the end of the year that the following classes of cases will also have been tried in Mil Gov Courts: (a) Crimes involving persecution of the Jews, (b) a political murder case, (c) a sterilisation [sic] case, (d) a euthanasia case."[33]

The documentation does not clarify why this was not carried out. It was even difficult to distribute the judgments from cases that had already been adjudicated, as "no written judgments suitable for distribution are in existence."[34] This surely dampened the raison d'être of the precedence cases.

---

30 Aachen High Court H. 677, German translation of sentence dated June 12, 1947 see HStA Düsseldorf – ZA Kalkum, Gerichte Rep. 89/255.
31 See "Der Aachener Brandstifterprozess. Die Anklage lautet auf Verbrechen gegen die Menschlichkeit," *Jüdisches Gemeindeblatt für die britische Zone*, June 11, 1947.
32 Memorandum "Crimes Against Humanity," August 14, 1947, TNA, FO 1060/1075.
33 Letter HQ Mil Gov Land North Rhine Westphalia, BAOR to L/R Det Cologne, Düsseldorf, Aachen, Münster, Arnsberg, Minden, December 19, 1946, HStA Düsseldorf, NW 928, Nr. 474.
34 Letter Land Legal Department, HQ Land NRW to Ministry of Justice NRW, March 4, 1948, HStA Düsseldorf, NW 928, Nr. 476.

As early as 1946, it was decided not to carry out a trial concerning denunciations. Instead, the British Legal Division referred to a post-war Berlin sentence against the informer Helene Schwärzel who had denounced Dr. Goerdeler, a participant in the July 20, 1944, plot to assassinate Hitler.[35] The German courts in the British Zone were thus entitled to instigate trials against informers based on CC Law No. 10 and Ordinance No. 47. Legal problems (there was no provision in the German penal code for informers) were to be referred to the central legal office in Hamburg. Placing these cases before special courts, such as the *Spruchgerichte* (denazification courts), was also considered, though the British preferred to have them tried by German ordinary courts. When some members of the German Administration of Justice demurred over the expected problems of these cases, the British Legal Division advised postponement. The prosecutors general of Lower Saxony opposed this option, saying: "The general view of the meeting was that it would not be desirable to postpone all denunciation cases, many of which aroused particular public interest."[36] Denunciation cases that had entailed severe consequences for the victims (concentration camp imprisonment, death sentences, and executions), would be given high priority.

Although the prosecutors were interested in indicting informers, the courts seemed less eager when it came to sentencing: "A proportion of Crimes against Humanity consists of denunciations by one German of another, resulting in serious consequences to the latter. The courts are reluctant to convict the accused in these cases because of the traditional maxim of German law '*nullum crimen, nulla poena sine lege*' [no penalty without a law], i.e. the denunciations did not constitute any offense against Criminal law at the time they took place."[37]

Apart from the legal problems, denunciation cases were potentially highly problematic for the investigators:

> Inquiries into denunciation cases were also beset with frustrations. Files had disappeared, and it was a common thing for an accused to state that it was not he who had made the denunciation, but that he had only been called as a witness. The sum and substance of all this was that public opinion regarded the Courts as 'reactionary'. Facts, however, had to be proved.[38]

---

35 Letter Legal Division, Zonal Executive Office, CCG (BE) to HQ Mil Gov Hannover Region, HQ Mil Gov North Rhine Westphalia Region, HQ Mil Gov Schleswig-Holstein Region, HQ Mil Gov Hansestadt Hamburg, November 21, 1946, HStA Düsseldorf, NW 928, Nr. 474; see also HStA Düsseldorf, Gerichte Rep. 255/275; Decree Legal Division, Mil Gov – Legal/MOJ/52 343/1 – of November 21, 1946, concerning adjudication of informers, in: Justizministerialblatt für das Land Nordrhein-Westfalen, September 1947, Nr. 5, 50-51.
36 Conference Chief Legal Officer, Lower Saxony, Ministry of Justice of Lower Saxony and Prosecutors General, December 18, 1947, TNA, FO 1060/1075.
37 Memorandum of J.F.W. Rathbone, March 8, 1948, TNA, FO 1060/740.
38 Inspection LG Aachen, March 16, 1949, TNA, FO 1060/1237.

When a case made it to court, it would encounter leniency, with the state prosecutor noting that "the lay members were 'milder' in their attitude than the judges; [and that] the passage of time was beginning to blur the bitter feelings and reactions felt in 1945."[39] The old adage that witnesses were a lot more forthcoming in front of the police than in court also held true here, as the senior prosecutor in Mönchengladbach remarked: "It was the experience of the Oberstaatsanwalt that 'witnesses knew less about the case when it came to trial than at the time they made their statements to the police.'"[40]

Fault was also found with the police. For the most part, they "were not well trained in the sphere of criminal investigation and ... their method of interrogation needed improvement. They accepted evidence which no Court would accept."[41]

From the beginning, implementation of CC Law No. 10 met with resistance from the German judiciary.[42] Many prosecutors assumed that they could use either CC Law No. 10 or German penal law *ad libitum* (as they pleased), but "the real trouble, in fact, [was] that in certain cases where the prosecution [had] only laid charges under German law, the latter [had] failed for technical reasons and the courts [had] acquitted and [had] declined to substitute a conviction under Control Council Law No. 10."[43]

The British Legal Division urged the German courts to get moving, writing that "we are convinced, and so no doubt are you, that the atrocities committed under the Nazi regime should be brought to trial swiftly and justly and that we all shall fail in our duty to see justice done and in our debt to the victims of these crimes if we let them go unpunished or if we let the processes of justice drag on indefinitely and inconclusively."[44]

The Legal Division still hoped that the German aversion to Control Council Law would abate in due time.[45] In their effort to convince German courts of the usefulness of CC Law No. 10, the British Legal Division tried to provide further definition: "As a result of certain reports appearing in German newspapers, it has apparently come to be fairly widely believed by the German legal profession that Control Commission Courts take a view of what constitutes a crime against

---

39 Ibid.
40 Inspection LG Mönchengladbach, March 16, 1949, TNA, FO 1060/1237.
41 Ibid.
42 Letter of W.W. Boulton, Ministry of Justice Control Branch to Legal Advice and Drafting Branch, November 24, 1947, TNA, FO 1060/1075.
43 Ibid.
44 Letter of E.G. Leonard, Legal Dept., Land NRW to Minister of Justice NRW, December 8, 1947, HStA Düsseldorf, NW 928, Nr. 475.
45 Letter Prosecutor General, Hamm, Dr. Kesseböhmer, to Land Legal Dept., North Rhine/Westphalia, October 30, 1947, TNA, FO 1060/1075; see also HStA Düsseldorf, NW 928, Nr. 475.

humanity very different from that taken by the German Courts."[46] Crimes against humanity were not necessarily mass atrocities; an individual could have become victim of a crime against humanity – "even if such person lacks moral and ethical qualities." "The destruction of a synagogue violates the religious feelings of the Jewish population and, therefore, offends against the dignity of mankind."[47] The German reluctance, however, was difficult to overcome.

The Implementation of Control Council Law No. 10 in the French Zone

While in the British Zone, final permission was given to German courts to adjudicate by using Control Council Law No. 10, among historians, confusion about the situation in the French Zone still looms large today. Regional military governments gave permissions at different times, sometimes only for individual cases. The French Military Government gave an early go-ahead to German courts in southern Baden, for the application of the law as far as German citizens were concerned.[48] Max Güde, prosecutor in Konstanz, assumed that this held true for the whole French Zone.[49] However, it is clear that courts were uncertain for some time as to how to proceed. This was partly due to the fact that the French Military Government did not encourage exchange between the heads of the German administration of justice and refused to have legal counsel or a common legal journal for the French Zone. Permission for the whole zone was not achieved until June 1, 1950.[50]

As for the British courts, the responsibility of the court was determined by the nationality of the victims. As explained earlier, prosecutors' offices and courts in the French Zone were not sure how to deal with these affairs. The Contrôle (department) in charge of German courts determined that the law was too vague

---

46 Letter Zonal Office of the Legal Adviser, Heford, to Legal Advisers to Regional Commissioners, HQ NRW, Niedersachsen, Schleswig-Holstein, Hansestadt Hamburg, October 15, 1948, HStA Düsseldorf, NW 928, Nr. 482.
47 Ibid.
48 Directive of Military Government Baden, Justice Director General, Baden-Baden, May 2, 1946, Amtsblatt der Landesverwaltung Baden, French Occupied Zone, Nr. 10, August 1, 1946, p. 49.
49 Max Güde, "Die Anwendung des Kontrollratsgesetzes Nr. 10 durch die deutschen Gerichte," *Deutsche Rechts-Zeitschrift* (1947), 111-118.
50 Decree No. 154 of the French Military Government, June 1, 1950, contained in *Amtsblatt der Alliierten Hohen Kommission*, p. 443.

to be used productively by German courts.⁵¹ It has been documented several times that the German courts had trouble applying the law.⁵²

Similar reports came from all echelons of the Württemberg legal service. CC Law No. 10 had been badly received and was considered obsolete, German penal law being considered sufficient.⁵³ The French Contrôle could not see that CC Law No. 10 had been integrated into German legal thinking. The law was applied very restrictively and only when no other legal possibilities remained. The punishments were mild, the application of the law unpopular.⁵⁴

As in the British Legal Division, the French Contrôle also thought for a time that the German courts would overcome their reticence. A monthly report from Württemberg put it succinctly: "The German courts do not like trying cases of crimes against humanity."⁵⁵

The longer the occupation lasted, the less the law seemed to take hold, and once again it remained unenforced.⁵⁶

The Discussion Concerning Control Council Law No. 10 in the American Zone

While British and French occupation authorities gave limited permission to German courts for the application of CC Law No. 10, the American Military Government never did so. Only American military courts in the American Zone were permitted to implement Law No. 10; German regular courts were allowed to use the German penal code only.⁵⁷

A member of the Bavarian ministry of justice stated on the occasion of a conference of the prosecutors general that the American Zone was the only part of

---

51 Monthly Report Baden, August 31, 1946, AOFAA, AJ 3679, p. 13, Dossier 7; see also Monthly Report for the French Zone (and Saar), August 1946, AOFAA, AJ 3679, p. 13, Dossier 7.
52 Monthly Report for the French Zone (and Saar), February 1948, AOFAA, AJ 3680, p. 21, Dossier 3.
53 Monthly Report Württemberg, April 1949, AOFAA, AJ 806, p. 619.
54 Report "Organisation Judiciaire de la Province du Wurtemberg-Hohenzollern" [undated, after June 1, 1949], AOFAA, AJ 806, p. 615, Dossier 2.
55 Monthly Report Württemberg, October 1948, AOFAA, AJ 806, p. 618; see also AOFAA, AJ 3680, p. 23, Dossier 2.
56 Monthly Report Württemberg, September 1949, AOFAA, AJ 806, p. 619.
57 Broszat, "'Siegerjustiz' oder strafrechtliche Selbstreinigung", 496; Henri Meyrowitz, *La Répression par les Tribunaux Allemands des Crimes contre l'humanité et de l'appartenance à une organization criminelle en application de la loi no. 10 du Conseil de Contrôle Allié* (Paris: Librairie générale et de jurisprudence, 1960), 120, Loewenstein, "Reconstruction of the Administration of Justice in American-Occupied Germany", 437.

West Germany where German penal judges did not apply CC Law No. 10.[58] Previously, a representative of the American Military Government had asked the Bavarian Ministry of Justice whether the application of CC Law No. 10 was considered desirable. A senior official of the ministry did not think so, stating that "most cases under Control Council Law No. 10 would also be punishable under the German criminal code. The only cases which presented difficulties were those of informants. Some of these cases could be tried under the Criminal Code by application of the principle of the 'indirect principal'."[59] The other cases could be transferred to the denazification tribunals, which were also entitled to mete out sentences of up to 10 years' imprisonment.

In Hesse, the absence of legal regulations concerning informers had cropped up, too, there being "no German law ... which covers these situations."[60] The military government of Hesse understood that any law created now would be retroactive and thus subject to criticism. They recommended transferring informers to the Counter Intelligence Corps (CIC) to be interned in camps. It was hoped that a settlement would come about "in a matter of a few weeks."[61]

At the end of 1946, Colonel Ernest L. McLendon, Chief of the Administration of Justice Branch of Legal Division, OMGUS, consulted the heads of the Legal Divisions in Bavaria, Hesse, Württemberg-Baden, Bremen, and the American Sector of Berlin regarding whether permission for the application of CC Law No. 10 by German courts should be granted for the American Zone, too.[62]

The chief legal officer of Bavarian Military Government, Richard J. Jackson, was in favor, maintaining that "on the basis of a recent increase of trials of Nazi crimes in Bavarian courts it is believed that the German courts would make full use of such an enactment."[63]

From Hesse it emerged that both the Legal Division and the Ministry of Justice were all for the introduction:

> In the view of this Division and of the Ministry of Justice the enactment of a Military Government Ordinance or Law similar to British Military Government Ordinance No. 47 is highly desirable and should be accomplished without further delay ... An example of the type of cases

---

58 Report on Conference of prosecutors general of the Western Zones in Schönberg near Kronberg/Taunus, February 1-2, 1949, NARA, OMGUS 17/197 – 3/13.
59 Minutes of Conferences with Bavarian Ministry of Justice, July 25, 1947, NARA, OMGBY 17/187 – 3/1.
60 Letter of OMGH to Ministry of Justice, Hesse, January 28, 1946, NARA, OMGH 17/210 – 2/6.
61 Ibid.
62 Letter of Ernest L. McLendon to Directors of Legal Division Bavaria, Gross-Hesse, Württemberg-Baden, Bremen and Berlin (US-Sector), November 27, 1946, NARA, OMGUS 17/217 – 2/3.
63 Letter of Richard J. Jackson to Chief, Administration of Justice Branch, Legal Division, OMGUS, December 9, 1946, NARA, OMGUS 17/217 – 2/3.

to which Control Council Law No. 10 might well be applied is furnished by the important insane asylum murder camp cases which so far could be prosecuted in German courts only under German law ... [However,] if Control Council Law No. 10 is to be applied in German courts the question needs to be considered whether Military Government Law No. 1, Article IV, which prohibits punishments for acts not expressly made punishable by law in force at the time of their commission, should be amended.[64]

The Bremen alter ego was far more reticent. In a letter to the chief of the Administration of Justice Branch, Legal Division, Robert W. Johnson (Chief Legal Officer, OMG for Bremen Enclave (US) writes:

Frankly, I have not yet reconciled my way of thinking so that it completely approves of the ex-post-facto features of the questions raised at Nuremberg. Apparently, the law retains such features in that it invalidates certain offenses admissible under certain laws, such as acts done under superior orders. It further seems to me that if we are abrogating existing German laws to further our own desires, occupation policies and aims, Military Government should do the job itself.[65]

From the Berlin Sector, the Legal Branch voiced the view that

adoption of an Ordinance in the American Zone of Germany similar to the British Ordinance in effect in the British Zone would seem to be in line with the announced policy of US Military Government to transfer more and more authority to German agencies and increasing their responsibility for setting their own affairs in order. However, in view of the situation in Berlin, where the German courts function under the supervision of the quadripartite Allied Kommandatura (Command), it would seem that more weight should attach to recommendations received from the Chief Legal officers of the Länder in the American Zone than any opinion which may be expressed for the US Sector, Berlin. If in due course it is deemed desirable by OMGUS to enact an ordinance for the US Zone similar to the British Ordinance, the effort will be made by the US Sector to secure city-wide implementation of such or similar law for city-wide application in Berlin. At this time this office is not in a position to anticipate what the reaction of the French and Soviet Military Government authorities may be although it stands to reason that the British Military Government authorities in Berlin would support such a measure for the Berlin courts.[66]

---

[64] Letter of Franklin J. Potter (Legal Division, OMGH) to Chief, Administration of Justice Branch, Legal Division, OMGUS, January 20, 1947, NARA, OMGUS 17/217 – 2/3.
[65] Letter of Robert W. Johnson (Chief Legal Officer, OMG for Bremen Enclave (US) to Chief, Administration of Justice Branch, Legal Division, OMGUS, December 10, 1946, NARA, OMGUS 17/217 – 2/3.
[66] Letter of Wesley F. Pape (Chief, Legal Branch, OMG for Berlin Sector) to Chief, Administration of Justice Branch, Legal Division, OMGUS, December 10, 1946, NARA, OMGUS 17/217 – 2/3.

The head of the German Justice Branch of Württemberg-Baden was wildly antagonistic:

> The enactment of legislation similar to British Military Government Ordinance No. 47 within the US Zone is not recommended at this time. It is believed that crimes against humanity are not defined with sufficient clarity in Article II, Paragraph 1 {c} of Control Council Law No 10 to make desirable the conferring of general jurisdiction on the German courts to try cases under that paragraph ... Murder, extermination, torture, rape etc. against Germans or stateless persons are capable of definition only in terms of German law in any event ... It is recommended that, when in any individual case, the remedy under existing German law is inadequate, and when from the facts of the case itself it appears that it is one in which justice may be achieved in the German courts under the provisions of control Council Law No. 10, the German courts be given specific authorization to try the case by Military Government under Article III, Paragraph 1 (d) of that Law.[67]

The Chief of the Legal Division in Württemberg-Baden

> transmitted to OMGUS adverse recommendation as to adoption of an ordinance similar to British Military Government Ordinance No. 47 making crimes against humanity under Control Council Law No. 10 triable in German Courts, on grounds that the definition of such crimes in the named law is so vague that authorizing its general adoption in German courts would depart from the principles of Military Government Law No. 1 ... It was recommended that the authority of the Offices of Military Government for the Land to authorize such trials in proper cases be continued.[68]

Within the Legal Division, OMGUS, expert opinions were also consulted. At first the Administration of Justice Branch was supportive of the idea of introducing CC Law No. 10 in German courts in the American Zone last but not least to unburden the American military courts.[69] Less than two months later, the opinion of the Administration of Justice Branch was diametrically opposed. Henry M. Rosenwald wrote in a memorandum: "I am ready to drop the proposed enactment, mainly because I feel that most crimes against humanity can actually be dealt with under the German Criminal Law."[70] Cases one could not handle under

---

[67] Letter of Ralph E. Brown (Chief, German Justice Branch, Legal Division, OMGWB) to Chief, Administration of Justice Branch, Legal Division, OMGUS, January 4, 1947, NARA, OMGUS 17/217 – 2/3.
[68] Juan A. Sedillo, Director, Legal Division, OMGWB, Weekly Report, November 10, 1947, NARA, OMGWB 12/135 – 2/2.
[69] Memorandum of Henry M. Rosenwald, Administration of Justice Branch, Legal Division, OMGUS to Chief, Legislation Branch, OMGUS, January 11, 1947, NARA, OMGUS 17/217 – 2/3.
[70] Memorandum of Henry M. Rosenwald, Administration of Justice Branch, Legal Division, OMGUS to Chief, Administration of Justice Branch, OMGUS, Haven Parker, February 28, 1947, NARA, OMGUS 17/217 – 2/3.

German penal law were to be handed over to military courts where CC Law No. 10 could be applied. Thus the legal gap could be closed without further legislation.

A decision was announced in August 1947. The directors of the legal divisions in the *Länder* were told that most crimes considered crimes against humanity were already punishable by German penal law, thus German courts would not need a specific authorization.[71]

It is difficult to ascertain why the American Legal Division opposed the application of CC Law No. 10. Whether they took the German arguments seriously (which will be discussed in greater detail in the next section), or whether the time factor played into their hands, they certainly had opened the German courts in their zone very early, with the first trials concerning Nazi crimes adjudicated in the summer of 1945. In mid-1945 they admonished German courts to "perform the duty of bringing to justice Germans or other non-United Nations nationals, other than major war criminals, accused of crimes against humanity, where such crimes are offenses against the local law and where the victims of the crimes are of German or other non-United Nations nationality."[72] Similarly, another directive pointed out the responsibility of the courts "to apprehend and bring to justice war criminals and all persons who have participated in planning or carrying out enterprises involving or resulting in atrocities."[73] By the time the decision was made in 1947, however, the Americans were already beginning to wind down their own war crimes trials program; their interests in occupation and denazification had already substantially eroded compared to the beginning of the occupation period.

The one notable exception in which CC Law No. 10 was being applied by German courts under American dominion was in the US sector in Berlin. This was a concession to the three other Allies, who had all permitted the German courts to go ahead with CC Law No. 10. For the handling of these cases, German courts applied to the Legal Division in the American sector, which would individually decide on cases. Even here, Americans were hesitant to give permission. Only cases of denunciations where grave consequences had resulted for the victim were acknowledged and allowed to be tried under CC Law No. 10.

---

[71] Letter of Alvin J. Rockwell to Directors of Legal Division, Military Government of Länder, August 5, 1947, NARA, OMGUS 17/215 – 3/10; see also Letter Alvin J. Rockwell, Legal Division, OMGUS to Legal Division, OMGWB, August 25, 1947, NARA, OMGWB 17/142 – 1/3.

[72] Directive "Administration of Military Government in the US Zone in Germany," July 7, 1945, quoted in letter of Alvin J. Rockwell to Directors of Legal Division with Military Government of the Länder, August 5, 1947, NARA, OMGUS 17/216 – 3/10.

[73] Directive Military Government, American Zone [undated], TNA, FO 1060/977.

While the non-application of Law No. 10 was a cause of some joy for German judges – it saved them a lot of heartburn – the adjudication of denunciations in the American Zone posed legal problems. On the whole, most legal procedures concerning denunciations ended without a trial; the state prosecutors terminated them because the deed had not been considered a crime during the Third Reich and thus no proof of a crime had been established. The only legal loophole for trying these cases under German penal law was in situations where the alleged informers had used false pretenses against the victim.

For severe cases of denunciations, the *Spruchkammern* were pulled in for help. Another legal possibility for the regular courts related to cases of indirect wrongful deprivation of personal liberty (if the victim had been arrested in the course of events following the denunciation) or negligent homicide. However, German courts were loath to try to adjudicate denunciations in such a manner, as cases were difficult to prove.

British criticism of the American method hinted at a major problem: "Such cases are dealt with under ordinary German law alone and there is every reason to suppose that a large number of these cases are going unpunished."[74]

Among the legal divisions, not everyone was content with the decision of non-application of CC 10 in the American Zone. Hans W. Weigert, a member of the Legal Division, received a letter from the sister of a victim of a denunciation who had been shot on April 27, 1945, her body thrown into the Danube near Deggendorf.[75] German proceedings had already started, but the sister learned that due to the non-empowerment of the German courts the informers (and main culprits in her eyes) could not be dealt with in court.[76] In a memorandum to the Legal Division, Weigert noted:

> I did not discuss with her the problems arising from our policy on Law No. 10 and I am therefore rather impressed with the contents of the letter which seems to me to express eloquently the reaction of the common people, especially those who are the victims of Nazi crimes. It seems to me that the letter is a strong argument in favor of our following the British and French example in regard to Law No. 10.[77]

---

74 Letter of J.F.W. Rathbone, Ministry of Justice Branch, Legal Division, ZECO, Herford to HQ Legal Division, Berlin, March 11, 1948, TNA, FO 1060/924; for a German translation see BAK, Z 21/2213.
75 Sentence in Rüter, *Justiz und NS-Verbrechen*, vol. I, No. 32.
76 Letter of Maria Nothaft to Hans Weigert, September 6, 1947, NARA, OMGUS 17/217 – 1/15.
77 Memorandum of Weigert for Alan J. Rockwell, Director, Legal Division, OMGUS, October 10, 1947, NARA, OMGUS 17/217 – 1/15.

There are several indications that the German public expressed a certain interest in the application of the law.[78] Nazi informers were hardly popular in German society, whether among victims or their relatives; journalists and politicians in the American Zone voiced their opinion in favor of the law. Even the president of the Oberlandesgericht, the chief prosecutor of the legal profession, and other members of the legal profession "deplored the fact that, at present, German courts in Bremen are not permitted to try denazification [sic], [read: denunciation] cases under Control Council Law No. 10."[79]

Hans Weigert continued to campaign for the application of the law by referring to experiences from the neighboring British Zone.[80] Experiences in Bremen and Hamburg convinced him that German jurists should be entitled to deal with the law.[81] The Legal Division insisted, however, that "certain crimes that might be tried under Law No. 10, notably denunciation cases, were not crimes under German law. We have felt that such matters could be dealt with adequately by the Spruchkammer as a general rule."[82]

Apart from *Spruchkammern*, victims could claim compensation for damages suffered in civil proceedings. Whenever a perpetrator was sentenced to payment for indemnification, the American Legal Division was impressed:

> This decision is of particular importance since it offers some redress to the victims of denunciators. It should be remembered that the German courts have no way at this time to punish a person that conveyed accurate information concerning political offenses to the Nazi authorities, since they did not violate any specific provision of the criminal code, and Control Council Law No. 10 cannot be applied by German courts. In the opinion of this office the German court is quite correct in the statement that the action of such a denunciator constitutes tort even if not a criminal offense.[83]

For several months, the British had tried to convince the American Legal Division to issue an ordinance like theirs. In the beginning, that looked like an easy task.[84] Rathbone of the British Legal Division suggested to the American Judge Advocate Division "that some form of Military Government legislation in your Zone

---

[78] Inspection LG Frankfurt, September 11, 1947, NARA, OMGH 17/209 – 1/2.
[79] Report of Hans W. Weigert, Legal Division, OMGUS about Field Trip to Bremen, Bremerhaven and Hamburg, July 4, 1947, NARA, OMGBR 6/62 – 2/60.
[80] Ibid.
[81] Ibid.
[82] Letter of John M. Raymond to Office of the Legal Adviser, Control Commission for Germany (British Element), Berlin, August 24, 1948, NARA, OMGUS 17/217 – 2/26.
[83] Letter OMGH to OMGUS, November 3, 1947, NARA, OMGH 17/210 – 3/4.
[84] Letter of J.F.W. Rathbone, Ministry of Justice Branch, Legal Division, Herford to HQ, Legal Division, Berlin, April 20, 1948, TNA, FO 1060/924.

is necessary for this delegation of authority to the Germans."⁸⁵ He felt that the discrepancies between the American and British zones regarding Law No. 10 were causing trouble for the German Administration of Justice, since it was "likely that the German Courts in the British Zone will be placed in the most embarrassing and unenviable position in comparison with their colleagues in the American Zone."⁸⁶ The British advised the American Legal Division to introduce Law No. 10 in the American Zone for use by the German courts – if necessary without considering "the views of the Land Ministers of Justice."⁸⁷

The British were disappointed to learn that their "efforts had been in vain and the American Legal Division would not agree to promulgate legislation or to issue a general authority to the German Courts to try these crimes."⁸⁸ The Americans told the British curtly (and not truthfully) that the "Germans have not yet made any request for authority to try any cases under Law No. 10."⁸⁹

Indeed, the German governments of Bavaria and Württemberg-Baden had asked at several points for permission to apply the law. To quote but one:

> The Minister of Justice, Württemberg-Baden, requested authorization to prosecute a case under Article III, 1 d of Control Council Law No. 10, representing that such authorization is desirable because it appeared doubtful whether or not application of the penalty as provided in German Criminal Code for breach of peace is possible, and because the question as to the definition of what constitutes a riotous crowd offered difficulties.⁹⁰

The Americans advised tersely that interpretation of the German law was up to the German courts. Once again, in the spring of 1948, a request came from Württemberg-Baden for the application of Law No. 10 concerning a denunciation. Again, OMGUS decided that "the request ... should not be granted."⁹¹

---

85 Letter of J.F.W. Rathbone to David I. Lippert, Judge Advocate Division, HQ EUCOM, August 11, 1948, TNA, FO 1060/148.
86 Letter of J.F.W. Rathbone, Ministry of Justice Branch, Legal Division, ZECO, Herford to HQ Legal Division, Berlin, March 11, 1948, TNA, FO 1060/924.
87 Ibid.
88 Letter Zonal Office of the Legal Adviser, Herford, to British Liaison Officer, Central Legal Office, September 6, 1948, TNA, FO 1060/148.
89 Letter of John M. Raymond, OMGUS, to Office of the Legal Adviser, Control Commission for Germany (British Element), August 24, 1948, NARA, OMGUS 17/217 – 2/26; see also TNA, FO 1060/148.
90 Report, September 20, 1947, NARA, OMGWB 12/135 –3/6.
91 Letter Legal Division, OMGUS to Legal Division, OMGWB, May 2, 1948, NARA, OMGWB 17/143 – 3/11-15.

The American Legal Division told the British that "our war crimes program and, we understand, your war crimes program, are drawing to a close."[92] With respect to this development, they were loath to entrust to the Germans a law that had explicitly been developed for the handling of war and Nazi crimes at exactly the point where this program seemed to be coming to an end. However, they had to admit that especially denunciations had fallen short of adequate attention noting that "many of these cases have presented jurisdictional and procedural questions not contemplated at the time when war crimes were being tried exclusively by war crime tribunals."[93] By the beginning of 1948, the ministers of justice in the American Zone were also opposed to the law, citing that "in principle a general and unlimited application of this law cannot be recommended because of the experiences in other zones. The reason of this recommendation lies not only in the difficult and doubtful legal and political principles involved in Law No. 10, but also in its contravention of the democratic principle of *'nulla poena, nullum crimen sine lege.'*"[94] This argument brings us to the position of the German judiciary.

German Jurists and Law No. 10

One of the central themes in discussion among the judicial guild, courts and law faculties was the application of Law No. 10 by German courts. Law gazettes and dissertations debated the merits and problems of the issue.[95]

One of the main defenders of the application of retroactive law was Gustav Radbruch. He emphasized that the legal legacy of the Third Reich was *gesetzliches Unrecht* (legal injustice) as well as supralegal law (übergesetzliches Recht), which was above the codified law.[96] Positivism had brought arbitrariness and foul

---

92 Letter of John M. Raymond, OMGUS, to Office of the Legal Adviser, Control Commission for Germany (British Element), August 24, 1948, NARA, OMGUS 17/217 – 2/26; see also TNA, FO 1060/148.
93 Report "The Administration of Justice in Bavaria," July 1, 1949, NARA, OMGBY 17/188 – 3/1.
94 Resolution ministers of justice in the American Zone, February 13, 1948, TNA, FO 1060/924; German translation BAK, Z 21/2213.
95 Von Hodenberg (SJZ 1947); Wimmer (SJZ 1947); Radbruch (SJZ 1947); Güde (DRZ 1947); Haensel (NJW 1947); Kiesselbach (MDR 1947); Meyer (MDR 1947); Graveson (MDR 1947); Strucksberg (DRZ 1947); Schönke (NJW 1948); Lange (DRZ 1948; SJZ 1948); von Weber (MDR 1949); Werner (NJW 1949); Dissertations: Johannsen (1948); Eberhardt (1950); Greim (1951); Lechleitner (1951); Lachmann (1951).
96 Gustav Radbruch, "Gesetzliches Unrecht und übergesetzliches Recht," *Süddeutsche Juristen-Zeitung* 1946, column 105-108.

laws. The purpose of laws is to create a principle of legal certainty, but also to aim at justice. If there were a discrepancy between positive law and justice, then justice would take precedence, as the law would have to be considered false.

Radbruch, however, was in doubt about how to deal with judges who had applied Nazi laws, since they had been educated in the positivist legal doctrine and were thus supposedly incapable of perceiving the legal wrong they were meting out. And even if they had understood that they were committing injustice, they could plead a state of emergency (§ 54 StGB, German Penal Code).

Not all German jurists were content with the idea of a supra-legal law; the president of the Central Legal Office called it the "nuclear bomb of legal order."[97]

The main opponent of the application of Law No. 10 was the high court president in Celle, Dr. Freiherr Hodo von Hodenberg. He told his colleagues at the high courts in the British Zone in no uncertain terms that Military Government Law No. 1 and Control Council Law No. 10 were contradictory: Law No. 1 stated that a deed could only be adjudicated if a law (against a crime or misdemeanor) had existed at the time when the act was committed, according to the old principle of *nulla poena sine lege*. But Control Council Law No. 10 would force German courts to act against exactly this legal principal as it, itself, had not been in effect when the Nazi crimes were committed. This, in his eyes, would lead to a shattering and diminution of the sense of right and wrong among the German population and would undermine the rule of law.[98] The Central Legal Office tried to convince the British Legal Division that German penal law was sufficient – with the exception of denunciations, which could either be dropped altogether at ordinary courts and handed over to the denazification tribunals or could be tried according to German penal law as "indirect" crimes. The Central Legal Office claimed it did not want to curtail the British occupying authorities' right to issue laws as they pleased; but German judicial personnel would thus be forced to decide against their conscience.

The British Legal Division did not sympathize with these particular pangs of conscience. In their opinion the German Legal profession was

> devoting far too much time and energy to academic discussion of the difficulties in bringing to justice Germans who have committed crimes against humanity or who have informed against other Germans in connection with their Anti-Nazi activities. This whole question is primarily one for the Germans and concrete proposals and action are now required from German lawyers rather than lengthy treatises on criminal law and jurisprudential concepts."[99]

---

97 Quoted in Gerhard Erdsiek, "Strafrecht," *Süddeutsche Juristen-Zeitung* 1948, column 42.
98 Letter OLG-Präsident Celle to OLG-Presidents of the British Zone, October 3, 1946, BAK, Z 21/784.
99 Letter of Legal Division to British Liaison Officer, ZJA, October 31, 1946, BAK, Z 21/784; see also BAK, Z 21/1352.

The British Legal Division acknowledged the legal problems but stressed that it was more important that wrongdoers not go scot-free.

The beacon of resistance against the application of CC Law No. 10 by German courts was raised by Freiherr Hodo von Hodenberg in a special edition of the *Süddeutsche Juristen-Zeitung* (published in the American Zone), which had a circulation of 10,000.[100] He argued that Law No. 10 was an international law that had served its purpose at the Allied tribunals, where no other law was available. German courts, on the other hand, could enact German penal law. The great majority of Nazi crimes (coercion, blackmail, assault, manslaughter, murder, etc.) were also punishable by German law, German penal law being authoritative and on the whole fully sufficient.[101] The definition of a crime against humanity (according to Article II, 1 c) was too vague for German jurists. It was rather a collective term for crimes that were already punishable according to other laws. Retroactive law was especially unlikely to be repudiated harshly as the Nazis had introduced retroactive laws themselves and thus violated the old principle of *nulla poena sine lege*. Von Hodenberg rejected the legitimation of retroactive law under the aspect of a higher justice; since objective justice could never be achieved, only subjective justice was possible. For understandable reasons, many people were now driven by a desire for revenge and demanded draconian punishment. Retribution, however, would have to fit into the framework of existing laws. Retroactive application of Control Council Law No. 10 would offend penal law. Referring to the denunciations, von Hodenberg pointed out that informing police or investigating authorities about facts was not a crime. Although some acted out of base motivations, this was morally reprehensible but not legally punishable. Further exceptions to the principle of *nulla poena sine lege* would lead to erosion of legal certainty. Furthermore, judges would be exposed to additional qualms. Not only had they been too compliant during the Third Reich, but now they would be forced to act against their legal notions. He recommended having denunciation cases referred to the denazification tribunals.

August Wimmer explained the stance of the British Legal Division: In the eyes of the Allies this was not retroactive law, as perpetrators had been told via foreign broadcasts that crimes would be prosecuted.[102] In England, only part of the penal law was fixed; common law drew on tradition, giving judges scope to form their own opinions. The principle of *nullum crimen sine lege* was not as important

---

[100] Hodo Freiherr von Hodenberg, "Zur Anwendung des Kontrollratsgesetzes Nr. 10 durch deutsche Gerichte," *Süddeutsche Juristen-Zeitung* 1947, column 113–124; see also Denkschrift des OLG-Präsidenten Celle, November 7, 1946, HStA Düsseldorf, NW 928, Nr. 474.
[101] Hodenberg, „Anwendung des Kontrollratsgesetzes Nr. 10," column 116.
[102] August Wimmer, "Die Bestrafung von Humanitätsverbrechen und der Grundsatz 'nullum crimen sine lege'," *Süddeutsche Juristen-Zeitung Sondernummer* 1947, column 123–132.

to English penal law as it was to German law. Rejecting retroaction would be a relapse into Nazism's legal positivism.

Further legal opinions and discussions followed. If Control Council Law No. 10 were to be applied by German courts, would it become German law, remain international law, or both? Was it also to be applied to crimes committed before the Nazi takeover of January 30, 1933? What was its relation to German penal law, i.e., should the two laws be applied jointly or exclusively?

The German administration of justice in the British Zone reluctantly gave in to the wish of the British Legal Division. The president of the Central Legal Office warned against not applying Law No. 10. It was a binding law issued by the Control Council; any judge who had been sworn into office was thus forced to apply it. For the adjudication of such unprecedented horrors as perpetrated under the Third Reich, exceptional measures were necessary.[103] He admonished a conference of presidents of district courts to apply the law and follow suit. Opposition to the law would counter popular sentiment, opinions, and expectations abroad. If pangs of conscience were torturing the judges, they had to remember that in a collision of duties one had to follow the higher calling. The task ahead was a patriotic duty that had to be mastered; failure could mean the loss of international understanding for a long time.[104]

Let it be said that throughout the whole occupation period, the debate on CC Law No. 10 and its application by German courts did not abate. Further problems cropped up as soon as German district courts began using the law for adjudication because judges were uncertain as to how to deal with the law. On the whole, the German administrations of justice in all Western zones were opposed to the application of the law by German courts for various reasons. Support from legal personnel in key positions in the British and French zones had at best been lukewarm, appealing to a sense of duty and obedience to Allied authority.

Contested cases started to come in to the Supreme Court of the British Zone. As judges were quite bewildered by the law, it often fell to the Supreme Court to define crimes against humanity and finally decide the cases. The Supreme Court assumed that Law No. 10 targeted political, racial, and religious mass persecution, rather than the isolated occasional misdeed. The perpetrator had to have committed the aggressive act consciously and willingly, intending to harm the victim. A grossly negligent crime against humanity or an attempted crime against humanity was, by definition, not possible. The deed also had to have been committed in connection with National Socialist rule, i.e., if the perpetrator identified with Nazi ideology

---

103 Advisory opinion Prof. Dr. Kiesselbach, Hamburg, [undated], BAK, Z 21/799.
104 Conference OLG-Presidents in Bad Pyrmont, November 26-27, 1946, HStA Düsseldorf, Gerichte Rep. 255/275.

and aims, or used them to further his own aims. The act would also have to have gravely infringed upon the victim's human rights, i.e., if the victim were killed or subjected to substantial mistreatment, grievous bodily harm or imprisonment. This also applied if a flippant desultory remark resulted in excessive consequences under Nazi courts. In addition, a perpetrator had to know about the unlawfulness of his act. According to the Supreme Court of the British Zone, German penal law and Law No. 10 were to be treated as concurrence of offenses, i.e., the burning of a synagogue during the pogrom of November 1938 would have to be treated as both arson (according to German penal law) and a crime against humanity (according to Law No. 10). If no German law was applicable (as was the case with denunciations) Law No. 10 was to be applied as a *lex specialis* (special law) that could stand on its own. The defense of "acting on orders" was to be considered in mitigation but would not preclude punishment as such.[105]

Though the Supreme Court of the British Zone outlined the guiding principles for jurisdiction by the lower courts, judges were reluctant to follow suit. They were "not keen on trying cases of Crimes against Humanity under Control Council Law No. 10 and violent disagreements between the judges arose during trials."[106] When adjudicating these cases, the judges meted out punishments that, in general, were less strict than what the state attorney had demanded.[107] The Legal Division summarized the situation saying: "The reluctance of certain judges to deal with Crimes against Humanity under Control Council Law No. 10 is already well known."[108] Thus, the legal office of the military government in Lower Saxony tried to imbue the senior state prosecutors with a sense of urgency considering prosecuting crimes against humanity.[109] In a letter to the Legal Division Headquarters in Berlin, Rathbone wrote:

> There is no doubt that the German legal authorities are not dealing with cases of Crimes against Humanity under Control Council Law No. 10 with adequate efficiency or expedition ... In my view and in the view of Legal Branch, this delay is due in the main to reluctance on the part of the German legal profession to deal with cases under Law No. 10, which allegedly infringes the doctrine of nulla poena sine lege.[110]

---

[105] Heinrich Jagusch, "Das Verbrechen gegen die Menschlichkeit in der Rechtsprechung des Obersten Gerichtshofs für die Britische Zone," *Süddeutsche Juristen-Zeitung* 1947, column 620–624.
[106] Inspection LG Lüneburg, Braunschweig, Göttingen, Hildesheim, Hannover, September 23 to October 8, 1947, TNA, FO 1060/247.
[107] Ibid.
[108] Ibid.
[109] Conference Legal Office, Land Lower Saxony, Ministry of Justice, Prosecutors general, state prosecutors, December 8, 1947, TNA, FO 1060/1075.
[110] Letter of Rathbone, Ministry of Justice Branch, to HQ Legal Division, Berlin, June 18, 1947, TNA, FO 1060/1036.

Five months later, W. W. Boulton wrote in another letter: "At the present time the rate of progress is painfully slow and there are grounds for believing that in some parts of the zone passive resistance is being offered by the Legal Civil Service to the disposal of crimes against humanity."[111] The Legal Division identified five reasons for this behavior of jurists:

1. "The majority of judges and prosecutors come from a right wing section of the population which has never had much sympathy with persons having a different political and religious faith from their own. The victims of crimes against humanity were Jews or persons with left-wing views and the sufferings which they have endured are not sufficiently appreciated by the courts."
2. Judges themselves were under threat. There were rumors that judges sentencing Nazi criminals would be "called to account" after the end of the Allied occupation.
3. Dissenting legal opinions on CC Law No. 10 (re: *nullum crimen, nulla poena sine lege*) would further complicate matters, as leading representatives of the German administration of justice were publishing critical articles in legal journals.
4. Central supervision was sorely missed. Remote regions, where control was looser than in metropolitan areas, had an even worse record in dealing with crimes against humanity.
5. The absence of lay elements at German courts contributed to the bad performance.[112]

The British Legal Division even accused the German Administration of Justice of deliberate obstruction. Boulton wrote: "Although direct evidence is difficult to obtain, there is every sign of a 'go slow' policy on the part of the German Courts, which cannot all be attributed to the doctrine of nulla poena sine lege because this objection does not apply to straightforward cases of murder, violence and ill treatment."[113] Worse still, "the judges and prosecutors have less sympathy for such persons than for the accused. The fact that millions of innocent persons were put to death by the Nazis seems to have made little or no impression on many legal officials."[114]

---

111 Letter of W.W. Boulton, Legal Division ZECO, CCG (BE), Herford to Chief Legal Officers, North Rhine/Westphalia, Lower Saxony, Schleswig-Holstein, Hamburg, November 13, 1947, TNA, FO 1060/1075
112 Ibid.
113 Letter of W.W. Boulton, Legal Division, ZECO, CCG (BE), Herford to Director, MOJ Control Branch, November 11, 1947, TNA, FO 1060/1075.
114 Ibid.

Moreover, the British Legal Division felt hoodwinked as jurists' meetings (which the Legal Division had suggested they hold) were used to polemicize against CC Law No. 10, prompting Boulton to continue: "It is suspected that advantage has been taken of this encouragement to hold meetings where the exponents of nulla poena have probably dominated the meetings."[115]

Still, the British Legal Division saw a clear demand for Law No. 10 in parts of German society.[116] The law also found some popularity outside of legal circles.

German courts in the British and French Zones tried to avoid the application of CC Law No. 10. Whenever possible, they preferred to use German Penal Law only, be it that they felt safer and more knowledgeable in its use, or that they were vehemently opposed to Law No. 10 for legal reasons. When it became obvious that the obnoxious behavior of German jurists regarding Law No. 10 would not subside, the British Legal Division – ever tolerant and ready for compromise – yielded ground, advising that

> as a general rule, such cases [crimes against humanity, E. R.] should be charged under German Law rather than under Control Council Law No. 10, although there may be cases (particularly where a long course of misconduct is shown by an accused) in which a charge under Law 10 is appropriate. Even so, it is usually advisable to lay an alternative charge or charges under German Law.[117]

Thus, after the American Legal Division rebuffed the British attempt to lure them into entitling German courts to application of Law No. 10, the Legal Division came to review its position.[118]

As soon as they understood that their efforts at proselytizing were in vain, the British made allowances for the German administration of justice. German jurists mocked CC Law No. 10 as an "alien presence in the German legal system"[119] and as a problem child (*Schmerzenskind der Strafjustiz und Rechtslehre*), which – like

---

115 Letter of W.W. Boulton, Legal Division, ZECO, CCG (BE), Herford to Director, MOJ Control Branch, November 11, 1947, TNA, FO 1060/1075.
116 Memorandum "Crimes Against Humanity," August 14, 1947, TNA, FO 1060/1075.
117 Letter Director of Prosecutions, Deputy Legal Adviser, Zonal Office of the Legal Adviser, Herford, to Legal Adviser, in Länder of the British Zone and British Sector Berlin, January 18, 1949, TNA, FO 1060/4.
118 Letter Zonal Office of the Legal Adviser, Herford to British Liaison Officer, ZJA, September 6, 1948, TNA, FO 1060/148.
119 Koblenz 2 Js 1051/47, AOFAA, AJ 1616, p. 801; see also Claus Seibert, "Abschied vom KRG 10," *Neue Juristische Wochenschrift* 1952, 252: "immer ein Fremdkörper, den viele mit einem Seufzer begrüsst haben und dem nur wenige eine Träne nachweinen werden."

no other – caused doubts, conflicts of opinion and legal misapprehensions.[120] They complained about the permanent influx of Anglo-Saxon legal thinking (*unaufhörliches Einströmen angelsächsischer Rechtsgedanken*)[121] since the International Military Tribunal at Nuremberg, problems of translation and the difficulties in explaining the differences between the German penal code and the code of criminal procedure.

If anything, things got more complicated when the German constitution, the Basic Law, was adopted. Article 103 (2) explicitly forbids the punishment of deeds that were not considered criminal when committed. Some courts were convinced that this article of the Basic Law made the application of Allied Law (specifically CC Law No. 10) untenable, and refused to open main hearings. But high courts abrogated these rulings. The British Legal Division decided that the Allied High Commission had accepted the Basic Law (and its ban on retroaction), but Control Council Law No. 10 was still valid.[122] The British Legal Division even intended to encourage broadening the area of application and asserted: "It is probably desirable to remove the present anomaly created by Law No. 10 whereby if the victim is not German or stateless, only a charge under ordinary German law can be preferred and only if the victim is German or stateless can a charge under Control Council Law No. 10 be preferred."[123]

Two years after the enactment of the Basic Law, the Control Council Law was nullified for the use in German courts; Chancellor Konrad Adenauer asked British High Commissioner Sir Ivone Kirkpatrick to withdraw the permission (of ordinance No. 47). Once again arguments against the law were reiterated. With the British Ordinance No. 234 (of September 1, 1951) the right of German courts to apply Law No. 10 was withdrawn. In Berlin, with its special status, a separate agreement had to be made. The French enacted similar arrangements. A final cancellation of Law No. 10 came with the first law for the clearing of occupation, May 30, 1956.

---

[120] Klefisch, "Die NS-Denunziation in der Rechtsprechung des Obersten Gerichtshofes für die britische Zone," *Monatsschrift für deutsches Recht* 1949, 324.
[121] Nadler, "Deutsches Recht vor dem Court of Appeal in Herford," *Monatsschrift für deutsches Recht* 1949, 17.
[122] Memorandum of Legal Divison, North Rhine/Westphalia for Legal Adviser, November 25, 1949, TNA, FO 1060/146.
[123] Letter of W.W. Boulton to Legal Adviser's Zonal Office, Herford, November 12, 1949, TNA, FO 1060/148.

The Phase-out of Allied Trials and Transfer to German Prosecution

While the Germans had initiated their prosecution of Nazi criminals, as the occupation period drew to a close, the Western Allies began transferring unsettled legal affairs into German hands. Again, each of them pursued the aim differently.

The American Point of View

The Americans were most intent on closing things down.[124] By 1948, it was obvious that a lot of cases had not been handled and these were by no means of lesser importance.[125]

It would be the task of the German legal system to deal with this material:

> Upon termination of the activities of the Military Tribunals which were conducted by the Judge Advocate in Dachau and by the Office of Chief of Counsel in Nuremberg, the German administrations of justice desire to try speedily such criminal cases which, while originally investigated by the aforementioned agencies, do not involve the safety and security of US and allied personnel and which therefore fall within the jurisdiction of German courts. Included are such mass atrocities cases which will not be prosecuted by the Judge Advocate.[126]

Indeed, work had already started.[127] To continue the prosecution and make sure that all culprits were held to account, it was essential to gain the cooperation of the German courts.[128]

The Judge Advocate proposed to give German authorities only limited access to files of the American war crimes trials program.[129] The Chief of Administration of Justice Branch was very much opposed to this idea, replying that: "Our war crimes trial program is ended. Our program of extradition of German war criminals to our allies is virtually ended . . . ."[130] Thus the German courts were "the only forum left to try the alleged murderers and perpetrators of other major

---

124 Letter of Alvin J. Rockwell to Chief of Staff, July 9, 1947, NARA, OMGUS 17/216 – 3/9.
125 Memorandum of John M. Raymond, October 29, 1948, NARA, OMGUS 17/213 – 2/46.
126 Ibid.
127 Ibid.
128 Ibid.
129 Letter of J. L Harbough (Judge Advocate) to John M. Raymond, January 19, 1949, NARA, OMGUS 17/213 – 2/46.
130 Letter of Mortimer Kollender, Chief, Administration of Justice Branch, to John M. Raymond, Chief, Legal Division, February 3, 1949, NARA, OMGUS 17/213 – 2/46.

felonies against Allied nationals, civilian and military, including American ..."[131] Therefore, it would be necessary to give complete access to the remaining documents.[132]

> With the end of our war crimes and extradition programs, presumably for valid reasons, the issue is not whether we or our Allies could better try these criminals than the Germans and thus avoid criticism, but rather whether they are to be tried at all or allowed to go free ...[133] But even if they [the Germans] were [too lenient], and even if we were unable to correct it in the exercise of our supervisory powers, it seems fairly obvious that some punishment for known common criminals, even if inadequate, is better than none at all ... Again, I think Colonel Harbough badly misreads the signs of the times in thinking that criticism by our Allies and people at home would be stilled or less indignant if they knew that these known criminals were to be allowed to go scot free without any punishment, rather than be tried and punished by the Germans."[134]

For the actual transfer of files from American to German hands, a commission (consisting of members of ministries of justice from Hesse and Württemberg-Baden, the Hessian denazification ministry and a member of the state prosecutor of Nürnberg-Fürth) was constituted to screen the material and pass it on to the competent German prosecuting authorities, e.g., incriminating evidence against former members of the Reich Ministry of Justice and the People's Court was handed over to Hessian prosecution agencies, while collected documents on the deportations of German Jews from Franconia or investigations against members of the Reichsministerium für die besetzten Ostgebiete (Reich Ministry for the Occupied Eastern Territories) and the German Foreign Office were passed on to the prosecutor at Nürnberg-Fürth.

Another approach was taken regarding those culprits who had already been sentenced by American military tribunals but who were also considered relevant for German adjudication, e.g., Ilse Koch, who had been sentenced to life imprisonment in the American Buchenwald trial. After review, the sentence was reduced to four years, leaving the Americans less than content, recommending that the case receive "not only ... a new trial by the Germans in the event we couldn't retry her, but also that we assist by turning over our files on the case."[135] While Koch's trial for crimes against Allied inmates of Buchenwald was complete and the sentence handed down, the issue concerning German victims was still open. General Lucius D. Clay, the military governor for the American Zone, referred the matter to

---
131 Ibid.
132 Ibid.
133 Ibid.
134 Ibid.
135 Ibid.

Bavarian Prime Minister Hans Ehard.[136] Previously "unintroduced evidence concerning Ilse Koch" had been analyzed, and although the American Legal Division found the material inadequate for an American trial, the situation was different for German proceedings.[137] The Judge Advocate was convinced that a German trial was sensible:

> A second trial of Ilse Koch by a German Court for any crimes in violation of German law would not be barred by the principle of double jeopardy. However, any prosecution against her in the German Courts should be limited to crimes in violation of German law committed against anyone before 1 September 1939 and against German nationals only after that date. She was not tried for such crimes in the Buchenwald case.[138]

German Courts Branch in Bavaria were critical of German attempts at Nazi crime trials, noting that "as time progresses, the prosecution and trial of these cases are met with greater difficulties because of the disappearance and forgetfulness of witnesses, a growing apathy on the part of the public and the courts to the past, and a general resurgence of Nazi influence and fears."[139] It probably would be better to close things down altogether. In his monthly report of November 1948, Richard A. Wolf suggested that

> the so-called political cases (breach of the peace, mistreatment of concentration camp inmates by capos) should be brought to an end in 1949, at least as far as the prosecutors' offices are concerned. Otherwise, the experiences of denazification might repeat: the more time passes by, the less witnesses know or want to know anything. The public opinion becomes disinterested; finally, persons severest incriminated will be punished less than those persons who were tried before.[140]

The British Stance

Like the American Legal Division, by the end of the 1940s the British competent authorities had lost interest in further war crime trials. In 1948 the Overseas Reconstruction Committee of the British cabinet decided that war crimes trials

---

136 Letter of Lucius D. Clay, to Jr. Col J.L. Harbough, Judge Advocate, February 7, 1949. NARA, OMGUS 17/213 – 1/13.
137 Memorandum of Wade M. Fleischer, Special Assistant for War Crimes, January 12, 1949, NARA, OMGUS 17/213 – 1/13.
138 Memorandum of J. L. Harbough, Judge Advocate, February 2, 1949, NARA, OMGUS 17/213 – 1/13.
139 Annual Report from July 1, 1947 to June 30, 1948, German Courts Branch, OMGBY, NARA, OMGUS 17/197 – 1/28.
140 Monthly Report, November 25, 1948, NARA, OMGBY 17/183 – 2/14.

should end by September 1, 1948. The foreign secretary suggested January 1, 1949, as the deadline for both British and German trials, putting the British Legal Division in somewhat of a quandary: On the one hand it was clear that the British war crime trials were more or less petering out, while on the other hand, because of the delays caused by ordinance No. 47 and legal disputes over CC Law No. 10 and crimes against humanity, German trials against Nazi criminals had barely begun. This lag would create an incongruous situation:

> It is clear that we cannot set a 'deadline' for the completion of cases by our own Courts if the Germans are allowed to try people for the same type of offence [sic] involving other Germans or stateless persons for a considerable time thereafter. Further is essential that Germans who have committed Nazi crimes against Allied nationals should not go unpunished if any Germans who have committed crimes against other Germans or stateless persons are still to be prosecuted.[141]

It would be difficult to come to an agreement as to when German courts should conclude their efforts at prosecuting Nazi crimes.[142]

Like their American counterparts, the British tribunals considered transferring their files to German investigating authorities.[143] New investigations ceased.[144] Parliamentary Under-Secretary of State for Foreign Affairs Lord Henderson informed the House of Lords in a speech on May 5, 1949, that no new trials had been initiated since September 1, 1948, apart from the last trial (against Field Marshal von Manstein), and only nine trials by Control Commission courts remained open.[145]

The British Legal Division was intent not only on ending its own trials but also on finishing the Nazi crime trials in German courts – not least because they probably never trusted the German judiciary to apply CC Law No. 10 correctly. From the end of 1947, the Legal Division raised ever more pressing questions as to when German courts would terminate Nazi crime trials – an ordinance pro-

---

141 Letter of Rathbone, Ministry of Justice Branch, Zonal Office of the Legal Adviser, Herford, to Director, Legal Advice and Drafting Branch, September 10, 1948, TNA, FO 1060/1241.
142 Ibid.
143 Letter, Director of Prosecutions, Deputy Legal Adviser, Zonal Office of the Legal Adviser, Herford, to Legal Adviser in Länder of the British Zone and British Sector Berlin as well as Prosecutions Sections, March 31, 1949, TNA, FO 1060/4.
144 Letter, Director of Prosecutions, Deputy Legal Adviser, Zonal Office of the Legal Adviser, Herford, to Legal Adviser in Länder of the British Zone and British Sector Berlin, January 18, 1949, TNA, FO 1060/4.
145 Transcript of Lord Henderson's speech in the House of Lords, May 5, 1949, TNA, FO 1060/149.

claiming the end would be imminent.[146] However, Germans were permanently initiating new investigations while the British were literally closing up shop as far as the trials were concerned. By the end of 1947 nearly 3,000 investigations were pending;[147] a year later, the number was not much reduced. In an October 1948 letter to the legal division in the British Zone, J. F. W. Rathbone pleaded with the German administration of justice: "It is the earnest wish of H.M. [His Majesty's] Government and of the Military Governor that these Crimes against Humanity should be disposed of as soon as possible."[148]

Meanwhile, the British tried to reduce the numbers by reminding the Germans of the actual criteria for crimes against humanity. They also advised that "it must be impressed upon prosecutors that, if they discontinue proceedings in cases where a conviction is very doubtful, the courts will be enabled to deal more justly and more expeditiously with really serious cases of crimes against humanity."[149]

One reason why things were not proceeding more swiftly was obvious to the Legal Division:

> A considerable period elapsed between the beginning of the occupation and the time when German courts could first exercise jurisdiction. During the interval many material witnesses left Germany or otherwise disappeared. The readiness of Germans to give evidence against German criminals which was apparent in 1945, has since largely evaporated. Witnesses are no longer willing to support statements which they made previously.[150]

Apart from the problems of investigating crimes going back 10-15 years, the complicated transfers of suspects from internment camps, the small numbers of staff at the courts, and the high overall crime rate hampered progress. In 1949, more than 1,000 investigations were still underway.[151] Of 1,380 investigations, indictments had been drawn up and main hearings were being planned in only 412 cases.[152] The prosecutors general and senior prosecutors were loath to order their

---

[146] Letter of W.W. Boulton, Legal Division ZECO, CCG (BE), Herford to Chief Legal Officers, North Rhine/Westphalia, Lower Saxony, Schleswig-Holstein, Hamburg, November 13, 1947, TNA, FO 1060/1075.
[147] Meeting J.F.W. Rathbone and Legal Officers of the British Zone in Herford, November 26, 1947, TNA, FO 1060/826; see also TNA, FO 1060/237.
[148] Letter of Rathbone, Zonal Office of Legal Adviser, Herford, to Legal Adviser in British Zone, October 6, 1948, TNA, FO 1060/4.
[149] Ibid.
[150] Memorandum, J.F.W. Rathbone, March 8, 1948, TNA, FO 1060/740.
[151] Letter of President Central Legal Office to Liaison Officer, Central Legal Office, May 20, 1949, TNA, FO 1060/148; see also TNA, FO 1060/1241.
[152] Letter of W.W. Boulton, Zonal Office of the Legal Adviser, Herford to Legal Adviser, HQ, Berlin, June 30, 1949, TNA, FO 1060/1240.

subordinates to end the trials; the Prosecutor General of Düsseldorf explained that he had not given a binding order to that effect.[153]

The Central Legal Office told the ministries of justice in the British Zone to ask all prosecutors' offices to check pending investigations regarding crimes against humanity and to remove trivial cases, once again reminding them of the criteria: malevolent intention of the perpetrator, a sense of unlawfulness on behalf of the perpetrator, a connection with the Nazi terror regime, inhumane consequences for the victim that would violate dignity of man and mankind as such and constitute gross injustice. An imprisonment of just a few days was not considered sufficient. Action of prosecutors should be governed by how likely they believed a conviction would be. Previously, prosecutors had been eager to indict and then leave it to the courts to decide, thus shifting the responsibility.

The prosecutors general thought that investigations and trials could be ended either in the spring or towards the end of 1949.[154] The minister of justice in Schleswig-Holstein refused to order the prosecutor general in Schleswig to terminate investigations, since previously neither prosecutors nor courts had proceeded too severely, but rather too mildly.[155] He did not want to reinforce this tendency to leniency.

However, the Central Legal Office wanted to avoid perpetual Nazi crime trials at all costs[156] and preferred to "restrict narrowly the continued prosecution of Crimes Against Humanity and of members of criminal organisations [sic], which threaten to drag on indefinitely."[157] In order to reduce the numbers, the Central Legal Office was intent on granting amnesty in all cases where a conviction was not likely or punishment would not exceed one year of imprisonment.

The summons came again in 1949: "H.M. Government welcomes the winding-up of trials of a political character in Germany and has made this a German responsibility."[158] The British found the long duration of trials quite unsettling and they spread warnings of gloom and doom: "If the matter is left to the Federal Government ... it may be years before it can devote time to bringing to a conclusion (assuming that public opinion approves) trials of Crimes against Humanity

---

153 Letter Central Legal Office to Liaison Officer, Central Legal Office, May 5, 1949, TNA, FO 1060/1727.
154 Letter Central Legal Office to Liaison Officer, Central Legal Office, January 12, 1949, TNA, FO 1060/148.
155 Letter of Minister of Justice of Schleswig-Holstein, Dr. Katz, to Legal Branch, HQ Land Schleswig-Holstein, November 9, 1948, TNA, FO 1060/148.
156 Memo Central Legal Office, June 10, 1949, BAK, Z 21/1310.
157 Letter of W.W. Boulton, Zonal Office of the Legal Adviser, Herford to Legal Adviser, HQ, Berlin, June 30, 1949, TNA, FO 1060/1240.
158 Ibid.

and members of criminal organisations [sic]."¹⁵⁹ They also distrusted the abilities of German jurists and politicians to reach "a satisfactory and co-ordinated solution."¹⁶⁰

To ease a coordinated transfer in February 1949, a conference with representatives of the British and French legal divisions took place in Baden-Baden. The French stated that about 300 cases of crimes against humanity were still pending in their zone. (It is unclear whether this number referred only to French or German courts or to both.) The French were very much opposed to transferring cases with French victims to German responsibility.¹⁶¹ Raymond Juncker, the head of the *Contrôle de la Justice Allemand* (Department of German Justice), issued a warning to the British when he "pointed out that the German prosecuting staff were obstructive, the judiciary were biased and undertook the trials reluctantly; evidenced by the fact that convictions only amounted to some 25 percent of the number of persons charged."¹⁶² The French Legal Division refused to give an exact date by which they were prepared to transfer cases to the German administration of justice. The head of the French Legal Division suggested that the British and Americans and French should find a joint solution. The British representative told him that the French matters were altogether different and that a joint settlement was out of the question "as the Americans have already solved it in their own way."¹⁶³ Thus a coordinated transfer of Western Allied judicial proceedings into German hands failed.

While in the British and American zones the Control Commission courts or military government courts continued to exist, they no longer tried National Socialist or war crimes anymore, only contraventions of occupation law.

The French Exception

As could be inferred from the above-mentioned conference between French and British legal divisions, the French Legal Division tried war criminals for a longer period than did the other Western Allies. French military tribunals were held in the former French Zone until the mid-1950s. The tribunal in Rastatt closed on

---

159 Ibid.
160 Ibid.
161 Letter of Nils Moller, Zonal Office of the Legal Adviser, CCG (BE), Herford to Principal Legal Adviser, HQ CCG (BE), Berlin, February 12, 1949, TNA, FO 1060/149.
162 Ibid.
163 Ibid.

March 5, 1956.[164] The American and British legal divisions even made use of this court once when Fritz Suhren, the former commander of Ravensbrück Concentration Camp, indicted in the British Ravensbrück trial, had fled from imprisonment in Hamburg. When he was seized some time later in Lower Bavaria living under an alias, the Americans extradited him to the French where he was tried by the military court in Rastatt, sentenced to death, and executed in June 1950 in Sandweier near Baden-Baden.

Allied Interventions in West German Trials

Military Government Law No. 2 gave the Allies considerable authority in the German administration of justice, be it via supervision of participation in main hearings and consultation of files, via control and possible cassation, or via suspension of judges and control of personnel, administration and budget. On the whole, interventions were relatively rare. Considering the fact that Germans had only recently supported and run a most murderous regime throughout Europe, the trust the Western Allies put into the West German legal system was astounding. American, British and French legal divisions made very sparse use of their right to alter, lift or nullify German rulings and intervened in literally only a handful of cases where German courts had erroneously tried nationals of the United Nations or dealt with cases of Allied victims. In only very few cases, interventions were triggered by what the Allies saw as blatant miscarriage of justice. The usual course of procedure then was a lifting of the sentence and a retrial by a German (or in a few instances, Allied) court.

Summary

Unlike in later years, none of the Nazi crimes adjudicated in the occupation period was subject to the statute of limitations. It was assumed that the limitation had been dormant during the Third Reich, thus causing a stretch of the appropriate time limit. In other words, a crime committed in 1933 against a Nazi opponent was not prosecuted during the Third Reich. The time limit to prosecute thus began after May 8, 1945 – or even later, according to the functioning of German courts. Then the usual deadlines applied. Hence, the perpetrators could be held account-

---

164 Yveline Pendaries, *Les Procès de Rastatt 1946-1954: Le jugement des crimes de guerre en zone française d´occupation en Allemagne* (Bern: Peter Lang, 1995), 291.

able, whether cases of murder, manslaughter, bodily harm, coercion, blackmail or breach of the peace.[165] The initial zeal for action should not be underestimated. In all Western zones, investigations concerning National Socialist crimes began in the summer of 1945. The British Legal Division commented on these early efforts:

> Many cases have been tried, which we should describe as crimes against humanity, but they have been disposed of under the Criminal Code and in some cases the Germans have not bothered to make a return on them. This is unfortunate because the Control Office is beginning to ask for information on the number of trials held by German Courts.[166]

Still, Allied observers noted that German courts lacked interest in these cases. When an American inspector inquired about the trial of Nazi crimes against Jews at courts in Lower Bavaria, he received the following answer: "It was explained to me by the Oberstaatsanwälte in Deggendorf and Passau that hardly any such crimes had been committed in their districts since 1933. The Oberstaatsanwalt in Passau insisted that during the Hitler period the population in his district had continued to regard the Jews highly and had therefore refrained from mistreating them."[167] The American Inspector wrote in his report that he was unable to check the validity of the statement. From an historian's point of view, the lack of relevant cases is probably best explained by the historically small number of Jews living in Lower Bavaria.

The minister of justice in Bavaria complained about the lack of enthusiasm, energy and speed when it came to the prosecution of Nazi crimes. He explained that National Socialist rule was a tyranny that cheated its way into government, abused legal institutions and asserted itself only by brute force. Resistance against the Nazis was thus acceptable and in order. The Nazi course of action against the Jewish population in November 1938 was in conflict with any basic principle of occidental law and civilization, and was thus illegal, regardless of whether organs of the state condoned or ordered crimes, did not prosecute them,

---

[165] For erroneous statements to the contrary see Irmtraud Heike, "Ehemalige KZ-Aufseherinnen in westdeutschen Strafverfahren," in *Schuldig: NS-Verbrechen vor deutschen Gerichten: Beiträge zur Geschichte der nationalsozialistischen Verfolgung in Norddeutschland*, ed. KZ-Gedenkstätte Neuengamme (Bremen: Edition Temmen, 2005), 89, or Gerd R. Ueberschär and Rolf-Dieter Müller, *1945. Das Ende des Krieges* (Darmstadt: Primus Verlag, 2005), 143.
[166] Letter of W.W. Boulton, Legal Division, Herford to Director, MOJ Branch, March 13, 1947, TNA, FO 1060/1026.
[167] Memorandum of Henry Urman, November 20, 1946, NARA, OMGUS 17/217 – 3/3.

or simply were not involved. He then ordered the state prosecutors to vehemently insist on a harsh punishment for National Socialist crimes.[168]

Western Allies and the German public often disliked the sentences because of their mildness. Thus "vivid reactions" from the public were recorded in Baden;[169] in Württemberg the lack of commitment concerning the investigation and prosecution of crimes against humanity was deplored.[170] The French collected verdicts they considered too mild with a view to eventual correction via quashing the sentence and giving more "orientation" to the German legal profession.[171] In the whole French Zone, an inappropriate indulgence seemed to have taken hold when it came to adjudicating Nazi crimes against humanity.[172]

The American legal officers in Bavaria stated that the Germans were very reluctant to testify against former Nazis because they considered the American occupation to be a transient affair, and advised caution.[173] By 1949, the French Contrôle thought that the public had already lost interest in the trials, although important cases still came up.[174]

While the number of investigations and trials initiated differs from court to court and prosecutor to prosecutor (and depends on a variety of factors, such as the attitude of the Allies, the zeal of the prosecutors, the number of crimes, the availability of documentation etc.), the total number is impressive indeed. From 1945 to 2005, in (West) Germany, 36,393 investigations and trials concerning Nazi crimes were initiated. Of these, about 13,600 were held between 1945 and 1949.[175] As has been pointed out above, hundreds of investigations had already begun in 1945. There were even 25 verdicts pronounced that year. In 1946 there were 257 and the following year 900 rulings were rendered. The peak was reached in 1948, when 2,011 (guilty) verdicts were delivered; the following year 1,474 judgments were passed, and in 1950 another 743.

---

168 Letter of Bavarian Minister of Justice Dr. Hoegner to prosecutors general München, Nürnberg and Bamberg, September 12, 1947, NARA, OMGUS 17/217 – 2/3; see also NARA, OMGBR 6/62 – 2/60 and Dossier 3: Prosecution of nationalsocialist crimes, General files 1093: Prosecution of still unpunished nationalsocialist crimes, Bavarian Ministry of Justice.
169 Monthly Report Baden, September 1947, AOFAA, AJ 3679, p. 20, Dossier 1.
170 Monthly Report Württemberg, October 1947, AOFAA, AJ 3679, p. 20, Dossier 2.
171 Ibid.
172 Summary of monthly reports for the French Zone (and Saar), October 1947, AOFAA, AJ 3680, p. 27, Dossier 2.
173 Report, August 12, 1946, NARA, OMGBY 17/183 – 2/12.
174 Monthly Report for Palatinate, November 1949, AOFAA, AJ 3680, p. 26, Dossier 3.
175 Eichmüller, "Die Strafverfolgung von NS-Verbrechen seit 1945".

Table 1. Number of investigations, trials, and dispensations by year

Year	Proceedings	Indictments	Convictions	Acquittals	Abatements
1945	382	120	25	2	0
1946	2,023	847	257	94	9
1947	4,135	3,029	900	554	28
1948	4,160	5,362	2,011	1,627	137
1949	3,346	3,975	1,474	1,426	326
1950	1,951	1,381	743	688	1,040

(Excerpt from statistics by Andreas Eichmüller, *Strafverfolgung von NS-Verbrechen – Zahlenbilanz*, 626)

What crimes did the German judiciary handle? As mentioned, Allied requirements limited the efforts of the German judiciary to cases involving German (and stateless) victims. This condition was also reflected in the categories of crimes (according to C. F. Rüter's classifications) that the Germans dealt with in the occupation period. The offenses usually took place within the borders of the Reich. Some of the crimes are difficult to categorize, others fall into two or three categories. A killing of concentration camp inmates towards the end of the war is both a war crime and a concentration camp crime. With all due precaution regarding these categorizations, the following percentages provide an overview of Nazi crimes handled in West German courts, both for the occupation period (1945–1949) alone and for the entire period from 1945 to 2005.

Table 2. Percentage of Nazi crimes by category

	1945–1949	1945–2005
Denunciation	38.3	17.9
Crimes at the end of the war	3.8	5.3
Euthanasia	0.7	1.2
Foreign workers	4.6	4.0
Justice	0.5	2.6
War crimes	1.2	12.9
Concentration camps/prisons	6.7	17.0
Mass extermination	1.2	12.5
Political opponents	16.3	8.9
"Reichskristallnacht"	15.4	6.8
Central authorities	0.2	1.0
Further Nazi crimes	7.8	9.4
Unknown/unspecified	11.3	8.8

Statistics by Andreas Eichmüller, *Strafverfolgung von NS-Verbrechen–Zahlenbilanz*, 628.

There is not much point in a further differentiation of penal action by zones or *Länder*. Law enforcement after 1945 was strongly dependent on regional peculiarities predominant even throughout the centrally organized Third Reich. Because more crimes against Jews were committed during the Nazi era in regions where traditionally many Jews lived, one will usually find a large number of so-called "Reichskristallnacht" trials. Thus, it would be pointless to reproach Schleswig-Holstein – where very few Jews lived – for its dearth of such trials, or to criticize Rhineland-Palatinate for the absence of concentration camp trials (none of the notorious main camps were located there), or the British Zone as such for the deficiency in "euthanasia" trials. As has previously been explained, hardly any denunciation cases were prosecuted in the American Zone before regular courts.

One could – with great effort – analyze the degree of penalty meted out. Again, the gain in knowledge would probably be limited. The degree of penalty is fixed in advance by the German Penal Code for certain offenses (breach of the private and public peace, coercion, deprivation of liberty, bodily harm, etc.), so the range of punishment was limited. Furthermore, in each case one would have to check to see whether the punishment was actually implemented, i.e., whether a prison sentence was served or suspended. Because of the lack of documentation, this is not possible in every case. This also holds true for the "personal dimension" of courts. The enormous quantity of legal records precludes a complete analysis of the judges and prosecutors involved in the adjudication of Nazi crimes. A consideration of the lay members of jury courts is beyond any probing as no files are available.

Part III: The Prosecution of Nazi Crimes Against Jews

[...] Thought I heard the thunder rumbling in the sky,
It was Hitler over Europe saying 'They must die',
We were in his mind, my dear, we were in his mind.

Saw a poodle in a jacket fastened with a pin,
Saw a door opened and a cat let in:
But they weren't German Jews, my dear, but they weren't German Jews...

W.H. Auden, Ten Songs (March 1939)

The following chapters will focus on three main themes of the prosecution of Nazi crimes against Jews. First: reconstruction of (historic) events by police and prosecutors. Each trial followed an investigation – often a painstaking undertaking by police, state attorneys and *Untersuchungsrichter* involving the interrogation of dozens of suspects, victims and witnesses, who would roundly deny, sometimes exaggerate or minimize their roles, or otherwise hold back or distort the truth. Thus, establishing "the truth" was often extremely difficult. Second: examination of the pogrom of November 1938, its motivations, peculiarities and efforts of judicial reckoning. Third: prosecution of deportation crimes.

We know from the statistics shown at the end of Chapter 2 that many Nazi crimes adjudicated in the West German courts during the occupation years concerned assault on political opponents, denunciations, crimes in concentration camps or "euthanasia" institutions, or crimes in the last frantic phase of the war – all of which involved Jews to a greater or lesser extent. However, only the adjudication of crimes that were idiosyncratic to Jews (i.e., where the vast majority of victims were Jews and where a substantial number of trials took place, thus providing a sound sample for analysis) will be discussed here. This yardstick holds true for only two of the three categories: the pogrom of 1938 and the deportations beginning in and following autumn 1941. Sticklers might object to this determination, pointing to the handful of non-Jewish victims incurred as collateral damage during the pogrom and the deportation of gypsies from the Reich, which was organized and implemented similarly to the deportation of Jews. Still, overall, only these two crime classifications had exclusively Jewish victims. Trials concerning extermination camps (another exclusively Jewish topic) were not very numerous during the occupation period. A short overview of these trials appears at the end of the chapter.

The Reconstruction of Nazi Crimes Against Jews

At first glance, it appears that we already know everything about the National Socialist crimes and atrocities committed against German Jews: the boycott of Jewish shops and the forced retirement of civil servants in April 1933; the infamous Nuremberg Laws of September 1935; the exclusion from economic life and "Aryanization"; the pogrom of November 1938; the mandatory move to *Judenhäuser* (Jewish houses); and deportation into ghettos and death camps have all been outlined and described in great detail. So what new facts could be gleaned from the perusal of judicial files? In fact, such a perusal reveals several new aspects. The above-named events generally reflect persecution by the state or the party, but little attention has been paid to the multi-facetted features of individual malicious acts that sometimes predated, exacerbated, and carried to extremes the official anti-Semitic policy. While the persecution carried out on orders of state and party (i.e., the Nuremberg Laws) on a national scale could hardly be fully prosecuted – the suspects who drew up the law, ratified it and put it into effect would number into the thousands – the individual local acts during the boycott or the pogrom could indeed be reconstructed and subsequently prosecuted. Although we shouldn't expect a full (and satisfactory) prosecutorial scheme, we should try to learn more by making use of the record about the Nazi crimes compiled by the judiciary. Rather than presenting a discussion of prosecution details, this section will focus on research into the investigation of Nazi crimes against Jews carried out in the early post-war years.

Early Excesses 1933

Jews were already the target of Nazi violence in March 1933. While the Nazis primarily went after political opponents at this point, Jews were also affected, either because they were also communists or social democrats, or simply because they were Jews. While the murder of the Jewish journalist Felix Fechenbach, editor-in-chief of the Social Democratic *Volksblatt* in Detmold, in August 1933 is well-known,[1] the destiny of fellow sufferers has largely been forgotten.

On March 7, 1933, in Wuppertal-Elberfeld, Oswald Laufer, the Jewish member of the pro-democratic *Reichsbanner*, was shot dead by storm troopers. Laufer, who was only 18 years old, had received a pseudonymous, orthographically bumbling letter in which his "permission" to continue living in Germany was "withdrawn."[2]

Another Jewish member of the *Reichsbanner* was shot and injured on March 5, 1933.[3] On March 12, 1933, (the day of local elections), Wilhelm Spiegel, the Jewish lawyer and head of the social democrats in Kiel, was shot to death in his house as the perpetrators shouted "police!".[4] The cattle-dealer Otto Selz from Straubing – who had been vilified by the infamous *Stürmer* newspaper since 1932

---

1 Paderborn 2 Js 980/45 = 2 Ks 1/48.
2 Wuppertal 5 Js 3641/46 = 5 KLs 61/48; HStA Düsseldorf – ZA Kalkum, Gerichte Rep. 240/190-192. An investigation initiated during the Third Reich against the unknown suspects ended due to the amnesty of March 21, 1933.
3 Wuppertal 5 Js 506/50, previously 5 Js 943/47, HStA Düsseldorf – ZA Kalkum, Gerichte Rep. 5/1297-1299.
4 Kiel 2 Js 344/45, LA Schleswig-Holstein, Abt. 352 Kiel; Nr. 4498-4499.

and who successfully fought in court for a retraction – was picked up by the SS in his house early on the morning of March 15, 1933, forced into a car, and killed near Mengkofen.[5] In Wiesbaden a Jewish businessman, Max Kassel, was shot to death during an attempted arrest on March 24, 1933.[6] On March 25, 1933, in Creglingen (Württemberg), members of the storm trooper unit from Heilbronn carried out house searches (for weapons) and abused 16 Jews in such that two of them subsequently died.[7]

In Kiel, Dr. Friedrich Schumm, a 31-year-old Jewish lawyer who practiced in Neidenburg, Eastern Prussia, was lynched during the boycott.[8] As access to his parents' furniture store was blocked by two SS men, Schumm entered through a side door. As he left the store, a brawl broke out in which SS-man Wilhelm Asthalter was seriously injured. In a panic, Schumm fled, but went to the police shortly afterwards and handed in his weapon. Around midday he was taken into police custody. Storm troopers and SS – who had been posted at other Jewish stores in Kiel – descended upon the furniture store, demolishing it and stealing money from the cash box (the money later shown to have been spent on food and bar hopping). As news of Asthalter's shooting spread, a gang of 40–50 SS men, augmented by storm troopers, Nazi Party members, and onlookers went to the police prison chanting "*Schumm heraus*" (out with Schumm). The police chief decided to have Schumm transferred to a nearby prison, but the move could not be carried out unnoticed. Shortly afterwards, SS men and storm troopers stormed the police prison and shot Schumm in his cell. According to the autopsy he had been hit at least 22 times.[9] Reporting the incident to the Prussian Ministry of the Interior, Police Chief Graf zu Rantzau stated that the crowd had been outraged because a Jew had shed the blood of a member of the German SS. Investigations against the perpetrators during the Third Reich ended because of an amnesty on August 12, 1933.[10]

---

5 Landshut 4 Js 895/49; Passau 2 Js 1407/45.
6 Wiesbaden 2 Js 847/45 = 2 Ks 4/48 (files disappeared).
7 Ellwangen 4 Js 10930-37/46 = Ks 8/49, KLs 21/49; Ellwangen 4 Js 6400-6401/46 = Ks 4/52.
8 See also Dietrich Hauschildt, "Vom Judenboykott zum Judenmord: Der 1. April 1933 in Kiel," in „*Wir bauen das Reich*": *Aufstieg und erste Herrschaft des Nationalsozialismus in Schleswig-Holstein*, ed. Erich Hoffmann and Peter Wulf (Neumünster: Wachholtz Verlag, 1983); Bettina Goldberg, *Abseits der Metropolen: Die jüdische Minderheit in Schleswig-Holstein* (Neumünster: Wachholtz Verlag, 2011), 300-311.
9 Kiel 2 Js 1454/46; 2 Js 508/47 = 2 KLs 6/47; 2 KLs 7/47; LA Schleswig-Holstein, Abt. 352 Kiel; Nr. 2649.
10 Kiel 4 J 504/33; Kiel 2 Js 345/45, LA Schleswig-Holstein, Abt. 352 Kiel; Nr. 4500-4501; also Kiel 2 Js 662/47 = 2 KLs 2/48, LA Schleswig-Holstein, Abt. 352 Kiel, Nr. 1697.

Other victims of Nazi violence were so intimidated that they took their own lives. Julius Frank had been arrested on March 7, 1933, in Worms and hanged himself in the prison of Dolgesheim. He had been the plaintiff in a trial against Nazis in Mainz in 1930 and feared repercussions.[11] After a pistol and 13 cartridges were found in Jacob Rose's house in Dornum in April 1933, he hanged himself in Norden prison.[12] Since German post-war investigations did not lead to a prosecution of those involved in Rose's initial arrest, Rose's son wrote sarcastically to the senior prosecutor: "I must say that I am delighted to see from your report that German legal practice has not changed in the last 15 years. I hope you never have to attend the trial of the murderers of your parents or children, but I wonder if you would have the same attitude and pronounce a similar sentence if that were the case."

Racial Defilement

While the Nuremberg Laws against racial defilement did not come into being until September 1935, the notion of the "illegitimacy" or of "illegality" of such relations between Jews and non-Jews existed much earlier.

Siegfried Reiter was a 47-year-old tailor from Hainsfarth in Bavaria. On August 6, 1933, he and his non-Jewish companion, Emma Baer, went for a swim in a pond in a forest in Brunn (near Nuremberg). Two men – one a high-ranking member of the National Socialist Flying Corps (NSFK) and the other a forest warden – were about to go hunting and happened on the pair. The warden forbade them from swimming because the waters were reserved for trout fishing. The Nazi official assumed that Reiter was Jewish and admonished his companion to intervene against him. The warden then asked for Reiter's papers. Reiter handed over a sports club membership card while the Nazi official searched his rucksack for further evidence. He finally asked Reiter directly whether he was Jewish. When Reiter replied in the affirmative, he was instantaneously insulted by both men as *Saujude* (pig-Jew) and Emma Baer as *Hure* (whore). They forced the couple at gunpoint to Brunn, where they were dropped off and held in custody at the mayor's office. The Nazi official telephoned for reinforcements. When the storm troopers arrived, the couple was removed from the mayor's office and forced to carry panels bearing insulting messages. On the front, Reiter's board read "I am a Jew and I defiled a German girl", and on the back, "I defiled the German forest." Emma Baer had to carry a placard bearing the words "I shall not let myself be

---

11 Mainz 3 Js 318/48 = 3 KLs 71/49, AOFAA, AJ 1616, p. 801.
12 Aurich 2 Js 1930/46, StA Aurich, Rep. 109 E 84/1-2.

defiled again by a Jew." An SA officer paraded them through Brunn. As this was a rather small provincial place where little public attention could be gained, the couple was forced into an open car and driven standing to and through Nuremberg. Storm troopers insulted them both and punched Reiter. In Nuremberg, Reiter was forced to bare his penis when a storm trooper uttered the wish to see the private parts of a Jew. Reiter was later mistreated such that he suffered a concussion and broken fingers, and went blind in one eye. He was taken to Dachau Concentration Camp where he was imprisoned for more than two years without trial or other legal proceeding.[13] Emma Baer was asked to appear again in Nuremberg on August 7, 1933. Her hair was shorn and photographs of her were taken with the intention of making her the laughing stock of the town.[14]

Reiter's was an extraordinary case of racially motivated violence, but by no means a singular one. Siegfried David from was suspected of a relationship with a non-Jewish girl named Lina Hübner – a crime he was to expiate with imprisonment in Dachau from January 1934 to December 1935.[15] In Worms on May 1933, a 28-year-old woman who was engaged to a Jew was arrested and dragged to a storm troopers' clubhouse, where her hair was shorn.[16] Conversely, when a Jewish cattle dealer engaged to a non-Jewish woman was arrested on March 1, 1934, in Detmold, he was mistreated at the police station and paraded through town wearing a vilifying placard calling attention to his "defiling" of German girls.[17] Thus, in 1933 the stigmatization of racial defilement by the Nazi mob had already taken shape.[18]

In Norden on July 22, 1935, Christine Neemann and her fiancé Julius Wolff were arrested separately by storm troopers and dragged to the troopers' local meeting place, where about 100 men were already assembled. There both were insulted and forced to carry placards, his reading *"Rasseschänder"* (racial defiler), and hers "I am a German girl and let myself be defiled by a Jew." They were then

---

13 Siegfried Reiter, born on March 19, 1886 in Hainsfarth, tailor from Nürnberg, was transferred from Nürnberg prison on August 26, 1933 to Dachau concentration camp, where he was kept in "protective custody" until November 29, 1935. See "Überstellung von Schutzhäftlingen nach KL Dachau," August 18 to December 30, 1933, p. 10 and alphabetic register Nr. 102, p. 370, archives of Dachau Concentration Camp Memorial. See also Michael Wildt, *Volksgemeinschaft als Selbstermächtigung: Gewalt gegen Juden in der deutschen Provinz 1919 bis 1939* (Hamburg: Hamburger Edition, 2007), 226.
14 Nürnberg-Fürth 3c Js 2031-32/49 = 921 KLs 342/50; StA Nürnberg, GStA beim OLG Nürnberg 198.
15 Bayreuth 1b Js 6851/46 = KLs 26/48, StA Bamberg, Rep. K 106, Abg. 1996, Nr. 842; see also inmates' database at Dachau Concentration Camp Memorial.
16 Mainz 3 Js 1429/49 = AG Worms 3 Ms 34/50 and 3 Ms 32/50.
17 Detmold 1 Js 2311/46 = 1 KLs 37/47; Detmold 3 Js 359/48.
18 This is contrary to the findings of Michael Wildt, *Volksgemeinschaft als Selbstermächtigung*, 226, who dates this development to the Nuremberg Laws and 1935.

marched through the town of Norden accompanied by a crowd of about 100 storm troopers singing anti-Semitic ditties while youth and by-standers joined in. After photographs had been taken, the couple was handed over to the police. Christine Neemann was put in protective custody together with Elisabeth Extra, who had been condemned for her relationship with another Jew, Richard Cossen. The Gestapo in Wilhelmshaven took Neemann to the women's concentration camp at Moringen, while Julius Wolff ended up in Esterwegen camp. Neemann was released from Moringen on August 30, 1935, after she had signed a statement confirming her intention to end the relationship with Wolff, who was discharged from Esterwegen at a later point and fled to the United States.[19]

Albert Fabian (born in 1897) had been received into the Catholic Church by baptism in 1934, which, in the eyes of the National Socialists, in no way affected his racial status as a Jew. On August 18, 1935, he was arrested in Frankfurt am Main on orders of the Gestapo in Karlsruhe because he was meeting with a non-Jewish woman, Maria Vogt, in a hotel (though they had separate rooms). The woman was released two weeks later, but Fabian was kept in police custody in Frankfurt until September 19, then transferred to Kislau (an early concentration camp), to Dachau in 1937, and to Buchenwald Concentration Camp in September 1938. He was released from Buchenwald on June 9, 1939, with the urgent order to emigrate and subsequently fled to Shanghai. As if illegal restraint and humiliation (he had been the butt of vile attacks in a special edition of *Der Stürmer* in January 1936) had not been enough, his economic downfall added insult to injury. Fabian's film business fell to a non-Jewish owner who had been granted general power of attorney thanks to a proxy power. He used Fabian's property to his own liking, selling film negatives and furniture at auctions, thus wasting between 20,000 and 30,000 RM.[20]

It is important to remember that all these parades, public humiliations, and arrests happened before the Nuremberg Laws were enacted in September 1935. After the laws were enacted, attacks went on with state approval. In Spangenberg, the Nuremberg Laws prompted a minor riot, with break-ins of Jewish homes.[21] In Saarbrücken in 1937, a man was denounced because of his relationship with

---

19 Aurich 2 Js 1541/46 = 2 Ks 7/49, StA Oldenburg, Best. 140-4 Nr 816 (alt. Acc. 13/79 Nr. 114); see also Bernhard Parisius and Astrid Parisius, "'Rassenschande' in Norden. Die Geschichte von zwei Fotos, die das Bild Jugendlicher von der NS-Zeit prägen," *Ostfreesland: Kalender für Ostfriesland* (2003), 131.

20 Frankfurt 8/3 Js 4823/48 = 57 KLs 7/50, HStA Wiesbaden, Abt. 461, Nr. 30070/1-5; see also "Ein Verrat blieb ohne Sühne. Freispruch im Fall Fabian mangels ausreichender Beweise," *Frankfurter Rundschau*, August 8, 1950; "Wenn das Blatt sich wendet. Ein Prozess aus alten Akten," *Frankfurter Neue Presse*, August 8, 1950.

21 Kassel 3a Js 74/46 = 3a KLs 1/50.

a Jewish woman and sentenced to one year and three months' in the penitentiary for breach of racial laws.[22] In October/November 1937, a Jewish woman was sentenced to two years' imprisonment for the same offense (and procuration). After serving her term, she was taken to a concentration camp, where she died in 1942.[23]

Racial defilement as a crime fell under the watch of the criminal police and their vice squad. In Hamburg, the vice squad concerned itself with the crime itself, as well as the crime of circumventing the prohibition against Jews employing non-Jews and forbidden marriages. Usually, the male partner was made accountable; non-Jewish women were interrogated as witnesses while Jewish women were arrested on orders of the Reich Security Main Office and sent to concentration camps. Rude interrogations concerning sexual practices occurred frequently; insults, threats and mistreatment were commonly used to extract confessions. In 1919, while a prisoner of war in the Soviet Union, Walter Hermannsen, married a Russian Jewish woman and converted to Judaism. After his wife died in 1939, Hermannsen moved in with a Jewish widow, Fanny Neumann, who cared for his four children. In 1941 he was interrogated on the allegation of racial defilement. He stated that he considered himself a Jew and as such felt innocent of any breach of racial laws. Not surprisingly, the Nazis considered him a non-Jew and in January 1942, sentenced him to one year in prison. When he was released in March 1942, Fanny Neumann and his four children had all been deported.[24]

Miss Geist, a secretary, was charged with having had sexual relations with her boss, the Jewish lawyer Dr. Max Eichholz (who in the 1920s had shared chambers with the lawyer Herbert Ruscheweyh). Dr. Eichholz was arrested around Easter 1939 in Hamburg. Geist first admitted to having had intimate relations only before the issue of the Nuremberg Laws, but conceded to a continuation of the intimacies after September 1935. In July 1939, Dr. Eichholz was sentenced to five years in the penitentiary; he was transferred to Auschwitz in December 1942, where he perished on January 12, 1943.[25]

---

[22] Saarbrücken 11 Js 88/48 = 11 KLs 16/48.
[23] Hamburg 14 Js 184/46 = 14 KLs 53/47; 14 Ks 36/48 (files no longer available); see also BAK, Z 38/518.
[24] Hamburg 14 Js 6/46 = 14 Ks 22/48, StA Hamburg, Best. 213-11, Nr. 15428/49.
[25] Hamburg 14 Js 158/48 = 14 Ks 9/50, StA Hamburg, Best. 213-11, Nr. 14112/52.

Excesses 1934–1937

The term pogrom in Nazi Germany is usually associated with *Kristallnacht* in November 1938. However, in several cases, pogroms – generally with lynch mobs – occurred much earlier.

In March 1934 in Gunzenhausen, about 250 to 300 storm troopers and SS members gathered, chanted anti-Semitic slogans, demolished a local inn owned by a Jew, mistreated and arrested whole Jewish families and dragged them into the local jail. When the riot was over, one Jew was found hanged, another stabbed to death.[26] A leading storm trooper was subsequently sentenced for breach of the public peace. Claiming to have been treated unjustly, he shot two Jewish witnesses who had testified against him in the trial, one of whom died.[27] In Langsdorf, Jews were mistreated and assaulted in their homes; one received a fatal gunshot wound in 1934.[28]

Bullying and harassment became a permanent feature. In April 1934 in Leiwen, storm troopers smeared the houses of two Jews with tar.[29] In Lohrhaupten, Hitler Youth chanted anti-Semitic songs in front of Julius Halle's house; Halle himself was hit in the face. The next day (June 28, 1934), while Halle was lodging a complaint with the police in Flörsbach, a National Socialist mob stormed his house and smashed the windows. Halle, his wife and son as well as his father-in-law were taken into "protective custody."[30] In Odenbach, an anti-Semitic rally was staged against the farmer and tradesman Albert Felsenthal. The windows of

---

26 Lagebericht SD-Hauptamt, Berlin, May/June 1934, in: Otto D. Kulka und Eberhard Jäckel, eds., *Die Juden in den geheimen NS-Stimmungsberichten 1933-1945* (Düsseldorf: Droste Verlag, 2004), 75.
27 Ansbach 82-105/35, GrSt 50/34, StA Nürnberg. The sentences against the perpetrators did not become legally binding during the Third Reich, thus in 1949/1950 renewed proceedings started against those still alive. For further investigations see StA Nürnberg, Staatsanwaltschaft Ansbach 1 Js 5696/47 and 1 Js 5697/47. Even the former Nuremberg police president, Dr, Benno Martin, pointed out that perpetrators during the Third Reich had not served their sentences: "The Office of the Chief of Council was informed by Martin, the former police chief of Nuremberg that Bär and Kaiser have not been punished for this crime. The Chief prosecutor found that under file AVZ 935, 950 and 951/34 Bär was found guilt of homicide and attempted homicide and sentenced to life imprisonment and 10 years respectively on October 1, 1934. Kaiser was sentenced for assisting homicide to four years in prison. The Minister of Justice released Kaiser on January 8, 1937, and Bär on November 19, 1938. Bär was killed on the Russian front in 1941 and Kaiser lives in Kirnach near Würzburg. The Chief Prosecutor will order Kaiser to continue his punishment suspended in 1937." Weekly report, November 16, 1946, NARA, OMGBY 17/183 – 3/13.
28 Giessen Js 1866/46 pol. = KLs 11/47, 2 Ks 7/49 joined with 2 Ks 6/49.
29 Trier 3 Js 477/49; AOFAA, AJ 1616, p. 806.
30 Hanau 3 Js 637/48, HStA Wiesbaden, Abt. 471, Nr. 37.

his home were smashed; his non-Jewish wife and their daughter were forced to flee. Felsenthal had been asked by a Jewish emigrants' organization in Mannheim to set up a training camp for Jews willing to immigrate to Palestine. Though he stepped back from the proposal, he was nevertheless mistreated badly enough that he asked for protective custody to escape from the mob.[31]

Everything Jews did or did not do could be followed by severe repercussions. Alfred Weil and Leo Nördlinger (both from Haigerloch) were put into protective custody in August 1935 for having boxed the ears of a Hitler Youth who had provoked them. On August 5, 1935, the *Hohenzollernsche Blätter* announced that if this should occur again, the majority of the population would no longer refrain from mob justice.[32] On February 4, 1936, the local Nazi head of Onstmettingen learned that Max Levi from Haigerloch had allegedly made snide remarks on the occasion of the burial of Wilhelm Gustloff. Levi was arrested forthwith and mistreated by the Nazi commander.[33]

Also on February 4, 1936, Heinrich Sämann's house in Neustadt an der Aisch was stormed by Nazis and he himself was mistreated. A war veteran had said to Sämann: "You pig of a Jew, are you going out again to cheat the peasants?" Sämann replied that he had to go to work because he had to take care of his sick wife and handicapped son, contrary to the war veteran whose pension was being paid by the state. The war veteran was so enraged that he recounted the incident several times in such an exaggerated way that the mob rioted before Sämann's house chanting "The Jew must come out!" or "Out with the Jew pig!" Sämann was beaten up during the incident and an ambulance was called but was blocked by the mob, who did not want a Jew to be loaded into it. Only the doctor's interference allowed Sämann to reach the car safely.[34]

Others were subjected to constant harassment. The local storm troopers of Wawern organized marches and boycotts every few weeks, smashing windows and urinating in the doorways. A local Polish-Jewish family was blackmailed on a regular basis.[35] In December 1937, about 400 residents of Feuchtwangen felt the urgent need to demonstrate and demand the expulsion of the local Jews, leading to the arrest of six Jews, who were taken into the so-called protective custody.[36]

It was no better for those who tried to document the torment. In March 1937, Ernst Ludwig Goldschmitt took photographs of the synagogue of Fürfeld, which

---

31 Kaiserslautern 7 Js 30/49 = KLs 45/49, AOFAA, AJ 3676, p. 38.
32 Hechingen Js 3754-3755/47, StA Sigmaringen, Ho 400 T2 Nr. 853.
33 Hechingen Js 1255-56/47 = KMs 1/49; StA Sigmaringen, Ho 400 T2 Nr. 585.
34 Nürnberg-Fürth 1a Js 268 a-h/47 = KLs 46/48, StA Nürnberg, StAnw Nürnberg 2106/I, II.
35 Trier 3 Js 346/47 = 3 KLs 16/48, LHA Koblenz, Best. 584, 2, Nr. 745-746.
36 Ansbach 2 Js 756/46 = KLs 23/48, StA Nürnberg, StAnw Ansbach 756/I-II.

had been damaged by members of the Hitler Youth. He had the photographs developed at a photo shop in Bad Kreuznach. A complaint by the rural state office (Landratsamt Alzey) got the Gestapo on the case and Goldschmitt was arrested for attempting to spread negative propaganda abroad. On March 31, 1937, Goldschmitt entered Dachau Concentration Camp as prisoner No. 11,985 and later transferred to Buchenwald. When he was released, he immediately immigrated to Palestine.[37]

Excesses in 1938, Before November

As the terror of the pogrom of November 1938 overshadows many previous events, even historians have not sufficiently pointed out the extent of persecution up to that point. The Rottweil synagogue was damaged in the spring of 1938, its doors and windows smashed. The pipe organ, chairs, carpets, ritual objects and books were thrown into the street. A Jewish couple was even forced to help the perpetrators drag the objects out and burn them.[38]

Not only in Rottweil, but also in Altenmuhr the Nazis ganged up on Jews. In March 1938 local Hitler Youth and civilians threw stones through the windows of the Jewish family Thormann. In autumn 1938, three Jewish women were molested; one of them was victimized in the street. In October 1938, about 20 perpetrators, led by the mayor and the head of the local Nazi Party, forced open the door of the synagogue and smashed the furniture; the attack also included the houses of Jewish families. The disenfranchising of the Jewish population led to a complete breakdown of morals and decency. When, during the pogrom, Jewish families were arrested, perpetrators forced their way into the home of the Mohr family and started to distribute their belongings to the waiting mob: beds, pillows, crockery, a piano, cupboards and other furniture were distributed outside.[39]

In August 1938, Max Strauss was assaulted in his house in Geisenheim by 20 to 30 Nazi activists who claimed that Strauss had insulted a certain Mrs. B. In fact, he had asked Mrs. B., who happened to be the wife of a storm trooper, to pay her bill of 9 RM.[40]

On September 29, 1938 – the day of the mobilization against Czechoslovakia during the Sudeten crisis – rioters, between 60 and 250 people (as cited by

---

37 Mainz 3 Js 719/48, AOFAA, AJ 1616, p. 803.
38 Rottweil 1 Js 831-34/46, StA Sigmaringen, Wü 29/2 T4 Nr. 219.
39 Ansbach 5 Js 10/48 = KLs 22/48, StA Nürnberg, StAnw Ansbach 734.
40 Wiesbaden 4 Js 639/46; Wiesbaden 4 Js 1907/46 = 4 KLs 15/49, HStA Wiesbaden, Abt. 468, Nr. 264.

different sources) targeted Hermann Wirth, head of the Jewish congregation in Gemünden, Hunsrück, who was forced out of his house, abused and forced to agree to never return.⁴¹

On September 28, 1938, a mob mistreated a Jewish couple in their home in Unsleben.⁴² On September 30, 1938, the interior of the synagogue of Mellrichstadt was smashed and a shop owned by a Jew was vandalized.⁴³ On October 8, 1938, the Jewish school and synagogue of Willmars were seized to be used for storing corn. The local Jewish residents were forced to vacate the buildings. This was accompanied by severe mistreatment.⁴⁴ The atmosphere of a pogrom loomed in many localities. On October 14, 1938, Hitler Youth bombarded the houses of Jews in Leutershausen with stones. Non-Jewish residents who had maintained friendly relations with Jews were insulted as *Judenfreund* (friend of Jews), their houses called *Judenherberge* (Jew hotel). Manure was heaped at the entrance of the synagogue and on October 16, 1938, the mob destroyed the building. Money from the *tzedakah* (charity) box was donated to the *Winterhilfswerk*.⁴⁵

A Jewish veterinarian and a non-Jewish doctor were paraded through Treysa on October 16, 1938, because they had collaborated on fighting foot-and-mouth disease among the local cattle.⁴⁶ Four weeks before the nationwide pogrom, Wehrmacht non-commissioned officers destroyed the synagogue of Leimersheim, throwing out books and Torah scrolls.⁴⁷ During the night of October 19, 1938, Nazi Party members and storm troopers in Ühlfeld chanted anti-Semitic songs and smashed windows at the home of Ludwig Schwab until his frightened family fled to stay with neighbors.⁴⁸ The synagogue of Zirndorf was broken into on the night of November 4, 1938; furnishings were demolished or stolen. A few days later, during the pogrom itself, a mob amassed in front of the house of Mr. Weinstein and demanded the surrender of apartments and houses inhabited by Jews – as these were considered to be particularly spacious and in good condition. The arrested Jews were promptly forced to vacate their homes. Events took such a violent turn that the local Jews begged to be taken to the Czech border in order to save their lives.⁴⁹

---

41 Koblenz 9 Js 345/49 = 3 KLs 39/50, LHA Koblenz, Best. 584, 6, Nr. 48.
42 Schweinfurt 4 Js 2645/47 = KLs 33/49.
43 Schweinfurt 2 Js 1913/47 = KLs 19/48.
44 Schweinfurt 2 Js 245/48 = KLs 31/48.
45 Ansbach 1 Js 4070/46 = KLs 23/47, StA Nürnberg, StAnw Ansbach 677; Activity Report, October 20. - November 2, 1947, NARA, OMGBY 17/183 – 3/15.
46 Marburg 4 Js 929/46 = 4 KLs 15/49.
47 Landau 7 Js 46/47 = KLs 44/48, AOFAA, AJ 3676, p. 38.
48 Nürnberg-Fürth 1d Js 4331/49 = 746 KLs 269/50, StA Nürnberg, StAnw Nürnberg 2912.
49 Nürnberg-Fürth 2 Js 1025/46 = KLs 105/47, StA Nürnberg, StAnw Nürnberg 1931/I, II.

As is known, the protection of Jewish tenants was lifted by a decree of April 30, 1939, thus making the termination of a rental lease considerably easier. Cancellations without notice became possible as long as there was an alternative housing for the Jews concerned. In Berlin, a Nazi (party member since 1925) demanded the expulsion of a Jewish woman from her flat; the housing society promptly obeyed, issuing her an eviction notice, as it was unacceptable for Aryans to continue having to share a roof with non-Aryans.[50] Gerhart Bock, a judge at the district court of Berlin, whose wife was Jewish, received a similar letter in November 1938, informing him of the cancellation of his lease, as non-Jews were to be spared from sharing housing with Jews.[51]

"Aryanization"

Recent years have seen much historical research on "Aryanization." The facts have been reconstructed primarily using restitution files or compensation records, i.e., those generated by post-war civil law procedures. The fact that Aryanization was a criminal act and thus also left some traces in penal trials has largely been ignored. Felonies like theft, deceit, embezzlement, coercion, extortion, or breach of trust were contained in the umbrella term "Aryanization." Post-war investigations and trials concerning these matters provide an additional source for analysis of this gigantic felonious transfer of property. The caveat, however, is that the only Aryanizations investigated were those whose criminal scope went far beyond the already malicious norms the Nazi state and party had introduced. Furthermore, after 1950, the statute of limitations applied. Nevertheless, the post-war penal investigations make clear the extraordinary leeway that Aryanization had given to non-Jews intent on depriving Jews of their property.

One region where Aryanization took particularly unsavory forms was the Nazi Gau (region) Saarpfalz under NSDAP Regional Commander Josef Bürckel. He created the *Saarpfälzische Vermögensverwertungs GmbH* (Saar Palatinate Trust, LLC), based in Neustadt an der Weinstrasse that, as a (sham) "rescue company," was to buy Jewish property and resell it to non-Jews. The Nazi law enforcement authorities were so disgusted by the corruption and venality of the vulgar Aryanizers that even they brought action against them in 1940.[52]

---

50   Berlin 1 P Js 1154/47 = 1 P KLs 60/48.
51   Köln 24 Js 180/49, HStA Düsseldorf – ZA Kalkum, Gerichte Rep. 231/312.
52   Reference to the Nazi trials for corruption of the years 1940/1941 is made in post-war files Frankenthal 9 Js 47/47 = 9 KLs 25/50; 9 KLs 64/52, AOFAA, AJ 3676, p. 38. See also Landau 7 Js 4/48 = KLs 8/49; AOFAA, AJ 3676, p. 37.

Another region where Aryanizers were particularly insolent was the NSDAP region Franconia. On November 11, 1938, the deputy NSDAP Regional Commander Holz ordered that all Jewish real estate be listed and its Aryanization initiated. With approval of the mayor of Fürth, Aryanizations took place in the town hall. Jewish property-owners were summoned – or even escorted – there by storm troopers and were compelled to sign a contract by which they offered the sale of their houses and plots of land to the Gauleitung at only 10 percent of the assessed value. If they agreed, the writs were drawn up by notaries immediately; if they refused they were roughed up by storm troopers in the cellar of the town hall. Only in Fürth did Aryanization take on such proportions that two notaries authenticated more than 200 documents in which about 510 plots of land changed hands. And yet, until the adoption of the "Regulation on the Use of Jewish Property" on December 3, 1938, no legal grounds existed for such proceedings. The main advantage for the NSDAP *Gauleitung* Franconia was financial, as they subsequently sold the illegally acquired real estate to non-Jews at conventional prices, thus amassing huge profits in a special account named after the deputy regional commander (*Sonderkonto Holz*).[53]

Jews arrested during the pogrom were sought out even in the Dachau Concentration Camp and forced to sign pre-contracts compelling them to sell their property at greatly reduced prices or face prolonged imprisonment in Dachau.[54]

Excesses After November 1938

Those spared during the pogrom were by no means safe. Fanatic storm troopers and Nazi activists were intent on continuing the threats and terror immediately after the riots. On November 11, 1938, the former president of the Berlin district court, Kurt Sölling, was driven out of his home at gunpoint in the town of Marzoll near Türk. After the incident, Sölling, who was married to a non-Jew, immigrated to Canada.[55]

A week after the pogrom, storm troopers in Kaldenkirchen demolished the house of a Jewish man named Lion, which had escaped damage on November 10 and where eight or nine other Jews had found sanctuary. As one of the perpetrators put it: "Now we want to 'tidy' up here as you were not affected on November 10." A 78-year-old woman was so terrified by the storm troopers smashing the

---

53 Nürnberg-Fürth 1a Js 2153/47 = 1115 KLs 297/49, StA Nürnberg, StAnw Nürnberg 2596/I-V.
54 For examples see Weiden 1 Js 6/49 = AG Weiden Ms 64/49 or Kaiserslautern 7 Js 134/49, AOFAA, AJ 3676, p. 38.
55 Traunstein 9 Js 391/49 = KMs 9/52 (files not traceable, probably destroyed).

furnishings and hitting Jewish residents that she jumped out of a second floor window and broke her leg.[56]

Landlords used the aftermath of the pogrom to evict their Jewish tenants. In Georgensgmünd, the local Nazi Party was asked by the county Nazi Party of Schwabach to create a *Judenhaus* in which all local Jewish residents were to be interned. The home of Rosalie Gerstle, a Jewish woman, was declared a *Judenhaus*, but not before Nazi Party members had dragged Jews from their previous homes and paraded them through town with a banner reading "Exodus of Israel."[57] Even attempts at a return to "normal" life were prevented by Nazi authorities. When Jews tried to re-open their shops in December 1938 in Detmold, Hitler Youth were ordered by the head of the *SD-Aussenstelle* to parade in front of the shops and chant anti-Semitic slogans.[58]

The pogrom had indeed been such a watershed as to outlaw Jews completely. Two examples illustrate hitherto unknown violence after the pogrom:

On November 16, 1938, a Jewish couple named Nathan and their adult daughter Irma Stein returned to their home in Nastätten, from which they had fled upon hearing of the impending riots. On the evening of their return, the family was assaulted in their home; guards posted at the doors prevented their escape. Reportedly, the family called for help for five hours. Mr. Nathan was atrociously mistreated; Irma Stein was sadistically raped and penetrated with an object such that her bed was sprayed with blood.[59]

On May 3, 1939, 81-year-old Hermann Bermann was beaten to death on the street in Osann. Four perpetrators had clubbed and kicked him until he broke down in a roadside ditch. Bermann had owned a shoe store in Osann until March 1939, but had moved to Trier. He had returned to Osann in order to sell a plot of land before his emigration. When local Nazi functionaries and storm troopers learned of his presence in the village, they followed him, insulted him, and beat him. An autopsy would establish that several ribs were broken, one lung and his heart had been damaged, his buttocks, testicles, bladder and abdomen bruised.[60] Because it had been such a blatant act of violence, five men were put to trial. Four were sentenced to one to two years' imprisonment; one was acquitted.

---

56 Krefeld 2 Js 1719/46 = 2 KLs 18/48, HStA Düsseldorf – ZA Kalkum, Gerichte Rep. 182/22-25.
57 Nürnberg-Fürth 1 Js 400/46 = 603 KLs 170/49, StA Nürnberg, StAnw Nürnberg 2494/I-III.
58 Detmold 1 Js 2314/46; Detmold 3 Js 531/48 = 3 KLs 12/48.
59 Koblenz 3 Js 580/48 = 9 KLs 7/49; LHA Koblenz, Best. 584, 1, Nr. 1239-1245.
60 Trier 5 Js 101/47 = 5 Ks 1/50, LHA Koblenz, Best. 584, 2, Nr. 825-829.

Violent Acts After the Beginning of the War

When Germany invaded Poland, German Jews were once more subjected to violence in their homes. In Burgen/Mosel the beginning of the war coincided with a pogrom initiated by the mayor and deputy party head; the pogrom led to the demolishing of the houses of four Jewish families. Doors were broken, windows smashed, furniture and the interior of the houses vandalized, belongings thrown into the streets. The occupants of the houses were insulted, menaced, and mistreated before being arrested.[61]

On or around September 3, 1939, Jews in Tauberbischofsheim were forced by storm troopers and NSKK-members to march with placards bearing the words "we are war-mongers" to the synagogue, where they were forced to kiss the floor. Then they had to go to a canal where they had to dunk their heads into the water and shout, "Thank you for the bath."[62] On September 5, 1939, a handful of young men decided to rough up the Jews of Edelfingen, striking several of them.[63] In Haren on September 7, 1939, the mayor and local Nazi Party chief accused Jewish veterinarian Dr. Philipp Sternberg of espionage and placed him in "protective custody," (Sternberg had looked into options for exile in the USA.)[64] On October 27, 1939, the commander (*Landrat*) of the province forced a Jewish clothing dealer to hand over 289 pieces of clothing to the Red Cross at a dumping price.[65]

Times of crisis, as well as anniversaries imbued with symbolic meaning for the National Socialist movement, were particularly ripe for excesses against Jews. After the attempt on Hitler's life on November 9, 1939, either the mayor or the local police chief of Haigerloch ordered the arrest of all male Jews, leading to the incarceration of 38 men. They were interrogated – beginning at midnight – and brutally mistreated. When the then state attorney was questioned as a witness in the post-war period, he admitted that he had not inquired into the cause of the arrests, saying he had assumed he would be powerless against party arbitrariness. He had not even bothered to alert the prosecutor general in Stuttgart of the incident. The district president (*Regierungspräsident* of Sigmaringen) and the chief executive of the province of Hechingen intervened, and the Jews were released from prison, but were forced to clean toilets, courtrooms, or the *Stürmer* blackboard on the following Sabbath (November 10-11, 1939). One Jew was blackmailed into paying 400 RM as an advance on the cost of imprisonment. Alfred

---

61 Koblenz 9/3 Js 971/47 = 9 KLs 11/51, LHA Koblenz Best. 584, 1 Nr. 1780; Nr. 1311.
62 Mosbach 1 Js 619/46 = KLs 10/46; Mosbach 1 Js 4811/46 = KLs 4/47; Mosbach 1 Js 1022/48.
63 Ellwangen 2 Js 10067/47 = KLs 26/48.
64 Osnabrück 4 Js 746/48, StA Osnabrück, Rep 945, Akz. 6/1983, Nr. 166-167.
65 Paderborn 3 Js 1267/46 = 3 KLs 4/48.

Levi, head of the Jewish congregation of Haigerloch, was forced to sign a check to the local Nazi Party to cover the costs of a meal for the Jewish captives and a storm troopers' celebration. The money was kept in an unofficial cash box – later confiscated by the Gestapo because of its illegality. The arrests were never questioned, even though not a single warrant of arrest had been issued and no accusations or charges had been made.[66]

In December 1939, Dr. Held and his wife were lured into the garden of their house in Röthenbach, hit over the head and knocked down; after a brawl near the fence, the mob left, only to return the next day as rumor spread that the Helds had attacked the storm troopers. Several items in the garden and house were demolished with an axe.[67]

Trapped in the "Judenhaus"

By 1940, the isolation of Jews had proceeded even further. Many Jews in the Reich had been driven from their previous lodgings and were now stranded in *Judenhäuser*, where they were easy targets for the Nazis.

At the beginning of 1940, 16 Jews were forcibly interned in the building at Wallstrasse 64 in Mönchengladbach, a so-called *Judenhaus*. One night in May 1940, shortly before midnight, the doorbell rang; an alleged air-raid protection unit was at the door. As soon as the occupants opened the door, three men – storm troopers and SS – entered and forced the residents to go to the cellar. Each of them was later summoned up to the kitchen, where the three men conducted interrogations, which included questioning about personal details and the meting out of several blows with a leather whip. The number of blows was decided on by the SS company commander, while the beating itself was carried out by the other two individuals. Men had to bare their buttocks while women were allowed to remain in their nightgowns; men were subjected to 10-20 blows while women underwent between one and three lashes of the whip. The five oldest residents (among them a 70-year-old man and a woman over 80 years of age) were not bodily harmed. Then the three men left the house. The victims reported the attack to the Jewish com-

---

66 Hechingen Js 223-229/47; Js 1604-1617/47 = KLs 32-42/47; StA Sigmaringen, Wü 29/2 T 4 Nr. 772; Rottweil 1 Js 2198/48 = KLs 155/48, StA Sigmaringen, Wü 29/2 T2 Nr. 985.
67 See Henry Friedlander, "Across the Stunde Null: the Continuity of German Law," in *Staatsverbrechen vor Gericht: Festschrift für Christiaan Frederik Rüter zum 65. Geburtstag*, ed. Dick de Mildt (Amsterdam: Amsterdam University Press, 2003). The suspects were indicted on June 25, 1940 (see Nürnberg-Fürth 1b Sg 119/40), the trial was postponed by a decree of June 10, 1941 until the end of the war. See Fürth 2c Js 185/47 = 13 KLs 83/47, StA Nürnberg, StAnw Nürnberg 1917/I-III.

munity the next morning. When the Gestapo head in Mönchengladbach learned of the incident, he declared it an isolated action of the SS company commander and his abettors. The company commander defended himself by claiming to have been drunk. Nevertheless, he insisted he had observed an iron rod being chucked out of house No. 64 and that he and his companions entered the house in order to investigate the incident. Only when he interrogated the terrified occupants and asked them for personal information did it become obvious to him that they were all Jews. Ostensibly, a fine of 20 RM was imposed on the SS man.[68]

Jews who were living in decent circumstances attracted envy. In Sprendlingen, a Jewish family named Schloss was terrorized by repeated assaults on their house where windows and roofing tiles were smashed. In 1941, Mr. Schloss was threatened with arrest for allegedly carrying out espionage and menacing Hitler Youth members. He hanged himself a few days later.[69] In 1941, the windows of Albert Bär's house in Rheinbrohl were smashed by a Nazi mob; china and furniture were demolished. The NSDAP district commander had taken offense that Jews in Rheinbrohl were still living in houses while the bombed-out population of Trier was dwelling in hovels and caves.[70]

On the night of May 15, 1941, the Nazi Party group of Solingen-Pfaffenberg attended a political lecture entitled "The settlement of German blood in the Ukraine." An evening of convivial drinking ensued. On his way home, a participant of both the instruction and the drinking spree mentioned that there were Jews living at Pfaffenberger Weg 190 in Solingen who ought to be taught a lesson. First, they smashed the windows. The (non-Jewish) owner of the apartment house noticed the commotion, stepped outside, and became involved in a brawl. Meanwhile, Nazi functionaries had entered the house and searched for Jews, mistreating those they found. Two elderly Jewish women were dragged from their beds and down the stairs. When police arrived, their beds and bedroom walls were speckled with blood, furniture damaged and doors broken. One of the elderly women, Miss Stock, suffered a broken arm and fingers and severe head wounds; the other woman, Miss Freireich, was bleeding from the abdomen. Another woman was wounded on her back and arm; one man sustained an injured shoulder.[71]

---

68 Mönchengladbach 6 Js 1243/47 = 6 KLs 5/48; HStA Düsseldorf – ZA Kalkum, Gerichte Rep. 10/59-61; see also "Mit dem Ochsenziemer verprügelt," *Freiheit*, May 18, 1948; "Unverständliches Revisionsurteil im Prozess Weller," *Jüdisches Gemeindeblatt*, May 6, 1949.
69 Mainz 3 Js 1528/47, AOFAA, AJ 1616, p. 802.
70 Koblenz 9 Ks 2/50, LHA Koblenz, Best. 584, 1, Nr. 1249-1252.
71 Wuppertal 5 Js 4238/46 = 5 KLs 32/47, HStA Düsseldorf – ZA Kalkum, Gerichte Rep. 240/69-71. Charges were pressed by the denazification committee Solingen on July 27, 1946 with the British Military Government to atone the crime ("ruchlose Tat"), as not only the United Nations but also

When the mayor of Laupheim learned that Jews from Stuttgart were to move to Laupheim he organized a "people's demonstration" against the Jews of Laupheim by handing lists of Jewish houses to the local storm troopers, who duly vandalized Jewish stores and homes.[72]

As the year went on, Jews were increasingly forced to live in the *Judenhäuser*, e.g., in Mühringen near Horb, where the forced move took place on November 8, 1941.[73]

Though the Jews were already severely reduced in all their living circumstances, the Nazis still found ways to humiliate and criminalize them. On April 25, 1941, a Jew who had been forced to vacate his 10-room-flat and move to a one-room apartment was arrested in Hannover. His offense: He was trying to sell his spare furniture. He was sentenced to three months' imprisonment for circumvention of the decree concerning the exclusion of Jews from economic life.[74]

Denunciations

Encounters with the authorities were potentially life threatening. Usually the victims were swiftly arrested, deported and murdered. On January 14, 1942, a 57-year-old man, Jakob Metzler, died after having been mistreated in the town hall of Gemünden on January 10.[75] Denunciations even cut through marriage bonds: The wife of Josef Woczinski met a non-Jewish man in 1941 in Berlin and took up an amorous affair with him. In order to secure Woczinski's acquiescence to a divorce, the lover stalked Woczinski and threatened him repeatedly. Woczsinski, however, feared deportation if he ended his marriage to a non-Jewish woman. The wife filed for divorce in March 1942, and left her husband the following month. The couple was divorced on July 7, 1942. Woczsinski was arrested on February 27, 1943, and deported to Auschwitz-Birkenau, where he perished.[76] Betty Wollfziefer was deported to Auschwitz after having been denounced and arrested by the Gestapo Düsseldorf on June 24, 1944, for "race concealment." The informant could not be traced because none of the files of the registration office in Düsseldorf-Kaiserswerth (which prompted the involvement of the Gestapo) survived.[77] In July

---

the greatest part of the German population expected atonement ("worauf mit Recht nicht allein die Vereinten Nationen, sondern auch der grösste Teil der deutschen Bevölkerung wartet.").

72 Ravensburg Js 9154-9170/47 = KLs 6-22/48; KLs 23-28/48, StA Sigmaringen, Wü 29/1 T 1, Nr. 6890.
73 Rottweil 6 Js 6651-53/47, StA Sigmaringen, Wü 29/2 T4, Nr. 668.
74 Hannover 2 Js 425/47 = 2 Ks 1/49.
75 Koblenz 9 Js 151/49 = Bad Kreuznach 3 Ks 9/50, LHA Koblenz, Best. 584, 6, Nr. 14 and 118.
76 Kiel 2 Js 152/49 LA Schleswig-Holstein, Abt. 352 Kiel; Nr. 1723.
77 Düsseldorf 8 Js 120/46, HStA Düsseldorf – ZA Kalkum, Gerichte Rep. 268/3.

1944, the Gestapo in Lübeck summoned Jewish businessman Emil Ronsheim from Hoisdorf, Kreis Stormarn, to prepare for deportation to Theresienstadt; he died during the transport. Either he had been denounced by an anti-Semitic Nazi couple (as he suspected and told an acquaintance before his deportation) or it was the recent death of his non-Jewish wife that had led to his enforced removal from Germany. As neither record nor witnesses were available, the alleged informers could not be tried.[78]

Denunciations, a permanent feature of the Third Reich, literally outlasted the Reich: Four women denounced a Jewish housemate for mentioning that when the war ended, times would change and the persecutors of the Jews would be feeling persecution, too. By the time the women informed on this comment, the battle over Berlin had already begun and the Allies were advancing day by day. The Jewish resident and his non-Jewish wife were arrested, and not freed from Charlottenburg prison until sometime after May 2, 1945.[79]

Bullying of Jewish Forced Laborers and Actions Against Jews in the Second Half of WW II

Following the pogrom of 1938, Jews were pressed into forced labor. In 1940, Albert Heumann, along with nine other Jews, was a street cleaner in Neuss. On February 12, 1940, his former neighbor, now a storm trooper, passed by on his bike and shouted to some bystanders that the air smelled of garlic – referring to the Jews. Heumann was upset by the remark, as he had given food to the former neighbor when the man had been a child – and pointed this out to him. The storm trooper was enraged and hit Heumann, who suffered from a heart condition. Heumann fell to the ground as the storm trooper rode away; he died two days later of a heart attack.[80]

Mistreatment of Jewish forced laborers was common. This could come in the form of fines or extra work; cancellation of days off and holidays; threats of complaints being lodged with the Gestapo (as occurred in Cologne, for example);[81] bodily harm (as testified to in Berlin);[82] or exposure to harmful working conditions, such as contact with poisonous sulfur (again as witnessed in Berlin.)[83]

---

78 Lübeck 14 Js 252/49, LA Schleswig-Holstein, Abt. 351 GStA Schleswig; Nr. 850.
79 Berlin 1 P Js 42/47 = 1 P KLs 120/47.
80 Düsseldorf 8 Js 160/46 = 8 KLs 3/47, HStA Düsseldorf – ZA Kalkum, Gerichte Rep. 372/9-11.
81 Köln 24 Js 302/46 = 24 KLs 4/48, HStA Düsseldorf – ZA Kalkum, Gerichte Rep. 231/103.
82 Berlin 1 P Js 104/49 (a).
83 Berlin 1 P Js 1529/47 = 1 P KLs 108/48.

Arguments at work could lead to arrest. After a violent quarrel, Samuel Baruch was imprisoned in Wuppertal for two and a half months before being deported to Auschwitz, which he luckily survived.[84]

As the war dragged on, the refusal to let Jews (mostly in "interracial" marriages) enter air raid bunkers became a frequent crime. The Jews were thus forced to search for alternative shelter or be left unprotected.[85]

One day after the July 20, 1944, assault on Hitler's life, a Jewish tailor in Berlin was dragged from his home and brutally mistreated, nearly drowning as a result. He escaped during the conclusion of an air raid, but died as a consequence of the abuse.[86] On November 4, 1944, Franziska Spiegel, a resident of Werfen, was abducted from her home by SS men and shot to death in a forest.[87]

As the war front flooded back to the Reich, mistrust and fear spread, again endangering Jews in particular. On March 15, 1945, Heinrich Prölsdorfer – married to a non-Jewish woman and thus "privileged" to have escaped deportation – was spotted in Munich by a local Nazi Party functionary chatting in English with a British POW (probably on a rubble-clearing detail) who had asked him the time. As Prölsdorfer was not wearing the obligatory Star of David and had obviously ignored the prohibition of fraternization with POWs, he was arrested by the police and handed over to the Gestapo, who transferred him to Dachau Concentration Camp on March 23, 1945. Prölsdorfer died as prisoner No. 146487 shortly before the liberation of Dachau.[88] Moritz Sommer had escaped deportation by hiding in a garden in Düsseldorf. During the night of April 14–15, 1945, he was discovered by an army patrol, accused of helping deserters, terribly mistreated, and hanged in Düsseldorf-Oberbilk.[89] The Jewish dentist Arthur Aronowski, whose wife was not Jewish, was arrested on April 25, 1945, by members of the 17th *SS-Panzergrenadierdivision "Götz von Berlichingen"* and later found shot dead in the forest.[90]

---

84 Wuppertal 5 Js 1148/47 = 5 KLs 78/48, HStA Düsseldorf – ZA Kalkum, Gerichte Rep. 191/75.
85 For Berlin see: Berlin 1 P Js 100/49 (a) = P KLs 11/50; Berlin 1 P Js 286/47 = 1 P KLs 126/47; see also Frankenthal 9 Js 65/47 = 9 KLs 2/48, AOFAA, AJ 3676, p. 38 (concerning Bad Dürkheim).
86 Berlin 1 P/P Js 118/50 = 1 PKs 3/51.
87 Bielefeld 5 Js 135/48.
88 München I 1b Js 1023/48 = 1 Ks 1/49, 1 KLs 156/48, StA München, StAnw 17413; Former Inmates' data base Dachau Concentration Camp Memorial.
89 Düsseldorf 8 Js 41/46 = 8 KLs 2/47; HStA Düsseldorf – ZA Kalkum, Gerichte Rep. 372/198-202.
90 Regensburg 1 Js 2172/46 = Ks 5/52; StA Nürnberg, GStA beim OLG Nürnberg 241.

The Fate of Jewish Children in Foster Care

Due to the racial nature of persecution, Jewish children were subjected to the same bullying, discrimination, exclusion, exile, or deportation as their parents. The Nazis went to greater lengths with half-Jewish children in foster-care. This concerned mainly children in precarious social circumstances, who were partly or fully orphaned or were at least "social orphans" whose parents could not or would not care for them, and who thus had been put into orphanages or placed with foster-parents. The following three examples will elucidate this assumption.

Horst Schmitt (born in 1930) and Helga Schmitt (born in 1933) from Frankfurt am Main stemmed from a so-called "racially mixed marriage." Their deceased mother had been Jewish, and their non-Jewish father had a criminal record for fraud, embezzlement, concealment of stolen goods, and forgery and failed to keep up his maintenance obligation for his offspring. The children were thus placed by the youth welfare office into a children's home. By 1943, maintenance costs for the siblings amounted to a then considerable 385 RM. On June 6, 1943, both were transferred from the children's home of Idstein to Hadamar, the infamous mental asylum. Horst Schmitt died the next day; Helga Schmitt died on September 21, 1943.[91] A similar fate befell the Strauss siblings. By the end of November 1941, the district youth welfare office in Diez filed an application with the local court of Bad Ems to place the pupils Willi Strauss (born in 1929) and Horst Strauss (born in 1931) into a public institution. They were the sons of Bernhard Strauss, a Jew who was imprisoned in a concentration camp, and a non-Jewish mother, Emmi Strauss (née Glasmann). The district youth welfare office gave theft of several notebooks and post-cards by the two children as the explanatory statement; alleged bad parental guidance provided further grounds, as the mother took little interest in them and the grandmother was overburdened with the task of caring for them. A teacher pronounced Willi Strauss to be a class troublemaker who was unruly, untidy, nearly completely bedraggled, mendacious and deceitful. The schoolmistress gave Horst Strauss a similar character reference. In January 1942, Emmi Strauss agreed to the temporary placement of her sons in a public welfare institution, which the local court of Bad Ems arranged. The brothers Willi and Horst Strauss were taken to the *Landesaufnahmeheim* Idstein; in spring 1942 both were placed as agricultural laborers with two farmers in Walsdorf. According to the available documentation they proved their worth and gave no reason for complaints. In autumn 1943, they were returned to the Idstein home to be transferred shortly afterwards to the mental home of Hadamar. Willi Strauss secretly wrote to

---

91 Frankfurt 4a Js 11/47, HStA Wiesbaden, Abt. 461, Nr. 30012 d; their death was also dealt with in the Hadamar trial in Frankfurt 4a Js 3/46 = 4 KLs 7/47.

his mother and stated that there were only eight children left in the mental home; he was sure that he and his brother Horst were to die during the coming week. Frau Strauss took the letter to the city council (*Stadtverwaltung*) of Bad Ems and a civil servant informed the NSDAP local group commander (*Ortsgruppenleiter*) of Bad Ems. The Nazi functionary asked Frau Strauss for the letter and also showed Willi Strauss's request for help to the deputy Nazi functionary on the district level in Diez. It remains unclear whether the Nazi functionaries indeed intended to help re-unite the family. Horst Strauss died on September 3, 1943, in Hadamar, his older brother Willi the day after.[92]

A similarly tragic story is that of Rita Vogelhut, as documented in East German files.

Rita Vogelhut was born in 1933 out of wedlock and placed shortly after her birth in foster-care with a non-Jewish family named Zänker at Kurfürstenstrasse 13, Magdeburg-Sudenburg. Her biological mother was Netti (or Nelly) Vogelhut, an unmarried Polish Jew from Bochnia who had been put under a legal guardianship in 1928, because she was feeble-minded. She died in 1940 in Poland; the father remained unknown. Luzie S. was in charge of handing out ration-cards for the house, and also dispensed household lists for the purposes of registration and official statistics. In spring 1943, the married couple Zänker was asked to complete a household list. Else Zänker placed only a dash in the appropriate column concerning her foster child. Luzie S. (who apparently took offense that a *Judenkind* was entitled to a ration card at all) returned the list and insisted that the foster child Rita be placed in the column "Jews." Else Zänker then filled in the rubric by adding the word *Mischling* (mongrel). Luzie S., a busybody, was not content and mentioned the case to the municipal economic office in Magdeburg. Frau Zänker was then requested by the authorities to hand in the birth certificate of Rita Vogelhut. The document ended up with the Gestapo, which was to ascertain the racial identity of the child. In March 1943, the foster mother requested the guardianship court to have her husband named legal guardian of the child (instead of the current Jewish warden) as well as to have German citizenship awarded to Rita Vogelhut, who until then was deemed stateless. The youth welfare office delivered all files into the hands of the Gestapo. In May 1943, the Gestapo conveyed their opinion that Rita Vogelhut was considered Jewish (*Geltungsjüdin*) according to the Nuremberg Laws and was to be taken from her foster home and placed elsewhere. Not surprisingly, the Gestapo's idea of "care" for Jewish children led to Rita's transfer to a collection point in Berlin on June 24,

---

92 Koblenz 9/3 Js 1488/48, AOFAA, AJ 1616, p. 804, Dossier 502.

1943, then to Theresienstadt ghetto. Soon all communication ceased, as she had been deported to Auschwitz-Birkenau on May 18, 1944.[93]

Desecration of Jewish Cemeteries

With so much human suffering, it may seem odd to focus attention on Jewish cemeteries. However, after the destruction or expropriation of synagogues and the deportation of the German Jews, these graveyards were quite frequently the only remnants of local German-Jewish history. While many Jewish cemeteries would remain unscathed during the Third Reich as far as the property question was concerned,[94] desecrations were nevertheless common. These acts of violence, though, have drawn less attention.

Desecration of Jewish burial sites is mentioned time and again in the files. The erosion of respect and sense of decency concerning graveyards worried the authorities less than the loss of international reputation. Given that in 1934, the wife of the head of the Jewish congregation of Neuhaus/Oste had had photographs made of the vandalization of eight graves in Wingst near Cadenberge, the *Landrat* of Otterndorf, fearing the exploitation of the incident for so-called Jewish atrocity propaganda, informed both the Gestapo and *Regierungspräsident*. When the (juvenile) delinquents were caught, a woman wrote to the investigators, "I am convinced that the kids would not have committed the deed if the graveyard had made a similarly proper impression to that of our cemeteries."[95]

Many vandalizations occurred around the time of the pogrom of November 1938, e.g., in Ilvesheim, Burgholzhausen, or Hemmendorf.[96] During the pogrom in Wuppertal-Elberfeld the mortuary at the Jewish graveyard was broken into and completely burned down; the vandals removed part of the roof to give the fire more oxygen. Gravestones were knocked down, graves devastated. While the morgue was burning, a mob chanted anti-Semitic songs. Though the fire brigade arrived, it did not intervene and even retrieved the hoses that had already been fixed to the hydrants. The brigade left the scene of the crime without taking any action.

---

[93] Magdeburg 2 Js 48/45 = 2 Ks 2/46, BStU, Mdg ASt 90/48.
[94] Andreas Wirsching, "Jüdische Friedhöfe in Deutschland 1933-1957," *Vierteljahrshefte für Zeitgeschichte* 50 (2002).
[95] Stade 4 Js 31/35, StA Stade, Rep. 171a Stade Nr. 238 (The file also contains the five photographs.).
[96] Mannheim Js 4831/45a; Giessen 2 Js 157/48; Hannover 2 Js 163/47 = 2 Ks 14/48.

During the night after the pogrom, the morgue at the Jewish cemetery in Solingen was blown up by storm troopers. Furthermore, graves were desecrated.[97] Similarly the mortuary at the Jewish graveyard in Mannheim was blown up.[98] Shortly after the pogrom, six youngsters set the mortuary of the Jewish cemetery in Aschaffenburg-Schweinheim ablaze.[99]

Desecration did not cease the year after. In Mühlen, a 15-year-old youngster "accidentally" toppled a Jewish gravestone, causing others to fall as well.[100] In Wittmund two male teenagers knocked down tombstones; later the fence was removed and the cemetery turned into a playground.[101] In Bamberg, the grave of a Jewish doctor was violated on June 21, 1939.[102] In April 1939, a Hitler Youth patrol ravaged the local cemetery of Ansbach. Of the 400 tombstones, 335 were overturned and smashed; windows and doors of the mortuary were torn open and smashed in, the roof was removed and holes were drilled into the walls.[103] Some of the damaged tombstones were sold (by the *Reichsvereinigung der Juden – Bezirksstelle Bayern*), but others were stolen by local interested parties.[104] As cemeteries continued to be vandalized over the years, their desolate states often served as a welcome pretext for a complete leveling. With the Reich's quest for raw materials, even the metal fences of cemeteries became coveted objects. In Lemgo, iron gates were removed by the local Nazi Party in the course of a war-inspired iron collection.[105] Similarly, tombstones and iron fences were dismantled in Kirchheim an der Eck.[106] In Göppingen and Jebenhausen the iron letters on gravestones were pried off.[107] Others effectively turned the graveyards into quarries and junkyards, where objects were dismantled and exploited. Damaged stones were handed out for free in Hagenbach;[108] in Stauffenberg a local stonemason was given permission by the local authorities to recycle the stones.[109] In

---

97 Wuppertal 5 Js 4131/46 = 5 KLs 62/47; HStA Düsseldorf – ZA Kalkum, Gerichte Rep. 191/35.
98 Mannheim 1a Js 3476/46.
99 Aschaffenburg 4 Js 28/49.
100 Rottweil 7 Js 982/48, AOFAA, AJ 804, p. 598.
101 Aurich 2 Js 557/47, StA Oldenburg, Best. 140-4 Acc. 13/79, Nr. 153.
102 Bamberg Js 1921/46 = KMs 7/48 (files not traceable).
103 Ansbach 5 Js 2/49 (files not traceable); Ansbach Ds 54/45, StA Nürnberg, StAnw Ansbach Ds 54/45.
104 Ansbach Ds 44/46 (files not traceable).
105 Detmold 1 Js 1430/47.
106 Frankenthal 9 Js 274-276/47 = 9 KLs 1/48, AOFAA, AJ 3676, p. 36.
107 Ulm (unknown file number) = AG Göppingen Ds 322/47 = AG Esslingen (unknown file number), the perpetrator was sentenced to four weeks' imprisonment by AG Esslingen for damage to property and unwarranted damage of graves. Case mentioned under NARA, OMGWB 12/137-2/7.
108 Landau 7 Js 17/47.
109 AG Giessen, LG Giessen 5 Ds 110/46, Ns 54/46.

1940, the head of the district Nazi Party propaganda office of Meppen asked a local stonemason (and Nazi Party member) to remove the Jewish gravestones; he pounded the (already damaged) stones to pieces. When the stonemason needed supplies again in 1943, he removed a further 66 tombstones and took them to his workshop.[110]

As soon as fences were gone, the floodgates swung open for – quite literally – the ghouls. The fence of the Jewish cemetery in Esens fell victim to a scrap metal collection, tombstones were overturned and the cemetery became a playground. In 1943, when the government-controlled Reich Association of Jews in Germany (*Reichsvereinigung der Juden in Deutschland*) sold the cemetery to a communal enterprise in Esens, the sale guaranteed the peace of the dead for 30 years. Sure enough, the mayor of Esens took a desecration by two men not as a cause to have the graveyard protected or reconstructed, but rather as a reason to have it leveled and used for storage.[111]

In other communities, the collection of scrap metal provoked uncontrolled devastation. On a Saturday afternoon in May or June 1940, the local beadle walked through Schupbach with a bell announcing that a communal work deployment was to take place on Sunday. About 60 to 70 residents turned up. One group was sent to the Jewish cemetery, where until 1938 Jews had been buried. The assembled townsfolk removed the tombstones with hammers, overturned gravestones and pulled away the perimeters. A hole was hacked into the wall of the cemetery and the iron gates at the entry were removed. The most impressive gravestones were used by the mayor as a boundary for his own property, while others were donated to the Reich Labor Service Camp Schupbach, where they were used as columns at the camp entrance. The deputy mayor chose a tombstone and carted it home on a trolley in order to display the stone at a wall of his house. The former mayor, who was responsible for the action, defended himself by saying that the scrap metal action had gotten out of hand when the mob decided on its own to vandalize the cemetery.[112] In Hettenleidelheim there were two Jewish cemeteries, an old one (used until 1865) and a new one. In 1938, the fence around the new cemetery was destroyed, the mortuary torn down and a few trees felled. In spring 1942, the old cemetery was turned into allotments; the gravestones were used as borders for paths or handed over to a stonemason. The local Nazi Party chief in Hettenleidelheim headed the scrap iron collection and had the iron gates removed. Toward the end of the war, gravestones served again as parts of anti-tank-obstacles; trees of the Jewish cemetery were felled, the communal trea-

---

110 Osnabrück 4 Js 56/47 = 4 KLs 5/48, StA Osnabrück, Rep 945 Akz. 6/1983, Nr. 585-586.
111 Aurich 2 Js 1978/46 = 2 Ks 3/48, StA Aurich, Rep. 109 E Nr. 119.
112 Limburg 5 Js 1022/47 = 5 KLs 16/47; HStA Wiesbaden, Abt. 463, Nr. 1228/1-2.

sury benefitted from the sale of the wood and the hearse for transporting the dead was sold as well.[113]

In Schlüchtern, the town bought the Jewish cemetery from the Jewish community in 1940. The mayor and district Nazi Party chief of Schlüchtern sold the compound for 6,000 RM to a soap factory (previously owned by a Jew but now Aryanized). Although the sale contract specified that a 30-year period applied (to guarantee the peace of the dead), the new owner used damaged and undamaged tombstones from the old Jewish cemetery for the foundations of an extension to his factory. At the entrance, gravestones were used with their inscriptions still legible. Another 25 tombstones from a newer part of the cemetery were sold to stonemasons; the money from the sale went to support the *Nationalsozialistische Volkswohlfahrt* (National Socialist Welfare).[114] After the last Jews had been deported, an innkeeper used the Jewish cemetery in Memmingen as a chicken run.[115]

The Reich Association of Jews in Germany had been ordered to surrender metal and iron from Jewish cemeteries, enabling scrap-metal dealers to demolish fences and gates and retrieve any other metal from the graveyards. In Haigerloch, the gates to the cemetery and the iron borders of graves were taken. In Hechingen, due to the previous vandalizing of the cemetery by Nazi Party members, scrap metal had already been piled up in a corner; the scrap dealer further removed the gates and the iron borders. One thousand thirty-five kilograms of metal were thus harvested in Haigerloch, 2470 in Hechingen.[116]

In 1943 in Binswangen, the municipality bought and razed the Jewish graveyard, as it had already been demolished by Hitler Youth members.[117] In Massbach, three teenagers desecrated the Jewish cemetery in 1944;[118] the same year saw the devastation of the graveyard in Bad Vilbel[119] and the vandalizing in Nördlingen.[120] The Jewish cemetery in Bremke was leveled in 1944 and gravestones piled in a heap.[121] In October 1944, gravestones and parts of the wall of the Jewish cemetery on Nuremberger Strasse in Bayreuth were removed to create a makeshift home

---

113 Frankenthal 9 Js 59/49, AOFAA, AJ 3676, p. 36.
114 Hanau 3 Js 56/46 = AG Schlüchtern Ds 97/46, HStA Wiesbaden Abt. 471, Nr. 9.
115 Memmingen Js 2917/46; Memmingen Js 2918/46; see also Memmingen Js 2881ff/46 = KLs 14/48, StA Augsburg.
116 Hechingen Js 2424/46; Js 2931/46; Js 2932/46 = KMs 3-5/47; StA Sigmaringen, Ho 400 T2, Nr. 574.
117 Augsburg 4 Js 284-89/49 (files probably destroyed).
118 Schweinfurt 3 Js 1142/48 = AG Münnerstadt Ds 24/49 Jug. (files probably destroyed).
119 Giessen 2 KMs 11/48 (files probably destroyed).
120 Augsburg 4 Js 2806-2815/47 =AK 5/48 (files probably destroyed).
121 Göttingen 3 Js 782/48 = 3 KMs 9/48.

for the son-in-law of SS Senior Commander (*Oberführer*) Eschold. Orders for the removal of the wall had come from the mayor of Bayreuth, although the city of Bayreuth had neither bought nor expropriated the Jewish cemetery or its wall.[122]

By the end of the war, countless centuries-old relics of Jewish culture had been demolished or converted beyond recognition. Cemeteries had been built over, as in Hann. Münden, where a sawmill covered the compound.[123] The graveyard of Medebach had been turned into a sheep-run, the gravestones used as the base of an apiary.[124] Gravestones from Obermockstadt were built into a canal;[125] remnants of tombstones from Gramm were on their way to becoming abutments until a local stonemason refused to use them.[126] In Trittenheim, a vintner paved his yard with remnants of the Jewish cemetery, claiming later that he had not been aware of their former use.[127] In Grebenau, Jewish gravestones, walls and perimeters were also turned into construction material.[128] In Bleckede the mayor wanted to do away with the carcass of a horse and considered the Jewish cemetery an appropriate location for the purpose.[129] In Haigerloch-Haag the location of the cemetery on a slope became a skiing hill for teenagers – knocking down 70 stones in the process.[130]

Even during the Third Reich, Jewish congregations notified the Nazi authorities of the vandalizations. In June 1941 the Jewish community of Hechingen wrote to their mayor that whole rows of gravestones had been knocked over, a building on the site vandalized, walls smeared with graffiti, and the ground defecated upon.[131] The municipal police of Hechingen ascertained that in the last week of May 1941 a large-scale devastation of the Jewish graveyard in Galgenweiher, a local sub-district of Hechingen, had taken place, leaving only 40 of some 200 graves unscathed; 160 gravestones had been lifted from their foundation pedestals using crowbars. While the perpetrators were never apprehended, local Nazi Party functionaries, members of Hitler Youth and *Reichsarbeitsdienst* (Reich Labor Service) as well as the SS from Tübingen were considered suspects.

Apart from desecrations during the Third Reich, cemeteries were also vandalized during the post-war period. The Jewish graveyard in Kleinheubach had been

---

[122] Bayreuth 1a Js 11585/46 = KLs 16/47, StA Bamberg, Rep. K 106, Abg. 1996, Nr. 839.
[123] Göttingen 4 Js 918/49.
[124] Arnsberg 3 Js 27/49 = 3 KLs 1/51.
[125] Giessen Js 2763/47 pol. = AG Nidda Ds 96a/47.
[126] Koblenz 9/3 Js 47/47 = 9 KLs 9/51, LHA Koblenz, Best. 584, 1, Nr. 1333.
[127] Trier 3 Js 535/47 = 3 KLs 18/48, LHA Koblenz, Best. 584, 2, Nr. 755-757.
[128] Giessen 2 Js 2499/49.
[129] Lüneburg 1 Js 57/47.
[130] Hechingen Js 4128/47, StA Sigmaringen, Ho 400 T2, Nr. 854.
[131] Hechingen Js 1333/47, StA Sigmaringen, Ho 400 T2, Nr. 850.

desecrated in 1938, 1941/1942 and was subjected to further vandalism in September 1946.[132] The Jewish burial ground in Mandel had suffered war damage but was reconstructed after 1945, only to have young boys overturn gravestones in 1948.[133] Traditional Jewish burial sites, as well as new graveyards (for concentration camp victims), became targets of anti-Semitic violence. The Jewish community in West Germany stated in an article that never before had so many gravestones been overturned as after May 8, 1945. About 77 violations had been reported by mid-1949.[134] Though this might have been an exaggeration, the vandalization as such had reached an alarming magnitude. This development would also upset the American Legal Division, which noted the desecration of Jewish graveyards in several of its reports.[135]

For the few survivors of deportations and concentration camps who would return to their homelands, the sight of devastated Jewish graveyards – the burial places of ancestors and relatives – must have been appalling. Their pleas to have the sites restored did not meet with immediate response. In Wallau, Ludwig Fried notified the authorities of the devastation of the Jewish cemetery and threatened to take the case to the Military Government to remedy the dilatory treatment of the affair.[136]

Most violations of the peace of the dead could not be prosecuted after 1945, since the perpetrators remained unknown or claimed ignorance of the fact that the stones they had used had belonged to Jewish cemeteries. Nearly systematic investigations were carried out in the Saar region where the cemeteries in Blieskastel, Dillingen, Homburg, Illingen, Merzig, Neunkirchen, Nohfelden-Gonnesweiler, Nohfelden-Sötern, Ottweiler, Saarbrücken, Saarlouis, Saarwellingen, St. Ingbert and Tholey had existed.[137] On the other hand, in most other German regions the vandalization of cemeteries during the Third Reich did not lead to extensive post-war investigations.

---

132 Aschaffenburg 4 Js 11/49.
133 Koblenz 2 Js 470/48, AOFAA, AJ 1616, p. 801.
134 "Judenhetze am Wirtshaustisch," *Jüdisches Gemeindeblatt*, May 6, 1949.
135 Schwanfeld, see monthly report December 25, 1948, NARA, OMGBY 17/183 – 2/14; Höchberg, see monthly report October 25, 1948, NARA, OMGBY 17/183 – 2/14; Königshofen, Neustadt and Karbach, see monthly report April 23, 1948, NARA, OMGBY 17/183 – 2/14; Regensburg, see monthly report July 26, 1948, NARA, OMGBY 17/183 – 3/15; Thalmässing, see monthly report June 26, 1948, NARA, OMGBY 17/183 – 3/15 Ansbach, see monthly report, April 25, 1948, NARA, OMGBY 17/183 – 3/15.
136 Letter mayor of Wallau to state attorney at local court Hochheim am Main, December 18, 1947, Wiesbaden 4 Js 81/48, HStA Wiesbaden, Abt. 468, Nr. 421.
137 Saarbrücken 11 Js 258/48; Saarbrücken 11 Js 27/48; Saarbrücken 11 Js 154/48; Saarbrücken 11 Js 61/48 = 11 KLs 31 – 35/48; Saarbrücken 11 Js 42/49; Saarbrücken 11 Js 52/48; Saarbrücken 11 Js 11/48; Saarbrücken 11 Js 86/48; Saarbrücken 11 Js 1/48.

Nevertheless, dozens of investigations, even some trials after 1945, did deal with the vandalizing of Jewish burial sites. Among the legal foundations were disturbance of the peace of the dead and willful damage to property, which are both punishable offenses according to the German penal code.

The following case exemplifies how the prosecution sometimes proceeded:

In 1947 the Jewish community of Osnabrück notified the authorities of the vandalization of the Jewish cemetery in Gildehaus. An article in the Osnabrück newspaper reported that the former Nazi Party district chief, Dr. Josef Ständer, had had gravestones removed from the cemetery in 1944. While Ständer denied any responsibility in his denazification proceedings, hints from residents and police investigations revealed that Ständer had had his yard paved with tombstones from the cemetery, the old Hebrew and German inscriptions facing downwards so as to remain hidden.[138]

In the denazification proceedings, Ständer was sentenced to four years' imprisonment for his affiliation with the Nazi Party. At the end of 1949 he was indicted in a regular penal court for vandalizing the cemetery. The deed was now characterized as misappropriation and concealment of stolen goods, as the cemetery was still the property of the Jewish community, thus the appropriation of tombstones equaled embezzlement. Of about 30-35 tombstones, six had clearly found use in Ständer's yard. Ständer claimed brusquely not to have known of the origins of the tombstones that the mayor had put at his disposal without informing him of where he had obtained them. Called as a witness, the worker who had paved the yard stated that the mayor purported that Ständer had explicitly asked for tombstones. Moreover, the tombstones stood upright in the courtyard for a few days so that the provenance was quite visible. The district court of Osnabrück considered it unlikely that Ständer, who was a resident of Gildehaus, had not learned of the destruction of the Jewish cemetery. In 1952, after the revision of a first sentence (based on the Control Council Law No. 10), Ständer was sentenced to one additional year of imprisonment for concealment of stolen goods.[139]

---

138 "Grabsteine als Hofpflaster. Der ehemalige Nazikreisleiter weiss von nichts," *Neues Tageblatt (Osnabrück)*, September 26, 1947.
139 Osnabrück 4 Js 2549/47 = 4 Ks 4/50, StA Osnabrück, Rep. 945 Akz. 6/1983, Nr. 402-406.

The Prosecution of the Pogrom

> The brown uniform, known as the SA, arrives in broad daylight or the dead of night, and rings the bell. Everyone is terrified by this ringing. ... And all of them are dragged from their houses to the accompaniment of shill cries, and taken away, put into camps and humiliated until their souls cannot go on and their bodies die.
>
> Veza Canetti, *The Tortoises*

Local Peculiarities of the Pogrom

The Nazi course of action on the Reich level during the pogrom has been reconstructed and need only be summarized here: the celebrations in commemoration of the Hitler coup d'état of 1923, with anti-Semitic speeches (following the assassination of the German diplomat vom Rath in Paris), official parades and line-ups, and the subsequent more casual get-togethers (sometimes with excessive consumption of alcohol); the turning to violence with the burning and devastation of synagogues, shops, flats, and houses; and the arrest and mistreatment, and even murder, of Jewish Germans. However, the local peculiarities that substantially influenced both the chain of events and the body of participants have not yet been considered sufficiently. I should like to address these by describing situations from which violence against German Jews erupted.

In Landstuhl, both active and reserve storm troopers had assembled in the market square for the Wehrmacht parade of the local garrison that was scheduled for November 10, 1938. Thus already organized and ready for action, two details of uniformed storm troopers marched in formation from the square into the town and destroyed the Jewish prayer room as well as several houses and flats. The NSDAP county commander, feeling pressed for time and fearing that the pogrom would coincide with the celebratory reception of the Wehrmacht, reproached those storm troopers who turned up late for the pogrom activities.[140] In Miehlen, the pogrom evolved from an event already in full flower: On the evening of November 9, 1938, a wedding celebration took place with many local National Socialists attending (indeed, the wedding couple had opted for the National Socialist wedding consecration instead of a church ceremony). The guests decided to conclude the celebration with a violent anti-Semitic attack against the local Jewish community, leading to the destruction of the synagogue, as well as several stores,

---

140 Zweibrücken 7 Js 3/49 = KLs 24/49, AOFAA, AJ 3676, p. 38.

a saddlery, and a butcher shop.[141] In some towns in the (Catholic) Rhinelands, the traditional St. Martin's procession – usually a feast with lit candles for small children and their parents – took place on November 11, 1938. In Düsseldorf, a Hitler Youth member admitted to having joined with storm troopers who rushed into the flat of a Jewish family at Erasmusstrasse 20.[142] Part of the pogrom also took place during the St. Martin's procession in Krefeld-Uerdingen,[143] and in St. Tönis.[144] In Hüls the pogrom started around six o'clock in the evening as the procession moved through the streets.[145] Joining up with the outdoor events was tempting because participants were already incited, mobilized, and equipped with the necessary tools. In other places, leaflets called on the population to stage rallies and to riot.[146]

As is known, riots took place before the nation-wide pogrom in Hesse and Saxony-Anhalt (East Germany). The events in Wachenbuchen (Hesse) provide a good example. On November 8 and 9, 1938, a mob assembled in front of the house of the Jewish teacher Sonneberg in Wachenbuchen. Storm troopers and other participants broke into the house and despoiled it, with the local party chief egging them on. The storm troopers, equipped with axes and picks, drove the teacher out of his house and demolished the abode completely – even removing the roof, tearing down walls, chucking furniture into the street and courtyard. While there were more than 35 rioters inside the house, the mob outside numbered about 300. On the evening of November 9, several hundred more people turned up in front of the house and demolished what was left of it; storm troopers forced the Jews of Wachenbuchen to tear down the sad remnants of the house on November 10. The trigger to all of this had been an anti-Semitic speech by the local Nazi Party head and mayor before a crowd of about 200–250 people, among them some 15–20 storm troopers.

The local Nazi Party chief had demanded that the Jewish school (where the teacher lived) be torn down as well and the teacher be given a "shellacking." (For quite a while, the municipality had been interested in purchasing the house in order to tear it down.) The head of the storm troopers in Wachenbuchen urged a more cautious approach in order to avoid the involvement of police and inquiries by state attorneys. Others had no such qualms: One storm trooper stole the Jewish

---

141 Koblenz 9 Js 132/49 = 9 Ks 1/50, LHA Koblenz, Best. 584, 1, Nr. 1305.
142 Düsseldorf 8 Js 164/46, HStA Düsseldorf – ZA Kalkum, Gerichte Rep. 268/14.
143 Krefeld 1 Js 70/48 = 1 Ks 2/48, HStA Düsseldorf – ZA Kalkum, Gerichte Rep. 8/41-44.
144 Krefeld 2 Js 402/48 = 2 Ks 2/48, HStA Düsseldorf – ZA Kalkum, Gerichte Rep. 30/109-111.
145 Krefeld 6 Js 655/48 = 6 Ks 1/48; HStA Düsseldorf – ZA Kalkum, Gerichte Rep. 30/118.
146 Kleve 5 Js 417/47 = 5 Ks 1/48; 5 KLs 1/48, HStA Düsseldorf – ZA Kalkum, Gerichte Rep. 107/7-8; see also Kleve 5 Js 568/48, HStA Düsseldorf – ZA Kalkum, Gerichte Rep. 7/906.

teacher's bike, another his wall clock; 50 preserving jars were handed over to the National Socialist Welfare (NSV).[147] When the district chief executive, Löser, learned of the attack on Sonneberg he asked why the man had not been arrested or battered to death. He argued that if Sonneberg were to go abroad, this would create a giant mess.[148]

Apart from the frequently described smashing of furniture and inventory items, the attacks often bore a very individual signature. In Gross-Auheim, the Nazi Party head incited several malefactors to demolish the dwellings and shops of certain Jewish families; the offenders set to the task with sledgehammers. Splinters and chips of glass and china littered the floor of the house until after the war. A picture of the son one of the Jewish families affected was torn from its frame, slashed, and doused with ink.[149]

In Kamp, a mob of political party heads, storm troopers, Hitler Youth, and civilians laid siege to the house of the Jewish Kaufmann family; the mob chanted "*Juda verrecke*" (Jews should die a horrid death) and "Jew! Open up!". In the course of events, the house was stormed; on the ground floor furniture and lamps were smashed, doors and stovepipes torn from their mountings. The actions of the mob in the attic caused part of the first-floor ceiling to collapse. At that point, the Kaufmanns, who had fled to the first floor, left the house and found refuge in the nearby Bornhofen monastery.[150]

In Fürth, storm troopers made their way to the main synagogue, dragged the Jewish lawyer Dr. Albert Abraham Neubürger from his nearby lodgings, and tried to ram the door of the synagogue open using his head. Only because the key to the door was found was Neubürger spared further tortures, but he was forced to watch while the devastation and arson took place. Neubürger committed suicide in February 1942, before his impending deportation.[151]

Property Offenses

Among the most frequent offenses of the pogrom – other than the riots – were looting and theft. The defense of "orders from above" sufficed for arson of synagogues, but the devastation of houses and shops, the arrest of Jewish citizens,

---

[147] Hanau 2 Js 828/46 = 2 KLs 3/47, HStA Wiesbaden, Abt. 471, Nr. 167/1-2; Hanau 2 Js 143/47 = 2 KLs 30/47, HStA Wiesbaden, Abt. 471, Nr. 168/1-2.
[148] Hanau 2 Js 143/47 = 2 KLs 30/47, HStA Wiesbaden, Abt. 471, Nr. 168/1-2.
[149] Hanau 2 Js 951/46 = 2 KLs 3/49, HStA Wiesbaden, Abt. 471, Nr. 175/1-2.
[150] Koblenz 9/5 Js 510/48 = 9 KLs 4/50, LHA Koblenz, Best. 584, 1, Nr. 1258-1259.
[151] Nürnberg-Fürth 1c Js 450/48 = 554 KLs 199/50, StA Nürnberg, StAnw Nürnberg 2860/I-III.

plunder, and theft were not covered by higher orders; they originated from very private motives. Personal enrichment was barely disguised by belated disposal of stolen goods to the NSV. In Bad Nauheim Jewish-owned shops were ransacked.[152] When the synagogue of Hof was devastated, the offenders pilfered 55 marks from a cash box. Silver candlesticks, a Torah shield, family pictures, a savings box, an accordion, a typewriter and a valuable watch were stolen from a neighboring flat – only some of which were returned later.[153] In Ludwigshafen three radios were stolen from Jewish families – and had to be given to the NSV.[154] In Spiegelau, storm troopers pillaged the house of a Jewish factory owner who had been arrested, stealing several objects of value.[155] The state prosecutor of Bonn initiated dozens of proceedings against residents of Weilerswist, Gross-Vernich, and Lommersum (county Euskirchen), euphemistically describing the offenders as being almost exclusively women who had not participated in the actual destructive event, but who had committed theft in already devastated houses.[156] In Neumarkt (Upper Palatinate) the pogrom offenders helped themselves freely to clothing, furniture, carpets, paintings, silver cutlery, jewelry, and objects from the synagogue and private homes of Jews, remarking that the Jews were being "tidied up."[157] In Düsseldorf a female suspect invited another woman to join in the pillaging of Jewish lodgings saying, "Come with me to town, the Jews are being worked over."[158] Elise F. recommended to Wilhelmine H. in Urbach that she fetch linens from the property of a Jew named Jakob. Miss H. then helped herself to duvets, pillows, linens, and spun wool, after which she bundled everything up and asked two other women to assist her in carrying home the loot. Shortly afterwards, the police confiscated all of it.[159] After the pogrom in Schwegenheim had ended, a woman took 12 pairs of ladies' and children's shoes from a Jewish-owned shoe store, along with two men's shirts and cloth for a child's dress. When summoned to hand in the objects, she complied.[160] In Aurich the rumor circulated that Nazi adherents had newly bedecked themselves by looting textiles during the pogrom.[161] The wife, daughter, and daughter-in-law of a man convicted in the post-war years for participation in the pogrom were, according to reports, wearing dresses made

---

152 Giessen 2 Js 2102/48 pol. = 2 KLs 4/49 pol.
153 Hof Js 3321/48 = KLs 4/51, StA Bamberg, Rep. K 107, Abg. 1987, Nr. 749.
154 Frankenthal 9 Js 51a-b/47 = 9 KLs 4/49, AOFAA, AJ 3676, p. 38.
155 Deggendorf 1 Js B 2593/46.
156 Bonn 7 Js 340/48, HStA Düsseldorf – ZA Kalkum, Gerichte Rep. 145/471.
157 Nürnberg-Fürth 1b Js 1667/48 = KLs 5/49, StA Nürnberg, StAnw Nürnberg 2316/I-III.
158 Düsseldorf 8 Js 73/47, HStA Düsseldorf – ZA Kalkum, Gerichte Rep. 268/24.
159 Koblenz 9/3 Js 226/47 = 9 Ks 5/50, LHA Koblenz, Best. 584, 1, Nr. 3237-3250.
160 Landau 7 Js 14/46 = KMs 14/47, AOFAA, AJ 3676, p. 37.
161 Aurich 2 Js 703/45 = 2 Ks 17/49, StA Aurich, Rep. 109 E 4/1-12.

from textiles looted from the Limburg synagogue.[162] Pillage on a huge scale was committed in Windsbach. The local party chief declared that Jewish property was free for the taking. He then had chandeliers, silver, textiles, and Torah Scrolls brought to his house.[163] In Badenweiler a defendant acquired a vacuum cleaner and two Persian carpets.[164] Others in Badenweiler helped themselves to valuable objects and jewelry belonging to a Jewish couple.[165] When the house of Jules Neuburger in Heidenheim was looted, a female culprit needed a handcart to carry textiles away. When confronted with this deed, she claimed to have taken the clothes in order to save them from pillage by the mob, intending to return them to their rightful owner. A man who had gotten hold of a large bowl in the same house claimed that this was not pilfering "as everybody took something." His daughter had grabbed a tablecloth as well. A few weeks later, the local party chief was ordered to collect the stolen items, but the enforced sequestration of stolen goods from their new owners yielded only a few items of minor value.[166] Other looters used a blowtorch to open a safe in Heidenheim.[167] In Ansbach, several chests with ritual objects and tallitot (prayer shawls) from the synagogue were kept by a participant in the pogrom.[168] In Trabelsdorf, pews, doors, staircases and beams from the gallery of the synagogue were carried away and used as firewood. The police report of August 1945 called the culprits *"minderbemittelt"* (which in German can mean both less well-off and mentally deficient).[169] In Nierstein, the lodgings of a Jewish businessman named Wolf were devastated; other offenders pilfered his stock of merchandise as well as his wine cellar.[170]

When the synagogue of Limburg was despoiled, the local population helped itself indiscriminately to both ritual and secular objects, which they either kept or destroyed. A defendant would later testify observing a constant stream of Limburg residents coming and going with various items. When he saw a pack of teenagers grabbing a copper cauldron, silverware, embroidered silk and a carpet runner, he immediately confiscated the stolen goods – and used them in his own household. Witnesses claimed that the defendant carted away cast-iron heating devices from the synagogue and the flat of the caretaker, as well as planks from

---

162 Limburg 3 Js 530/46, HStA Wiesbaden Abt. 463 Nr. 1166.
163 Ansbach 1 Js 2500/46 = KLs 25/47, StA Nürnberg, StAnw Ansbach 682/I-V.
164 Freiburg 1 Js 134/49 = 1 Ks 5/49.
165 Freiburg 1 Js 238/49.
166 Ansbach 5 Js 74/49; StA Nürnberg, StAnw Ansbach 5 Js 74/49.
167 Ansbach 5 Js 114/48 = KLs 26/49; StA Nürnberg, GStA beim OLG Nürnberg 150.
168 Ansbach 1 Js 5396/47 = Nürnberg-Fürth KLs 129/48, StA Nürnberg, StAnw Nürnberg 2171/I-IV.
169 Bamberg Js 40/46, StA Bamberg, Rep. K 105, Abg. 1995, Nr. 661/1-2.
170 Mainz 3 Js 1300/47, AOFAA, AJ 1616, p. 806.

the ground floor, bricks, a ladder, a tin vat, a mattress and bedding.[171] In Oberlustadt, a man stole clothing and linens from the flats of two Jewish families (among them the Weils) and later claimed brashly they had been given to him as a present since he had once helped Mrs. Weil open a wardrobe.[172] In Ingelheim, Lina Koch was robbed of furniture, pictures, and other belongings during the pogrom.[173] In 1946, the head of the welfare office in Solingen-Ohligs initiated an investigation, having discovered formerly Jewish-owned furniture in the flat of the brother-in-law of the local Nazi Party head. During the pogrom, the Wertheim warehouse was ransacked; the local Nazi Party later bought a complete bedroom set – two beds, two bedside tables, a dressing table, two chairs, mattresses, pillows, duvets, a tea trolley, and four sets of bed linen, ornamental tea cloths – from the loot.[174] In Landau, the SS Sturmbann settled cozily in the house that had belonged to the Jewish ophthalmologist Dr. Frank, whose janitor got a flat there as well – completely furnished with objects and inventory stolen or "confiscated" from Jewish homes and shops during the pogrom. The SS left the lodgings in mid-1941, taking most of the furnishings with them, but leaving some oil paintings, curtains, cutlery, linens, tables, a briefcase and a laundry wringer with the caretaker for "safekeeping." When the janitor moved to new lodgings, he took it all with him; the objects were found during a house search in January 1946. Only reluctantly did the wife of the caretaker admit that the items did not belong to them and that they had intended to keep them indefinitely.[175]

Linens and clothing were exhaustively stolen after the pogrom in Hassloch. On orders of a storm trooper, the entire stock of Mr. Loeb's textile store was loaded into a car. Members of the municipal administration had to bring blankets and men's briefs into the *Sturmführer's* lodgings, purportedly to have them distributed to storm troopers in need. As there were also ladies' underwear, knickers, and stockings among the items, one wonders what immediate need the storm troopers might have had. Eventually, most of the textiles ended up with the NSV and were – ostensibly – sold. Some were carted away by an SA troop commander and distributed among fellow storm troopers who had missed out on the plundering. In addition to the textiles, a refrigerator and a desk from Loeb's were pilfered. Some offenders tried to cover the theft by providing receipts: A Nazi Party official "bought" a table, a tea trolley and a stove from Loeb for 50 RM. The post-war court would judge the "purchase" to be an actual seizure because the plight of the

---

171 Limburg 3 Js 794/45 = 3 KLs 5/45, HStA Wiesbaden, Abt. 463, Nr. 904.
172 Landau 7 Js 70/47, AOFAA, AJ 3676, p. 37.
173 Mainz 3 Js 111/48, AOFAA, AJ 1616, p. 802.
174 Wuppertal 5 Js 81/47 = 5 KLs 44/48, HStA Düsseldorf – ZA Kalkum, Gerichte Rep. 191/43-44.
175 Landau 7 Js 1/47 = KMs 10/47, AOFAA, AJ 3676, p. 36.

Jewish proprietor was exploited, rendering the legal transaction invalid according to civil law. An investigation also revealed that the Nazi official had stolen the items first and only later had sent an intermediary to conclude a contract of purchase.[176] The *Sturmführer* also stored a desk, a bookcase, bedroom furniture, and other furnishings from Jewish homes, only to remove the items when, shortly after the pogrom, the Nazi Party initiated inquiries as to where the loot had gone. Several bottles of wine stolen by Nazi Party members were later handed over to the NSV.

For some the pogrom was lucrative even if they had not had sticky fingers themselves: One Nazi Party official received a lump sum of 2,000 RM from the Nazi treasury as well as a daily allowance of 93 RM in compensation for an accident he incurred on November 11, 1938. According to his own statement, he was patrolling destroyed Jewish flats and stores in the Nazi Party district of Hombüchel in order to prevent plunder. At around three o'clock in the morning, in the course of these duties, he slipped on bits of broken glass at the entrance of the synagogue in Wuppertal-Elberfeld, sustaining a severe cut on his left arm and requiring hospital treatment. Contrary to his version of events, witnesses stated that he had been present when the synagogue was blown up and had been injured by the resulting splinters.[177]

Sometimes objects were acquired, but not put to use by any "*Volksgenossen*" (German citizens, i.e., ethnic Germans). In Seibersbach, the textile stock of the Jewish Wolf family was pilfered and put on a truck. Although groceries owned by the family were promptly distributed by the NSV, the textiles were stored in the town warehouse in Dörrebach where they eventually fell victim to moth damage.[178] Maybe the clothes were simply forgotten, or maybe the Nazi Party functionaries thought it best to conceal the stolen goods as long as possible lest police or Gestapo started sniffing around.

Some wrongdoers used the pogrom for their own private campaign of revenge. In Trier-Euren the Nazi Party chief proclaimed, "Today a general reckoning will be held."[179] The wife of one storm trooper owed back debts to Albert Strauss, the Jewish storeowner in Oestrich. When the Nazi Party chief learned of this, he reproached the storm trooper for still buying from Jews; the storm trooper

---

[176] Frankenthal 9 Js 235/49 = 9 Ks 5/50; AOFAA, AJ 3676, p. 38.
[177] Wuppertal 5 Js 3591/46 = 5 KLs 82/48; HStA Düsseldorf – ZA Kalkum, Gerichte Rep. 240/261- 265; see also "Synagogen-Brandstifterprozess in Wuppertal-Elberfeld," *Jüdisches Gemeindeblatt für die britische Zone*, September 10, 1948.
[178] Koblenz 9/2 Js 1433/48 = Koblenz 9 KLs 35/49; Bad Kreuznach 2 KLs 28/50, LHA Koblenz, Zg. 94/04, Bündel 4.
[179] Trier 2 Js 496/48 = 2 KLs 26/49, AOFAA, AJ 1616, p. 805.

took his revenge during the pogrom when he tripped Albert Strauss as he was fleeing from his persecutors.[180]

In Dierdorf, a 17-year-old boy forced himself into the house of Moritz Salomon, in revenge for the compulsory enforcement of debt collection against his parents, who owed money to Salomon.[181] In Wiesbaden-Biebrich, a landlord joined the mob to destroy his Jewish tenant's store and flat.[182]

Others used the pogrom for "debt relief," by burning I.O.U.s as, for example, in Schöllkrippen.[183] In Achim two cattle traders removed pages from the account book of the Jewish cattle dealer Ansbacher in order to erase their debts.[184] Similarly, a father and son approached Leopold Strauss in Oestrich and tore the page with the documentation of their own debts from Strauss's journal.[185] In Treuchtlingen, Lina K., heavily indebted to a Jew named Neuburger, broke into his house and tried to destroy the account books.[186] Things were handled more conveniently in Aufsess, where citizens who had debts with Jews were picked up by car from various villages to confront the Jews, who were then forced to issue receipts of allegedly repaid debt or alternatively sign renunciations, forfeiting repayment. The receipts were retained by the SS, most probably to make further use of them, either to squeeze at least some money from the original debtors or to blackmail them for their continued trade relations with Jews. When other peasants learned of the debt relief, they intruded into the house of the more than 70-year-old, bedridden Karl Fleischmann in Aufsess and demanded their debts (from 1,200 to 1,600 RM) be waived as well. On the same day, November 11, 1938, a notary and the second mayor of the commune of Aufsess approached Fleischmann in order to compel him to sell his plot of land to the municipality. The second mayor forced another Jew to pay a further 350 RM for the demolition of the synagogue (which the municipality had bought in September 1938).[187]

A Nazi Party member who still owed 2,000 RM to the Jewish cattle dealer Markus Stern went to Stern's flat in Frankfurt – accompanied by the Gestapo – and demanded the son, Jonas Stern, be arrested as Markus Stern was not present. Jonas Stern was imprisoned in Buchenwald until January 9, 1939.[188]

---

180 Wiesbaden 4 Js 2393/46 = 4 KLs 9/49, HStA Wiesbaden, Abt. 468, Nr. 262/1-5.
181 Koblenz 9 Js 228/49 = 9 Ks 8/50, LHA Koblenz, Best. 584, 1, Nr. 1278.
182 Wiesbaden 2 Js 3090/45 = 2 KLs 20/49; HStA Wiesbaden, Abt. 468, Nr. 260/1-7.
183 Aschaffenburg 4 Js 7/49 = KLs 7/51.
184 Verden 6 Js 311/47 = 6 Ks 1/48; StA Stade, Rep. 171a Verden, Nr. 587.
185 Wiesbaden 4 Js 2393/46 = 4 KLs 9/49, HStA Wiesbaden, Abt. 468, Nr. 262/1-5.
186 Nürnberg-Fürth 1 Js 70/46 = KLs 16/46, KLs 138/46, StA Nürnberg, StAnw Nürnberg 1809.
187 Bayreuth 1b Js 6851/46 = KLs 26/48, StA Bamberg, Rep. K 106, Abg. 1996, Nr. 842.
188 Frankfurt 55/7 Js 2985/49, HStA Wiesbaden, Abt. 461, Nr. 30026.

Others went straight to blackmail: In Varel, two storm troopers tried to force a Jew named Weinberg – who had been compelled to sell a house a few days previously for 2,000 RM – to hand over the money.[189] In Montabaur, Jews had to sign a list saying that certain items – office furniture and equipment, typewriters and bookcases – were left "voluntarily" to the storm troopers. The storm troopers immediately picked up the objects by truck.[190]

In Frankfurt am Main, a man had entertained trade relations with a Jew named Löwenstein. Due to the man's debt, Löwenstein had had his postal checking account confiscated. On November 10, 1938, the man appeared in Löwenstein's lodgings and demanded the return of the confiscated account as well as 50 RM "expenses," which the intimidated creditor handed over. Thus encouraged by the success, the offender went on to the flat of a Jew named Rosenthal and demanded money for an accident that Rosenthal reputedly had had with him. Rosenthal gave him a check amounting to 320 RM. This extortionate robbery was viewed with distaste even among Nazi authorities: In 1939, the offender stood trial in a local court in Frankfurt: He was acquitted concerning the Löwenstein case but sentenced to six weeks' imprisonment for the Rosenthal case. In 1948 he was to face a court anew, this time for breach of the peace upon entering Rosenthal's flat together with a mob of 15-20 men.[191]

In Hennweiler, the offenders seized the day to debt collection: The Nazi Party head of Hennweiler (*NSDAP-Stützpunktleiter*) went with an alleged creditor to the family of Kahn, who allegedly owed him 100 RM dating back to a cattle deal in 1928. The creditor assumed that all Jewish property would be seized and thus wanted to have his account settled immediately. Kahn issued an I.O.U., which the proud "creditor" bragged about later at an inn. This encouraged the creditor and the NSDAP party chief of neighboring Hahnweiler to approach Kahn again in the evening to have the I.O.U. exchanged for cash.[192]

In Ermetzhofen a Jew named Hugo Österreicher was forced to pay 65 RM to the NSDAP party head of Neuherberg; furthermore, he was forced to cede a request for payment of an outstanding rent bill (owed by a farmer) – the sum amounted to 60 RM – to the Nazi Party of Neuherberg. The Party then collected the debt from the farmer.[193]

---

189 Oldenburg 10 Js 888/48 = 9 Ks 15/50, StA Oldenburg, Best. 140-5, Nr. 1162.
190 Koblenz 9/3 Js 1648/48 = 9 KLs 62/49, LHA Koblenz, Best. 584, 1, Nr. 1236.
191 AG Frankfurt 6 b Ms 32/39; AG Frankfurt 3 Ms 19/48 HStA Wiesbaden, Abt. 461, Nr. 32492 (Restakt).
192 Koblenz 9/2 Js 449/47 = 9 KLs 52/49; LHA Koblenz, Best. 584, 6, Nr. 34.
193 Ansbach 2 Js 586-591/47 = KLs 24/48, StA Nürnberg, StAnw Ansbach 769.

In Achim, the extorted money – more than 4,000 RM – was paid into a special account and then transferred to the storm troopers (*Reiter-Standarte 62*) in Bremen, who remitted the amount to the SA group Nordsee. The further whereabouts of the money remained unclear.[194] In Emden a family was arrested; during their enforced absence their lodgings were used for a looting binge. The storm troopers made ample use of wine and cigarettes and a house search led to the disappearance of more than 8,000 RM and expensive jewelry.[195] In Norden, the seized money was paid into a special account of the storm trooper unit (*SA-Sturm Norden*) at the district savings bank Norden (*Stadtsparkasse*) and then transferred to a special account in the name of the Nazi local head of Norden. The account amounted to 21,364.32 RM, all stemming from Jewish property.[196] In Nuremberg, the SA Area Headquarters 14 acquired 40-42,000 RM during the pogrom – money later to be transferred to the NSDAP regional headquarters.[197] Siegbert Einstein, one of the few survivors of the Jewish community of Buchau (which had once numbered 200 members), stated that 39,000 RM had been extorted from the Jewish congregation during the pogrom – the NSDAP district then freely dispensing with the money.[198]

The Ritual of Public Degradation

Apart from plunder, theft, and blackmail, acts of what Peter Loewenberg termed "Public Degradation Ritual" can be found frequently in the files.[199]

Often in the course of the excesses of *Kristallnacht*, Jews were forced to shout self-incriminations and anti-Semitic insults. In Rosbach, the arrested Jews were put into the fire engine house, had to listen to anti-Semitic ranting and then line up in front of a mob and say aloud, "We are the world's biggest swine."[200] In Meppen many of the Jews had been arrested early in the morning in great haste and were thus dressed haphazardly. Some were forced to walk barefoot over the broken glass of smashed shop windows. They were taken to the SA area headquarters and brought to the cellar, where they were forced to answer the question

---

194 Verden 6 Js 311/47 = 6 Ks 1/48; StA Stade, Rep. 171a Verden, Nr. 587.
195 Aurich 2 Js 191/46 = 2 KLs 4/47, StA Oldenburg, Best. 140-4 Acc. 13/79, Nr. 63.
196 Aurich 2 Js 862/45 = 2 Ks 7/50, StA Aurich, Rep. 109 Nds. Nr. E 341/1-12.
197 Nürnberg-Fürth 1d Js 2134/49 = KLs 122/49, StA Nürnberg, StAnw Nürnberg 2455/I-III.
198 "Der Buchauer Synagogenprozess. Entschuldigungen für die Täter," *Unsere Stimme*, February 21,1948; Ravensburg Js 8439-57/47 = KLs 126-142/47; KLs 146/47; KLs 29/48, StA Sigmaringen, Wü 29/1 T 1, Nr. 6889
199 Loewenberg, "The Kristallnacht as a Public Degradation Ritual".
200 Bonn Js 1838/45 = 7 KLs 5/46, HStA Düsseldorf – ZA Kalkum, Gerichte Rep. 195/921-928.

of who they were with the words "We are the swine Jews" or "We are the murderers of vom Rath"; then they were mistreated brutally with bottles, sticks and poles.[201] The demolished Jewish houses in Neuenhaus were affixed with placards bearing the words "*Rache für vom Rath*" (revenge for vom Rath).[202]

On the morning of November 10, 1938, 10 to 20 male Jews from Sinzig and surroundings were compelled to march through town. One had to carry a placard saying "We do not tolerate assassins! Out with the Jews!" Nazi functionaries accompanied the parade with anti-Semitic chanting.[203] In Saarburg, arrested Jewish men had to walk with a placard saying "We are the murderers of Gustloff and vom Rath." A non-Jewish lawyer who was considered a Nazi opponent and had Jewish clients was forced to participate in the parade and carry the placard intermittently.[204] In Regensburg, at least 40 Jews were incarcerated in the motor-sports school; younger Jews had to strip naked and do physical exercises while older ones had to do military-style exercises. Subsequently they were led through town; two had to walk with a placard that read "Exodus of the Jews." Sixty-six-year-old Jakob Lilienthal, whose nose had been broken during his arrest and who was no longer able to walk due to the abuse he had suffered at the hands of the storm troopers, was pulled along on a handcart. The local newspaper did not pass up the opportunity of photographing the procession.[205] In Laupheim, the arrested Jews had to sing in front of the burning synagogue, perform physical exercises and listen to the rant of an SA colonel before being forced to disclose their assets and liabilities in the town hall.[206] In Emden, Jews – among them women and children – were forced to do military-style exercises in a schoolyard under orders of the adjutant of the *SS-Standarte* Emden; they had to prostrate themselves under threat of death. They also had to sing a popular German folk song while marching and cleaning the schoolyard of leaves and rubbish.[207] In Saarbrücken, a procession of Jews was led through town; they were ceaselessly

---

201 Osnabrück 4 Js 22/48 = 4 Ks 8/49, 4 Ks 9/49, StA Osnabrück Rep 945 Akz. 6/1983 Nr. 114-128; see also "Pogromprozess in Osnabrück. Vorbildliche Arbeit der Gemeinde und des Weltkongresses," *Jüdisches Gemeindeblatt*, May 16, 1949; see also Osnabrück 4 Js 450/49 = 4 Ks 3/50, StA Osnabrück, Rep 945 Akz. 6 Nr. 93-96.
202 Osnabrück 4 Js 690/48 = 4 Ks 4/49, StA Osnabrück, Rep 945 Akz. 6/1983 Nr. 71-73.
203 Koblenz 9/2 Js 1153/47 = 9 KLs 7/51, LHA Koblenz, Best. 584, 1, Nr. 1316.
204 Trier 3 Js 449/47 = 3 KLs 17/48, LHA Koblenz, Best. 584, 2, Nr. 752-754.
205 Regensburg 1 Js 539/47 = Ks 1/51, StA Nürnberg, GStA beim OLG Nürnberg 228.
206 Ravensburg Js 8439-57/47 = KLs 126-142/47; KLs 146/47; KLs 29/48, StA Sigmaringen, Wü 29/1 T 1, Nr. 6889.
207 Aurich 2 Js 193/46 = 2 Ks 5/49, StA Aurich, Rep. 109 Nds. E Nr. 339/1-9.

insulted and mistreated.[208] Similar shaming parades are documented for Kehl,[209] Offenburg[210] and Rheinbischofsheim,[211] to name but a few.

Frequently, Jews were forced to take part in the destruction of the synagogues of their hometowns. In Leiwen 50 to 80 villagers first destroyed the apartments of three Jewish families and the synagogue. Subsequently, the Jews of Leiwen were made to carry candlesticks, candles, ritual garments and Torah Scrolls to the Mosel River to be burned.[212] In Boppard, Jews also were compelled to partake in the devastation of the Jewish house of prayer.[213] In Bosen, Jews were coerced with blows to bring saws, axes and hatchets and put them to use on the furniture of the synagogue and ritual objects, chuck them into the street and burn books and Torah Scrolls.[214] In Haren an der Ems Jews were forced to reveal the location of "walled-in Torah Scrolls" and destroy them (which is described somewhat clumsily by German investigators after 1945: It was probably the opening of a *Geniza*, the Hebrew term for a temporary repository for damaged or aged liturgical writings. Texts containing the name of God cannot be thrown away but rather must eventually be buried).[215]

In Krumbach 15 to 20 Jews were forced to come to the synagogue where, under threats and mistreatments by Gestapo and Security Service, they had to load books and other texts onto a truck. The next day the pilfering continued; Jews were compelled to cover their heads with kippot or top hats, adorn themselves with Stars of David, scissors or bells and sing songs. They were also photographed in shameful or ridiculous poses, e.g., sticking their tongues out. Two men were beaten into writing fake accounts of racial "defilement." One Jew had to mount the hearse, which was drawn by two Jewish women who later had to clean up the mess in front of the ruined synagogue.[216]

In Hamburg-Harburg, the morgue in the Jewish cemetery was set afire; the hearse, also in flames, was pulled out and drawn around by Hitler Youth members. A mob grabbed prayer books, robes and headdresses that were then burned in the market place of Harburg.[217] In Nastätten a high ranking storm trooper was responsible for arresting Jews in their lodgings and dragging them to

---

208 Saarbrücken 11 Js 37/48 = 11 KLs 24/49.
209 Offenburg 2 Js 820/47 = 2 Ks 2/49.
210 Offenburg 1 Js 447/48 = 1 Ks 6/48.
211 Offenburg 2 Js 824/47 = 2 Ks 2/48.
212 Trier 3 Js 544/47 = 3 KLs 19/48; LHA Koblenz, Best. 584, 2, Nr. 747-751.
213 Koblenz 9/3 Js 218/48 = 9 KLs 3/51, LHA Koblenz Best. 584, 1, Nr. 1317.
214 Koblenz 9/2 Js 147/48 = Bad Kreuznach 3 Ks 6/50, LHA Koblenz, Best. 584, 6, Nr. 4-13.
215 Osnabrück 4 Js 22/48 = 4 Ks 8/49, 4 Ks 9/49, StA Osnabrück, Rep 945 Akz. 6/1983 Nr. 114-128.
216 Memmingen Js 12142/47 = KLs 74/47, StA Augsburg.
217 Hamburg 14 Js 70/46 = 14 Ks 7/49, StA Hamburg, Best. 213-11, Nr. 22701/54 (Bd. 1-11).

the synagogue. Two of them were forced to collect glass and china splinters from the streets so that their hands were bleeding. Others had to carry a sofa on which storm troopers were sitting. Jews from neighboring Welterod were driven with blows to board a truck and taken to the synagogue of Nastätten, where all assembled Jews had to sing the children's song "*Fuchs, Du hast die Gans gestohlen*" (Fox you stole the goose/give it back to me/or the hunter will shoot you/with his gun.) substituting "*Jud*" for "*Fuchs*." The storm trooper addressed them in the synagogue and announced that there was an end to Jewry; that they were to cease to exist. Then he hit the Eternal Light with his riding crop. The excesses reached such an extent that even in the post-war judgment the "thoroughness and brutality" of the perpetrators found special mention, as unmatched in other places in the Rhineland and Nassau.[218]

In a pub frequented by the SS, a drunken lawyer, Dr. H., asked the SS squad leader in Landau to let him see the incarcerated Jews in the prayer room in order to see "what faces the imprisoned Jews are putting on." In the library of the prayer room, Dr. H. summoned a Jew named Rosenblum, punched him in the face, menaced him with a revolver and threatened to shoot him. Then he forced Rosenblum to spit three times on a Torah Scroll, while he himself spit several times into Rosenblum's face. Then he compelled two Jews to fill their mouths with water and to spit it in each other's faces.[219] During the pogrom in Drensteinfurt, Jews were also forced to ridicule Jewish rites.[220]

In other towns, Jews were deliberately locked into places reserved for cattle or abattoirs. In Aurich, 100 to 200 Jews were deprived of their liberty and mistreated in an agricultural hall. One had to shout, "I am a race defiler" ("*Ich bin ein Rasseschänder*"). Others were coerced to work on the drainage of a sports field while being harassed. Nosey bystanders observed as the humiliations continued. On their forced march to the court prison, the arrested Jews – 42 men – were forced to sing the German folk song: "*Muss i denn, muss i denn, zum Städtele hinaus*" while the mob accompanied them. In Leer, the arrested Jews from that town as well as Bunde and Weener were imprisoned overnight in the stockyard designated for small livestock; on November 11, 1938, they were carted off on a cattle truck to Oldenburg.[221] In Oldenburg, Jews were imprisoned in the horse market; reportedly they were also incarcerated under humiliating circumstances in toilets. Storm troopers then marched them via the destroyed synagogue to the prison; this parade was also photographed. A storm troop captain (*SA-Haupttrupp-*

---

218 Koblenz 3 Js 580/48 = 9 KLs 7/49, LHA Koblenz, Best. 584, 1, Nr. 1239-1245.
219 Landau 7 Js 44/47 = Ks 3/50, AOFAA, AJ 3676, p. 36 and AJ 3676, p. 37.
220 Münster 6 Js 726/47 = 6 KLs 36/48.
221 Aurich 2 Js 75/48 = 2 KLs 2/51, StA Aurich, Rep. 109 Nds. E Nr. 310/1-4.

führer) shouted: "Look at the criminals! Beat them to death!" Female bystanders shouted: "Behead them!"[222] In Norden the Jews were taken to the abattoir where they were to be the first to be butchered according to kosher tradition. The Jews were corralled into stockyards; they had to put their faces into pig feces while they were hit with batons and electric cattle prods.[223] In the evening of November 10, 1938, the Jewish teacher Klein in Norden was forced to set fire to the pile of ritual objects heaped up in the destroyed synagogue.[224]

Apart from the destruction of religious symbols embodying Judaism, the erasure of commemorations of Jewish military honors was a recurring theme. In Memmingen, the marble plaque bearing the names of Jewish soldiers killed in action during the World War I was smashed to smithereens by the *NSDAP-Kreisamtsleiter* (county office commander).[225] A Jewish veteran commented on the pogrom in Kirn: "For this Germany I was a soldier in the war for four years."[226]

A further element in degradation was the parading of Jews in insufficient clothing in public, sometimes combined with a sadistic sexual component. A deputy commander of the Nazi *Frauenschaft* (women's association) in Düsseldorf, wanting to further shame a Jewish man named Cohen, who was more than 70 years old and had been driven from his flat, lifted up the only garment he had on – a shirt – exposing him to a gawking mob.[227] In Idar, a 70-year-old Jew named Neuhäuser had to stand naked in front of his tormentors who hit his genitals with a stick and then went on insulting and mistreating him.[228] In Witten it was a Jewish married couple that had to strip naked to be hit and chased through a moat.[229] In Diepholz the 86-year-old Jewish butcher Carl Samenfeld – who at the time was bedridden – was torn out of his bed and lodgings and pulled on a handcart to the local courthouse. He was only wearing a nightcap, a shirt and underpants.[230] In Meppen an old Jewish woman was arrested in her nightgown and had to walk through the streets in this attire.[231]

In other places, Jews were stigmatized and marked by cropping of their hair: A Jewish woman who protested against the arson of the synagogue in Osthofen

---

222 Oldenburg 9 Js 4/49 = 9 Ks 14/50, StA Oldenburg, Best. 140-4 Acc. 13/79, Nr. 205.
223 Aurich 2 Js 862/45 = 2 Ks 7/50, StA Aurich, Rep. 109 Nds. E Nr. 341/1-12.
224 Aurich 2 Js 156/48 = 2 Ks 8/48, StA Aurich, Rep. 109 Nds. E Nr. 338/1-6.
225 Memmingen Js 2881ff/46 = KLs 14/48, StA Augsburg.
226 Koblenz 9 Js 49/49 = Bad Kreuznach 2 KLs 41/50, AOFAA, AJ 1616, p. 805.
227 Düsseldorf 8 Js 144/46, HStA Düsseldorf – ZA Kalkum, Gerichte Rep. 268/14.
228 Koblenz 9/2 Js 147/48 = Bad Kreuznach 3 Ks 6/50, LHA Koblenz, Best. 584, 6, Nr. 4-13.
229 Bochum 2 Js 581/48 = 2 KLs 60/48 = 2 Ks 18/49.
230 Verden 6 Js 305/47 = 6 KLs 21/47, StA Stade Rep. 171a Verden, Nr. 589 (I-III).
231 Osnabrück 4 Js 22/48 = 4 Ks 8/49, 4 Ks 9/49, StA Osnabrück, Rep 945 Akz. 6/1983, Nr. 114-128.

was shorn.²³² In Fürth, several hundred male Jews were imprisoned in a former concert hall called Berolzheimerianum. A storm trooper cut one Jewish man's hair with nail clippers while remarking, "Now your communist curls are coming off!"²³³ Other remarks point to sexual envy due to the alleged success with the opposite sex. A storm trooper and member of the SA Headquarters 24 in Fürth asked an arrested Jew: "Don't you know me any more, you know what's up. This [flirting] with Christian girls in the Bayer pub will stop now." Then he hit him in the face and kicked him as he fell.²³⁴

Women were treated with particular brutality. In Wusterhausen (East Germany), a Jewish woman was tarred and feathered; a doctor had to administer to her in prison where the life-threatening tar was removed.²³⁵ In Niederwerrn a woman was raped.²³⁶ Certain remarks hint at further possible acts of violence: A staff sergeant of the Motor Corps (*Nationalsozialistisches Kraftfahrkorps*) who had entered the lodgings of Jews in Bad Kreuznach, Freilaubersheim and Fürfeld remarked that one Jewish woman had lain down on the floor and spread her legs in order to prevent the demolition of her home.²³⁷

In part, the cultural debasement was driven by the hunt for trophies. Unlike damaged property, the trophies had small or non-existent material value. Trophies were meant to hurt the victim personally. One of the most frequently sought objects of anti-Semitic trophy hunters were photographs that showed the victims being humiliated, bedecked with shaming placards or in embarrassing poses, or that depicted destroyed synagogues or other buildings. As the taking of photographs was not yet a common (or inexpensive) affair, perpetrators had to go to some lengths to document their deeds. In Rülzheim, the owner of a cinema was summoned by the SS to take photographs. As he was considered politically unreliable by the local Nazi Party head, his camera was sequestered afterwards in order to control the spread of the photographs.²³⁸ In Vallendar, Jewish men were attending a prayer service when members of the Nazi Party Koblenz (*NSDAP-Gauleitung* Koblenz) appeared and forced them to stand at the wall of the synagogue with their prayer shawls and ridicule the Jewish prayer rites. A civil servant (*Regierungsoberinspektor*) and Nazi Party functionary (*NSDAP-Organisationsleiter*) took photographs of the event, though the photographs were consid-

---

232 Mainz 3 Js 815/47 = 3 KLs 92/48.
233 Nürnberg-Fürth 1a Js 2153/47 = 1115 KLs 297/49, StA Nürnberg, StAnw Nürnberg 2596/I-V.
234 Nürnberg-Fürth 1a Js 2153/47 = 1115 KLs 297/49, StA Nürnberg, StAnw Nürnberg 2596/I-V.
235 Neuruppin, Zweigstelle Brandenburg 2 Js 614/45 Wu = 2 Ks 1/46, BStU, Pdm ASt StKs 29/48; see also Neuruppin, Zweigstelle Brandenburg Aufs. 580/48 = StKs 4/49, BStU, Pdm ASt St AR 2/49.
236 Schweinfurt 4 Js 2963/47 = KLs 70/49.
237 Koblenz 9 Js 293/49 = Bad Kreuznach 2 KLs 11/50, LHA Koblenz, Best. 584, 6, Nr. 106.
238 Landau 7 Js 38/48 = AG Landau Ls 40/50, AOFAA, AJ 3676, p. 36.

ered botched.[239] Pews, chairs and carpets were destroyed, chandeliers, altar and *Mikvah* (ritual bath) demolished in the presence of the assembled Jewish population. The Jews were then taken by cattle car to Koblenz; in their absence the synagogue was burned down on the night of November 12-13, 1938.[240] In Quakenbrück, two Jews were photographed during their arrest; the three or four images were given away as presents (the son of the mayor of Alfhausen received a copy as a present during a drinking binge with a storm trooper).[241] In Koblenz, a Jew named Süssmann was photographed in his nightgown during the pogrom. The next day, Friday, November 11, 1938, the "Nationalblatt" (the Nazi Party press organ in Koblenz) vilified him with a set of three further photographs that allegedly showed groceries he had hoarded (60 eggs, 14 pound butter, uncounted pounds of flour and sugar, as well as olives and palm oil). The "Nationalblatt" did not let the opportunity pass without the critizism that there were still businessmen who sold groceries to Jews in large quantities.[242]

Similarly, perpetrators had their own photographs taken after the "work" was done: When the devastations of Jewish houses in Hönningen were completed, the perpetrators went to a pub and had a photograph taken with rolled-up sleeves.[243] On the other hand, photographs of Jews in Jewish private homes were often torn or befouled even if the victims explicitly asked to spare photos of already emigrated family members; it is also well known that Jewish-owned photography shops were destroyed and cameras, binoculars and other optical instruments stolen.[244]

In Berge the flat of Albert Neublum was raided; photographs, a letter and an account book were confiscated and exhibited "for propaganda purposes" during a public party meeting in an inn.[245] In Wilhelmshaven, objects allegedly taken from the synagogue were exhibited in the street for further scrutiny One picture particularly struck a newspaper journalist as he reported on the occasion: the biblical David's "cowardly" "Jewish slaying" of the giant Goliath.[246] Breaking from Christian tradition, the Nazis portrayed David as a cowardly killer.

---

239 Koblenz 9 Js 11/49 = 9 KLs 13/50; 9 KLs 14/50, LHA Koblenz, Best. 584, 1, Nr. 1329; 1285-1288.
240 Ibid.
241 Osnabrück 4 Js 252/49, StA Osnabrück, Rep 945 Akz. 6/1983, Nr. 445.
242 Koblenz 9/5 Js 411/47 = 9 KLs 8/51, LHA Koblenz, Best. 584, 1, Nr. 1300-1303; 1332.
243 Koblenz 9/3 Js 191/47 = 9 KLs 16/50, LHA Koblenz, Best. 584, 1, Nr. 1337.
244 Mannheim 1a Js 3886/48 = 1 KLs 38/48; Mannheim 1a Js 400/48 = 1 KLs 26/48; Detmold 1 Js 1425/46 .
245 Osnabrück 4 Js 2474/46 = 4 KLs 8/48 StA Osnabrück, Rep 945 Nr. 94.
246 "Wilhelmshavens Synagoge brannte nieder. Spontane antijüdische Kundgebungen in unserer Kriegsmarinewerft – Juden wurden in Schutzhaft genommen – Erregte Demonstrationen vor den Judengeschäften," *Wilhelmshavener Zeitung*, November 11, 1938.

In Bad Kreuznach, perpetrators cut off the beard of Rabbi Dr. Alfred Jacobs; the Nazi Party head of Bad Kreuznach displayed the black beard – which was kept in an envelope bearing the address of the Jewish Community of Bad Kreuznach – while announcing: "This is the first trophy we acquired this morning" or "We made a good catch today; this is the rabbi's beard we cut off."[247] The cutting of the rabbi's beard was accredited to several people, one of them an auxiliary policeman nicknamed *"Judenschreck"* (Jew scarer)[248] and another, a storm troop lieutenant (*SA-Oberscharführer*).[249] In Bad Ems the local rabbi allegedly also suffered the loss of his beard.[250]

Five days before the pogrom, after a drinking binge, the drunken offenders broke into the local synagogue through a window in search of a statue of Moses which was allegedly located there. Unsurprisingly, due to the ban in the Hebrew Bible on depictions of humans no such sculpture was found. The intruders thus stole a pillow with honorary decorations and ridiculed it until the police confiscated it. Ritual objects from the synagogue, which was first damaged and later burned down, were used in a mocking parade. When in summer 1939 the local Nazi Party leader took the metal items from the synagogue to Andernach to be sold as scrap, he mockingly affixed the Star of David from the synagogue to his truck.[251] Stars of David on synagogues always attracted particular attention because of their symbolic character. At the instigation of the mayor of Königstein, a member of the fire brigade who had a reputation as a daredevil picked the Star of David off the roof of the synagogue.[252] At the risk of his life, a teenager climbed the dome of the synagogue in Mainz and removed the Star of David with a metal saw. He tore away the star to the applause of a jeering crowd. The star was later taken by the SS to the rooms of the *SS-Standarte*.[253] During the arson of the morgue at the Jewish cemetery in Osternburg,[254] as well as during the devastation of the mortuary in Niederbieber,[255] the Star of David was removed from the roof.

In Wallau, ritual objects were loaded onto the hearse belonging to the Jewish community and carted through the town before being burned on the sports field.[256] In Dromersheim, the furniture from the synagogue was heaped on a

---

247 Bad Kreuznach 2 Js 232/50 = 2 KLs 4/51, LHA Koblenz, Best. 584, 6, Nr. 58-60.
248 Koblenz 9/2 Js 285/48 = 9 KLs 21/49, LHA Koblenz, Best. 584, 1, Nr. 1232.
249 Koblenz 9 Js 41/49 = 9 KLs 32/49, LHA Koblenz, Best. 584, 6, Nr. 18.
250 Koblenz 9/5 Js 103/46 = 9 KLs 24/50, LHA Koblenz, Best. 584, 1, Nr. 1318-1327; 1328.
251 Koblenz 9/2 Js 350/48 = 9 KLs 37/49, LHA Koblenz, Best. 584, 1, Nr. 1108.
252 Wiesbaden 4 Js 391/45 = 4 KLs 22/49, HStA Wiesbaden, Abt. 468, Nr. 265/1-7.
253 Mainz 3 Js 1157/47, AOFAA, AJ 1616, p. 802.
254 Oldenburg 10 Js 1420/48, StA Oldenburg, Best. 140-5, Nr. 329.
255 Koblenz 9/3 Js 300/47 = 9 Ks 10/50, LHA Koblenz, Best. 584, 1, Nr. 1078-1080; Nr. 1084.
256 Wiesbaden 4 Js 2440/48 = 4 KLs 17/49, HStA Wiesbaden, Abt. 468, Nr. 263.

hand truck and burned in a field.²⁵⁷ In Hof a municipal car and two company cars were decorated with ritual objects from the synagogue and driven through town as a parade – accompanied by music and some 70 to 90 SS-men. The objects were burned near the river Saale while the SS held hands and sang an SS chant (*"SS-Treuelied"*).²⁵⁸ In Haren, storm troopers from the Emsland camps paraded through town with a Star of David and sang anti-Semitic songs.²⁵⁹

A certain perverse curiosity drove a Nazi Party functionary (*NSDAP-Blockleiter*) to return at night to the still smouldering synagogue in Solingen, where he and a storm trooper (*SA-Mann*) rummaged through the ashes and rubble in search of a "Talmud," as both of them had heard a lot about the book.²⁶⁰ The NSDAP propaganda functionary of Bentheim took a "Talmud" in German as he intended to read it, but instead delivered it promptly to the *Grenzpolizeikommissariat* (border police) Bentheim.²⁶¹

In Kastellaun, workers from a nearby emergency camp Roth took garments and prayer books from the synagogue and brought them to the pub.²⁶² A storm trooper in Gruiten took prayer books and said disparagingly: "This trashy literature we want to take with us."²⁶³ After the demolition of the synagogue of Rülzheim by perpetrators from Landau, local townspeople stood several hours in front of the synagogue to satisfy their curiosity as they had never observed the interior of a synagogue.²⁶⁴

An SA sergeant major took bread for the Sabbath celebration from the kitchen of rabbi Martin of Hassloch.²⁶⁵ Another man was said to have taken an altar cloth from the synagogue of Windecken as well as a book in Hebrew type. The man admitted to having visited the synagogue out of curiosity but denied the theft as the items had held no value for him.²⁶⁶ A storm trooper in Konz cited his quenchless curiosity when entering the Jewish house of prayer during the pogrom.²⁶⁷ In Krumbach, the perpetrators stole tefilin, parchment scrolls, and a mezuza.²⁶⁸ During the pogrom in Andernach, a storm trooper retrieved the wooden tablets

---

257 Mainz 3 Js 52/47 = 3 KLs 70/48, AOFAA, AJ 1616, p. 802.
258 Hof Js 3321/48 = KLs 4/51, StA Bamberg, Rep. K 107, Abg. 1987, Nr. 749.
259 Osnabrück 4 Js 22/48 = 4 Ks 8/49, 4 Ks 9/49, StA Osnabrück, Rep 945 Akz. 6/1983 Nr. 114-128.
260 Wuppertal 5 Js 954/47 = 5 KLs 22/48, HStA Düsseldorf – ZA Kalkum, Gerichte Rep. 191/62.
261 Osnabrück 4 Js 344/46 = 4 Ks 15/49, StA Osnabrück, Rep 945 Akz. 6/1983, Nr. 106-108.
262 Koblenz 9/2 Js 531/47 = 9 KLs 10/51, LHA Koblenz, Best. 584, 1, Nr. 1334.
263 Wuppertal 5 Js 224/46 = 5 KLs 3/48, HStA Düsseldorf – ZA Kalkum, Gerichte Rep. 191/28-30.
264 Landau 7 Js 49/46 = KLs 55/48, AOFAA, AJ 3676, p. 38.
265 Frankenthal 9 Js 235/49 = 9 Ks 5/50; AOFAA, AJ 3676, p. 38.
266 Hanau 3 Js 689/47, HStA Wiesbaden, Abt. 471, Nr. 19.
267 Trier 3 Js 403/47 = 3 KLs 43/48, AOFAA, AJ 1616, p. 802.
268 Memmingen Js 12142/47 = KLs 74/47, StA Augsburg.

with the Ten Commandments from the ruins of the burned-down synagogue. A couple of weeks later, he invited an SA Troop Administrator to inspect the boards with the Decalogue. Later he kept the boards behind his bathtub, from whence they eventually got "lost."[269] The local Nazi Party leader of Osnabrück kept a menorah hidden in a cupboard in the air raidshelter.[270] In Mühringen the whole air raid shelter was outfitted with pews from the synagogue.[271] Others took interest in the material value of the objects: After the war, four Torah Scrolls were discovered in a dairy in Vettweiss – the silver shields, however, had been removed.[272]

Part of the public degradation was the mocking of Jewish rites in synagogues and in the streets. In Germany, this was and remains an offense known as *religionsbeschimpfender Unfug* (disrespect for religious tradition). In St. Goar, teenagers vested themselves with prayer shawls from the house of God and roamed the streets.[273] During the excesses in Euskirchen, an offender fitted himself out with a prayer robe and jumped around the synagogue in an attempt to imitate a "temple dance."[274] (The wording – taken from the post-war sentencing – shows how preciously little German courts knew of genuine Jewish rituals.) A storm trooper in Quakenbrück ridiculed the Jewish religion by adorning himself with a rabbi's gown and hat, taking a Torah Scroll into his hand and attempting to imitate Jewish worship rituals in front of the open window for the amusement of the crowd outdoors.[275]

In Hamburg-Harburg, indicted storm trooper Willy S. took a black gown and a "hymn-book" in order to imitate a rabbi, later describing it as a sort of carnival joke.[276]

Luise D., who lived opposite the synagogue in Oberlustadt, helped the perpetrators by handing them an axe with which they could break down the synagogue door. She was given several Torah Scrolls to carry outside, where she chucked them into the fire. She then adorned herself with a rabbi's prayer scarf, performed mocking gestures, and burned it, too, along with the *Ark* (ritual cabinet) of the Torah shrine.[277] A civil servant from the rural district office Saarburg, who

---

269 Koblenz 9/2 Js 1100/47 = 9 Ks 9/50, LHA Koblenz, Best. 584, 1, Nr. 1296-1298; 1336 (quote from first sentence, 1950).
270 Osnabrück 4 Js 1045/48 = 4 Ks 14/49, StA Osnabrück, Rep 945 Akz. 6/1983 Nr. 553.
271 Rottweil Js 4834/46, StA Sigmaringen, Wü 29/2 T 4, Nr. 573.
272 Aachen 9 Js 768/49 = 9 KLs 3/53, HStA Düsseldorf – ZA Kalkum, Gerichte Rep. 89/227.
273 Koblenz 9/3 Js 1861/48 = 9 KLs 15/49, LHA Koblenz, Best. 584, 1, Nr. 1827.
274 Bonn 7 Js 1137/47 = 7 KLs 12/47, HStA Düsseldorf – ZA Kalkum, Gerichte Rep. 195/333-334.
275 Osnabrück 4 Js 1628/47 = 4 KLs 4/48; StA Osnabrück, Rep 945 Akz. 6/1983, Nr. 65-70.
276 Quoted from Egon Giordano: "Hamburger Synagogenschänder-Prozessss. NSDAP sorgte für die 'Bestrafung' der Synagogenschänder," *Jüdisches Gemeindeblatt*, April 8, 1949.
277 Landau 7 Js 81/46 = KLs 60/47, AOFAA, AJ 3676, p. 38.

in keeping with his official duties had received the key to the local synagogue, opened it for the Gestapo from Saarburg, which initiated the destruction. He himself entered the building and blew the ritual *shofar* (ram's horn).[278] In Hemmerden the *yad* (ritual pointer used for the reading of the Torah) was thrown on the floor.[279] In Kempen a storm trooper, who in civil life was a member of the local employment office, stole a silver-pointed yad from the synagogue and roamed the streets, while children romped around him, boasting of his participation in the demolition and arson of the synagogue. He then proceeded to smash the shop window of the Jewish butcher Winter and a lamp in the lodgings of Sally Rath. He went to two other Jewish flats, stealing an offertory box decorated with a Star of David from one of them. He would show the box around afterwards, claiming that because it bore the "Soviet star," it had served to collect monies for the Soviets. The *yad* he kept for a few more days on his desk at the employment center.[280]

The perpetrators placed their deeds in a plethora of references and contexts. A participant in the pogrom in Oestrich who – with others – had pilfered the house of the wine trader Rosenthal, became completely drunk and threw flour and eggs out of the window shouting "Attention! Here comes German flour!" and "Look out for the German eggs!" He toasted himself by shouting "Drink German wine."[281] An SA squad leader cut the duvets of the Hirschberger family in Rüdesheim and threw the feathers out the window, referring to the Grimm's fairytale as he screamed "Mother Holle is shaking her feathers out!"[282] Religiously motivated anti-Judaism is evident in the words of a man who told a Jewish woman in Rüdesheim, "You nailed our savior to the cross, this is our revenge."[283] An SS man took a Hebrew Bible in his hand and uttered mockingly "The Lord saw the deeds of his son and said that it is well done."[284] In Ulm, the local Jews were – in a sort of perverted baptism – forced to get into an empty fountain trough.[285] The deeds of the Nazi Party functionary from Weisweiler were clearly those of one well-acquainted with Christian rites and liturgy (he had been sexton in the church of St. Anna in Düren until 1937). He forced a 70-year-old Jew named Leyens to carry a short piece of wood (from the ruins of the prayer room) on his shoulders.

---

278 Trier 3 Js 449/47 = 3 KLs 17/48, LHA Koblenz, Best. 584, 2, Nr. 752-754.
279 Mönchengladbach 6 Js 2085/46 = 6 KLs 4/48; HStA Düsseldorf – ZA Kalkum, Gerichte Rep. 10/201; 204; 205.
280 Krefeld 6 Js 136/47 = 6 KLs 3/48, HStA Düsseldorf – ZA Kalkum, Gerichte Rep. 8/72-75.
281 Wiesbaden 4 Js 2393/46 = 4 KLs 9/49, HStA Wiesbaden, Abt. 468, Nr. 262/1-5.
282 Wiesbaden 4 Js 417/46 = 4 KLs 25/48, HStA Wiesbaden, Abt. 468, Nr. 258/1-8.
283 Ibid.
284 Mönchengladbach 6 Js 912/46 = 6 KLs 4/51, HStA Düsseldorf – ZA Kalkum, Gerichte Rep. 72/25-28.
285 Ulm 5 Js 6192-95/46 = KLs 4/46; Ulm 4 Js 463-97/50; Ulm 7 Js 16375/58.

He also spit into Leyens's face. Leyens had to carry the beam on his shoulders and walk to the market place where other objects from the prayer room such as pews, chairs, and prayer books were already being burned. From the spitting to the carrying of the beam, the march through town and the following auto-da-fe, the episode reads like a mix between Christ's Passion and a foray through medieval Christian persecutions of heretics and Jews.[286]

Others were content with symbolic liquidations. As objects from the synagogue of Hagenbach were being burned, a man stood on the steps of the synagogue and announced: "Now we are burning the Jew." Then he kicked a rabbi's head covering into the fire and chucked a prayer book into the flames as in the– probably Hebrew–book "everything was written backwards."[287]

In Nuremberg, storm troopers beheaded display dummies in several Jewish textile stores.[288]

Deportations in the Course of the Pogrom

As is known, perpetrators threatened the enforced removal of Jews. A storm trooper in Kappeln said to a family upon entering their house: "Open up, you swine hounds, you are supposed to be sent on your way" or: "Open the door, your game is over; your train is at five o'clock."[289] During the pogrom, about 26,000 Jews were arrested across the whole Reich and subsequently taken to the concentration camps in Buchenwald, Dachau and Sachsenhausen.

Furthermore, in some places advanced deportations not only affected adult Jewish men, but also women, children, and the elderly. This is particularly notable in the NSDAP Saar-Palatinate region (later named Westmark).

On November 11, 1938, the newspaper *Pfälzer Anzeiger* clamored loudly that the deportations were the right decision.[290] In Speyer, Jewish women and their non-Jewish partners were forced – allegedly on higher orders from the Reich Security Main Office (RSHA) – to leave the town and district on November 10, 1938.[291] The next day, in Ingenheim and Heuchelheim, Jewish women and men were brought by bus to Landau train station, were taken to the right banks of the

---

286 Aachen 9 Js 321/49 = 9 Ks 1/50, HStA Düsseldorf – ZA Kalkum, Gerichte Rep. 89/143-144.
287 Landau 7 Js 15/47 = AG Landau Ls 36/50, AOFAA, AJ 3676, p. 38.
288 Nürnberg-Fürth 2 Js 681/46 = 70 KLs 271/47, StA Nürnberg, StAnw Nürnberg 2033a.
289 Flensburg 2a Js 93/48 = 2a KLs 9/48, LA Schleswig-Holstein, Abt. 354 Flensburg; Nr. 965.
290 Article contained in Landau 7 Js 21/47 = KLs 42/48, AOFAA, AJ 3676, p. 37.
291 Frankenthal 9 Js 53/49 = 9 KLs 17/50, AOFAA, AJ 3676, p. 37.

Rhine and not allowed to return for a week.[292] In Göllheim, 21 Jews were arrested during the pogrom and taken to Kirchheimbolanden; the mayor tried to scare the others away by threatening them and urging them to leave by the next morning at latest. One Jewish man was so frightened by this eruption of threats that he fled to Mannheim and hid for six weeks.[293] Those Jews of Schwegenheim who had not been arrested were told that they had to leave. They were first brought to Lingenfeld, then to Karlsruhe, and were allowed to return only after four weeks.[294] In Pirmasens, the Jews were arrested and had to hand in valuables and money. Older Jews were then dismissed, while the younger ones were taken by bus to the French border near Hilst and compelled under threat of violence to cross the French border. The French police brought them back to Schweix; from there they had to walk to Pirmasens, only to be incarcerated again and forced to forfeit their possessions.[295] In Landau, the families of arrested Jews were requested by the SS to appear at the railway station. Those who showed up on time were forced to board a train; those who turned up later were subjected to strip searches and luggage searches. Victims were stripped of money, jewelry, valuables, and documents.[296]

In Hochspeyer, 70-year-old Jewish Mrs. Rubel was abducted to Mannheim. She had returned to her former home in Hochspeyer on November 11, 1938, as the Jewish community's old age home in Neustadt an der Haardt had been burned down during the pogrom. The mayor and local Nazi Party head inquired of the district Nazi Party what should be done with her. He was told that the NSDAP regional commander had ordered the Saar-Palatinate to be made *judenfrei* by midnight. The local Nazi Party leader and his deputy decided to take Mrs. Rubel by car from Hochspeyer to Mannheim (in the adjacent Gau Baden) where Mrs. Rubel had relatives. They reached Mannheim at around 10 o'clock in the evening, dumped the elderly woman with a policeman whom she was to ask for directions to her relatives' home. As a "farewell" the mayor and Nazi Party head told Mrs. Rubel that she was never to return to Hochspeyer. They then left her to her own devices.[297] Thus, certain cases seem to anticipate the nationwide deportations as early as autumn 1941.

---

292 Landau 7 Js 21/47 = KLs 42/48, AOFAA, AJ 3676, p. 37.
293 Kaiserslautern 7 Js 151/49, AOFAA, AJ 3676, p. 37.
294 Landau 7 Js 43/46 = KLs 49/48, AOFAA, AJ 3676, p. 38.
295 Zweibrücken 7 Js 107/49 = KLs 1/50, AOFAA, AJ 3676, p. 36.
296 Landau 7 Js 44/47 = Ks 3/50, AOFAA, AJ 3676, p. 36 and AJ 3676, p. 37.
297 Kaiserslautern 7 Js 107/47 = KLs 22/48, AOFAA, AJ 3676, p. 37.

Perpetrators

Alien or local culprits?

A major question for those researching into the pogrom is obvious: Who were the perpetrators? Starting in the Third Reich, but even more so in the post-war years, excesses were blamed on perpetrators from "outside." According to post-war testimonies, offenders preferred to come at night in cars or lorries, with blackened faces and in scruffy old clothes, often already equipped with weapons, tools, petrol or fire accelerants, thus rendering the local (oh-so peace-loving) inhabitants powerless against the crimes. A typical indictment (by the state attorney of Bonn) read "The perpetrators were without exception nonlocals who were fetched with cars while only very few locals participated."[298] Similarly, a state prosecutor stated that "As experience teaches, with all so-called Jew actions the main protagonists were non-local persons. This holds true also in Hessloch."[299]

Non-local perpetrators do in fact appear in many post-war investigations. Excesses in Kirchheim/Eck were blamed on rabble from Frankenthal.[300] In Alsenz, Reich Labor Service (RAD) men from Bad Münster had come on a truck to participate in the pogrom.[301] Frequently in southwest Germany, workers contracted to build the Westwall (Siegfried Line) were incriminated, i.e. in Nalbach and Diefflen,[302] in Neumagen,[303] Ettlingen,[304] in Konz,[305] in Rülzheim,[306] or Bergzabern.[307] Nazi Party functionaries and party organizations such as storm troopers or SS were natural suspects. The pogrom in Geroda was apparently the work of SS members from the Wildflecken military training ground.[308] The destruction of the Jewish prayer house in Bentheim was blamed on members of the Grenzpolizeikommissariat Bentheim, consisting of younger SS men from southern Germany or Austria who were stationed only briefly in the North of Germany.[309] The excesses in Rheinbischofsheim were allegedly committed by the Austrian

---

298 Bonn 3 Js 1015/47 = 3 Ks 2/49, HStA Düsseldorf – ZA Kalkum, Gerichte Rep. 145/471.
299 Mainz 3 Js 2607/46 = 3 KLs 97/48, AOFAA, AJ 1616, p. 802.
300 Frankenthal 9 Js 227/47, AOFAA, AJ 3676, p. 37.
301 Kaiserslautern 7 Js 18/49 = KLs 75/49, AOFAA, AJ 3676, p. 37.
302 Saarbrücken 11 Js 239/48 = 11 KLs 4/51.
303 Trier 3 Js 253/47 = 3 KLs 5/48, LHA Koblenz, Best. 584, 2, Nr. 741-744.
304 Karlsruhe 1 Js 88/46 = 1 KLs 19/46.
305 Trier 3 Js 403/47 = 3 KLs 43/48, AOFAA, AJ 1616, p. 802.
306 Landau 7 Js 38/48 = AG Landau Ls 40/50 AOFAA, AJ 3676, p. 36.
307 Landau 7 Js 4/46 = KLs 18/49, AOFAA, AJ 3676, p. 37; AJ 3676, p. 36.
308 Würzburg Js 1760/46 = KLs 70/48.
309 Osnabrück 4 Js 344/46 = 4 Ks 15/49, StA Osnabrück, Rep 945 Akz. 6/1983 Nr. 106-108.

members of the border patrol in Kehl.[310] The lodgings of the four or five Jewish families in Offenbach am Glan fell victim to members of the storm troopers or SS from Kusel.[311] The pogrom in Oberbieber was planned by the head of the district Nazi Party in Neuwied, who also organized transport in trucks.[312] In Fellheim, the devastation of the local synagogue was blamed on a group of trainee cheese makers from neighboring Boos who arrived at night on bicycles and in cars.[313]

Sure enough, Nazi Party members and storm troopers instigated non-local perpetrators who had fewer inhibitions when it came to attacking victims who were unknown to them. However, we should not underestimate the local participation and sometimes even local initiation of the pogrom. In Osann, a gang of storm troopers and Nazi officials from Wittlich had driven Jews from their lodgings, devastated houses, furnishings, and the synagogue. The local storm troopers felt compelled to join in and continue the destruction.[314]

In some places, it was the workforce of local enterprises or employees of authorities who became engulfed in the pogrom. The workforce of the local Mauserwerke – together with storm troopers – destroyed the house and shoe store of Josef Eppstein in Oberndorf.[315] The head of the employment center in Münsingen and a member of the district office put the torch to the synagogue in Buttenhausen.[316] In Offenbach am Glan, the head of the tax office released employees from work early in order to allow their participation in the pogrom.[317] When the SS Colonel Trier looked for compliant participants, they recruited members of the tax office in Bitburg (as an SS troup commander was director of the tax office).[318] In Vallendar it was the municipality that had been invited by the NSDAP regional headquarters in Koblenz to rummage through the houses of the Jewish residents and arrest them.[319] The main culprits in the arson of the Kobern synagogue were administrative employees of the mayor's office in Winningen who had come on their bikes to Kobern. The order for the arson came from the mayor of Winningen himself.[320] When the synagogue of Tübingen was burned down, both a member of the local medical insurance plan (Allgemeine Ortskrankenkasse) and a janitor of

---

310 Offenburg 2 Js 824/47 = 2 Ks 2/48.
311 Koblenz 9 Js 277/49 = Bad Kreuznach 3 KLs 2/51, LHA Koblenz, Best. 584, 6, Nr. 56.
312 Koblenz 9/5 Js 1262/48 = 9 KLs 7/50, LHA Koblenz Best. 584, 1, Nr. 1282.
313 Memmingen Js 3406/46 = KLs 15/48, StA Augsburg.
314 Trier 5 Js 225/47 = 5 KLs 3/48; LHA Koblenz, Best. 584, 2, Nr. 882-884.
315 Rottweil 2 Js 1351-63/46; 4369-75/46 = KLs 32-38/48, StA Sigmaringen, Wü 29/2 T 1, Nr. 954.
316 Tübingen 1 Js 2468-76/46 = KLs 59/47; StA Sigmaringen, Wü 29/3 T 1, Nr. 1608.
317 Koblenz 9 Js 277/49 = Bad Kreuznach 3 KLs 2/51, LHA Koblenz, Best. 584, 6, Nr. 56.
318 Trier 5 Js 335/48 = 5 KLs 23/48; LHA Koblenz Best. 584, 2,, Nr. 901.
319 Koblenz 9 Js 11/49 = 9 KLs 13/50; 9 KLs 14/50, LHA Koblenz, Best. 584, 1, Nr. 1329; 1285-1288.
320 Koblenz 3 Js 1043/45 = 9/3 KLs 49/46, LHA Koblenz, Best. 584, 1, Nr. 3206-3209.

the town hall were involved.³²¹ In Kirn it was also the local municipal administration and workers from a local enterprise who had been requested via loudspeakers to come to the main square. One participant became involved after a colleague shouted: "Peter, come here, we are marching against the Jews. Those not joining in will be dismissed without notice."³²² In Emmerich, the tools for destruction were handed out from the tool reserve of the municipal building yard; the head of the public utility company apparently had called for participation in the pogrom.³²³ In Höhr-Grenzhausen, workers in the local pottery Dümler&Breiden ceased work after an appeal, assembled in the factory yard and marched into town while chanting anti-Semitic songs.³²⁴ The interior of the synagogue in Uerdingen was smashed by workers from the sugar factory Pfeifer&Langen in Krefeld, who had come equipped with hammers, chisels and hatchets.³²⁵ In Freudenberg a group of workers from another company demolished the interior of the synagogue.³²⁶ In Tirschenreuth it was the head of the local Nazi Party who urged members of the workers' council to join in the pogrom.³²⁷

Frequently, the "outsider" perpetrators needed local guidance in their destructive work: The local Nazi Party commanded lists of Jewish residents. In Baisingen apparently the local police forced Jewish residents to close their window shutters in order to make their homes identifiable to the brownshirts.³²⁸

In Nuremberg a party functionary (*NSDAP-Blockleiter*) who was responsible for overseeing Ostendstrasse 12–48, led nine or ten storm troopers to Ostendstrasse 46, where Jewish families were living. The storm troopers demolished furniture with hammers and axes. Then the party functionary pointed out another flat occupied by a Jewish family in Ostendstrasse 38. There was quite some leeway for action: The Nazi Party functionary did prevent the demolition of yet another flat by saying that there were no Jews living there, while in fact a Jewish woman who was married to a non-Jew lived there.³²⁹ In Relsberg it was the local Nazi Party head who led the demolition squad.³³⁰ In Winnweiler, a local storm trooper happened upon a posse of 20–25 storm troopers unknown to him; they asked him

---

321 Tübingen 1 Js 2987/46 = KLs 46/46, StA Sigmaringen, Wü 29/3 T 1, Nr. 1515.
322 Koblenz 9 Js 49/49 = Bad Kreuznach 2 KLs 41/50, AOFAA, AJ 1616, p. 805.
323 Kleve 5 Js 1102/48 = 5 Ks 1/50; 8 Ks 3/50, HStA Düsseldorf – ZA Kalkum, Gerichte Rep. 224/44-45.
324 Koblenz 9/3 Js 929/48 = 9 KLs 10/50, LHA Koblenz, Best. 584, 1, Nr. 1257.
325 Krefeld 1 Js 70/48 = 1 Ks 2/48 HStA Düsseldorf – ZA Kalkum, Gerichte Rep. 8/41-44.
326 Mosbach 1 Js 659/46 = KLs 8/46.
327 Weiden Js 948/46 = KLs 9/48, StA Nürnberg, GStA beim OLG Nürnberg 191.
328 Rottweil 1 Js 3805-3813/47, StA Sigmaringen, Wü 29/2 T4, Nr. 551.
329 Nürnberg 1c Js 2861/48 = KMs 33/48, StA Nürnberg, StAnw Nürnberg 2096a.
330 Kaiserslautern 7 Js 152/49 = KLs 15/50, AOFAA, AJ 3676, p. 37.

where Jews lived in the town. Instantly, he was ready to help and led them first to the house of the Jewish Ruben women, then to the store and lodgings of a Jewish woman named Allmann. There he threw eggs on Mrs. Allmann and snatched banknotes she had hidden under her shirt; he then mistreated her to the point that she became unconscious. The Rubens and Mrs. Allmann died a few years later in a concentration camp.[331] In Ichenhausen the SS Captain (*Hauptsturmführer*) and deputy NSDAP District Commander of Günzburg, Franz Haggenmiller, questioned a local Hitler Youth leader to learn the addresses of local Jews in order to arrest them. When the arrests were carried out, 60–80 local people assembled before the town hall; some in the mob hit the Jews with sticks and insulted the victims as *Saujuden* (pig-Jews). While mistreatment of the Jews continued in the town hall, the mob turned to the synagogue, which they devastated; a local NSDAP cell commander (*Zellenleiter*) stole ritual objects.[332] In Bausendorf it was a civil servant with the municipality who showed the houses of local Jews to an SS gang from Traben-Trarbach.[333] In Bengel, near Wittlich, it was also a low-level civil servant who led an SA Colonel (*Standartenführer*) to the Jewish homes.[334] In Oberlustadt it was Lydia K. who came equipped with a hatchet to break into the synagogue, which had been violated by perpetrators from outside the town. She continued with her destructive acts in the synagogue and then turned to the (already utterly wrecked) home of Salomon Frank, hitting Frank with a club.[335] A functionary of the German Labor Front (*DAF-Zellenwart*) in Koblenz, who lived at Kaiser-Friedrich-Strasse 53, was observed demolishing the dwellings of three Jews living in the same house.[336] The couple R. lived in the same house on Lingenerstrasse in Meppen with Ludwig Alexander. When they saw a gang of storm troopers prowling about, they called out, that there was yet another Jew to turn the storm troopers' attention to Mr. Alexander.[337] In Nuremberg it was the janitor of Herbartstrasse 44 who prompted six uniformed storm troopers to arrest August Mainzer. (The storm troopers did not comply with the wish).[338] Two brothers who were storm troopers inhabited a flat in Ammannstrasse 7 in Nuremberg, which did not inhibit their violence when it came to their neighbors. They forced their way into the flat of the Jewish family Alexander in the same house and demolished objects. They were joined by another perpetrator from the neighborhood,

---

[331] Kaiserslautern 7 Js 149/48 = KLs 34/49 AOFAA, AJ 3676, p. 38.
[332] Memmingen Js 2826ff/46 = KLs 61/47, StA Augsburg.
[333] Trier 5 Js 253/47 = 5 KLs 6/48; LHA Koblenz, Best. 584, 2, Nr. 534.
[334] Trier 5 Js 373/49, AOFAA, AJ 1616, p. 805.
[335] Landau 7 Js 81/46 = KLs 60/47, AOFAA, AJ 3676, p. 38.
[336] Koblenz 9/5 Js 411/47 = 9 KLs 8/51, LHA Koblenz, Best. 584, 1, Nr. 1300-1303, 1332.
[337] Osnabrück 4 Js 22/48 = 4 Ks 8/49, 4 Ks 9/49 StA Osnabrück, Rep 945 Akz. 6/1983, Nr. 114-128.
[338] Nürnberg-Fürth 2f Js 2007/48 = KMs 30/48, StA Nürnberg, StAnw Nürnberg 2091.

living in Ammannstrasse 14. When they were finished with the Alexanders, they went to terrorize a Jewish widow named Welsch in Ammannstrasse 9.[339] Willy Feingold, living in Schonerstrasse 8 in Nuremberg, who would die in the Sachsenhausen Concentration Camp in 1942, recognized one of the perpetrators who insulted and mistreated him and wrecked his flat as a neighbor.[340]

An SA senior troop commander (*Obertruppführer*) in Nuremberg had been given a wedding present by the Lamel family – this, however, would not stop him from heading a group of about eight drunken men to assault the both the bedridden Karl Lamel and his son in their home and wreck the whole flat at half past three in the morning.[341]

In Lichtenfels, Frau Pauson recognized one of the perpetrators and called out: "Herr [...], you are also taking part? Herr Neighbor, leave us alone!" to which he replied: "Keep your trap shut, old Jewish sow, we will batter you to death."[342] In Schnaittach, when Emma Ullmann was arrested, she said to a storm trooper: "Hans, leave me alone. I was your classmate." To which he retorted: "Just you wait, you Jewish slut, I will show you a real classmate."[343] A cattle trader and storm trooper who was participating in the arrest of his former school buddy Hermann Wolff in Geistingen near Hennef justified his action by stressing that it was precisely his friendly feelings for Wolff prompted him to the action, as he wanted to to render him a good service and assist him. The more credible reasoning followed: There had been disciplinary proceedings before the party tribunal (*Gaugericht*) against the storm trooper, which had motivated him to prove his worth by participating in the pogrom.[344]

When Mr. Metzler in Sobernheim was confronted by a storm trooper who wrecked his lodgings, he was so shocked that he asked: "Herr Studienrat, what have we done to you?"[345] In Hoya, a storm trooper and teacher in Schwarme asked explicitly to carry out the arrest of a particular Jew because he knew him quite well.[346] In Nuremberg the non-Jewish doctor Christian Potzler tried to find help as his Jewish wife was chased barefoot in her nightgown through the streets. He

---

[339] Nürnberg-Fürth 1c Js 2341/48 = KLs 279/48, StA Nürnberg, StAnw Nürnberg 2291.
[340] Nürnberg-Fürth 2c Js 1722-23/48 = 155 KLs 255/48, StA Nürnberg, StAnw Nürnberg 2268a.
[341] Nürnberg-Fürth 3c Js 62/49 = KLs 253/49, StA Nürnberg, StAnw Nürnberg 2559.
[342] Coburg 7 Js 1373/49 = KLs 6/49, StA Coburg, StAnw Coburg Nr. 556-562.
[343] Nürnberg-Fürth 2c Js 121/48 a-u = KLs 203/48, StA Nürnberg, StAnw Nürnberg 2231/I-III. Emma Ullmann was found hanged in Gestapo custody on November 12, 1938.
[344] Bonn – Zweigstelle Siegburg Js 2476/45 – Sgb. = 6 KLs 1/47, HStA Düsseldorf – ZA Kalkum, Gerichte Rep. 2/320.
[345] Koblenz 9/2 Js 445/47 = 2 KLs 39/50 LHA Koblenz, Best. 584, 6, Nr. 44-47.
[346] Verden Js 305/47 = 6 KLs 21/47, StA Stade, Rep. 171a Verden, Nr. 589 (I-III); see also Verden 6 Js 349/49 = 6 Ks 6/49, StA Stade, Rep. 171a Verden, Nr. 605.

addressed NSDAP District Commander and SA Senior Leader (*Oberführer*) Hans Zimmermann, whom he knew. Zimmermann barked at him: "You, as member of a student corps, aren't you ashamed to be married to something like that?"[347] In Gruiten the district's suggestion of attacking the Jewish butcher Walter Kussel met with enthusiasm from the assembled storm troopers and Nazi Party members. After the Kussel family's flat had been completely wrecked, a Nazi Party functionary said to the non-Jewish wife: "This is what happens to German girls marrying Jews."[348] A storm trooper who was ordered to join others in breaking into the lodgings of the Jewish family Zeiller in Nuremberg first argued that he did not want to enter this particular house as his wife Gretl had been a parlor maid there. Eventually he joined in, allegedly to prevent worse measures. In a letter to his father-in-law (dated November 14, 1938) he admitted his participation: "I was even woken up at three o'clock in the morning and had to serve during the retaliation action against the Jews; I was present with Zeiller where Gretl used to be."[349]

A member of the storm troopers in Nuremberg offered to demolish the lodgings of a Jew whom he knew as a neighbor and from whom he had leased a plot of land.[350] In Rückersdorf about 20 storm troopers wrecked the flat of a Jewish couple; one of the culprits hacked to pieces a table that he had actually manufactured himself as a carpenter and sold to the couple.[351]

In Bad Ems, the action against the Jews got even further out of hand. Initiated by the storm troopers of Bad Ems, the riot soon drew an uncontrollable mob. Teenagers stormed into the hatter shop Bernstein, looted it and played wildly with hats and caps. A veritable pogrom sight-seeing tour began as visitors came across the scene and egged the perpetrators on: "They drove there by car to enjoy this free spectacle and thus supported it initially through their curiosity, later by cheering on the masses and creating peer pressure."[352] Neither the police nor the mayor intervened, although – according to the sentence he received – at least the latter would have been expected to step in, as such violence would endanger the reputation of the city as an international spa.[353]

In several places there was no outside impulse necessary; the action ignited from within as local storm troopers, Nazi functionaries, or dignitaries incited the populace to violence. In Treuchtlingen and Ellingen, it was solely "indigenous"

---

347 Nürnberg-Fürth 3a Js 2229/48 = KLs 12/49; StA Nürnberg, StAnw Nürnberg 2334.
348 Wuppertal 5 Js 224/46 = 5 KLs 3/48, HStA Düsseldorf – ZA Kalkum, Gerichte Rep. 191/28-30.
349 Nürnberg-Fürth 2e Js 2692/48 = KLs 29/49, StA Nürnberg, StAnw Nürnberg 2365/I-II.
350 Nürnberg-Fürth 2c Js 158, 249, 280, 282, 302/47 = 35 KLs 123/47 joined with 13 KLs 150/47, StA Nürnberg, StAnw Nürnberg 1945/I-III.
351 Nürnberg-Fürth 1d Js 213-223/49 = KLs 151/49, StA Nürnberg, StAnw Nürnberg 2479/I-II.
352 Koblenz 9/5 Js 103/46 = 9 KLs 24/50, LHA Koblenz, Best. 584, 1, Nr. 1318-1327, 1328.
353 Ibid.

perpetrators who damaged the houses and stores of their Jewish neighbors, mistreated them, and burned down their synagogues. Some of the women even encouraged the storm troopers to return to already damaged houses if the wreckage did not seem sufficient. Nora A. said: "With Gutmann not enough damage has been done so far." Amalie B. similarly called on the storm troopers to continue wreaking havoc in the house of Dr. Meyerson: "Look, it's not yet enough for the Jewish swine. We have to get the storm troopers in again." Dr. Meyersohn was arrested and abused; he committed suicide a few days later.[354] In Neumarkt (Upper Palatinate) there was no order by storm troopers or party; the participants were mostly civilians who, for the most part, were not even party members – still, the synagogue was demolished, as were the lodgings of a Jew named Baruch; several Jews were arrested and one of them died of unknown causes on November 10, 1938.[355]

Besides the above-mentioned pogrom "tourism," some places turned the action into a free-for-all or a community pursuit. In Hüffenhardt the synagogue was torn down by order of the NSDAP local group commander and mayor; the furnishings were burned in the street. About 40–60 people participated in the action. The wooden parts of the building were burned in the evening at a site outside the village with many villagers present; a band played and the mayor (and local Nazi Party functionary) delivered a speech declaring the destruction of the synagogue an expiation of the murder of vom Rath. Some perpetrators even received money from the village treasury for their participation in the transport of beams or supervision of the demolition.[356] In Bergen-Enkheim the mayor allegedly paid for two jugs of cider to be consumed during the demolition of the local synagogue, while the NS women's auxiliary served coffee. The local Nazi Party functionary had first incited a group of youths to do the wrecking; in the evening locals and people from other towns joined in so that 60–70 people, or – as witnesses put it – half of Bergen[357] participated.

In Oestrich the perpetrators were so familiar with the homes of their victims that they emptied and then demolished the wine cellar of the wine merchant Eduard Rosenthal, prompting the mayor and local Nazi Party head to exclaim: "Dammit, quit stealing from a Jew! You may smash everything, but don't steal." Several groups of criminals were coming and going. The first to arrive – around

---

354 Nürnberg-Fürth 1 Js 70/46 = KLs 16/46, KLs 138/46, StA Nürnberg, StAnw Nürnberg 1809. See also "Erster Prozess wegen Judenprogrom," *Jüdisches Gemeindeblatt für die Nord-Rheinprovinz und Westfalen*, May 6, 1946; and "Urteil gegen Pogromteilnehmer," May 24, 1946.
355 Nürnberg-Fürth 1b Js 1667/48 = KLs 5/49, StA Nürnberg, StAnw. Nürnberg 2316/I-III.
356 Heidelberg 1a Js 2206/46 = KLs 14/46.
357 Frankfurt 5 Js 104/46 = 5 KLs 15/47, HStA Wiesbaden, Abt. 461, Nr. 30021/1-8.

five or six o'clock in the evening – were "unknown" alien culprits; between 7:00 and 7:30 p.m. the locals arrived; around midnight storm troopers from Eltville turned up, shown the way by local residents. Within a short time several perpetrators were completely drunk; some continued their binge in local pubs.[358] In Colmberg the perpetrators of the pogrom were treated to complimentary beer (paid for by the NSDAP) at an inn.[359] In Rüdesheim the perpetrators had planned their deeds in a pub, to which they returned for free beer after having torn down the synagogue.[360] Similarly, free beer was served during the pogrom in a pub in Andernach.[361]

Age, occupation and gender

As explained earlier, it is difficult to make quantitative and qualitative assertions about the perpetrators because post-war investigations and trials inevitably involved only a fraction of the total number of perpetrators. Thus the following remarks can offer highlights, but cannot claim to be comprehensive. Many investigations and trials mention that adolescents were participating in the pogrom. In Geisenheim, young storm troopers (in civilian clothing) who were students at the agricultural college for viniculture carried stones in their briefcases and threw them into the window of a Jewish store, shouting "*Juda verrecke!*" (Death to the Jews!).[362] In Königstein, the wreckage of the homes of several Jewish families was attributed to pupils of the local school. Reportedly, some 20–30 children and adolescents smashed windows and tore down a fence.[363] In Liblar, a 17-year-old Hitler Youth leader participated in the pogrom by smashing a kitchen cupboard with a hammer and throwing a radio out of the window. Later he would explain that his attendance was due to his "curiosity."[364] Five of six defendants indicted for the pogrom in Schupbach were born in the years 1921 and 1922, thus only 16 and 17 years old at the time of the offense.[365]

Few investigations and trials supply reliable information on the occupations of the perpetrators. First of all, people changed jobs. For a statistical analysis one would have to differentiate between the professions people had at the time of the

---
358 Wiesbaden 4 Js 2393/46 = 4 KLs 9/49, HStA Wiesbaden, Abt. 468, Nr. 262/1-5.
359 Ansbach 5 Js 36/49, StA Nürnberg, StAnw Ansbach 5 Js 36/49 .
360 Wiesbaden 4 Js 417/46 = 4 KLs 25/48, HStA Wiesbaden, Abt. 468, Nr. 258/1-8.
361 Koblenz 9/2 Js 1100/47 = 9 Ks 9/50; LHA Koblenz, Best. 584, 1, Nr. 1296-1298; 1336.
362 Wiesbaden 4 Js 1907/46 = 4 KLs 15/49 HStA Wiesbaden, Abt. 468, Nr. 264.
363 Wiesbaden 4 Js 391/45 = 4 KLs 22/49, HStA Wiesbaden, Abt. 468, Nr. 265/1-7.
364 Bonn 7 Js 4037/47 = 7 Ks 1/49, HStA Düsseldorf – ZA Kalkum, Gerichte Rep. 195/67-68.
365 Limburg 2 Js 1207/45 = 2 KLs 16/46, HStA Wiesbaden, Abt. 463, Nr. 1163.

crime and their post-war occupations because denazification temporarily banned many from continuing in their former trades. The primary problem is that few sentences are detailed enough to fulfill this criteria, even though a short description of the living and working circumstances of the defendants is included in each trial. Secondly, the information can be quite misleading: A vague wording such as "Kaufmann" (businessman) can refer to a wholesale dealer as well as to a corner shop owner. Only further research into local circumstances could solve the riddle, making only preliminary remarks possible.

In some places, we find that certain jobs appear frequently among the perpetrators. This applies on the one hand to persons in professions where there was a strong rivalry with Jews (e.g., cattle dealers or wine traders), and on the other hand to members of occupational categories that were overrepresented within the ranks of Nazis (e.g., elementary school teachers). In Rachtig and Zeltingen it was ostensibly the winemakers' guild that decamped to demolish the houses and farms of their Jewish neighbors (and business competitors).[366] The five culprits named their occupations as "vintner, vineyard owner, or wine commission agent." Similarly in Veldenz, out of 14 defendants, 10 were vintners, vineyard owners, or employees in a winery.[367] In Mittelheim, where the Jewish vintner Arthur Hallgarten had his estate, both his stock of wine in the cellar and his winepress were demolished by storm troopers and SS men who had been shown the way by local residents.[368]

The participation of medical doctors in the pogrom was not rare; in Bechhofen the main culprit was a doctor (who happened to also be a storm trooper).[369] In Solingen, Dr. Rüppel, whose flat and surgery had been wrecked because he had previously been married to a Jewish woman (who still lived with him after a feigned divorce) recognized among the evildoers a colleague who was a dentist and storm trooper.[370]

Teachers were also not reluctant to engage in crime, as for example in Röllbach[371] and in Dierdorf (where the teacher involved also happened to be the NSDAP local group commander).[372] In Reilingen, a teacher led his class into a

---

366 Trier 3 Js 800/47 = 3 KLs 8/50, AOFAA, AJ 1616, p. 799, Dossier 166.
367 Trier 3 Js 202/49 = 3 KLs 10/50, LHA Koblenz, Best. 584, 2, Nr. 907.
368 Wiesbaden 14 Js 1534/46 = 4 KLs 24/48, indictment under NARA, OMGUS 17/198 – 1/2.
369 Ansbach 2 Js 766/46 = KLs 21/47, StA Nürnberg, StAnw Ansbach 675.
370 Wuppertal 5 Js 82/47 = 5 KLs 43/47; HStA Düsseldorf – ZA Kalkum, Gerichte Rep. 191/97; see also Wuppertal 5 Js 3369/46 = 5 KLs 34/48, HStA Düsseldorf – ZA Kalkum, Gerichte Rep. 191/72.
371 Aschaffenburg 4 Js 5/49.
372 Koblenz 9 Js 228/49 = 9 Ks 8/50, LHA Koblenz, Best. 584, 1, Nr. 1278.

Jewish home, where they demolished the furnishings.³⁷³ In Neustadt-Gödens (Ostfriesland) two teachers allegedly encouraged their pupils to chant *"Juda verrecke"* when the arrested Jews were taken out of town; in Sande a teacher had his pupils chant "Throw the whole Jewish gang out from our fatherland" (*"Schmeisst die ganze Judenbande/raus aus unserem Vaterlande"*).³⁷⁴ A technical instructor at the occupational school in Essen-Steele (who was also the NSDAP branch officer) took his pupils to see the demolished synagogue "for reasons of discipline."³⁷⁵ In Altenbamberg pupils refrained from turning up for school lessons because they saw their teacher (and local NSDAP commander) participating in demolishing the furnishings of the synagogue.³⁷⁶ In Mainz a teacher led the pupils entrusted to his care to Jewish department stores, which they jointly demolished.³⁷⁷

In Wiebelskirchen a teacher allegedly put pupils up to smashing the window of a Jewish store.³⁷⁸ In Horb, a sports teacher (also a Hitler Youth leader) had his pupils line up and listen to his speech on the assassination of vom Rath. He was also suspected of having encouraged pupils to throw stones at Jewish homes and to smash in the windows of a Jewish store with a beam.³⁷⁹ In Kaiserslautern, a sports teacher walking with his class to the athletic field happened upon the lodgings of the Jewish family Feibelmann where a mob was already smashing in windows and throwing objects into the street. Both pupils and teacher entered the house, too, until the teacher called the pupils back outside.³⁸⁰ In Fürstenau there was no synagogue, but only a simply furnished room for prayer in a private home. The pews, the reed organ, a podium, three Torah Scrolls, two silver candleholders and two pointers were demolished by teachers and pupils of the local elementary school – and SS members.³⁸¹ In Bad Bentheim, pupils of the elementary school, the middle school, and the agricultural college smashed the prayer room; their action could only be stopped when police turned up and intervened.³⁸² In 1948, a teacher at the high school Rheydt-Odenkirchen was sentenced by the Mönchengladbach district court to 10 months in prison for demol-

---

373 Mannheim 1a Js 4832/47 = 1 KLs 35/47; the case is also mentioned in a report dated November 12, 1947, NARA, OMGWB 12/137 – 2/7.
374 Aurich 2 Js 2000/46 = 2 Ks 10/49, StA Aurich, Rep. 109 E Nr. 115/1-5.
375 Essen 29 Js 82/47 29 KLs 26/47 29 Ks 9/48, HStA Düsseldorf – ZA Kalkum, Gerichte Rep. 105/274.
376 Kaiserslautern 7 Js 49/49 = KLs 4/50, AOFAA, AJ 3676, p. 36.
377 Mainz 3 Js 685/47 = 3 KLs 38/48.
378 Saarbrücken 11 Js 61/49.
379 Rottweil 7 Js 3916/47, StA Sigmaringen, Wü 29/2 T4, Nr. 557.
380 Kaiserslautern 7 Js 36/49 = KLs 44/49, AOFAA, AJ 3676, p. 38.
381 Osnabrück 4 Js 729/49, StA Osnabrück, Rep 945 Akz. 6/1983, Nr. 479-480.
382 Osnabrück 4 Js 344/46 = 4 Ks 15/49, StA Osnabrück, Rep 945 Akz. 6/1983, Nr. 106-108.

ishing apartments of Jewish tenants or owners, and the arson at the synagogue of Hochneukirch; he was later acquitted for lack of proof.[383] Similarly, a grammar school teacher in Nuremberg who trespassed with storm troopers into the lodgings of a Jewish carpet dealer was acquitted for lack of proof.[384] A teacher and storm trooper from Gross-Krotzenburg received a two-year jail sentence for severe breach of the peace. The charges included inciting about 100 people – among them several elementary school students – armed with axes, hatchets, and similar tools to wreck the local synagogue, the Jewish school, the Jewish teacher's flat, as well as the homes of other Jewish residents. The lodgings of the Jewish teacher were so completely looted that afterwards the family had to beg for such necessities as bedsheets and household items. The defendant himself had urinated into the synagogue and arrested several Jews in the town.[385] The headmaster of the school in Deidesheim received a three-year sentence for crimes against humanity in connection with breach of the public peace and breach of domestic peace. It seems that during the pogrom, school children had asked whether they were allowed to smash windows at the house of the Jewish family Reinach. The answer proved superfluous as the headmaster himself pounded a door to pieces with a hatchet, smashed a pot containing curdled milk and cheese, and threw shoes from the family's shoe store into the street. He hacked a wardrobe to pieces, shattered the petrol tank of the motorbike owned by Reinach's son, and cut up the duvets in the house of another Jewish family.[386] In Horb, a teacher led a gang of pupils in demolishing the house of prayer and removing books, Torah Scrolls, and pews to be burned.[387]

Even members of the judiciary did not abstain from criminal deeds. In Frankfurt am Main a clerk with the court was suspected of participation because he had been present during the burning of the synagogue on Börneplatz.[388] In Neumagen, employees of the local court partook in the excesses.[389] An employee of the state attorney at Trier had also aroused suspicion of participation in the pogrom.[390] Apparently, suspicions against members of the judiciary ran so high in the postwar years that after he had learned that a judge from Höxter had been involved as

---

[383] Mönchengladbach 6 Js 621/46 = 6 Ks 6/48, HStA Düsseldorf – ZA Kalkum, Gerichte Rep. 10/133,135
[384] Nürnberg-Fürth 2 Js 681/46 = 70 KLs 271/47, StA Nürnberg, StAnw Nürnberg 2033a.
[385] Hanau 2 Js 224/47 = 2 KLs 9/48; HStA Wiesbaden, Abt. 471, Nr. 172/1-4.
[386] Frankenthal 9 KLs 1/49, AOFAA, AJ 3676, p. 36.
[387] Rottweil 1 Js 883-96/46 = KLs 65-84/48, StA Sigmaringen, Wü 29/2 T4, Nr. 224.
[388] Frankfurt 5 Js 5394/48 = 5 KLs 3/49, HStA Wiesbaden, Abt. 461, Nr. 31971.
[389] Trier 3 Js 253/47 = 3 KLs 5/48, LHA Koblenz, Best. 584, 2 Nr. 741-744; see also Trier 3 Js 424/49, AOFAA, AJ 1616, p. 805.
[390] Trier 2 Js 526/49, AOFAA, AJ 1616, p. 805.

a sentry in the street during the event, the president of the high court in Hamm required all judges of all courts in his district to declare in an affidavit whether they had participated in the "action" against the Jews in November 1938.[391]

In Nuremberg two storm troopers broke into the lodgings of Jews and destroyed furniture – not an unusual occurrence during the pogrom, except that the culprits had both been state attorneys in their civil professions.[392] In Amberg, it was State Attorney Dr. Robert R. who had participated in the local pogrom and who was sentenced to three months in prison for breach of the public peace.[393] In Kaiserslautern, investigations were directed against the former president of the district court, who had ordered the arrests of Jewish residents.[394]

A particularly striking characteristic of progrom perpetrators is their heterogeneity. In general, Nazi crimes shared the same demographic as non-politically motivated crimes: The perpetrators were young and male. However, the pogrom is somewhat different in this respect: There were a substantial number of women involved (in the post-war years 65 women were sentenced for crimes during the pogrom) across an enormous age span ranging from the very young to the quite elderly. It is also, to my knowledge, the only Nazi crime complex in which a significant familial factor is visible. In a considerable number of trials and investigations, the defendants were related.

Telling the tale

In spite of the shameful behavior of the perpetrators, their recollections of the pogrom were embellished with much bragging and recounting of one's exploits.

Directly after the pogrom, participants boasted of their acts; in other cases their absence from the workplace had been noted. In Nuremberg, one of the storm troopers wore a shirt speckled with blood and bragged about his "accomplishments."[395] Others were injured in the violence. An SA colonel (*Standartenführer*) was sent flying through the door in the detonation of a petrol bomb in the Rüdesheim synagogue, and was injured so badly that he had to consult a doctor.[396] Another storm trooper in Kirn was hit in the head by splinters of glass

---
391 Letter OLG-President Hamm, Dr. Wiefels, to Minister of Justice, Northrhine-Westphalia, February 10, 1948, HStA Düsseldorf, NW 928, Nr. 476.
392 Nürnberg-Fürth 1 Js 1075/46 = Amberg KLs 1/49.
393 Amberg 1 Js 4871/46 = KLs 26/47, StA Nürnberg, GStA beim OLG Nürnberg 146; see also Activity report, November 2, 1947, NARA, OMGBY 17/183 – 3/15.
394 Kaiserslautern 7 Js 174/48.
395 Nürnberg-Fürth 3b Js 2181/47 = 72 KLs 225/47, StA Nürnberg, StAnw Nürnberg 2011.
396 Wiesbaden 4 Js 417/46 = 4 KLs 25/48, HStA Wiesbaden, Abt. 468, Nr. 258/1-8.

while demolishing the flat of a Jewish family and had to be taken to the hospital.³⁹⁷ In Würzburg it was a forestry official who – while smashing the chandelier in the flat of Rabbi Dr. Siegmund Hanover – hit a storm trooper in the eye with a stick. The storm trooper had to be treated by a doctor.³⁹⁸

Others flashed their newly acquired booty: A storm trooper arrived late for work at the post-office in Bad Kreuznach sporting three valuable rings – his previous financial situation had not allowed him to even buy a wrist-watch.³⁹⁹ Criticism of the pogrom was not welcomed: The NSDAP district commander of Norden, Everwien, upon hearing that a lawyer had made snide remarks about the behavior of the storm troopers, demanded that said lawyer come to the county office, where he was insulted as a *"Judenknecht"* and *"Judenbüttel"* (servant of the Jews). Then the commander boasted about his role: "Let me make it clear to you: I put the torch to the Jewish church [sic] ... I stand up for what I did. The order came from my own soul, and my Führer approves ... We will cope with the Jews."⁴⁰⁰ In Gelsenkirchen, a festive advent evening at the swimming club was embellished with a detailed description of the arson of the local synagogue. Later the recounting was turned into a skit containing the lines, "He rides a car from time to time/and puts the torch to synagogues". The skit was printed and even sung at the club.⁴⁰¹ Others were more concerned about the official side of things: How to represent the event properly? The local Nazi Party of Hüttenbach wrote a letter to the NSDAP county office at Lauf and attached the following draft for the entry in the party chronicle.

> At 5 o'clock in the morning [November 11, 1938] Kreisleiter Pg, Mayor Pg, Kreispropagandaleiter Pg and Sturmführer turned up and torched the Jewish temple. Party members of the Ortsgruppe supported the action. Now party members have criticized this sentence in this respect, as it should read that it was not party members who set the synagogue on fire, but the people. Right. But as the author of a chronicle I ought and must report the truth. It would easily be possible to remove this page and insert another text. I beg you, my Kreisleiter, how should I deal with this entry? Heil Hitler!⁴⁰²

---

397 Koblenz 9 Js 49/49 = Bad Kreuznach 2 KLs 41/50, AOFAA, AJ 1616, p. 805.
398 Würzburg Js 763/46 = KMs 5/46, StA Würzburg, StAnw 352.
399 Koblenz 9 Js 41/49 = 9 KLs 32/49, LHA Koblenz, Best. 584, 6, Nr. 18.
400 Aurich 2 Js 156/48 = 2 Ks 8/48, StA Aurich, Rep. 109 Nds. E, Nr. 338/1-6.
401 Essen 29 Js 19/48 = 29 KLs 6/48, HStA Düsseldorf – ZA Kalkum, Gerichte Rep. 105/277.
402 Nürnberg-Fürth 2c Js 121/48 a-u = KLs 203/48, StA Nürnberg, StAnw Nürnberg 2231/I-III.

Investigation of Pogrom Crimes During the Third Reich

The title of this section seems to be a contradiction in terms, as it is known that investigations of pogrom crimes during the Nazi dictatorship were more or less immediately cut off by the Gestapo and the courts. The Reich Ministry of Justice ordered the state prosecutors to cease investigating or indicting individuals for material damage to synagogues, cemeteries and stores; inquiries concerning pilferage, killings, assaults, and devastations of Jewish homes were to be left to the Gestapo.[403]

However, several incidents had already been recorded by the appropriate authorities in Germany, be it police or fire brigade, and thus had to be dealt with. The crimes were often recorded in detail by the local police and/or fire brigade and the reports sent on to the local authorities to eventually reach the state attorneys. Investigations were usually terminated by the Gestapo.

The Gestapo transferred its collected investigations to the Highest Party Court. This led to 16 trials by February 13, 1939. Three of these were sexual offenses; the 13 others concerned the killings of 21 Jews.[404] Then the Highest Party Court (Oberstes Parteigericht) signaled that further trials in this regard were to be avoided – unless there was evidence of self-serving or criminal actions.[405] The Highest Party Court's idiosyncratic interpretation of the term "criminal" left considerable leeway.

In fact, the ordinary courts did carry out legal proceedings, despite the above-named order of the Reich ministry of justice. The number of these trials is unknown and further research into the matter seems futile as so few judicial record stemming from the Third Reich survived. What can be said from random Third Reich sources unearthed while searching for post-war judicial files is that the National Socialist ordinary courts targeted perpetrators for property offenses – thus neither arson, nor breach of the public or private peace, nor deprivation of liberty were part of the charge-sheet, leaving only theft. In other cases, perpetrators benefitted from the amnesty issued on September 9, 1939, were subject to reprimands and admonishments by the Nazi Party, or were expelled from the party.

I will cite just a few examples: In Lommersum, a Jewish department store named Kain had been ransacked. On November 12, 1938, Family E. was found in possession of two cartloads of merchandise (among them a sofa, six chairs, a fire screen and clothing (31 pairs of men's trousers, 67 men's sweaters, 12 petti-

---

[403] See Lothar Gruchmann, "Reichskristallnacht" und Justiz im "Dritten Reich," *Neue Juristische Wochenschrift* (1988), 2857.
[404] Ibid., 2859-2860.
[405] Ibid., 2860.

coats), linens, duvets, stockings, curtains, table cloths, fabric, pillows, and three bikes). A laundry basket contained crockery, cutlery, a vase, a clock, preserving jars, more clothing, blankets and a bread cutter. Wilhelm E. contested the notion that he had dragged all the items into his home and claimed that other people had thrown the goods over his fence, while he had only collected the wares in his barn, allegedly in order to give them back to Kain upon his return from protective custody. He remarked that he had not reported the incident to the police because he felt bound to Kain, who had saved him from a bankruptcy auction with a loan of 8,500 RM. Only in the trial did Wilhelm E. own up that he had broken into the Kain department store three or four times and had taken armfuls of merchandise each time; his wife Maria E. confessed to having taken clothing, underwear, and home textiles. As the criminal intent was obvious – the mayor of Lommersum having ordered the pilfering to stop by one o'clock in the morning because these acts were "unworthy" of Germans, subsequent demands to hand in the loot having been ignored by the couple – Wilhelm E. was sentenced by a jury court in Bonn to five months' imprisonment, Maria E. to five weeks for theft.[406]

A storm trooper in Sinzenich first tried to hinder the pilfering (and largely destroyed the goods), but when temptation got the better of him he stole three sacks of linens and shared the contents of a cash box with a 16-year-old apprentice; he took 590 RM while the apprentice received 210 RM. When the police demanded that the looters turn in the stolen goods, the storm trooper only surrendered part of the loot and buried the rest in a stable, where it was found during a search. The local court in Bonn sentenced him on May 30, 1939, to eight months in prison for theft.[407] In post-war Germany, his deeds caught up with him again: On March 25, 1949 he was sentenced to two years – minus the eight months he had already served on the theft charge – in the penitentiary for crimes against humanity in conjunction with breach of the public.[408] A similar procedure was applied in East German courts after the war: An NSDAP party functionary in Neuruppin had been sentenced to eight months' imprisonment for embezzlement of several hundred Reichsmark during the pogrom in April 1939. In April 1948 he was confronted with new charges, this time for crimes against humanity and contravention of Control Council Directive 38 and in June 1948 was sentenced to five years in the penitentiary for crimes against humanity.[409]

---

[406] Bonn 2 Js 411/38 = 2 Ms 5/39; HStA Düsseldorf – ZA Kalkum, Gerichte Rep. 2/195-196.
[407] Bonn 2 Ms 16/39.
[408] Bonn 7 Js 335/48 = 7 Ks 3/49, HStA Düsseldorf – ZA Kalkum, Gerichte Rep. 195/329-330.
[409] Neuruppin 5 Js 701/38 pol. = 5 KMs 5/39; Neuruppin, Zweigstelle Brandenburg Aufs. 233/48 = StKs 89/48; BStU Pdm ASt, StKs 89/48.

Similarly in Hanau, where Jewish stores and houses had been devastated and the synagogue had been burned, NSDAP District Commander Max Else was sentenced in West Germany to 9,5 years in the penitentiary (for severe breach of the public peace). The sentence included a penalty meted out by the special court (*Sondergericht*) Kassel (3 KLs 27/40) for eight years in the penitentiary, issued on July 4, 1940.[410]

As inquiries concerning the loot were looming and house searches imminent, some perpetrators resorted to more elaborate means of concealment. In August or September 1939, Babette H. was visited in her flat in Hof by a storm trooper, who asked whether he could enter her apartment – of which he had been the previous tenant. He then proceeded to loosen a tile in the ceramic stove in order to remove valuables that stemmed from the ransacking of the local synagogue.[411] In Kaiserslautern, Elisabeth K. convinced Mrs. Löwenstein shortly before the pogrom to bring furniture and valuables to her house for safekeeping and to sign a feigned transfer of property to Elisabeth K's daughter Lieselotte. In the enforced absence of the Löwenstein family after the pogrom, Elisabeth K. appropriated further property, such as linens, clothes, mattresses, silver, china, a radio, oil paintings, jewelry, and a savings account book and hid the items. Upon the return of the Löwenstein family, she referred to the alleged gift and refused to surrender the goods. She embellished her refusal with flimsy lies such as having chucked everything out when a broadcast warned that storing of Jewish property was forbidden, and that unknown burglars had then stolen everything. The Löwenstein family demanded a house search, which led to the discovery of several items hidden in mattresses and behind pictures. A carpet was found nailed under the bottom of a cupboard. While the first trial during the Third Reich (on charges of concealment, betrayal of trust, and attempted blackmail) ended due to the aforementioned amnesty of September 9, 1939, Elisabeth K. had to stand trial again and was sentenced to one year in prison for crimes against humanity in conjunction with embezzlement and failure to meet an expectation.[412]

As has become obvious from the above-mentioned cases, both the party courts and the ordinary courts during the Third Reich were only interested in punishing theft, but not the other offenses and crimes committed during the pogrom. Punitive action of the courts affected only those most brazen thieves who ignored any demands that they hand over the loot to the Nazi authorities. It was probably not so much the theft as such – the damaged third parties were after all "only Jews" – but ignoring the authority of the Nazi state enraged both the law

---

[410] Hanau 2 Js 603/47 = 2 KLs 7/48; HStA Wiesbaden, Abt. 471, Nr. 171/1-5.
[411] Hof Js 3321/48 = KLs 4/51, StA Bamberg, Rep. K 107, Abg. 1987, Nr. 749.
[412] Kaiserslautern 7 Js 180/47 = KLs 75/47; AOFAA, AJ 3676, p. 37.

enforcement agencies and the Nazi Party, and therefore called for teaching the more stubborn and delinquent among the *Volksgenossen* a lesson.

First Post-War Trials

On September 5, 1945, the state attorney at Limburg charged six defendants with breach of the public peace and deprivation of liberty during the pogrom in Villmar. Members of the local NSDAP had devastated the homes of two Jewish families and the Jewish men had been arrested by constabulary and storm troopers' auxiliary police. The local court of Weilburg issued the verdict a week later, on September 12. The court bemoaned the "moral squalor" of the defendants, who had considered the Jews outside the law due to the reckless National Socialist propaganda. The constable was reproached for deprivation of liberty, as he should not have arrested the Jews, but rather the criminals.

> It could be that, like most Germans, years of propaganda had undermined their power of moral judgment and blinded them to the damnability of their actions. As is well known, November 1938 was the start of crimes unparalleled in history, crimes for which there can be no human atonement. However, one would do injustice to the defendants if one did judge their deeds under the influence of subsequent crimes – as difficult as it is to refrain from such judgments today.[413]

This verdict shows the problems the German judiciary was facing: reversed ethical values, the collapse of the rule of law, a reappraisal of events that had taken place several years earlier, as well as the general question of how to deal adequately with such crimes.

Though the Weilburg sentence was delivered early, it is not by any means the first post-war pogrom trial in the Western Zones that we know of: In the summer of 1945, the county master builder of Forchheim was indicted for the blasting of the local synagogue and sentenced to five years in the penitentiary for violation of the Explosives Act (though he would be acquitted by district court Bamberg after the appeal in 1946).[414] First investigations had been conducted by the Military Government in July 1945; the case was then handed over to the local court of Forchheim. The later appeal was also granted as the judge in charge at the local court was

---

[413] Limburg 2 Js 641/45 = AG Weilburg DLs 3-8/45 = Limburg 5 KLs 2/52, HStA Wiesbaden, Abt. 463, Nr. 1201.
[414] Bamberg Js 36/45 Fo = AG Forchheim DLs 1/45 = LG Bamberg Ns 9/46 (files not traceable).

convicted for attempted coercion and possession of procurement authorizations shortly afterwards. Nor did the public prosecutor prove to be beyond reproach.[415]

In Hesse, where courts were functioning anew from early on, several pogrom cases had already been brought and tried in summer, fall, and winter of 1945. On August 17, 1945, the state attorney of Darmstadt pressed charges against five defendants at the local court of Offenbach. The accused were suspected of having participated in the pogrom at Neu-Isenburg. The court assumed that the statute of limitations applied and the case was dismissed, only to be picked up again and adjudicated by the district court of Darmstadt in 1946.[416] The first interrogations concerning the local pogrom by the Darmstadt Criminal Investigation Department are dated June 21, 1945; in early August 1945 the investigations were handed over to the public prosecutor; on August 25 the indictment was drawn up; the verdict was pronounced on October 23, 1945. The defendant was sentenced to three years in the penitentiary for severe breach of the public peace.[417] The defendants in the pogrom in Gross-Zimmern were indicted on October 5, 1945, and the case was adjudicated on December 14, 1945.[418] The defendants guilty of ransacking of the synagogue in Limburg – situated just opposite the courthouse – were indicted on October 17, 1945, and sentenced on November 20.[419] The mistreatment of Jews and damage to Jewish property in Weyer was the subject of an indictment dated December 4, 1945; the sentence was issued on December 18.[420]

On November 2, 1945, the prosecutor general in Oldenburg ordered the public prosecutors in Oldenburg, Osnabrück, and Aurich to commence criminal proceedings immediately.

"This deed [the pogrom] had the gravest consequences and thus caused thorough disgust in the salubrious feeling of that part of the German population that was still healthy ... The German people, but also the world public expect that all those criminals partaking – if found guilty – will get the deserved punishment."[421] While the letter did encourage the initiation of penal action, not all would follow the call for action. In Wildeshausen the synagogue had been torched and burned down – yet it would take an order from the military government in Oldenburg to

---

415 See also NARA, OMGUS 17/262-2/15.
416 AG Offenbach 2 DLs 57/45 (files not traceable), NARA, OMGH 17/211-2/1.
417 Darmstadt Js 1070/45 = KLs 18/45.
418 Darmstadt Js 2907/45 = KLs 27/45.
419 Limburg 3 Js 794/45 = 3 KLs 5/45, HStA Wiesbaden, Abt. 463, Nr. 904.
420 Limburg 2 Js 839/45 = 5/2 KLs 7/45, HStA Wiesbaden, Abt. 463, Nr. 922.
421 Oldenburg 3 Js 2861/45 = 9 Ks 8/49, StA Oldenburg, Best. 140-5, Nr. 342; letter also under Oldenburg 3 Js 2865/45, StA Oldenburg, Best. 140-5, Nr. 28; and Oldenburg 5 Js 1308/47, StA Oldenburg, Best. 140-5, Nr. 97.

the prosecutor general on March 27, 1947, to get criminal proceedings started.[422] In other parts of Germany, investigations also got off the ground early. In Paderborn in July 1945, the public prosecutor summoned the police to investigate the pogrom of Salzkotten.[423] Some resumed investigative activities more or less as soon as the war was over: The Losheim constabulary's first interrogations concerning anti-Semitic excesses in Losheim and Greimerath started in May 1945.[424] Not much later, in June 1945, the district administrator of Steinfurt demanded that evidence of the pogrom in Rheine be preserved. The police finished their interrogations in February 1946; the record were held up at the municipality level and penal procedures ground to a halt, only to be recommenced in August 1947 when the town administration transferred the investigations to the state prosecutor.[425]

In Württemberg-Baden the head of the German justice branch summoned the Ministry of Justice to conduct investigations on the anti-Semitic upheaval in Ulm.[426] The Bavarian minister of justice, Dr. Wilhelm Hoegner, feeling that Nazi crimes were not prosecuted with the necessary energy and speed, appealed to the conscience of the prosecutors general in Munich, Nuremberg, and Bamberg. The state prosecutor's hesitancy was attributed to a misunderstanding of the legal position. He wrote:

> National Socialist rule was by its very nature a tyranny, ascended to rule by fraud and sustained under misuse of legal authority and by brute force. According to the doctrine of natural justice, resistance against the Third Reich was permitted and in order ... The National Socialist course of action against the Jewish population in November 1938 was in contradiction to basic principles of occidental rule of law and civilization and was thus unlawful no matter what and whether state organs participated, covered up, ordered or retrospectively did not prosecute.[427]

The investigation was not just a legal or moral duty. Damage caused by the devastation of the synagogue in Schlüchtern amounted to 30,000 RM; the cost for

---

422 Oldenburg 5 Js 711/47; StA Oldenburg, Best. 140-5, Nr. 80.
423 Paderborn 5 Js 234/48 = 7/5 Ks 2/49; see also "Verbrechen gegen die Menschlichkeit: Die Zerstörung der Salzkottener Synagoge. Von sieben Angeklagten wurde nur einer verurteilt.", *Jüdisches Gemeindeblatt für die britische Zone*, March 11, 1949.
424 Saarbrücken 4 Js 116/46 = 11 KLs 6/48.
425 Münster 6 Js 475/47 = 6 KLs 10/48.
426 Letter of Ralph E. Brown to Ministry of Justice Württemberg-Baden, December 3, 1946, NARA, OMGWB 12/131 – 2/6.
427 Letter Bavarian Minister of Justice, Dr. Hoegner to prosecutor generals in München, Nürnberg, Bamberg, September 12, 1947, in: Dossier 3: Prosecution of nationalsocialist crimes, General files 1093: Prosecution of still unpunished nationalsocialist crimes, Bavarian Ministry of Justice.

repair had to be covered by public means.⁴²⁸ If for no other reason, there was the need to find the culprits in order to hold them accountable for the material damage. Literally hundreds of municipalities now burdened with the financial cost of the restoration hoped to recoup at least part of the expense from the perpetrators. Thus a criminal investigation of the arson of the synagogue and devastation of Jewish shops that was blamed on the former mayor of Regensburg was initiated by the department of the city council and handed over to the state prosecutor in 1947.⁴²⁹ In 1947, the city director of Bonn pressed charges against the Nazi Party chief and former mayor for arson of the synagogue and the Jewish parish hall. At the same time, newspapers appealed to the public to report their eyewitness accounts of the pogrom.⁴³⁰ The city director of Gelsenkirchen pressed charges against that city's former mayor for torching the local synagogue.⁴³¹

More pronounced than the (occasional) charges originating from municipal authorities were the reports of erstwhile victims or their families, who were chiefly interested in a speedy clarification and prosecution. Several proceedings were initiated by reports of emigrants or former Jewish residents. The prosecution of the arson of the Bochum synagogue might not have taken place without the insistence of Dr. Oscar Koppel, a lawyer in Bochum until 1933, who had immigrated to the United States where he became a professor and government official. In 1945 he was part of the prosecutors' team of the International Military Tribunal in Nuremberg. He died in 1947 in Washington, DC.⁴³² Charles W. Anrod from Chicago, who until 1935 (under his birth name Karl Aron) had been a judge at local and district courts in the Rhineland and Hesse pointed out the devastation of the Jewish cemetery, and in particular the graves of his parents and brother, in his home-town of Niederbieber.⁴³³ The German justice branch supported the investigations by contacting witnesses of the pogrom or of anti-Semitic excesses who had fled to the United States.⁴³⁴

Survivors living in Germany approached the authorities with their concerns. Ludwig Fried appeared several times at the office of the mayor of Wallau and

---

428 Hanau 3 Js 33/46, HStA Wiesbaden, Abt. 471, Nr. 7.
429 Regensburg Js 500/47 = KLs 82/47.
430 Bonn 3 Js 1015/47 = 3 Ks 2/49; HStA Düsseldorf – ZA Kalkum, Gerichte Rep. 145/471; charges were pressed by the Oberstadtdirektor on April 23, 1947. On September 2, 1947, the Bonn state attorney informed the Cologne prosecutor general that the suspects (among them the former district party chief and the former mayor of Bonn) could not be found guilty.
431 Essen 29 Js 34/49, HStA Düsseldorf – ZA Kalkum, Gerichte Rep. 105/280.
432 Bochum 2 Js 1883/48.
433 Koblenz 9/3 Js 300/47 = 9 Ks 10/50, LHA Koblenz, Best. 584, 1, Nr. 1078-1080, 1084.
434 Monthly report, February 3, 1948, NARA, OMGWB 12/139 – 3/22.

reproached him for not undertaking any steps toward the investigation and prosecution of those responsible for the desecration of the synagogue and cemetery.[435]

Charges also were pressed by the Jewish communities. For example, the Jewish Community of Saarbrücken notified the authorities of all destroyed synagogues and defiled cemeteries of the Saar region.[436] Other notifications came from the National Association of Jewish Communities of the North Rhine province in Düsseldorf or from victims' associations. Political parties might also take up the cause: On November 22, 1945, the organization of the Social Democratic Party in Wiesbaden handed in a report on the pogrom to the law enforcement agencies.[437] Newsletters and bulletins were used to search for witnesses, e.g., in Hanau.[438]

On October 1, 1948, notices appeared at different places around town requesting witnesses to come forward if they had information on the role of a particular storm trooper and member of the municipality of Papenburg during the pogrom (and the city director in the post-war years).[439]

Charges reached police and state prosecutors via letters from all over the world. The pogrom in Vettweiss was reported by Isidor Schwarz, a native of Vettweiss who had emigrated to Sao Paolo, Brazil.[440] Hugo Weil from the Netherlands made the report on the devastation of the flat of his father-in-law Oskar Mayer in Kusel. Mayer had immigrated to the Netherlands, been deported and later murdered in Sobibor.[441] Salomon Schwarz and Ferdinand Rubel were living in the United States when they wrote a letter admonishing the prosecutor with the denazification authorities in Rockenhausen to avenge the excesses in Rockenhausen and Steinbach am Donnersberg.[442] In Kappeln it was the British Sergeant John Blunt who took care that the crimes against the Jewish family Eichwald were not forgotten: He had been born into the Eichwald family in 1923 in Kappeln and his parents and grandparents had been deported subsequently to Minsk.[443] Sol. Schubach, now a resident of New York, reporting on the pogrom of Dauborn, wrote: "I hope that the people receive a just punishment for the atrocious crimes

---

[435] Wiesbaden 4 Js 2440/48 = 4 KLs 17/49, HStA Wiesbaden, Abt. 468, Nr. 263.
[436] Saarbrücken 11 Js 62/48 = 11 KLs 43/48.
[437] Wiesbaden 2 Js 3090/45 = 2 KLs 20/49; HStA Wiesbaden, Abt. 468, Nr. 260/1-7.
[438] Hanau 2 Js 603/47 = 2 KLs 7/48, HStA Wiesbaden, Abt. 471, Nr. 171/1-5.
[439] Osnabrück 4 Js 1071/48, StA Osnabrück, Rep 945 Akz. 6/1983 Nr. 64; Osnabrück 4 Js 1640/46 = 4 Ks 8/48; StA Osnabrück, Rep 945 Akz. 6/1983, Nr. 46-49.
[440] Aachen 9 Js 768/49 = 9 KLs 3/53, HStA Düsseldorf – ZA Kalkum, Gerichte Rep. 89/227.
[441] Kaiserslautern 7 Js 188/49, AOFAA, AJ 3676, p. 36.
[442] Kaiserslautern 7 Js 56/49, AOFAA, AJ 3676, p. 38. The letter of Salomon Schwarz dates of February 7, 1949, the letter of Ferdinand Rubel, now resident in New York, of January 2, 1949, April 30, 1949 and November 30, 1949.
[443] Flensburg 2a Js 93/48 = 2a KLs 9/48, LA Schleswig-Holstein, Abt. 354 Flensburg; Nr. 965.

they perpetrated. In my opinion they ought to be sentenced to life-long penitentiary or death penalty."[444]

Perseverance was certainly an asset. Hugo Günzburger, the trustee of the Jewish Community in Memmingen, was told by the public prosecutor in the town that there was no legal basis on which to proceed against the perpetrators already named by Günzburger. Only when a critical article appeared in a newsletter of the Social Democratic Party were investigations begun.[445] In Neitersen, house of Siegfried Seligmann – nephew of Amalie Stern – had been completely wrecked in November 1938. He notified the mayor in Weyerbusch on August 3, 1945; on March 27, 1946, the state attorney in Koblenz informed him that police interrogations had determined that the suspected arsonists and those responsible for malicious damage were no longer living in the Neitersen area. Enraged, Seligmann retorted on April 5:

> I first want to point out that I cannot understand how it was asserted that the suspected arsonists and wrongdoers are missing or still POWs. According to my personal ascertainment the following persons are still present in lieu [names given] ... These perpetrators are still living in Neitersen. If the state prosecutor still should not have enough documentation, I name for the complete elements of crime the following witnesses ... I will not shirk any work or means to seek clarification in this matter now, as the courts are re-opened for the purpose of inquest. I must, however, observe that the matter is not as fast and as diligently dealt with as the Nazi criminals did with our property and lives. If I will not in the shortest time be absolutely certain that the investigations are being carried out fast and thoroughly, I will arrange for matters to be taken further.[446]

Not only victims clamored for elucidation of past crimes: In 1948/1949, the public prosecutor in Hanau received several anonymous letters concerning events in Marköbel – where the synagogue had been torn down during the anti-Jewish riots – and naming several suspects. The missives demanded urgently that perpetrators be detained in order to squeeze information from them. In the letters, the pogrom was called a shameful affair that should be handled without delay. All decent people would be waiting for punishment of the guilty persons. Rather provocatively, the senior prosecutor was asked if his intention was to hush things up. Another anonymous letter went to the Ministry of Justice in Wiesbaden complaining about the the Hanau prosecutor's lack of interest in prosecuting.

When questioned concerning the charges, the usual reaction of suspects was denial. Some tried to acquire helpful documentation. One suspect, bold as brass,

---

444 Limburg 3 Js 778/48, HStA Wiesbaden, Abt. 463, Nr. 1226.
445 Memmingen Js 2881ff/46 = KLs 14/48, StA Augsburg.
446 Koblenz 2/3 Js 1315/45 = 9/2 KLs 34/47, LHA Koblenz, Best. 584, 1, Nr. 3216-3217.

sent a letter to a victim in Milwaukee demanding an attestation of good behavior during the pogrom of Sobernheim as he had conducted himself in a "very reserved" manner and entered the house of Eugen Feibelmann only under pressure from a storm trooper.[447]

Problems of Investigation and Legal Problems

Post-war investigations faced extraordinary difficulties. The detailed reconstruction of activities was nearly impossible because many Jewish families who had been victim of the anti-Jewish riots of November 1938 either had been murdered or were living abroad. Those still alive – and willing to testify – could not answer certain questions such as who had given orders, where and when the action had started, and which buildings or families had been targeted in what sequence. The clarification of these aspects, however, was crucial for the prosecutors as it would influence the legal assessment of affairs and the role of individual perpetrators, who were understandably not inclined to shed light on their own roles, and onlookers and bystanders were either incriminated themselves or not interested in clarification of the event.

As the Minister of Justice in North Rhine-Westphalia complained,

> Some witnesses apparently cannot remember while others consciously (and so ostentatiously) withhold the truth that their impediment of justice stuck out like a sore thumb. But the obstacles could not be overcome. Yet another portion of the witnesses – sad to say – keep silent as they fear to become involved in criminal procedures because these witnesses themselves were incriminated ... Unfortunately, experience tells us that, as time passes, a big part of the population is – for reasons not to be discussed here – no longer willing to take part in the elucidation of these offenses.[448]

A similar lament came from the Bavarian Minister of Justice:

> Clarification often demands a lot of time, in many cases the offenders are unknown, often a part of the main culprits or important witnesses are no longer available as they either died in the war, are still captive or have gone into hiding. In other cases, the guilty [parties] were interned in camps administered by the Americans in 1945 and 1946 and thus not available to the German law enforcement authorities.[449]

---

447 Koblenz 9/2 Js 445/47 = 2 KLs 39/50, LHA Koblenz, Best. 584, 6, Nr. 44-47.
448 Speech of Minister of Justice, Dr. Artur Sträter, in the Diet of Northrhine-Westphalia on November 8, 1949, 3383.
449 Speech of Minister of Justice Dr. Josef Müller, in the Bavarian Diet, March 15, 1948, 1093.

To add to the complications, the riots occasionally took place over many hours and frequently overnight. Different gangs attacked many abodes, synagogues, and shops at different times, which made the identification of perpetrators difficult. In some cases, there were different "waves" of onslaught discernible, with party members or storm troopers from other localities – with "official" orders – initiating the attacks, joined by local functionaries and authorities, schoolchildren causing mischief and/or women who scavenged the shops and houses for usable items. The sheer number of participants was bound to make investigations nearly futile. In Langenselbold, the report listed the number of participants as "several hundreds."[450] In Sobernheim, the mob numbered between 80 and 100 people, who – some in plain clothes, others in uniform – marauded through the synagogue and houses of Jews. Only a fraction of the wrongdoers could be traced. Still, 36 defendants were indicted, but the proof was not considered sufficient in 23 of those cases.[451] In Memmingen, the Nazi Party chief wanted to convert the synagogue for secular use, perhaps as a public swimming pool or youth hostel. As the building proved unsuitable, he decided to tear it down, which involved the employment of an architect, several building contractors and laborers – in all about 200 people. (The cost for the demolition and a "ploughman's lunch" for the laborers – some 12,000 RM – was billed to the Jewish community.) Furthermore, 23 flats of Jewish families and three Jewish stores were devastated, witnessed by yet another crowd of bystanders.[452] Post-war investigations led to an indictment of 36 persons in Memmingen.

In addition to the great number of participants (in different roles and at different times), other circumstances created trouble for the investigators. Crimes often happened in autumnal early darkness or at night (with switched-off or smashed street lamps). Many culprits had gone underground, were dead, or missing. Some had already been arrested by the Allies for other crimes when their crimes of 1938 were revealed. The former NSDAP local group leader of Osnabrück, a master watchmaker, was arrested in Heilbronn in the American Zone for black-marketeering. He was suspected of having taken several gold and silver items during the burning of the synagogue that he then used in his workshop.[453] Investigations sometimes stretched beyond the borders of the Western Zones, but ran into difficulties finding witnesses and locating perpetrators, as in the case of

---

450 Hanau 2 Js 456/46 = 2 KLs 1/47, HStA Wiesbaden, Abt. 471, Nr. 166.
451 Koblenz 9/2 Js 445/47 = 2 KLs 39/50 LHA Koblenz, Best. 584, 6, Nr. 44-47.
452 Memmingen Js 2881ff/46 = KLs 14/48, StA Augsburg.
453 "Übler Osnabrücker Terrorist gefasst: Zu Unrecht des Schwarzhandels verdächtigt – aber als Naziführer erkannt," *Neues Tageblatt*, January 17, 1947; see also Osnabrück 4 Js 1045/48 = 4 Ks 14/49; StA Osnabrück, Rep 945 Akz. 6/1983, Nr. 553.

the shooting of the Jewish businessman Dr. Leo Levy by storm troopers in Bad Polzin, Pomerania.[454]

Moreover, the anything but clear situation of the German administration of justice was unsettling. Lack of confidence in responsibilities and/or in the interest of the Allies in investigations caused further delay. Files were handed over to the military government authorities, where they were sometimes lost or were misplaced, forcing new investigations to be initiated or the procedures reconstructed from copies.[455] In parts of the French Zone, the authorities had planned to carry out their own trials concerning the pogrom. Due to overwork or other more pressing problems, the investigations were put on hold for months and even years. From July 1945 to July 1947, the French investigations of the local pogrom of Koblenz had come to a standstill. When the German investigations began, witnesses and suspects claimed that it was all so long ago.[456] The arson of the Jewish senior citizens' residence in Neustadt an der Haardt – where two women had lost their lives – had been the subject of investigations since October 1945; the coroner's preliminary hearing had opened in October 1946, but in June 1947 the French judicial authorities took over, which led to the termination of the German preliminary hearing in July 1947. It was not until March 1949 that the German administration of justice once again took up the investigations.[457]

In other cases, suspects were under French arrest – and thus removed from German judicial intervention.[458] In Schlüchtern, the German police ascribed difficulties in their inquiries to the fact that in September 1945, the American Counter Intelligence Corps (CIC) had already conducted interrogations, thus forewarning participants who now were extremely reluctant to be forthcoming.[459] At times, sheer lack of manpower hindered or delayed judicial proceedings: The president of the district court of Nürnberg-Fürth, Camille Sachs, himself a victim of the pogrom, mentioned several pogrom trials under way in his district, but pointed out that there were hundreds of suspects whose cases had not yet been deliber-

---

454 Hannover 2 Js 462/56 (previously Oldenburg 10 Js 710/48).
455 For an example see Kleve 5 Js 417/47 = 5 Ks 1/48; 5 KLs 1/48, HStA Düsseldorf – ZA Kalkum, Gerichte Rep. 107/7-8. The file was lost with Land Legal Department NRW and replaced by new investigations initiated by the Jewish Community in Northrhine-Westphalia.
456 Koblenz 9/5 Js 411/47 = 9 KLs 8/51, LHA Koblenz, Best. 584, 1, Nr. 1300-1303, 1332.
457 Frankenthal 9 Js 39/49 = 9 KLs 31/49.
458 Trier 3 Js 800/47 = 3 KLs 8/50 AOFAA, AJ 1616, p. 799. The main culprit had been in French arrest for four months in 1947.
459 Hanau 3 Js 33/46, HStA Wiesbaden, Abt. 471, Nr. 7.

ated. "Still yet it was impossible to prosecute those cases for want of police officials, prosecutors and investigating judges."[460]

The files give an impressive glimpse of the obstacles the police, state attorneys, and courts had to overcome. Criminal Investigation Department Kempen complained that their research into the pogrom in St. Tönis had run aground because many witnesses did not want to recall the events; the members of the fire brigade of St. Tönis – all of them former Nazi Party members and storm troopers – being especially reluctant.[461]

In Bad Ems, where the Jewish home for the aged had been ransacked to such an extent that jewelry and memorabilia of residents were found a few days later by the police under heaps of rubble and a thick layer of bed feathers had covered the street in front of the institution, so that the actual course of events could only be reconstructed to a modest degree. At fault were the defendants themselves – reluctant witnesses – as well as the attitudes of people who knew more than they were willing to say – not to mention the death or disappearance of several perpetrators during the war and the absence of statements from victims who had either died in concentration camps or had moved abroad without an address.[462]

Investigators scrutinizing the course of the pogrom in Syke, Twistringen, Diepholz, Lemförde, and the *Grafschaft* Hoya stated that both defendants and witnesses were obviously loath to come clean.[463]

In Alzenau it was sheer aversion to the investigation on the part of the population. The state attorney had no choice but to terminate investigations against 44 suspects for lack of proof and asserted resignedly that other inquiries were useless, as the population of Alzenau stuck together and was tired of the perpetual interrogation in this affair. The interrogated did not understand the state attorney's prosecution, as the affair was considered to have been settled by the denazification courts (*Spruchkammer*).[464] A senior state attorney in Freiburg noted in his diary on January 17, 1946: "Investigation about the arson of the synagogue of 8–9 November 1938 – the guilty party is 'forever unknown.'"[465]

The deaths of perpetrators, witnesses, and victims were bound to hinder sweeping investigations. In some cases, the suicide of a perpetrator was attributed to his role during the pogrom. The brother of Albert H. in Hausberge stated that

---

460 Letter of President LG Nürnberg-Fürth, Sachs, to OMGBY, April 15, 1946, NARA, OMGBY 17/183 – 3/13.
461 Krefeld 2 Js 402/48 = 2 Ks 2/48, HStA Düsseldorf – ZA Kalkum, Gerichte Rep. 30/109-111.
462 Koblenz 9/5 Js 103/46 = 9 KLs 24/50, LHA Koblenz, Best. 584, 1, Nr. 1318-1327; 1328.
463 Verden 6 Js 305/47 = 6 KLs 21/47, StA Stade, Rep. 171a Verden, Nr. 589 (I-III).
464 Aschaffenburg 4 Js 8/49.
465 Bader, "Der Wiederaufbau," 62.

Albert H., a storm trooper, confessed his participation in the pogrom and admitted to having smashed – accompanied by two local butchers – the dwellings of several Jews in Hausberge, Steinbergen, and Vlotho. The brother reproached him and gave him a good dressing-down. Albert H. took the words to heart, succumbed to alcoholism, neglected his family, and hanged himself a few weeks later.[466] The arson of the synagogue in Schötmar went unpunished as the main culprit died during the investigations – possibly by suicide – after he had named other suspects. The suspects then simply denied the accusations unwaveringly.[467]

Dealing with witnesses was always tricky. In 1947, charges were pressed against two persons for demolishing the synagogue in Geinsheim, a part of Neustadt. A witness who had claimed to the police that he could clearly identify the perpetrators withdrew his statement in the interrogation by the judge.[468] The constabulary of County Saarburg ascertained that they had been able to shed light on the course of the anti-Semitic excesses in Wawern, but had failed to investigate all involved persons.[469] The Criminal Investigation Department Cloppenburg determined that inquiries were very difficult as individuals were either reluctant or completely unwilling to make statements. The department considered it hard to believe that there was always talk of "unknown storm troopers."[470]

The state attorney at Koblenz was so annoyed with the inadequate interrogations, believing he had been given a lot of blarney by the police, that he returned the files to the police of Idar-Oberstein. He simply refused to tolerate such naive interrogations in which one Nazi Party leader claimed to be unsuspecting and another unknowing while fires were burning all around them. The police had even dared to present an innocent old party member (i.e., with a membership dating back before 1933). He voiced his opinion in no uncertain terms that the police had simply recorded nonsense and thus put the purpose of their own task in question. He urged them to either conduct serious investigations in the matter, or state that the police were not up to the task.[471]

In Kamp, the interrogations conducted by police officers in 1945 and 1946 were considered full of flaws and thus nearly worthless as the (newly recruited) police had had no practical experience at the time. Things did not improve much when the police wrote their final report. Testimonies of witnesses were very

---

466 Testimony of Wilhelm H., November 18, 1946, Bückeburg Js 256/47, StA Bückeburg, L 23 B Nr. 537.
467 Detmold 1 Js 1447/46.
468 Frankenthal 9 Js 224-225/47, AOFAA, AJ 3676, 38.
469 Trier 3 Js 346/47 = 3 KLs 16/48 LHA Koblenz, Best. 584, 2, Nr. 745-746.
470 Oldenburg 5 Js 1308/47, StA Oldenburg, Best. 140-5, Nr. 97.
471 Koblenz 9/2 Js 147/48 = Bad Kreuznach 3 Ks 6/50, LHA Koblenz, Best. 584, 6, Nr. 4-13.

restrained, which was not only due to the poor recollection of witnesses, but also to their reluctance to incriminate others.[472] The facts of the pogrom in Alpen were extraordinately obfuscated because suspects perennially changed their statements.[473] The police report by the constabulary of Oberbieber gives insight into pent-up misery and frustration:

> Current interrogations were carried out under disadvantage and difficulties. Suspects or participants barely remembered or did not at all want to recall the course of events. Nobody wants to know who gave him the orders. And nobody wants to admit having had a hand in the excesses. All interrogations generated so many antinomies that it is absolutely clear that the suspects did not tell the truth in their hearings.[474]

In Bergen-Enkheim the indictment even mentioned the difficulty of the investigations. Witnesses feared being suspected of betrayal, thus making enemies, and therefore held back information.[475] The investigation of the pogrom in Bad Dürkheim (where 25 houses and stores had been ransacked) simply determined that clarification of facts was no longer possible. This was attributed to the passage of time, but especially to the reluctance of suspects and witnesses to make statements. The examining magistrate was frequently told that the residents of Bad Dürkheim did not understand why these incidents were being re-opened after such a long time.[476] The criminal investigation department of Bad Homburg noted that investigations were extremely difficult, since the suspects were mostly former storm troopers who, as a tight-knit community, never betrayed each other. Many suspects and also witnesses did not – given the passage of time – want to recall either details or participants. Those participants confronted with their own statements made to the Gestapo (during investigations of 1939) stated that they had been compelled to make statements and guilty pleas as they were being incarcerated, hit and threatened with imprisonment in concentration camps. They did not own up to these confessions, either.[477]

The police in Vallendar reported that research into the events of November 1938 was a "disagreeable, time-consuming and hard task." To get any leads, it was necessary interrogate a plethora of witnesses, particularly from former Jewish neighborhoods. Many witnesses had since died, and others – especially business people and acquaintances of the suspects – did not want to recollect the events.

---

472 Koblenz 9/5 Js 510/48 = 9 KLs 4/50, LHA Koblenz, Best. 584, 1, Nr. 1258-1259.
473 Kleve 5 Js 417/47 = 5 Ks 1/48; 5 KLs 1/48, HStA Düsseldorf – ZA Kalkum, Gerichte Rep. 107/7-8.
474 Koblenz 9/5 Js 1262/48 = 9 KLs 7/50, LHA Koblenz, Best. 584, 1, Nr. 1282.
475 Frankfurt 5 Js 104/46 = 5 KLs 15/47, HStA Wiesbaden, Abt. 461, Nr. 30021/1-8.
476 Frankenthal 9 Js 25/50 = 9 Ks 6/50, AOFAA, AJ 3676, p. 37.
477 Frankfurt 56/8 Js 3389/49 = 56 KLs 15/52, HStA Wiesbaden, Abt. 461, Nr. 32030/1-6.

Suspects probably had arranged among themselves to make no statements, or only inconsequential ones, to the police. A considerable part of the population, particularly those with leftist inclinations, rejected making statements in the affair on principle, being of the belief that the authorities are only going after the "small fish," while the "big fish" are being left alone. They were not content with the current political system and thus refused to make any statements, making it very difficult to find even a limited number of witnesses for the prosecution. To find all suspects would not be possible even for the prosecutor in Koblenz, since the suspects – apart from a certain A., a shoemaker named F., and another party functionary L. – were not known and their identity could not be determined. One cannot help thinking that only with the further arrests of several highly implicated persons would clarification be possible.[478]

An officer from the Nievern constabulary recounted his attempts to locate a radio that had been stolen from Rudolf Strauss. Each of the suspects claimed to have no knowledge of the current whereabouts of the device. The defendants showed little remorse and portrayed themselves as innocent. The population also denied having seen the "Jewish action" although a great number of them looked on during the incident.[479]

In some cases, law enforcement authorities were able to identify some suspects who had clearly lied. In Bergen-Enkheim, where the synagogue had been torn down, several people were arrested and sent to jail for their false statements. A wife who had encouraged her husband to lie – which promptly led to his arrest – apologized and said that she (and her family) had feared being shunned as traitors in Bergen.[480] In another case, the state attorney suspected verbal agreements between the accused, since they had already been arrested once in 1946/1947 by the American Counter Intelligence Corps (CIC) and had been imprisoned in the local court prison of Alsfeld.[481] The criminal investigation department of the *Land* Rhineland-Palatinate (located in Koblenz) suspected similar arrangements among defendants who were accused of having been responsible for the defilement of the synagogue in Nastätten. Former storm troopers would meet from time to time for an "exchange of ideas." Witnesses accordingly said very little, since Nastätten was still considered to be "80 percent National Socialist," with the population still living in fear of the former rulers whose influence – despite the end of the war – was estimated to considerable.[482]

---

478 Koblenz 9 Js 11/49 = 9 KLs 13/50; 9 KLs 14/50, LHA Koblenz, Best. 584, 1, Nr. 1329, 1285-1288.
479 Koblenz 9 Js 129/49 = 9 KLs 11/50, LHA Koblenz, Best. 584, 1, Nr. 1253-1254.
480 Frankfurt 5 Js 104/46 = 5 KLs 15/47; HStA Wiesbaden, Abt. 461, Nr. 30021/1-8.
481 Giessen 2 Js 1761/49.
482 Koblenz 3 Js 580/48 = 9 KLs 7/49; LHA Koblenz, Best. 584, 1, Nr. 1239-1245.

The coroner of Frankenthal wrote to the prosecutor general in Neustadt about the difficulty and complexity of the investigation concerning the incidents of November 1938. Inquiries had been only partially successful, since the perpetrators flatly denied having a role and the line of argument always ran into heavy obstacles. In general, the most valuable material witnesses turn out to have been co-perpetrators.[483]

The judgment concerning the pogrom in Hechingen even stated that perpetrators and witnesses were equally tainted. Despite extensive preliminary inquiries, only some of the perpetrators could be located; material witnesses – former storm troopers – made statements that were considered by the court to be utter nonsense, even to the point that witnesses and perpetrators could be switched arbitrarily without substantially affecting the trial. The court thus refrained from using witnesses' testimony, and instead based its findings on the plea of the defendants (who either denied any involvement or blamed storm troopers who had died or been killed in action.)[484]

A similar observation was made by a senior prosecutor in Koblenz, who said that pogrom cases shared the same weakness, as defendants blamed those who were either dead, killed in action, or gone missing. Witnesses did not want to remember the incident. The senior prosecutor ascribed this to the fact that most of the participants in the "*Judenaktion*" had gone unpunished, led blameless lives and enjoyed a good reputation in civil life, thus making the witnesses reluctant to come up with the truth as they feared being viewed as informants. He suggested that it was necessary for the press to inform the public about the "correct" assessment of the pogrom.[485]

In Freudenburg, the mayor and NSDAP local group commander was charged with having been one of the main participants in the pogrom. He was seen holding prayer books and a candlestick in his hands as he left the synagogue during the pogrom. The local Nazi Party chief defended himself by saying that he had taken Torah Scrolls and prayer books to his office to preserve them from further havoc and mischief. The main hearing showed once again how unreliable witness accounts were. Witnesses often gave bold evidence when interrogated by the police because they assumed the culprit was far away; as soon as they were asked to repeat their statements under oath in court (with the defendants and their counsel present) they clammed up. One witness admitted that he only knew from hearsay about the charge and was not really a witness; another declared

---

[483] Frankenthal 9 KLs 1/49, AOFAA, AJ 3676, p. 36.
[484] Hechingen Js 358-359/46; Js 2029-2033/48 = KLs 123-128/48, StA Sigmaringen, Ho 400 T2, Nr. 584.
[485] Koblenz 9/2 Js 445/47 = 2 KLs 39/50 LHA Koblenz, Best. 584, 6, Nr. 44-47.

that he always "imagined" that the Nazi Party leader was involved due to his function. Proof was thus not possible.[486]

Sometimes delayed remorse led to pleas of guilt. A member of the National Socialist motor corps (Nationalsozialistisches *Kraftfahrkorps*, NSKK) who had already been sentenced for participation in the pogrom (breach of the public and private peace, assault in two cases) made a complete confession in which he charged several people, which led to additional investigations. He admitted that his testimony in court had been about 90 percent lies (upon the advice of his likewise indicted brother, the former local NSDAP group commander, mayor, and head of the fire-brigade of Oestrich).[487]

With investigations dragging on for months and sometimes years, even witnesses for the prosecution lost interest. The devastation of the flats of Jewish families in Landau could not be atoned for, as an immediate material witness died suddenly before she could be questioned by a judge. The statement she had made to the police could not be used by the court for a main hearing due to standard judicial rules. Several attempts were then made to obtain sworn statements from two survivors in the United States. Finally in September 1949, a New York attorney sent two questionnaires to the two female witnesses but received no answer and told the state attorney in Landau that there was obviously no further interest on behalf of Jews in the United States in prosecuting these crimes.[488] Similarly, the pogrom in Issel near Schweich remained unpunished as two witnesses for the prosecution, Julius Jakob (resident of New York) and Tilly Jakob Marx (living in Detroit) – who had been identified by the Jewish community of Trier – could not be found; rogatory letters to the United States were returned unopened.[489] Another investigation was terminated for lack of proof, although the guilt of the suspects was considered to have been proved; Isidor Kahn, the main witness to the pogrom in Kirf, could not appear in person for the main hearing and the temporary interrogation (*kommissarische Vernehmung*) was considered insufficient.[490]

Apart from the investigation difficulties, the legal evaluation was also a challenge. One of the primary demands for a conviction is the full investigation of the circumstances of the case. Yet, establishing the truth in a quagmire of rumors often proved beyond the ability of the court. Some acts were considered morally reprehensible, but were not penal offenses. A woman who witnessed the pogrom

---

[486] Trier 3 Js 404/47 = 3 KLs 45/48, AOFAA, AJ 1616, p. 802.
[487] Wiesbaden 4 Js 2393/46 = 4 KLs 9/49, HStA Wiesbaden, Abt. 468, Nr. 262/1-5.
[488] Landau 7 Js 9/47, AOFAA, AJ 3676, p. 38.
[489] Trier 3 Js 634/47, AOFAA, AJ 1616, p. 801.
[490] Trier 3 Js 541/48, AOFAA, AJ 1616, p. 804.

in Solingen-Ohligs declared this to have been the most wonderful night of her life; she had insulted Miss Goldschmidt, who was trying to gather her duvets from the street where the mob had thrown them saying: "Take your duvets and sleep well." The state prosecutor deemed the remarks crude and distasteful, but exempt from punishment.[491]

One problem was that a single deed could be perceived in a number of different ways. Entering the house of a Jewish family during the pogrom could be interpreted as the first act of a breach of the private peace, as material damage or theft, or as the attempt to suppress violence against the residents or express concern about their welfare. The ban against destroying objects could again stem from very different motives. When the windows of the synagogue in Weyer were smashed by youths, Alice E., who lived nearby, intervened. However, it was not outrage over the senseless destruction or empathy with the tortured Jews that drove her, but rather self-interest. She cried, "Stop it, you boys; this could become a BDM (Bund Deutsche Mädel–the female branch of the Hitler Youth) home one day!" She was a BDM member herself.[492] In Burghaslach, the flat of a Jewish woman named Bernheimer was not demolished – the NSDAP local group commander intended to buy the house himself and thus had prevented its destruction.[493]

In Trier, the local NSDAP group commander for Trier-Süd, who was also a member of the municipal administration in Trier and who used lists of Jewish residents to direct the vandalizing gangs on the pogrom night, would shortly afterwards move into the house of a Jew who had been coerced into selling it (according to the *Verordnung über den Einsatz des jüdischen Vermögens* (Ordinance on the Use of Jewish Property) of December 3, 1938 (RGBl. I, 1709)).[494] A storm commander (*SA-Sturmführer*) checked whether the synagogue in Bückeburg could be used as an office for the storm troopers; allegedly, a placard was posted saying, "This building has been entrusted to the storm troopers. Property damage will be penalized!" The declaration was in vain. The synagogue was burned down.[495]

The legal assessment was hampered by the fact that some perpetrators claimed they had assumed their acts of deprivation of liberty to be legal since the police or other authorities had ordered "protective custody" for the Jews and since the storm troopers – as an auxiliary police force – were entitled to make arrests.

---

491 Wuppertal 5 Js 81/47 = 5 KLs 44/48; HStA Düsseldorf – ZA Kalkum, Gerichte Rep. 191/43-44.
492 Limburg 2 Js 839/45 = 5/2 KLs 7/45, HStA Wiesbaden, Abt. 463, Nr. 922.
493 Nürnberg 2c Js 316/47 = KLs 238/47, StA Nürnberg, StAnw Nürnberg 2016/I-V.
494 Trier 2 Js 121/49 = 2 Ks 9/50, LHA Koblenz, Best. 584, 2, Nr. 851.
495 Bückeburg Js 257/47, StA Bückeburg, L 23 B Nr. 538.

Arson (or accessory to arson) was usually committed by just a handful of perpetrators. Presence at the scene of the crime did not constitute an offense. But how to distinguish between gawkers and arsonists? Damage to property – despite its enormous frequency – was often not prosecuted because victims did not press charges. This was probably due to the fact that damage to property was considered a lesser crime compared to deprivation of liberty, arson, and breach of the public peace. It could also be due to the fact that prosecutors were more interested in "public" damage, than in private damage suffered by individual victims. The courts also had difficulty in assessing the pogrom as a breach of the public peace. The assumption for this legal categorization is a "gathering together" of a number of people. If the participants in the pogrom were clearly a limited number of people (composed of NSDAP, storm troopers, SS members) who had gathered according to an order, the offense was not deemed by certain courts to have been a public breach of the peace. In Remscheid, gangs of six or seven storm troopers ransacked several stores and dwellings. As it could no longer be ascertained whether civilians had joined in with the limited group of storm troopers (thus creating the gathering together of an arbitrary mob according to § 125 StGB) the district court decided to sentence according to Control Council Law No. 10 rather than the German penal code.[496] In Trier, the penal chamber of the court also could not establish evidence of a public gathering together, as storm troopers, SS, and NSDAP members had been ordered to line up, were informed about the purpose, and organized into gangs. It could not be established that other people assembled or joined in. Thus, the judgment was again pronounced according to Control Council Law No. 10.[497] In Zweibrücken a similar argumentation concerning the pogrom in Landstuhl, where two uniformed storm trooper gangs had committed the crimes, also led to a decision made according to Crimes against Humanity. This met with protest from the state prosecutor, prompting the supreme court in Neustadt to change the sentence in that respect and declared that a breach of public peace had also occurrred, since according to § 125 StGB it made no difference whether it was an accidentally assembled mob or people ordered to line up; instead, the number of people and the threat they exuded were deemed relevant.[498]

---

496 Wuppertal 5 Js 1099/47 = 5 KLs 51/47, HStA Düsseldorf – ZA Kalkum, Gerichte Rep. 191/138, similarly also Trier 3 Js 253/47 = 3 KLs 5/48, LHA Koblenz, Best. 584, 2, Nr. 741-744 and Mönchengladbach 6 Js 2085/46 = 6 KLs 4/48; HStA Düsseldorf – ZA Kalkum, Gerichte Rep. 10/201; 204; 205.
497 Trier 2 Js 496/48 = 2 KLs 26/49, AOFAA, AJ 1616, p. 805.
498 Zweibrücken 7 Js 3/49 = KLs 24/49, AOFAA, AJ 3676, p. 38.

During the pogrom in Bad Kissingen, houses and a Jewish children's sanatorium were demolished and the synagogue burned down.[499] The state attorney pleaded that the excess disgraced the German people and that the crimes had been punishable at the time they were committed, thus making atonement necessary. Defense counsel argued that during the Third Reich, a latent state of breach of public peace had prevailed, thus a disturbance of public order was not possible, which made the defendants blameless. Furthermore, they had only obeyed orders, had been interned in Allied camps and had only been incriminated by denunciation. Indeed, the NSDAP district commander of Bad Kissingen, the county administrator, the commander of the storm troopers and the head of the SD branch (Security Service) were acquitted as the court could not bring itself to define the above-mentioned crimes as a breach of the public peace. Only a storm troop colonel (*SA-Standartenführer*) was sentenced to two years and six months in the penitentiary for incitement to arson.

Even indifference towards organs of law and order in the face of obvious crimes was not punished. A member of the police and a member of the voluntary fire brigade were given credit for non-involvement (they had learned of the impending arson and had not yet ordered police and fire-brigade to intervene) as they had acknowledged that by intervening they would be in contravention with the National Socialist state. Their failure to act was not considered worthy of penalization.[500]

Others questioned the character of synagogues as houses of (active) prayer. On November 10, 1938, the synagogue of Petershagen was demolished. However, the responsible district court refused to schedule a main hearing for the case because it was considered doubtful that the barn-like and already quite derelict edifice could still have been considered to be a synagogue. Thus, according to the court, violation of religious feeling, the freedom of religion of Jews, or the crime of destroying a building used for religious services were not applicable. Because the Jewish community had offered the premises for sale in 1927 and had last used the building in 1937, the perpetrators were given the benefit of the doubt; it was considered unlikely that they knew that the building was used for religious services. The culprits argued further that they had "only" demolished the interior in order to prevent worse destruction, as the local Nazi head had been being pressured by the NSDAP district to act.[501]

No excuse offered by the perpetrators was cheap and nasty enough. In Osnabrück a member of the SS claimed that he had been headed for the brothel when

---

[499] Schweinfurt 3 Js 365/46 = KLs 43/49.
[500] Koblenz 9/2 Js 1100/47 = 9 Ks 9/50; LHA Koblenz, Best. 584, 1, Nr. 1296-1298, 1336.
[501] Bielefeld 5 Js Pol 114/47.

he decided to make a detour to the burning synagogue where he stayed for about two hours – according to his statement – naturally without participating in any demolishings.[502] A former member of the constabulary claimed never to have heard of the pogrom in Schupbach until he was confronted with the bill of indictment charging him.[503] Guilt feelings were in short supply. In Mönchsroth near Dinkelsbühl the home of the Levitte family (who had lived in the town since 1776) was ransacked and one storm trooper (a teacher at a high-school in Dinkelsbühl) mistreated Elkan Levitte. In a post-war interrogation the suspect stated: "I could not see a crime in my acts at the time, as I was ordered to service by my superior [*SA-Sturmbannführer*]."[504]

Not infrequently, penal chambers of courts were positively glowing with benevolence towards the perpetrators. They abetted acquittal or terminations by themselves supplying the most outrageous explanations. The arson of the synagogue of Twistringen – committed by an SA senior company commander and a deputy mayor – was described with a contradiction in terms as an "excess of inconsequential range, which can occur anywhere in times of political agitation."[505]

Even when details given by perpetrators were verifiably incorrect – e.g., the court was able to prove that the NSDAP district commander of Oldenburg had given orders by telephone even before he had received the call from the NSDAP regional commander of Weser-Ems, Röver, from Munich – the chamber could not bring itself to a conviction. In this case, the proof (beyond reasonable doubt) for a conviction was missing; as the person in question had been in contact with the NSDAP district commander of Friesland, Emden, and Norden, it was not possible to prove that he incited them to arson.[506] The former NSDAP of Oldenburg himself claimed that his calls to other district commanders had been intended as calls for moderation in the anti-Semitic actions.

A conviction was not certain even if the circumstances of a deed were obvious, the perpetrators unmistakably guilty, and the legislation clear. In Neustadt an der Aisch, about 100 storm troopers assembled in the market place in the morning and formed gangs of about 4–12 men who then went to the dwellings of the five Jewish families of Neustadt. The sentence lauded the storm troopers on their behavior as they "limited" themselves to intrusion into dwellings and the smashing of china and tumbling of furniture, while excesses elswhere had been a lot

---

502 Osnabrück 4 Js 582/49 StA Osnabrück, Rep 945 Akz. 6/1983, Nr. 621.
503 Limburg 2 Js 1207/45 = 2 KLs 16/46, HStA Wiesbaden, Abt. 463, Nr. 1163.
504 Vernehmung 5.5.1949, Ansbach 5 Js 45/49 = Ms 66/49; StA Nürnberg, StAnw Ansbach 956.
505 Verden 6 Js 305/47 = 6 KLs 21/47; StA Stade, Rep. 171a Verden, Nr. 589 (I-III).
506 Oldenburg 9 Js 3/49 = 9 Ks 16/50, StA Oldenburg, Best. 140-4 Acc. 13/79, Nr. 204.

worse. One reason for "moderation" was that the local Nazi Party head was interested in the purchase of the house of a Jewish family – which he acquired shortly afterward. A retroactive expiation was not deemed necessary by the court as the culprits were ill, they were POWs, or had suffered other deprivations since the crime. The former NSDAP district commander was complimented for his moderation as he had not given orders to torch the synagogue and had limited the riots to the few "Jewish families." (Whether the court did not understand the anti-Semitic nature of the pogrom, or whether the judges wanted to point out that it was better to direct violence against human beings than against objects, I do not know.) As the former district commander had also acted on orders and spent three years in internment, the court felt obliged to terminate the procedure by applying the amnesty of December 31, 1949.[507]

Other courts allowed for the denazification sentences to be deducted from the penal sentences. In Nuremberg, storm troopers had been ordered to smash the store of Mr. Gutmann at the Josefsplatz. When they arrived, they found that the shop had already been destroyed. As they moved on to their next target – a flat – they found again that others had been there first. The state attorney pleaded for three months' imprisonment; the court, however, terminated the trial on the grounds that the perpetrators had already atoned for their deeds in the denazification trial, therefore principles of justice would not demand a further atonement.[508]

A trial against a local Nazi Party chief based in Nuremberg-Wöhrd was similarly unsatisfactory. Storm troopers had looked him up at night and asked him for addresses of Jewish families. During the night he toured the town in a car and inspected devastated Jewish facilities, among them the burned-down synagogue in the Essenweinstrasse. He then succeeded in obtaining a printing machine from the Phönix Club (located on the Prinzregentenufer), bringing it to the offices of the NSDAP local group headquarters, and hiding it in a vault until it was destroyed in an Allied air raid in January 1945. The court did not see that a crime had been committed: There was no proof of breach of the peace, i.e., the accused had not taken part in the intrusion of houses and synagogues. There were no witnesses accusing him of assault or violence. There was no looting or theft because there was no intention of appropriation in the taking of the printing machine because he had brought the machine to the offices of the NSDAP local group headquarters. Furthermore, the statute of limitations applied.[509]

---

507 Nürnberg-Fürth 1d Js 2682-90/48 = 485 KLs 173/50; StA Nürnberg, StAnw Nürnberg 2839/I-III.
508 Nürnberg 2c Js 2155/48 = KMs 6/49, StA Nürnberg, StAnw Nürnberg 2319.
509 Nürnberg-Fürth 2d Js 1894/48 = KLs 126/49, StA Nürnberg, StAnw Nürnberg 2459.

In Duisburg a former storm trooper (who had been expelled from the SA for a theft from his own comrades) had participated in the smashing of the Jewish prayer room, nabbed a woman's handbag containing jewelry in a shop, and 4–5 boxes of cigarettes from a tobacconist. The court credited him with "inexperience" (while the state attorney had seen monetary gain and a dishonorable intention in the behavior).[510]

A janitor couple in Landau (already mentioned above) who had made use of objects belonging to Jewish families also remained unpunished despite concealment; they profited from an amnesty despite the fact that the husband had even guarded the arrested Jews for several hours and had accompanied their transport to the Dachau Concentration Camp. His contribution to the crime – accessory to deprivation of liberty in coincidence with crime against humanity – was considered so negligible as to benefit from the amnesty of June 18, 1948.[511]

If perpetrators were actually convicted and sentenced, the punishment meted out was unbelievably mild. On top of that, the prison terms did not have to be served, due to the amnesty law of December 31, 1949. In Aurich, two perpetrators were found guilty of crimes against humanity in coincidence with severe breach of the public peace, grave deprivation of liberty, and extortionate robbery. Yet the court was reluctant to punish them and sentenced them to the lowest possible prison term – one year. The actual execution of the sentence was pronounced inappropriate by the court as the deeds had been committed before September 15, 1949, and none of those convicted had acted out of cruelty, a dishonorable disposition, or greed. The following reasoning bordered on the absurd: The defendants either had obeyed orders or had been "carried away in the spirit of comradeship by the momentum of the action," as the sentence put it. Although one defendant hauled off a candlestick (thus injuring the religious sensibilities of Jews), this was apologetically explained as the fruit of many years of anti-Semitic propaganda. Another forced a Jew to hand over a desk. His behavior was exculpated as his insight regarding his own deed had been obfuscated by the "events" and his "altruistic" motivation, since all he wanted was to acquire a desk for the Aurich storm troopers' office. The court did not consider this so reprehensible as to be considered dishonorable or mercenary.[512] In 1950, the high court of Oldenburg revised the decision of district court Aurich and ordered the enforcement of the punishment. The district court Aurich tried to avoid the execution of sentences in other cases as well – with similar explanations: no particular cruelty was detected, since perpetrators "only" arrested Jews but did not otherwise mistreat

---

510 Duisburg 21 Js 332/49 = 14 Ks 8/50, HStA Düsseldorf – ZA Kalkum, Gerichte Rep. 319/71-72.
511 Landau 7 Js 1/47 = KMs 10/47, AOFAA, AJ 3676, p. 36.
512 Aurich 2 Js 703/45 = 2 Ks 17/49, StA Aurich, Rep. 109, Nds., Nr. 4/1-12.

them; the deeds were not committed from disreputable dispositions as no hate, envy, vindictiveness, vandalism/lust for destruction, lust for power or blood were discernible.[513]

Mitigating circumstances were found even for hardened criminals. Juvenile offenders were considered so brainwashed by Nazi propaganda that they could no longer distinguish right from wrong.[514] Adults benefitted from considerations such as having received and obeyed, experiencing difficult family situations, or having been in a state of inebriation.

If execution of the sentence and a prison term actually loomed, perpetrators implored the authorities to temper justice with mercy. The NSDAP local group commander who had deported a 70-year-old Jewish woman from Hochspeyer to Mannheim and had been sentenced according to crimes against humanity in conjunction with deprivation of liberty to a mere four months in jail asked for a suspension of the sentence – which both court and police, and even the senior prosecutor in Kaiserslautern, were willing to grant. Only the intervention of the head of the French Control for German Justice – in the form of a letter to the regional head for Rheno-Palatinate – made it clear that this leniency was unacceptable and that he should serve at least part of the term.[515]

American observers, too, were outraged about the mild pleas of even the state prosecutors:

> For the lenient qualifications of the crimes in this case are not only the judges, but in the first place the prosecutor (Dr. Kretschmer, no party member) to blame.[516] ... It is well known that judges are too lenient in the sentencing of former Nazis; it will, however, serve them as a bad example if the prosecutors themselves qualify the crimes so favorably for those criminals.[517]

On the other hand, there were a few rare trials where severe punishments were meted out. Two perpetrators found guilty of arson and material damage during the pogroms in Darmstadt, Eberstadt, Griesheim, and Gräfenhausen were each

---

[513] Aurich 2 Js 720/48 = 2 Ks 7/48; StA Aurich, Rep. 109 Nds. E, Nr. 142/1-6.
[514] Limburg 2 Js 1207/45 = 2 KLs 16/46, HStA Wiesbaden, Abt. 463, Nr. 1163.
[515] Kaiserslautern 7 Js 107/47 = KLs 22/48, AOFAA, AJ 3676, p. 37.
[516] Activity report, October 5, 1947, NARA, OMGBY 17/183 – 3/15. The reference is made to Nürnberg-Fürth 2c Js 38/47 = KLs 53/47, StA Nürnberg, StAnw Nürnberg 1895/I-V.
[517] Activity report, October 5, 1947, NARA, OMGBY 17/183 – 3/15.

sentenced to seven years' imprisonment.[518] In Offenburg, the NSDAP district commander was sentenced in the first instance to five years.[519]

Although most trials wound up within a few months, some did take longer. In Schweinfurt, it took nearly 10 years to reach a valid final sentence. A first judgment was passed in 1947 (six months for breach of the public and private peace), but an appeal with the high court in Bamberg led to a renewed hearing and a new sentencing in 1949 (one year and six months' imprisonment for continued breach of the public and private peace). The trial resumed in 1956, when two witnesses for the prosecution softened their accusations. The case eventually ended in acquittal.[520] A similarly drawn-out affair was a Düsseldorf trial in which the charges were brought in 1948; after postponements, an appeal, and resumption, an acquittal was obtained in 1955.[521] In Hanau, 10 years would pass from the date of the first sentence in 1947 until the final dismissal of the case in 1957. By that time, both the victim, Benzion Adler from Ostheim (who had emigrated to Kapstadt) and one defense attorney had died.[522]

Semantics of Sentences

Although legal language is standardized to a large degree, the semantics of some of the judgments make it obvious that words did not come easily to the post-war judges in describing the pogrom. While many judgments start stereotypically ("Like everywhere in Germany, excesses occurred also in . . .") there are some sentences that make clear how judges were at a loss for words and how they tried to make sense of the riots or attempt to explain the inexplicable. As in the description of the pogroms of Weier, Nochern, and Lierschied, they used florid language to invoke German history, false ideologies, fanatization by propaganda, and the violation of human rights.[523]

---

518 Darmstadt Js 5719/46 = KLs 97/46; see also rubric "Aus aller Welt," *Jüdisches Gemeindeblatt für die Nord-Rheinprovinz und Westfalen*, November 9, 1946. One of the convicted ringleaders fled the internment camp Darmstadt and took refuge in the Soviet Occupied Zone respectively the German Democratic Republic and thus did not serve the term. He died in Leipzig in 1960.
519 Offenburg 1 Js 2112/46 = 1 Ks 1-3/48; see also "Verbrechen gegen die Menschlichkeit," *Jüdisches Gemeindeblatt für die britische Zone*, July 14, 1948.
520 Schweinfurt 1 Js 1201/46 = KLs 16/47.
521 Düsseldorf 8 Js 9/48 = 8 Ks 6/49; 8 Ks 1/55 HStA Düsseldorf – ZA Kalkum, Gerichte Rep. 372/478-480.
522 Hanau 3 Js 141/47 = 3 KLs 5/47; HStA Wiesbaden, Abt. 471, Nr. 212/1-5.
523 Koblenz 3 Js 210/48 = 9 KLs 42/49, LHA Koblenz, Best. 584, 1, Nr. 1823.

Others racked their brains to understand the origins of the pogrom: "How could this aberration occur in Vallendar? All defendants were people with no criminal history". Sentences explained the commotion with the instigating propaganda ("*aufputschende Propaganda*").[524] For Deidesheim, the court determined that the defendants had succumbed to mass psychosis.[525] In addition, the motivation for the adjudication is broached in the sentences, i.e. necessary atonement.[526] When meting out punishment, courts took into consideration "that the defendants had participated in a crime that for a long time besmirched the name of Germany the world over. Thanks to the defendants and their peers, people beyond our borders have spoken of Germans with anger and loathing for 10 years now."[527] In Landau, the presiding judge pointed out that the events under investigation had been dishonest and disreputable for the German people and thus had incurred the hatred of the entire civilized world against them.[528]

Dealing with the Jewish religion itself was a delicate matter for the courts; knowledge of Judaism, its rites, and traditions was patchy at best. Anyone familiar with the religion would have been bewildered by the awkward formulations. Police recorded in the charges concerning the arson of the synagogue in Zoppot as "Injured party: Jewish Christian community in Zoppot."[529] Describing the Torah Scrolls was also a challenge. One judgment mentioned that they were "wrapped in kid/goat or pigskin."[530] In Osnabrück the sentence included an explanation the Torah. The result was a well-meaning, but totally ignorant description of the scroll as a parchment of pigskin.[531] Perpetrators often mentioned the "Jewish church" when referring to the synagogue[532] or during the pogrom demanded hidden "church treasures."[533] The seating in the synagogue was described as "*Kirchenbänke*" (church benches),[534] books taken from the synagogue were referred to as "*Kirchenbücher*" (church books).[535] Witnesses fared

---

524 Ibid.
525 Frankenthal 9 KLs 1/49, AOFAA, AJ 3676, p. 36.
526 Hanau 2 Js 951/46 = 2 KLs 3/49, HStA Wiesbaden, Abt. 471, Nr. 175/1-2.
527 Hechingen Js 358-359/46; Js 2029-2033/48 = KLs 123-128/48, StA Sigmaringen, Ho 400 T2, Nr. 584.
528 "Das Urteil im Synagogenbrand-Prozess," *Vorderpfälzer Tageblatt*, April 21, 1950; Landau 7 Js 44/47 = Ks 3/50; AOFAA, AJ 3676, p. 37 and AJ 3676, p. 36.
529 Kiel 2 Js 808/47, LA Schleswig-Holstein, Abt. 352 Kiel, Nr. 4497.
530 Aachen 4 Js 53/46 = 4 Ks 3/49, HStA Düsseldorf – ZA Kalkum, Gerichte Rep. 89/219-221.
531 Osnabrück 4 Js 1521/46 = 4 Ks 7/48, StA Osnabrück, Rep 945 Akz. 6/1983, Nr. 54-55.
532 Köln 24 Js 884/47, HStA Düsseldorf – ZA Kalkum, Gerichte Rep. 231/92; also Wuppertal 5 Js 3369/46 = 5 KLs 34/48, HStA Düsseldorf – ZA Kalkum, Gerichte Rep. 191/72.
533 Wuppertal 5 Js 3591/46 = 5 KLs 82/48; HStA Düsseldorf – ZA Kalkum, Gerichte Rep. 240/261-265.
534 Bonn 3 Js 1015/47 = 3 Ks 2/49; HStA Düsseldorf – ZA Kalkum, Gerichte Rep. 145/471.
535 Bonn 7 Js 1137/47 = 7 KLs 12/47, HStA Düsseldorf – ZA Kalkum, Gerichte Rep. 195/333-334.

no better. One was referred to with aplomb as "racially Jewish."⁵³⁶ Frieda Kahn from Freudenburg was unabashedly marked as *"Judenmädchen"* (a Jewess).⁵³⁷ Curiously lacking as well was a name for the anti-Semitic outrage of November 1938. The judgments took refuge with *"Judenaktion,"* the term used during the Third Reich, or used euphemistic descriptions as in Hamburg where the "notorious days of glass" or a rather minimized "window-smashing action" frequently appeared.⁵³⁸

Even observers not too familiar with the German language were repelled by the semantics: "The observation was made that in bills of indictment where Jewish people are involved (mostly as victims in pogrom cases), the phraseology is used: 'the Jew N.N.' It is felt this practice should be discontinued."⁵³⁹ The language used was sometimes linked to the staffing of the chambers and courts as such, as the American Military Government noted:

> At the Landgericht Mosbach an acute shortage of judges exists. Your instruction to the effect that only politically unimplicated judicial personnel should participate in trials with political backgrounds cannot be enforced since none of the judges, with the exception of the Landsgerichtspräsident, posesses the above-mentioned qualification. As a result, three judges classified as 'followers' were scheduled to try a case of arson of a synagogue on 4 September 1947. Upon objection by our staff inspector, the Landsgerichtspräsident attempted to get at least one politically unimplicated judge from another court and it is believed that he finally succeeded in securing Amtsgerichtsrat Muench from Buchen. This instance illustrates the serious personnel situation in Mosbach, and prompt remedial action is indicated as necessary.⁵⁴⁰

Even toward the end of the occupation, American observers recognized that, "Antisemitism [sic], covert in most cases, but openly expressed from the bench even recently, still exists and requires positive action by Military Government."⁵⁴¹

Adjudicating the Killings

The number of Jews killed during the pogrom is not known; one number – including the territory of the then Reich, i.e., Austria and the Sudetenland – cited in

---

536 Trier 2 Js 266/46 = 2 KLs 24/48; LHA Koblenz, Best. 584, 2, Nr. 850; AOFAA, AJ 1616, p. 799.
537 Trier 3 Js 316/49, AOFAA, AJ 1616, p. 805.
538 Hamburg 14 Js 535/48, StA Hamburg, Best. 213-11, Nr. 18800/64.
539 Weekly report, May 3, 1947, NARA, OMGBY 17/183 – 3/14.
540 Letter of Ralph E. Brown to Minister of Justice Württemberg-Baden, August 28, 1947, NARA, OMGWB 12/140 – 1/1-20.
541 Report Legal Division [undated; presumably 1949], NARA, OMGBY 17/188 – 3/1.

official statements of the National Socialists is 91.⁵⁴² Jews who died of injuries sustained during the pogrom or who committed suicide because of it are not contained in the count, nor are those who died in the concentration camps (Buchenwald, at least 233; Dachau, at least 185; and Sachsenhausen, where numbers were not documented) subsequent to their arrests. A survey of the places where pogroms led to the murder of Jewish women and men is presented in the book *Fire!*.⁵⁴³

It seems that most of these murders were investigated and – if possible – tried in the post-war years after initial investigations (by National Socialists) had been quashed. It is difficult to distinguish between clear-cut cases of murder or manslaughter where victims were shot, stabbed or hanged and those where death was caused by abuse either during the pogrom or shortly thereafter. Prosecutors and courts were often unable to tie the actions of assailants to the fatal consequences for victims.

In the territory of Western Germany, the following judicial proceedings after 1945 dealt with deaths during the pogrom categorized as either murder, manslaughter, grievous bodily harm resulting in death, or suicide:

---

542 Report of the Highest Party Court of the NSDAP to Göring, February 13, 1939, IMT, vol. 32, PS-3063, 20-29.
543 Nachama/Neumärker/Simon (editors), *Fire! Anti-Jewish Terror on 'Kristallnacht' in November 1938*, 89.

Table 3. Number of victims of murder, manslaughter, or grievous bodily harm resulting in death or suicide during the pogrom according to West-German judicial proceedings (1945-1949)

Ahlen	1	Goslar	1	Neustadt an der Weinstrasse	2
Altengronau	1	Grebenau	1*	Neuwied	1
Aschaffenburg	2	Hanau	1	Nordheim	1
Bamberg	1	Hilden	6 H	Nuremberg	7
Beckum	1	Höxter	1	Oberdorf	1
Bremen	5	Horn	1	Peine	1
Cologne	1	Kaiserslautern	2**	Regensburg	1
Darmstadt- Arheilgen	2	Karlsruhe	1	Seesen	1
Düsseldorf	1	Kitzingen	2	Solingen	1
Eberstadt	1	Landau	1	Wallertheim	1
Emden	1	Lichtenfels	1	Wöllstein	1
Felsberg	1	Lünen	3	Würzburg	1
Frankenberg/Eder	1*	Munich	1		
Frankfurt am Main	1	Neumarkt (Upper Palatinate)	1		

*Died in Buchenwald **1 died in Dachau H 5 Jews; 1 non-Jew

As has been explained, this enumeration cannot be complete. In addition, because I have focused on the trials and investigations conducted in the occupation years, I have omitted proceedings initiated after 1950 that may contain inquests into pogrom crimes and murder.

Case Study: The Trial Concerning the Killing in Würzburg

In Würzburg, the NSDAP Cell Commander Heinrich Vates was ordered to arrest Ernst Elias Lebermann in Würzburg. A mob of allegedly 400 to 450 people accompanied him through the streets of Würzburg uttering rallying cries. Lebermann, 65, was battered so badly that he died the next day. A block leader, Franz Völker, and Alois Neuberger, an NSDAP functionary and civil servant participated in the assault. In November 1946, Heinrich Vates and Franz Völker were sentenced to one and one and a half years of penitentiary respectively for grave breach of the public peace; in March 1947 Alois Neuberger received one and a half years' jail time for the same offense. The Bavarian Ministry of Justice petitioned the Military Government to suppress the judgments of November 1946 and March 1947 citing Law No. 2, Article VII, number 12c, as neither the finding of guilt nor the degree of penalty were in accordance with the state of affairs and the legal position.⁵⁴⁴ The court had referred to an autopsy carried out by a pathologist, Prof. Dr. Karl W. of the University of Würzburg, on November 15, 1938. He had rendered an expert opinion concluding that Lebermann died of heart failure due to a clogged artery; the injuries to head and buttocks were not considered to have been causal (*ursächlich*) to Lebermann's death. (The state prosecutor contemplated pressing charges against the pathologist for favoritism.⁵⁴⁵) The medical opinion had obviously been worded with the deliberate intent to prevent an inquest into manslaughter or assault with fatal consequences. In the main hearing in November 1946, the pathologist disavowed his former expertise and declared that the death had been caused by mistreatment and emotional agitation. A further expert opinion diagnosed heart failure after mistreatment as cause of death. However, in both the November 1946 and the March 1947 sentences, the court had referred to the autopsy report of 1938⁵⁴⁶ in which the abuse was not seen as the cause of death. The court had not even produced a conviction for assault with fatal consequences. The Bavarian Ministry of Justice considered this an error in the finding of guilt; furthermore, the punishment meted out was considered too lenient: the convicts had not even been deprived of their honorary civil rights. The legal division with the American Military Government in Bavaria (OMGBY) passed the minister of justice's petition to the legal division of the American Military Government (OMGUS), where it was decided that the sentence was to be overturned for being in "flagrant violation of MG policies."⁵⁴⁷ Hans W. Weigert wrote:

> This case is the first judgment of a German court to be nullified for more than technical reasons. It is also the first case in which a German administration of justice has taken the initiative to request that Military Government make use of its powers vested in it under Article VII, 12c. For these reasons it is felt that proper publicity should be given to this matter. It should be stressed that Military Government is actually exercising its powers of control and supervision in regard to the German judiciary and also that the German authorities have been cooperating fully with Military Government.⁵⁴⁸

The American Legal Division pondered how they would justify their intervention and decided on an analysis of American policy: "I believe that if a rather strong

---

544 Letter Bavarian Ministry of Justice to Legal Division, Military Government for Bavaria, July 8, 1947, NARA, OMGBY 17/183 – 3/12.
545 Letter Prosecutor General Bamberg to Paul J. Farr, German Courts Branch, Bamberg, July 30, 1947, NARA, OMGBY 17/183 – 3/12.
546 Letter Prosecutor General Bamberg to Bavarian Ministry of Justice, June 20, 1947, NARA, OMGBY 17/183 – 3/12.
547 Letter of John M. Raymond, Legal Division, OMGUS, to OMGBY, August 28, 1947, NARA, OMGBY 17/183 – 3/12.
548 Memorandum of Hans W. Weigert, August 25, 1947, NARA, OMGBY 17/183 – 3/12.

statement of our basic policy and War crimes Program were made in some such way and appropriate publicity given to it, it might tend to bring other courts into line without attacking the judgment of the court on the case presented to it." The invalidation was thus to be worded in such a way as to give no grounds for suspicion that the Americans "were either acting as a Supreme Court or acting as the Nazi Ministry of Justice used to act in dictating the judgments and sentences that ought to be pronounced in certain cases. Any possibility for criticism along these lines must be avoided at all costs." Any further intervention, i.e., against the penal chamber or the court for miscarriage of justice (as suggested by Hans W. Weigert) was rejected by Legal Division.[549] Colonel Raymond, chief of the Legal Division OMGUS, criticized Weigert's approach in a letter to Alvin Rockwell: "As to the present case, I did not like the expressions of personal opinion injected in the summary of the case prepared by Mr. Weigert."[550] Weigert, as director of the German Courts Branch, OMGUS, had traveled to Würzburg and checked out the judges concerned; he learned that two had been members of the NSDAP since 1937 and one judge in training had also been affiliated with Nazi organizations and had benefitted from the denazification youth amnesty.[551] Weigert insisted on the latter's removal from the penal chamber. The president of the responsible high court in Bamberg, Dr. Thomas Dehler, rejected the demand to have the two judges removed from their posts.[552] The President of the Würzburg district court, Lobmiller, declared that then it would be impossible to staff any penal chamber in the Würzburg district court.[553] In a memorandum, the Americans declared that typically no nullification would have been considered until a high court had decided about the appeal, and as the deadline had passed, normal procedures were no longer possible: "Normally, this Division refuses to consider Military Government intervention in such a case until appeal to, and final disposition by, the Oberlandesgericht."[554]

After the quashing of the sentence by the Military Government, a new main hearing before the district court of Bamberg could be held. The prosecution was

---

549 Letter of John M. Raymond, Legal Division, OMGUS to Alvin J. Rockwell, September 2, 1947, NARA, OMGBY 17/183 – 3/12.
550 Ibid.
551 Letter Richard A. Wolf, German Courts Branch, OMGBY, to Director OMGBY, October 24, 1947, NARA, OMGBY 17/183 –3/12.
552 Letter Thomas Dehler to Richard Wolf, German Courts Branch, OMGBY, October 27, 1947, NARA, OMGBY 17/187 – 1/6.
553 Letter of President of district court Würzburg, Lobmiller, to President of High court Bamberg, October 24, 1947, NARA, OMGBY 17/187 – 1/6.
554 Memorandum of Legal Division, OMGUS, to Director OMGBY, November 1, 1947, NARA, OMGBY 17/183 – 3/12.

represented by Senior Prosecutor Dr. Johann Ilkow;[555] District Court President Dr. Weinkauff and two other judges formed the penal chamber. Neither the prosecutor nor District Court President Weinkauff was affected by the Law of Liberation (denazification). Finding staff for the penal chamber proved difficult: "The entire district of Bamberg has no judges or *Assessoren* who do not fall under the liberation law besides the two judges mentioned above."[556]

On March 4, 1948, in the main hearing at Bamberg district court, Vates was sentenced to three years and six months, Völker to three years and Neuberger to four years in prison for severe breach of the peace. (The state attorney had pleaded for sentences between six and eight years' imprisonment.) Interest in the case had repercussions far beyond Würzburg or the high court of district Bamberg. The former rabbi of Würzburg, Dr. Siegmund Hanover, now living in New York City, wrote that he had followed the case with rapt attention "and I was glad to learn the ridiculous verdict was quashed by Military Government."[557] Still, once again, the main hearing did not result in a sentencing for murder, manslaughter, or grievous bodily harm.

Public Reaction to the Trials

The Western Allies and the German public viewed the trials with interest but also with reservation. Representatives of the German Justice Branch partook as observers at several criminal trials of Nazis who had committed atrocities and other crimes for racial and political motives during the Nazi regime. Such trials were usually held before packed courtrooms and under the close scrutiny of the German press. German judicial authorities emphasize the importance of such trials and apparently welcome the attendance of Military Government representatives.[558]

A member of a UN commission traveled from London to observe a trial by the district court of Paderborn concerning the mistreatment and blackmail of a

---

[555] Dr. Johann Ilkow was married to a Jewish wife who had survived Theresienstadt ghetto. Due to his marriage Ilkow had been pensioned off as a state attorney in Brünn (Brno) in March 1943. He was then put into a forced labout camp in Bohemia in 1944. See personal file Dr. Johann Ilkow, HStA München, MJu 25339.

[556] Letter Richard A. Wolf, German Courts Branch, OMGBY to Director, OMGBY, February 7, 1948, NARA, OMGBY 17/183– 3/12.

[557] Letter Dr. Siegmund Hanover to Kurt Eyerman, German Courts Branch, Legal Division, OMGBY, March 17, 1948, NARA, OMGBY 17/183 – 3/12.

[558] Weekly Report, October 25, 1946, NARA, OMGWB 12/135 – 2/4.

Jewish horse trader in Warburg in the spring of 1938.[559] The American Legal Division stated for Bavaria: "The undersigned has noticed a definite tendency among judges and prosecutors in the Oberlandesgerichtsbezirk [Nuremberg] to evade the prosecution and trial of Nazis who have committed crimes against anti-Nazis and Jews in 1938 and April 1945."[560]

Some of the shortfalls were based on misunderstandings. The senior prosecutor in Amberg procrastinated because he was unsure of how to deal with certain aspects:

> The Chief Prosecutor has been handling the case of the destruction of the Amberg synagogue by SA men. He did not draw the indictment, however, up to date because he was waiting for the verdict in the Nuremberg War Crimes Trial for the reason of *ne bis in idem* [not being tried twice for the same offense]. The undersigned made it clear to him that the guilt of individual SA men participating in the destruction of the synagogue has little to do with the question whether the SA is to be considered a criminal organization or not.[561]

As one of the defendants was the former state attorney and storm trooper company commander Dr. Robert R., his colleague probably also felt inhibited. Legal personnel dealing with the arson of the Ansbach synagogue faced the same problem: "The Prosecutor declined to sign the charge sheet considering himself prejudiced in the case Chief because he had worked together with LG-Rat G. [Dr. Otto G., defendant and SA troop commander] for a number of years. The Prosecutor General ordered prosecutor Göppner of Rothenburg (branch office of Ansbach) to sign the charge sheet."[562]

On the whole, however, observers thought that state attorneys and judges did get things going, leading to a true avalanche of investigations and trials concerning the pogrom. The American Legal Division reported for the year 1948: "The Landgericht [Giessen] has recently been flooded with Landfriedensbruch [breach of the peace] cases which originated between 1933 and 1945. These cases are causing a great deal of work for which purpose Staatsanwalt Dr. Lipschitz from Dillenburg had been given a temporary assignment as Landgerichtsdirektor of a second new Strafkammer [criminal court]."[563] For Giessen in Hesse, the number of pogrom trials ready for main hearing was given as 60 (of which 27 had actually

---

559 Paderborn 2 Js 338/46 = 2 KLs 18/47; "Ein deutsches Urteil," *Jüdisches Gemeindeblatt für die britische Zone*, October 24, 1947.
560 Weekly Report, November 16, 1946, NARA, OMGBY 17/183 – 3/13.
561 Weekly Report, September 28, 1946, NARA, OMGBY 17/183 – 3/13.
562 Monthly Report, February 24, 1948, NARA, OMGBY 17/183 – 3/15.
563 Inspection LG Giessen, March 23, 1948, NARA, OMGH 17/209 – 1/2.

been tried).[564] In April 1948, a second penal chamber and in autumn 1948, a third were established at Giessen district court to tackle the pogrom cases.[565]

The American Legal Division was fully aware of the inherent difficulties: "Some of these trials are held up because the main offenders are still in internment camps."[566] The Legal Division tried to be accommodating in single cases by letting the suspects be interviewed in the camps.[567] Sometimes main hearings were delayed as the penal chamber had to be re-constituted in the search of judges unencumbered by a Nazi past. In some places Jewish victims of the Third Reich returned as judges. Dr. Fritz Valentin, the presiding judge in the Hamburg-Harburg pogrom trial, had emigrated with his family to Britain in 1939 because he had been expelled from his profession as a judge in 1934.[568] In rare cases it was the former perpetrators who returned: The second co-chair of the chamber at Ravensburg District Court that dealt with the arson of the synagogue in Laupheim was Edmund Stark, who had previously worked as prosecutor at the notorious Nazi People's Court.[569]

The American Military Government knew how important witnesses were for the trials. "The difficulties to try these cases are manifold: most principals and many witnesses are still in a Lager."[570] Or, "Germans seem generally very reluctant in testifying against Nazis. It is said time and again that one does not know how long Americans will occupy the country; therefore it is better to be careful."[571] A report on one of the first pogrom trials in Nuremberg ran: "In this connection it must be stated that according to experience from the past it is exceptionally hard in the district of the Oberlandesgericht [Nuremberg] to find prosecution witnesses for such cases."[572] When the desecration of the synagogue in Windsbach was tried, American observers stated that hardly any evidence had come from the witnesses because they had been "unusually timid and reticent" in their statements. A conviction of the defendants would not have been possible if they had

---

564 Inspection LG Giessen, April 21, 1948, NARA, OMGH 17/209 – 1/2.
565 Inspection LG Giessen, October 19, 1948, NARA, OMGH 17/209 – 1/2.
566 Inspection LG Darmstadt, June 12, 1947, NARA, OMGH 17/209 – 1/2.
567 Letter of Ralph E. Brown to Interrogation Section, January 2, 1947, concerning interrogations of suspects in internment camp Moosburg and Dachau re. riots in Weinheim, NARA, OMGWB 12/133 – 2/4.
568 Hamburg 14 Js 70/46 = 14 Ks 7/49, StA Hamburg, Best. 213-11, Nr. 22701/54 (Bd. 1-11).
569 Ravensburg Js 9154-9170/47 = KLs 6-22/48; KLs 23-28/48, StA Sigmaringen, Wü 29/1 T 1, Nr. 6890.
570 Report, September 2, 1946, NARA, OMGBY 17/183 – 2/12.
571 Report, August 12, 1946, NARA, OMGBY 17/183 – 2/12.
572 Weekly Report, March 14, 1947, NARA, OMGBY 17/183 – 3/13.

not owned up to their deeds themselves.⁵⁷³ Many witnesses would also give in to insinuations and pressure of defense counsel, "which is in no way balanced out by the weak presentation of the prosecution."⁵⁷⁴

One of the reasons given by the Americans for the reluctance of witnesses for the prosecution was that former Nazis were bringing libel charges against those who had given evidence against them before the *Spruchkammern*.⁵⁷⁵

A representative of the German justice branch in Hesse reported the same problem when looking into pogrom trials: "It has been the experience of the undersigned [Littman] that, on one hand, the judges in Landfriedensbruch trials often face a solid block of poker-faced local witnesses who do not remember anything pertaining to the events after 1933, and on the other hand, the best evidence available is sometimes only an affidavit from abroad on the part of the emigrant."⁵⁷⁶ A suggestion was made to develop a principle of statutory declaration to enable witnesses living in the United States to make sworn statements before a judge (rather than a notary as for an affidavit) thus increasing their value as evidence because these statements could then be made available to German courts. Although the principle was difficult and costly in terms of labor, Inspector Littman hoped that it might stem the rapidly increasing number of acquittals.

Most acquittals met with harsh criticism. When two former state attorneys and storm troopers suspected of involvement in the pogrom in Nuremberg walked away scot-free, the chief of the legal division in Bavaria spoke his mind about what he termed an "erroneous sentence which was given unpleasant publicity in the German newspaper edited in Nuremberg."⁵⁷⁷ Upon the conviction of a medical doctor who as a storm trooper had been involved in the arson at Bechhofen synagogue, the Americans found fault with the procedure, maintaining that the court had not arrested him immediately after the sentence, thus revealing insecurity on the part of the administration of justice.⁵⁷⁸ Indulgent judges and mild sentences also met with disapproval:

> The court was so lenient because the Jews were not beaten and only damage to property was done and because the defendants were a 'well disciplined' lot ... The German press in Nuremberg commented with some sarcasm on this unusual leniency of the court ... The Chief Prosecutor – who is a half Jew – and who represented the charges at the trial told the

---

573 Report, October 19, 1947, NARA, OMGBY 17/182 – 3/9; see also NARA, OMGBY 17/183 – 3/15.
574 Report, August 9, 1947, NARA, OMGBY 17/182 – 3/9.
575 Report, February 17, 1947, NARA, OMGBY 17/183 – 2/12.
576 Activity Report, March 23, 1948, NARA, OMGH 17/209 – 1/2.
577 Report, January 24, 1948, NARA, OMGBY 17/182 – 3/9; Report, October 19, 1947, NARA, OMGBY 17/182 – 3/9; Monthly report, January 24, 1948, NARA, OMGBY 17/183 – 3/15.
578 Report, November 20, 1947, NARA, OMGBY 17/182 – 3/9.

undersigned that according to his opinion the courts are so lenient in these cases because the judges are convinced that all these defendants would be tried again by the denazification boards where they would be sent to labor camps anyway for these deeds; thus if they obtain severe sentences at the courts, too, they actually would be punished twice for the same crime. This assumption of the German courts is completely false. Experience in the field has shown that denazification boards have been lenient to the greatest extent. They have shown their weakness repeatedly.[579]

The French Legal Division was also displeased with the carrying out of pogrom trials, commenting on the notorious mildness for hardened Nazi members who took part in the persecution of Jews and the destruction of synagogues, even though the higher authorities – such as ministries of justice – encouraged the German courts to more severity. The French, however, had put the "fox in charge of the henhouse": The judges – themselves former Nazi Party members – could hardly be expected to be severe with their former comrades and condemn the same deeds that they had not criticized at the time of their commission. Special courts – denazification commissions, jury courts – would have been better qualified to deal with these cases.[580] The French police kept close watch on judgements concerning the pogrom, making sure a police officer was present in the courtroom when the judgement was read.

Simultaneously, it was mentioned that the public in Tiengen would expect a severe punishment; previous "mistakes" of the district court Lörrach (where the trial had been pending before appeal) were not to be repeated.[581] It was noted with satisfaction that several prison terms were imposed, but the French lamented the lack of a reaction by the German press.[582]

In Württemberg, the Military Government representative made analogous observations when reporting on the pogrom trials in Buchau and Laupheim at Ravensburg District Court. The trial had met with great interest (contrary to the Tübingen euthanasia case of Grafeneck and the Hechingen deportation case – the latter to be discussed later).[583] The atmosphere at the trial had been calm but extremely laborious.[584] About 300 people had been present at the main hearing and had followed the case with greatest interest. Punishments meted out had been mild, with even the longest sentence not exceeding a year. The lesson to be

---

[579] Report, August 23, 1947, NARA, OMGBY 17/183 – 3/15.
[580] Monthly Report Baden, July 1947, AOFAA, AJ 3679, p. 18, Dossier 2; see also Summary Monthly Report for the French Zone (and Saar), July 1947, AOFAA, AJ 3680, p. 27 (2).
[581] Monthly Report Baden, September 1947, AOFAA, AJ 3679, p. 20, Dossier 1.
[582] Monthly Report Baden, October 1947, AOFAA, AJ 3679, p. 20, Dossier 2.
[583] Monthly Report Württemberg, January 1948, AOFAA, AJ 806, p. 618.
[584] Monthly Report Württemberg, February 1948, AOFAA, AJ 806, p. 618.

learned from the big political trials was always the same: Although the higher members of the judiciary would reach sentences independently based on laws and their consciences and the personae of the judges involved were impeccable, the majority of German judges had belonged to the Nazi Party or their organizations and did not disapprove – neither at the bottom of their hearts nor by their outward behavior – of the persecution of the Jews during the Third Reich. If they were now involved in such trials as judges, they were caught in a bind: If being particularly harsh, they had to fear that their own political past would be pointed out to them; if being very mild, they would be decried as old adherents of the Hitler regime. Thus: "Quel que soit leur jugement, ils sont certains d'être critiques (no matter what they decided, they would be criticized)."[585]

The British Legal Division also observed pogrom trials in their zone and voiced criticism at neglect or omission. In Blumenthal the synagogue had been torched; more than a dozen Jewish men were forced to pose for a photograph in front of the Nazi Party headquarters in Hellenthal, were derided and forced to listen to an insulting speech before being taken to Sachsenhausen Concentration Camp.[586] The Military Government asked the Ministry of Justice in North Rhine-Westphalia when the indictment would be drawn up and why none of the suspects had been arrested so far.[587] They continued to follow the course of the trial until 1952.[588]

Not only the Allies, but also the German population watched the trials. This confrontation with their inglorious past was often literally fieldwork, as it took place in or near where the pogrom had actually happened, rather than in the courtrooms of the district courts. The pogrom of Oberbieber was adjudicated in nearby Neuwied; for clarification of the events of the riots in Sobernheim the district court traveled in situ. The courts convened in local courtrooms in Altenkirchen, Elmshorn, or Idstein, as well as in gymnasiums as in Idar-Oberstein, or in pubs as in Altengronau, in Oestrich, in Stadtkyll, or Osann. In deciding the sentence for arson of the synagogue of Esens, the penal chamber of Aurich traveled to Esens. In Deidesheim the court, defendants, defense counsel, witnesses and the audience convened in the local vocational school; in Wallau it was the assembly hall of the municipality, in Geisenheim the town hall. The penal court of Bochum

---

585 Ibid.
586 Aachen 11 Js 57/49 = 11 KLs 13/52, HStA Düsseldorf – ZA Kalkum, Gerichte Rep. 89/13-17.
587 Legal Division to Ministry of Justice Northrhine Westphalia, March 17, 1949, HStA Düsseldorf – ZA Kalkum, Gerichte Rep. 145/473.
588 Aachen 11 Js 57/49 = 11 KLs 13/52, HStA Düsseldorf – ZA Kalkum, Gerichte Rep. 89/13-17.

travelled to Witten for the trial of the pogrom of Witten.[589] At main hearings, the audience was large.[590] As mentioned before, the adjudication of the pogrom of Buchau and Laupheim drew a crowd of about 300. Sentences were received with emotion not only on behalf of the defendants but also by the audience. In 1947, when the cases regarding the devastation of the synagogues of Altenkunstadt and Burgkunstadt were tried and the punishments meted out (prison sentences of one and a half years for two culprits), the American Legal Division noted: "It was reported that the populace were excited and enraged demanding a more severe punishment of the wrongdoers."[591] The American Legal Division was all for greater publicity on the Nazi crime trials – in the above-mentioned trial by the local court of Lichtenfels, the main hearing had taken place in a tiny courtroom where only eight visitors could sit.[592] A trial concerned with the riots against Jews in Bünde, which ended with an acquittal of a former SS First Lieutenant caused demonstrations in which as many as 2,500 people were said to have participated.[593]

German discussions on the trials are, to some extent, reflected in the German press (which was subject to Allied censorship). It also happened that journalists expressed diametrically opposed opinions in their articles. While the editors of *Hamburger Allgemeine* felt that events surrounding the pogrom of Hamburg-Harburg[594] remained shrouded in darkness, a mere three days later the *Hamburger*

---

[589] Bochum 2 Js 581/48 = 2 KLs 60/48; 2 Ks 18/49; see also "Sühne für Verbrechen gegen die Menschlichkeit," *Jüdisches Gemeindeblatt für die britische Zone*, October 8, 1948.

[590] E.g. "Zuchthausstrafen für Synagogenbrandstifter," *Die Freiheit*, April 24, 1950: "Am Donnerstagnachmittag wurde unter grossem Publikumsandrang das Urteil im Synagogenbrand-Prozess verkündet." Landau 7 Js 44/47 = Ks 3/50, AOFAA, AJ 3676, p. 36-37.

[591] Report, February 24, 1947, NARA, OMGBY 17/183 – 2/12; criticism was directed at the trial AG Lichtenfels Ds 82/46; Ds 216/46; later Coburg 2 Js 546/47 = KMs 5/47 a, b, KMs 5ab/47, StA Coburg, StAnw Coburg Nr. 142. See also: "Drei Monate Gefängnis für Synagogen-Schänder," *Jüdisches Gemeindeblatt für die Nord-Rheinprovinz und Westfalen*, February 21, 1947.

[592] Report, April 7, 1947, NARA, OMGBY 17/183 – 2/13.

[593] Bielefeld 5 Js Pol 188/47 = 5 KLs 10/48; "Der teutsche Oberstudienrat – Die Bünder Kristallnacht vor dem Bielefelder Schwurgericht," *Volks-Echo*, January 29, 1949; "Freispruch im Pogrom-Prozess," *Volks-Echo*, February 5, 1949; "Massendemonstration gegen Bültermann – 2500 protestieren in Bünde gegen Bielefelder Urteil," *Volks-Echo*, February 14, 1949; "Was vor zehn Jahren in Bünde geschah," *Jüdisches Gemeindeblatt für die britische Zone*, February 4, 1949; "Was vor zehn Jahren in Bünde geschah – Die Urteile im Bielfelder Prozess," *Jüdisches Gemeindeblatt für die britische Zone*, February 18, 1949; and "Verfolgte protestieren gegen 'Rechtssprechung' im Bündener Synagogenprozess," *Jüdisches Gemeindeblatt für die britische Zone*, February 18, 1949; further: "Bültermann spielt auch vor dem Spruchgericht den Harmlosen. So viel Lügen sind selbst dem Gericht noch nicht vorgekommen," *Jüdisches Gemeindeblatt*, May 27, 1949.

[594] Hamburg 14 Js 70/46 = 14 Ks 7/49; StA Hamburg, Best. 213-11, Nr. 22701/54 (Bd. 1-11). See also: "Sie 'schützten' die Synagoge. Der grosse Hamburger Synagogenschänderprozess," *Jüdisches*

Freie Presse noted that light was being shed on the matter.[595] Relatives of the perpetrators complained about the severity of sentences, while the press castigated their incomprehensible mildness. The daughter of a former NSDAP local group leader wrote in a letter to a politician that the sentence against her father in a pogrom trial was reminiscent of Nazi judgments by the notorious *Volksgerichtshof* (People's Court). "How could a court in current times deliver such a harsh sentence? The sentence of three years and six months prison is a downright death sentence; it would have been more humane to immediately return such a verdict and execute it."[596]

The press often traced untrue statements and polemicized about the chronic amnesia that befell the perpetrators.[597] It was remarked in the case of Bätzner, the former district commander of Horb, (concerning the destruction of four synagogues),[598] that he insolently seemed never to be able to recall events that incriminated him, but could easily recall those that exonerated him.[599] Others remarked on the inconsistent and conflicting stories that were presented before the court.[600] On a trial in Detmold[601] it was remarked how perpetrators squirmed "like snakes" to appear guiltless.[602]

Frequently, the court itself was under attack. In the case of the Buchau pogrom, the senior prosecutor tried to distinguish between greater and lesser wrongdoers. In the press he was accused of being apologistic when it came to

---

Gemeindeblatt, March 25, 1949; "Hamburger Synagogenschänder-Prozess: NSDAP sorgte für die 'Bestrafung' der Synagogenschänder," *Jüdisches Gemeindeblatt*, April 8, 1949; "Harburger Synagogenschänderprozess: 16 Angeklagte verurteilt," *Jüdisches Gemeindeblatt*, May 6, 1949.
595 "Die Kristallnacht bleibt dunkel," *Hamburger Allgemeine*, March 23, 1949; "Die Harburger Kristallnacht lichtet sich endlich," *Hamburger Freie Presse*, March 26, 1949.
596 Letter Annemarie R. to Herrn Heile, January 2, 1948, Verden 6 Js 305/47 = 6 KLs 21/47; StA Stade, Rep. 171a Verden, Nr. 589 (I-III).
597 "'Es kommen auch mal wieder andere Zeiten.' Keine Sühne für die Miehlener Judenpogrome – Angeklagte litten unter chronischem Gedächtnisschwund," *Die Freiheit*, May 24, 1950; see also Koblenz 9 Js 132/49 = 9 Ks 1/50, LHA Koblenz, Best. 584, 1, Nr. 1305.
598 Rottweil 1 Js 883-96/46 = KLs 65-84/48, StA Sigmaringen, Wü 29/2 T4, Nr. 224.
599 "'Unschuldige' Brandstifter vor Gericht," *Unsere Stimme*, June 23, 1948.
600 "Die Horber 'Juden-Aktionen' fanden ihre Sühne. Der ehem. Kreisleiter Bätzner zu 1 Jahr 6 Monaten Gefängnis verurteilt – Dietz erhielt 1 Jahr 3 Monate Gefängnis," *Schwäbisches Tagblatt*, June 22, 1948.
601 Detmold 1 Js 1412/46 = 1 KLs 2/48.
602 "Verbrechen gegen die Menschlichkeit," *Jüdisches Gemeindeblatt für die britische Zone*, May 22, 1948.

the perpetrators.[603] In Hildesheim[604] threats against judges and state attorneys (intended to to prevent future cases by browbeating the courts) were made during recesses in the trials.[605]

The communist paper *Unsere Stimme*, conjecturing about the mild sentences against perpetrtors of the pogrom in Buttenhausen, said things would not have turned out that way if a church had been involved.[606] The main hearing concerning the riots in Andernach also met with harsh criticism: some old National Socialists obviously took pleasure in the helplessness of the judges, which led to an inevitable solidification of the fairytale of unknown perpetrators and a ridiculing of the witnesses for the prosecution, as the prosecutor seemed weak.[607]

In Tübingen the trial against the former NSDAP district commander almost turned into a trial against the penal chamber.[608] The defense counsel pointed out that if the offender were accused of arson, one would also have to prosecute the former prosecutors who had not pursued justice as the law demanded. The audience applauded at this point, so the presiding judge reprimanded them. Senior prosecutor and judges protested against this view and explained that they themselves had not been prosecutors at the time.[609] Similar analogies between post-war justice and Nazi justice were drawn in the case of the burned-down synagogue in Amberg[610]: "Defense counsel Dr. Grühl of Amberg (Party member since 1931) tried to compare this court with the Sondergerichte of the infamous [Oswald] Rothaug und [Rudolf] Oeschey, sentenced to life in prison by the Nuremberg Military Tribunal."[611]

---

603 "Der Buchauer Synagogenprozess. Entschuldigungen für die Täter," *Unsere Stimme*, February 21, 1948; Ravensburg Js 8439-57/47 = KLs 126-142/47; KLs 146/47; KLs 29/48, StA Sigmaringen, Wü 29/1 T 1, Nr. 6889.
604 Hildesheim 2 Js 1984/47 = 2 Ks 4/48.
605 "Synagogenbrandstifter vor dem Schwurgericht. Provokationen und Drohungen im Gerichtssaal," *Jüdisches Gemeindeblatt*, December 24, 1948.
606 "Unverständliche Milde," *Unsere Stimme*, October 29, 1947; see also Tübingen 1 Js 2468-76/46 = KLs 59/47; StA Sigmaringen, Wü 29/3 T 1, Nr. 1608.
607 "Die Unbekannten," *Die Freiheit*, September 15, 1950; Koblenz 9/2 Js 1100/47 = 9 Ks 9/50; LHA Koblenz, Best. 584, 1, Nr. 1296-1298, 1336.
608 Tübingen 1 Js 1952/49 = Ks 8/49, StA Sigmaringen, Wü 29/3 T 1 Nr. 1764.
609 "Zweieinhalb Jahre Zuchthaus für Rauschnabel," *Schwarzwälder Heimat-Post*, May 23, 1949.
610 Amberg 1 Js 4871/46 = KLs 26/47, StA Nürnberg, StAnw beim OLG Nürnberg 146.
611 Monthly report, December 24, 1947, NARA, OMGBY 17/183 – 3/15.

The Balance and Remarks on the Investigation and Trials

Overall, West German courts and state prosecutors initiated 2,468 investigations and trials in conjunction with the pogrom, involving 17,700 suspects and defendants.[612] In East Germany (Soviet Occupied Zone/German Democratic Republic) about 300 trials took place.[613] Due in part to a different legal basis – Control Council Directive 38 – some rather flimsy procedures concerning preservation of evidence (hardly any Jewish witnesses had returned to East Germany), and the whole outlay of the trials, a concrete comparison is not advisable. In Austria, 370 defendants were put on trial concerning the pogroms in Vienna, Innsbruck, Linz, and Graz.[614] Again, different legal general outlays, i.e., the combination of denazification proceedings and penal justice in Austria, make a direct comparison difficult. Of these 2,468 West German proceedings, 1,174 were actual trials. The great majority of sentences, namely 1,076, were passed in the years 1945 to 1950. A final pogrom trial took place in 1992 in Paderborn; the second to last in 1964 in Bremen. Regionally, the trials are to be broken down as follows:

>Bavaria: 262 trials with 1,854 defendants
>Rhineland-Palatinate: 219 trials, 1,524 defendants
>Hesse: 210 trials, 1,516 defendants
>Baden-Württemberg: 183 trials, 690 defendants
>North Rhine-Westphalia: 180 trials, 828 defendants
>Lower Saxony: 76 trials, 543 defendants
>Saarland: 30 trials, 236 defendants.
>Schleswig-Holstein, Berlin, Bremen, and Hamburg each held fewer than ten trials.

Trials usually concerned the events of November 1938 as occurred in the vicinity of the district court. A very small number of cases concern the pogrom outside the territory of the Western Zones and the Federal Republic of Germany, i.e., East Germany or further former German territories in the East. A tiny percentage concerns pogrom activities other than November 1938, i.e., in March 1938 or in 1939.

Though 2,468 investigations and trials with 17,700 suspects and defendants might sound impressive, the reality is somewhat less admirable. Investigations and trials serve a legal purpose. While historical reconstruction of events is part of the sentence, it is not the primary aim of a judge to do the historian's task. In

---

612 Database by IfZ.
613 Ibid.
614 Thomas Albrich and Michael Guggenberger, "'Nur selten steht einer dieser Novemberverbrecher vor Gericht:' Die strafrechtliche Verfolgung der Täter der so genannten 'Reichskristallnacht' in Österreich," in *Holocaust und Kriegsverbrechen vor Gericht: Der Fall Österreich*, ed. Thomas Albrich, Winfried R. Garscha and Martin F. Polaschek (Innsbruck: StudienVerlag, 2006), 26-56.

numerous cases many different versions of the course of events were in circulation: victims, perpetrators, witnesses, and bystanders all had differing experiences and differing versions to tell. Thus to some extent, reconstruction was virtually impossible. Yet beyond the legal material many of the trials contain important sources: construction plans of synagogues (to demonstrate the outlay of the location); city maps (with the former lodgings of Jews marked); letters of emigrants who recount their recollections; and last but not least, photographs of the burning or demolished synagogues. These are impressive records of German Jewry on the brink of destruction. On the other hand, the quality of the investigations varies. In 1938, about 500 Jews had lived in Koblenz. Post-war inquiries could not come up with a full picture of all families and stores affected by the anti-Semitic furor of the pogrom; the demolition of only 13 Jewish stores and 35 flats could be proved.[615]

Simultaneously, one must caution against the assumption that the total number of investigations and trials reflects the total number of crimes committed during the pogrom. Mainly in German metropolitan areas, such as Hamburg[616] and Munich,[617] inquiries usually proved abortive. Though Berlin held more trials,[618] many are inconclusive and directed against very few defendants, even though perpetrators must have numbered in the hundreds. With the turmoil of war – air raids and evacuation of schoolchildren and German families to undamaged areas outside the big cities – the population turnover had been so substantial that post-war inquiries literally found nothing to grasp. The situation is better for mid-sized cities such as Düsseldorf and Frankfurt am Main where several trials took place; others, like Nuremberg, were thoroughly combed through by investigators. On the whole, however, investigations were usually more successful in smaller towns and villages.

---

615 Police report of March 31, 1949, Koblenz 9/5 Js 411/47 = 9 KLs 8/51, LHA Koblenz, Best. 584, 1, Nr. 1300-1303, 1332.
616 Hamburg 14 Js 291/47 = 14 KLs 31/47, StA Hamburg, Best. 213-11, Nr. 2/48; another trial concerns the pogrom in a then suburb of Hamburg (Harburg): Hamburg 14 Js 70/46 = 14 Ks 7/49; StA Hamburg, Best. 213-11, Nr. 22701/54 (Bd. 1-11).
617 München I 1 Js 1063/51, StA München, StAnw 6655; München I 1c Js 1430/53, StA München, StAnw 21045; München I 115 Js 1/64, StA München, StAnw 21870; München II 10a Js 112/61, StA München, StAnw 34613; München I 1 Js Gen. 108/50, Generalstaatsanwaltschaft München Nr. 4815. The only trial concerns a suburb of München (Planegg): München I 1 Js 273/45 = 1 KLs 24/46, StA München, StAnw 18672.
618 Berlin 1 P Js 131/48 (a) = P KLs 40/49; Berlin 1 P Js 1392/47 = 1 P KLs 199/47; Berlin 1 P Js 1427/47 = 1 P KLs 22/48; Berlin 1 P Js 439/47 = 1 P KLs 122/47; Berlin 1 P Js 535/47 = 1 P KLs 140/47; Berlin 2 P\7 P Js 47/49 (f) = 2 P KLs 5/50; Berlin P Js 104/48 (b) = 1 P KLs 24/48; Berlin P Js 248/48 (r) = P KLs 97/48; Berlin 1 P Js 1336/47 = 1 P KLs 192/47.

Also, only 30 West German trials are concerned with the 91 acknowledged murders associated with the pogrom. Only a comparison with the Austrian and East German trials could establish how thorough the investigations of all these deaths have been.

Moreover, the statute of limitations applied for most crimes concerning the pogrom. There was no reckoning for *Kristallnacht* in Augsburg because the first investigations did not take place until 1962.[619] There are further imponderabilities: It is more likely that witnesses recalled the participation of the local elementary school teacher (or another local dignitary) than that of lesser known residents of a town; they were also more likely to recognize the NSDAP district commander, who was an important figure in public life, than a simple NSDAP member. Also, people who returned to their hometowns (and scene of the crime) ran a higher risk of being identified and punished. Thus the number of participants in the pogrom has to be calculated at a much higher number than the above-mentioned 17,700 suspects and defendants. Frequently, state attorneys did not bother to include the name of a perpetrator in their list of suspects if the person was verified as dead.

Moreover, investigations were routinely destroyed. The pogrom against the Jews in Celle – which involved the attempted arson of the synagogue, the devastation of the *tahara* house (place where the ritual washing of a corpse took place before burial) at the cemetery, and destruction of shops and dwellings – was the object of interrogations that filled three binders with inquests of not less than 64 suspects, among them the NSDAP district commander of Celle. As no proof could be established, the investigation was terminated and the files were destroyed in 1955.[620] In Bad Lippspringe, Jews had been forced to gather in a hotel and were insulted while being forced into the Lippe fountain in the park of the spa. It is impossible to extract further information on the case because the records have disappeared.[621] The records of the arson of the Schierstein synagogue are gone,[622] as are those concerning the synagogue in Hagenbach – a trial against no less than 10 defendants.[623]

The records of another trial concerning the pogrom in Hagenbach, Wannbach, and Pretzfeld against an additional nine culprits also disappeared without trace.[624] "Loss of files" is also the reason for our ignorance of further details con-

---

619 StA Augsburg, Augsburg 7 Js 240/62.
620 Lüneburg 1 Js 40/47.
621 Paderborn 7 Ks 1/49 (files not traceable), see also Paderborn 4 Js 614/47.
622 Wiesbaden 2 KLs 4/46 (files not traceable); copy of the sentence with Yad Vashem TR 10/484; for the trial see "Zuchthaus für Synagogenschänder," *Jüdisches Gemeindeblatt für die Nord-Rheinprovinz und Westfalen*, May 24, 1946.
623 Bamberg Js 1185/46; Js 1205/46 = AG Forchheim DLs 25 a-k/46; files not traceable.
624 Bamberg Js 1879/47 = KLs 63/47; files not traceable.

cerning the anti-Semitic riots in Hassfurt, Westheim, and Kleinsteinach (involving 24 defendants).[625] We will also never be able to learn more about events during *Kristallnacht* in Forchheim, Adelsdorf, and Mühlhausen as reconstructed in a trial (with 19 defendants, among them the NSDAP district commander of Forchheim).[626] Another trial against the NSDAP district commander of Forchheim and five other defendants concerning the pogrom in Ermreuth, where Jewish families were severely mistreated, has also gone missing.[627] Historical research will also have to do without a trial against eight former storm troopers from Bamberg who terrorized the Jewish population in Demmelsdorf, Zeckendorf, and Schesslitz during the riots of November 10, 1938 (Fixed Date).[628] The destruction of the synagogue in Hochheim was tried once in August 1946 and again in 1947 – but the records are gone.[629] A jeweler was suspected of having acquired Jewish property, as she received substantial quantities of silverware from storm troopers in 1938 and did not register them in her inventory – but further insight is prevented due to the loss of the files.[630]

The Prosecution of the Deportations

> One had to forget – because one could not live with the thought that this graceful, fragile, tender young woman with those eyes, that smile, those gardens and snows in the background, had been brought in a cattle car to an extermination camp and killed by an injection of phenol into the heart, into the gentle heart one had heard beating under one's lips in the dusk of the past. And since the exact form of her death had not been recorded, Mira kept dying a great number of deaths in one's mind, and undergoing a great number of resurrections, only to die again and again, led away by a trained nurse, inoculated with filth, tetanus bacilli, broken glass, gassed in a sham shower bath with prussic acid, burned alive in a pit on a gasoline-soaked pile of beechwood. ...
>
> Vladimir Nabokov, Pnin

> Wednesday, [April] 8, at around half past six we received the message that our parents were to report on Thursday 9 early in the morning with their luggage at the appropriate police station. This message hit us even harder as we all had trusted in the reclamation [i.e., exemption from deportation] and thus had not prepared anything. My father immediately

---

[625] Bamberg Js 846/46 = KLs 24/48; files not traceable.
[626] Bamberg Js 2886/48 = KLs 70/48; files not traceable.
[627] Bamberg Js 657/48 = KLs 69/49; files not traceable.
[628] Bamberg Js 478/45 = KLs 79/47; files not traceable.
[629] Wiesbaden 2 Js 2224/45 = 2 KLs 11/46; 2 Ks 4/48, NARA, OMGUS 17/198 – 1/3.
[630] Bamberg Js 1790/46 = AG Bamberg Ds 177/46; files not traceable.

called Dr. Skowronek who came at 9 o'clock in the evening to Breslau. He probably will have written to you that all attempts he initiated were in vain. My sister and I accompanied my parents on Thursday to the police and from there to the general collection point. I will spare you and me to go into greater detail as far as this haunting day is concerned. Renate [her sister] and I had to stay back, and the calmness that my father and also my mother kept can only be explained by the fact that they hoped until the very last moment for the great miracle of a reclamation ... I have, despite several attempts, not been able to see or speak my parents again. My father, however, succeeded in having two letters delivered to us from the collection point. Both are very courageous. In the second he writes that only now, Sunday, it has become clear to him that his hopes will not be fulfilled and that both parties, my parents as well as we two, will not see each other again for a long, long, maybe incalculably long time ... My parents send their best farewell wishes. Your files are with the attorney Dr. Quabbe.[631]

With this letter dated April 15, 1942, to a client of her father, the 16-year Anita Lasker described the deportation of her parents on April 9–10, 1942, from Breslau to Auschwitz.[632]

The following chapter delves into the attempts the West German state prosecutors and courts undertook in the first post-war years to prosecute the deportation of German Jews from the Reich. For reasons of conciseness, I will not include the deportations before autumn 1941, i.e., the deportation of more than 6,500 Jews from Southwest Germany in the course of the so-called Wagner-Bürckel action on October 22, 1940 (named after two regional commanders, Robert Wagner of Baden and Josef Bürckel of Saarpfalz), or the deportation of about 1,000 German Jews from Stettin into the General Gouvernement in February 1940. Also, the mass arrests and subsequent committal to concentration camps after the pogrom, as well as isolated cases of deportations following denunciations are not being discussed; similarly the deportations of so-called gypsies cannot be considered here. The illegality of deportations – perpetrated by members of the Gestapo according to the guidelines of the Reich Security Main Office, relying on the cooperation of several official and party authorities, among them municipal offices of cities, communities and districts, local courts, fiscal authorities, customs authorities, police, Nazi Party, SS, Reichsbahn – was beyond doubt.[633] The deportations

---

631 Essen 29 Js 205/60, HStA Düsseldorf – ZA Kalkum, Gerichte Rep. 169/81-83. Due to a complex and long-winded trial with an amount in dispute which amounted to several million goldmarks, the lawyer Dr. Alfons Lasker had been permitted to continue work for a non-Jewish client by the Reich ministry of justice.
632 Anita Lasker-Wallfisch, *Ihr sollt die Wahrheit erben: Die Cellistin von Auschwitz: Erinnerungen* (Reinbek bei Hamburg: rororo, 2000).
633 See also letter of the prosecutor general in München, Dr. Roll, to the office of the land commissioner for Bavaria, December 15, 1949, NARA, OMGUS 17/217 – 2/4.

represented at least three qualifying characteristics of a crime: the dispossession of the deported, the deprivation of liberty, and finally murder. Furthermore, there had never been a legal basis for the deprivation of liberty.[634] The deportations also constituted other offenses and crimes according to the German Penal Code, such as the persecution of innocent people, accessory to murder, extortionate robbery (as the Jews were robbed of most property before deportation), bodily injury (during arrests), coercion, embezzlement, and forced statements (i.e., for the tracing of hidden Jews).

I will cover all West German deportation trials taking place in 1945–1949/50 and give an overview of what happened after 1950. As approaches to this complex of trials differed from zone to zone, the chapter is based on a geographic organizing principle. Unlike the proceedings concerning the pogrom trials, several sentences (though not all) appear in the volumes of *Justiz und NS-Verbrechen*.[635]

Deportation Trials in the French Zone

The Hechingen Case

The first trial in the French occupation zone took place in Hechingen (southern Württemberg). From the start of the investigations, the proceedings met with discontent. One witness complained about the whole "Jewish affair" being reopened.[636] The following is a short description of one local deportation procedure, as all deportations from the Reich beginning in autumn 1941 followed more or less the same pattern.

From November 1941 to August 1942, a total of 290 Jews had been deported from Hechingen and neighboring Haigerloch. The Gestapo in Stuttgart forced the Jewish Community of Württemberg (which had its headquarters in Stuttgart) to

---

634 Neither the "Verordnung des Reichspräsidenten zum Schutz von Volk und Staat" of February 28, 1933 nor the "Verordnung zur Sicherstellung des Kräftebedarfs für Aufgaben von besonderer staatspolitischer Bedeutung" of February 13, 1939 nor other decrees covered the deportations in a legal respect.
635 Hechingen see under vol. I, Nr. 22; vol. III, Nr. 80; Mainz see under vol. X, Nr. 347; Würzburg see under vol. IV, Nr. 138 and vol. VIII, Nr. 283; Nürnberg-Fürth see under vol. IV, Nr. 140 and vol. XI, Nr. 363; Düsseldorf see under vol. IV, Nr. 142 and vol. V, Nr. 148; Frankfurt am Main see under vol. VI, Nr. 207 and vol. XI, Nr. 367; Köln see under vol. XII, Nr. 403; München see under vol. XIII, Nr. 411; Münster see under vol. XVII, Nr. 503; Darmstadt see under vol. XXII, Nr. 611 and 613; Stuttgart see under vol. XXII, Nr. 615; Berlin see under Nr. 956 and Weimar/Erfurt see under Nr. 959 (in preparation).
636 Hechingen Js 1138-1139/47, StA Sigmaringen, Ho 400 T2, Nr. 845.

put together lists of deportees and send a letter to each person on the list containing the guidelines for deportation. The letter dated, November 19, 1941, sent out by the Jewish Congregation of Württemberg, ended with the words: "Finally we beg you not to give up hope; the achievements of the members of our community especially in labour employment encourage the aspiration that this new and most difficult task, too, can be mastered. Jewish Congregation Württemberg, registered association." On November 18, 1941, the chief administrative officers of the districts concerned received a decree of the Gestapo Stuttgart informing them of the impending evacuation: "In the context of the de-judaization [sic] of the whole of Europe, regular railway transports with 1,000 Jews each are currently leaving the Altreich in direction of the Reichskommissariat Ostland." The decree also mentioned that the envisaged settlement area did not contain even the minimum material required to install or maintain existence and thus called for the bringing along of construction equipment, tools, kitchenware, stoves, buckets and sanitary materials. The administrative preparation of the deportation according to the orders of the Gestapo lay in the hands of the district administrator of Hechingen. This encompassed the timely assembly of the victims, the seizure of property, the strip search of deportees, and the control of luggage, as well as transfer to the collection point – the transit camp in Stuttgart. The district administrator transmitted the decrees to the mayors of Hechingen and Haigerloch, ordered means of transport, initiated the medical examination of sick and handicapped by a public health officer to check their capacity to travel, had the confiscation order delivered by bailiff, and arranged for the assembly and strip search of all deportees. On November 27, 1941, the railway coaches (which had been attached to a regularly scheduled train of the Württembergische Landesbahn) left Hechingen at 11:21 a.m. At 12:07 p.m. deportees from Haigerloch boarded the train, which was to reach Stuttgart at 4:26 p.m. the same day. The luggage of the deportees had been assembled in a barn in Haigerloch and the parish hall in Hechingen on November 24, 1941. After the Jews had been forced from their homes, the lodgings were searched for hidden weapons, ammunition, blasting agents, poison, foreign currency and jewelry. This first deportation affected 122 Jews, 111 from Haigerloch, 11 from Hechingen. During the strip search even elderly women were forced to undress completely. A housewife from Rexingen who helped conduct the strip search forbade the Jewish women to bring along prayer books on the deportation train, saying, "Leave it here, where you are going, you will not be in need of one of these."[637] On November 27, 1941, 122 Jews from Hechingen and Haigerloch were deported to the Reichskommissariat Ostland (i.e., Latvia); on April 24, 1942, a another 27 were deported "to the East;" ten to the General Gouvernement on July

---

637 Rottweil 4 Js 6948/47, StA Sigmaringen, Wü 29/2 T4, Nr. 676.

10, 1942; 138 to the Ghetto Theresienstadt on August 19, 1942. Of more than 290 deportees, only eight are reported to have survived.

In April 1947, five participants in the deportations were indicted, namely the former *Landrat* of Hechingen, the former public medical officer (*Amtsarzt* of Hechingen) and three women belonging to either public relief or the Nazi women's organization (NS-Frauenschaft).[638] This trial, apart from being the first in the Western zones to center on the deportation, is also a rarity because it is concerned with the role of the civil administration in the course of the deportations from the Reich. The three indicted women had searched the Jewish women at the collection points during the deportations of November 27, 1941, April 14, 1942, and August 19, 1942, and had relieved them of money, jewelry, or other valuables. The head of the public health office (*Gesundheitsamt*) had declared three Jews fit for travel even though the attending physician had denied their transportability. The district administrator had handed the decrees of the Gestapo to the competent communes of Haigerloch and Hechingen and had orders for sequestrations and confiscations issued and submitted. The rather odd composition of defendants in the trial in Hechingen resulted from the fact that the deportation of Jews from Hechingen and Haigerloch had been ordered and (partly) organized by the Gestapo unit in Stuttgart, but were outside the French Zone and thus beyond the legal reach of the Hechingen court.

On November 3, 1946, Selma Weil from Haigerloch, a survivor of the deportation who had returned to her hometown, notified the French constabulary in Tübingen.[639] The Sûreté Hechingen had already investigated the persecution of Jews in Hechingen and Haigerloch and had submitted their findings. In February 1947, the senior prosecutor of Hechingen and the director of the district justice department (*Landesjustizdirektion*; known later as the ministry of justice) of Tübingen) were asked to report to the French justice authority, where they were ordered to carry out investigations speedily.[640] Two days later, suspects were arrested, and in mid-February 1947 the coroner Rudhardt, questioned witnesses.[641]

We are quite well informed about the further proceedings, since the Administrator General of the French Zone, Émile Laffon, took great interest in the trial and

---

638 Hechingen Js 230-231/47 = KLs 23-27/47, StA Sigmaringen, Ho 400 T2, Nr. 575-576; see also Rüter, vol. 1, Nr. 22.
639 Monthly Report Württemberg, December 1946, AOFAA, AJ 806, p. 616.
640 Monthly Report for the French Zone (and Saar), February 1947, AOFAA, AJ 3680, p. 27 (1).
641 Monthly Report Württemberg, January 1947, AOFAA, AJ 806, p. 616.

asked the Sûreté to observe the development and scrutinize the investigation files closely to ensure that the prosecutor had done his homework.[642]

The French thus kept a keen watch over the proceedings even before the charge had been brought. They complained about the delay, which led them to suspect that police and justice officials were interested in stalling the investigation or keeping it as low-key as possible.[643] They even suspected – among other motivations – anti-Semitic predispositions in the Hechingen district to be the root of the problem. In their eyes, the coroner had been too timid in the questioning of residents of Hechingen and Haigerloch. The French were particularly annoyed and reproached the coroner for not arresting the heavily charged but popular District Administrator Schraermayer. Coroner Rudhardt was thus replaced by an examining magistrate named Andreischock. Due to the anticipated impression the sentence might make in international Jewish circles, the French occupation authority – probably Jean Ebert, *Chef du Contrôle de la Justice Allemande* (Chief Supervisor for Geman Justice) – advised recomposing the penal chamber at the district court of Hechingen. Two former party members were thus replaced by two unencumbered judges from the local courts who stood in at the district court.[644]

At this point the Hechingen district court formed two penal chambers, one of which was intended to deal only with crimes against humanity.[645] The presiding judge was Dr. Alexander von Normann, who had been an attorney at law in Königsberg.[646] Though none of the members of this penal chamber were considered to have been Nazis, the new composition would prove inauspicious. As early as June 1947, Franz Gog would leave the chamber because of bias, as he became too involved with the cases of the defendants.[647]

Even before the first day of the trial, the Sûreté knew that emotions were running high: 90 percent of the population of the Hechingen district favored former District Administrator Schraermayer, who enjoyed particular support from the conservative party and the clergy.[648] The German judges, therefore, felt uneasy with the adjudication of the case. The Sûreté prophesied doom, fearing that the German judges would not be up to their job, which would mean that

---

642 Letter L'Administrateur Général, Laffon, to Délégué Supérieur, Wurtemberg, February 13, 1947, AOFAA, AJ 806, p. 615, Dossier 1a.
643 Monthly Report Württemberg, January 1947, AOFAA, AJ 806, p. 617.
644 Monthly Report Württemberg, March 1947, AOFAA, AJ 806, p. 616.
645 Decision of District court Hechingen, May 6, 1947, AOFAA, AJ 804, p. 597, Dossier 15.
646 Curriculum Vitae von Normann, November 18, 1946, Dossier Alexander von Normann, AOFAA, AJ 3683, p. 55.
647 According to the Monthly Report of Württemberg, December 1948, Gog practiced again as an attorney. AOFAA, AJ 3680, p. 23, Dossier 4.
648 Report Sûreté de Hechingen, June 4, 1947, AOFAA, AJ 804, p. 597, Dossier 15.

French military courts would have to take responsibility.⁶⁴⁹ Functionaries of the conservative party (CDU) and clergy were unanimously of the opinion that the indictment was baseless, and that such a trial would be a miscarriage of justice from the outset. They criticized the members of the Administration of Justice ferociously, the Sûreté noted, as the Administration had been responsible for Schraermayer's arrest. Schraermayer's successor in the office of district administrator of Hechingen, Dr. Speidel, complained that the Schraermayer case was causing as many problems as was the requisitioning of the reduction of food rations.

On May 6, 1947, charges were brought against the district administrator, the public health officer and three women from either Welfare or the Nazi women's organization. In several cases the indictment read "crimes against humanity." The Landrat was charged with ordering the crimes, the doctor with aiding and abetting them by declaring three Jews fit for deportation though the attending physician had clearly stated the opposite.

The main hearing opened one month later on June 6, 1947, at 9 o'clock. About 50 spectators appeared. The defendants looked composed, according to the Sûreté, and listened to the testimonies of the few surviving Jews of Haigerloch without visible emotions. The Sûreté, however, was up in arms against Judge Franz Gog, who had been asked to give regards to the defendant Schraermayer from a common acquaintance who had intimated to Schraermayer's defense counsel that he (Gog) would do his utmost for his client. Gog allegedly had advised the counsel for the defense, *Rechtsanwalt* Schellhorn, not to annoy the presiding judge, von Normann, and alienate him against the defendant.⁶⁵⁰

Schraermayer was called to the witness stand during the main hearing on June 9, 1947. He testified that he had firmly believed in an "evacuation" rather than a "deportation." During the questioning he started to weep, saying that in his quandary he had intended to give up his office, but friends, some of whom were Jews, had implored him to stay on, arguing that everything would get worse if a Nazi were to take the post of district administrator.⁶⁵¹ He insisted that everything he had done had been done in the firm belief that he could justify his deeds before God and his own conscience.⁶⁵² Furthermore, he said that if he had refused to collaborate he would have been sent to a concentration camp. He only obeyed the evacuation order out of fear of the Gestapo. He also said that he had joined the Nazi Party in 1937 out of dread, having had a reputation for being "Jew friendly"

---

649 Report Sûreté de Hechingen, June 4, 1947, AOFAA, AJ 804, p. 597, Dossier 15.
650 Report Sûreté, June 6, 1947, AOFAA, AJ 804, p. 597, Dossier 15.
651 Ibid.
652 Report Sûreté, June 9, 1947, AOFAA, AJ 804, p. 597, Dossier 15.

and clerical, which had lead to the inclusion of his name on a blacklist. If the Nazis had won the war, he figured he would have been shot.

The third day of the main hearing drew 60 curious onlookers. Defense counsel had motioned for evidence to prove that Schraermayer had been an opponent of the Nazis. Two telegrams – from the Archbishop of Freiburg and the Ministry of the Interior in Tübingen – were read as testaments his character, describing the Landrat as an observant Catholic who had simply followed Gestapo orders and was himself a victim of Nazi arbitrariness. The presiding judge, von Normann, opined that the motions for evidence were unnecessary and suggested a limitation of the gathering of evidence as these two characterizations did not meet the rules of the German court system. Subsequently, correspondence from the Nazi Party of Balingen that emphasized the clerical attitude of the Schraermayer family was read.[653]

The fourth day of the main hearing – with yet another audience numbering about 60 people – began with the withdrawal of Judge Gog. He declared himself biased because he had met privately with the defendant and his counsel. The courtroom became agitated; the audience engaged in animated discussion.[654]

The French occupation authority saw the trial as one example of the major influence the church still exerted on the German administration. Of the three judges involved, only the presiding judge, von Normann, had lived up to the challenges of the trial as he was the only one who felt bound by his conscience; the others had been out of their depth. This behavior did not endear him to his contemporaries nor to the local populace. He had been advised anonymously to leave Hechingen at the earliest possible moment:[655] With the trial, the presiding judge concluded, he had become the black sheep of town:[656]

Having no illusions as far as the behavior of the German administration of justice was concerned and having declared confidentially that the German administration of justice had not changed since the Third Reich (during the war, the Nazi regional commanders would try to influence the trials; now it was the Archbishop of Freiburg and the Ministry of the Interior), von Normann considered asking for protection from the Sûreté. The clergy would exert pressure through these interventions; furthermore, the local clergy and members of the

---

653 Report Sûreté, June 10, 1947, AOFAA, AJ 804, p. 597, Dossier 15.
654 Dossier Franz Gog, AOFAA, AJ 3681, p. 39.
655 Report of the Sûreté, June 11, 1947, AOFAA, AJ 804, p. 597, Dossier 15.
656 Ibid. Anonymous threats are known also from other trials, see Cord Gebhardt, *Der Fall des Erzberger-Mörders Heinrich Tillessen: Ein Beitrag zur Justizgeschichte nach 1945* (Tübingen: Mohr Siebeck, 1995), 219.

church had tried to influence witnesses and the Archbishop of Freiburg had tried to influence the court.

The trial was suspended for about 10 days after Gog declared himself biased. The Sûreté used this interruption to survey the local population. They determined that the trial was being discussed passionately, with the great majority of the population clearly on Schraermayer's side. The presiding judge, on the other hand, was accused of having provoked the trial. The military government of the Hechingen district found that invitations to the trial were being sent to all important sympathizers of the former district administrator in hopes of creating a favorable atmosphere in the courtroom. Three dignitaries in the district, a member of parliament, an architect, and the priest of Hechingen were particularly in favor of Schraermayer. The common opinion in Hechingen was that the delay in the trial would cause a prolonged imprisonment for the defendants.[657]

Even before the sentence was announced, the French occupation authority summarized its opinion: First, the trial no longer concerned Schraermayer, but rather procedural law in a great political trial and the comportment of the German administration of justice as such. The confidence of French authorities in the German ability to try the case had been sadly disappointed. Second, an acquittal of Schraermayer would severely damage the image of the French occupation power in the eyes of the German population. Only two years after the end of the war, the whitewashing of the testimony of one person by the administration of German justice could not be understood from a humane, rational, or legal standpoint, while several minor Nazi functionaries and others unlucky to have been arrested shortly after the capitulation had been punished harshly by the French Military Government courts. In addition, Jewish organizations in the French and particularly the American Zone of occupation would look askance at an acquittal.[658]

On June 23, 1947, the trial resumed with a newly composed penal chamber, still headed by President von Normann.[659] We know from the monthly reports that the atmosphere against the presiding judge was less hostile, but also that fewer visitors attended.[660] Once again, witnesses for the defense – mainly political dignitaries and members of the local clergy – were called to testify. The French side was dismayed that this amounted to propaganda. A priest from Burladingen

---

[657] Report Délégué du Cercle de Hechingen for Délégation Supérieure pour le Gouvernement Militaire du Wurtemberg, June 14, 1947, AOFAA, AJ 804, p. 597, Dossier 15.
[658] Report Sûreté, June 18, 1947, AOFAA, AJ 804, p. 597, Dossier 15.
[659] In the published version of the sentence the main hearing is thus dated on June 23-28, 1947. (Rüter, vol. I, Nr. 22).
[660] Monthly Report Württemberg, June 1947, AOFAA, AJ 806, p. 617.

had even had the nerve to contact a Jewish witness to ask for a contribution to the construction of the local church.[661]

The Sûreté's final report about the last two main hearings is full of praise for the German court for having resolved the difficult task of the trial with flying colors. This may have been the first time in the French Zone that the German judges had dared to act against public opinion and make a choice between their popularity and their duty as judges. Again on June 27, 1947, some 50 people were present in the courthouse, among them many women. One of the female defendants wept uncontrollably. The counsels for the defense spoke of a mass psychosis that had emerged and accompanied the trial. The final day of the trial (June 28, 1947) lasted – with interruptions – from 8:00 a.m until 6:30 p.m. The defense counsel for Schraermayer stressed once again that the district administrator had assumed the deportation was to result in resettlement, not extermination.

Schraermayer was sentenced to two years and three months' imprisonment for his role as an accessory in a crime against humanity. The court was convinced that the he had known about the final purpose of the measure. The first deportation had taken place at the beginning of winter: Even the well-equipped German Wehrmacht feared the winter in the Baltic states; it was known – from the Gestapo letter – that no material for construction or basic subsistence was available at the destined locations. The third transport encompassed mostly infirm, weak, feeble-minded, and handicapped people; the fourth transport included more than 40 percent septuagenarians, even some octogenarians.

When reading out the sentence, von Normann explained that the court did not deal with terms like "bad luck" or "tragedy", but with "responsibility" and "guilt." Nothing else could matter for the Germans but world opinion. It would do Germany a disservice to play German public opinion against world public opinion. Schraermayer broke down and shouted aloud; another defendant wept. The audience left the room without further incident. The French observers were not deceived; the German audience was not content. Rumor had it that the sentence was being compared to the crimes against humanity of the Third Reich as the first crime against humanity in the new democracy.[662] The French head of the district of Hechingen agreed that 90 percent of the population was convinced that Schraermayer had fallen victim to obscure machinations.

The most hated man in Hechingen was von Normann, the presiding judge, who – due to his provenance (from Eastern Prussia) – was seen as an intruder.[663] The trial was mentioned several times in the monthly reports of the French judi-

---

661 Report Sûreté, June 25, 1947, AOFAA, AJ 804, p. 597, Dossier 15.
662 Report Sûreté, July 1, 1947, AOFAA, AJ 804, p. 597, Dossier 15.
663 Report Délégué du Cercle de Hechingen, July 11, 1947, AOFAA, AJ 804, p. 597, Dossier 15.

cial control and was said to have caused quite a commotion; overall, the resonance was considered unflattering.[664] The press and certain segments of the population would accuse the judicial system of being meek; politicians – especially from the conservative party – would emphasize the excessive callousness of the courts.[665]

The first sentence against a member of the civil administration for participation in the deportation of Jews would not be long-lasting. The Sûreté had told the Military Government of Württemberg in January 1948 that Erich Nellmann, the prosecutor general at the high court of Tübingen, had already announced that the sentence would be lifted and the case sent back to a district court. Indeed, on January 20, 1948, the high court in Tübingen lifted Schraermayer's sentence and acquitted the three women who had participated in the strip searches of Jewish women and had been sentenced to jail terms of one to four months.[666]

The occupation authority was thus not surprised by the sentence of the high court; the presiding judge of the district court, von Normann, expected that the prosecutor general himself would plead for an acquittal. The Sûreté claimed that the prosecutor general in Tübingen, Nellmann, had essentially said to von Normann: "What do you want? Mr. Schraermayer is a good Catholic and he has always defended the faith."[667] The ministry of justice in Tübingen would even try to remove von Normann from the judicial service.[668] The judges of the chamber concerned with crimes against humanity at the district court of Hechingen, wanted to avoid having the case sent back to them.

After the revision at the high court Tübingen, the case was not tried again in Hechingen but rather in the Tübingen district court. Schraermayer was acquitted there on August 12, 1948. The judgement now declared that objectively the deed was a crime against humanity, furthermore a severe case of deprivation of liberty. However, Schraermayer had credibly assured the court that he had considered the measures a "resettlement." He alledged that the victims of the deportations had even told him that they expected an improvement of their lives compared to Germany where they were being humiliated and suffering discrimination. The bringing along of tools and equipment as well as the final sentence of the letter of the Jewish Community had encouraged this reasoning. Schraermayer's story that he had not suspected the planned aim of extermination of the Jews was thus to be

---

[664] Monthly Report Württemberg, October 1947, AOFAA, AJ 3679, p. 20, Dossier 2.
[665] Ibid.
[666] Publication of the sentence of the High Court Tübingen in *Neue Juristische Wochenschrift*, 1947/1948, issue 18, 700-701.
[667] Report Sûreté, January 15, 1948, AOFAA, AJ 804, p. 599, Dossier 20.
[668] Ibid.

believed. On the other hand, he had known that the deportations were the result of racist motives and were characterized by such concomitant circumstances that the death of many people would have been predictable. The actions had not been motivated by racial hatred – the judgment called him a warm-hearted man and civil servant and an outspoken opponent of National Socialism. Several "acts of resistance" were recounted (the patronage of a Catholic procession against storm troopers, the warning of priests against impending spying by the Gestapo etc.), which seemed to classify him as politically unreliable in the Nazi sense. Subjectively, he had not committed a crime against humanity as he lacked an inhuman mindset; he had committed deprivation of liberty under the extenuating circumstances of the state of emergency. The press – with the notable exception of the communist press – and the German population welcomed the judgment, but enquiries of the Sûreté led them to conclude that the acquittal was received with some reservation.[669]

The most disappointed party was probably the French. They remarked bitterly that the erstwhile most important political trial in Württemberg-Hohenzollern, which had resulted in four convictions (Schraermayer and the three women), was now to end in a general absolution.[670] They immediately called for enforced control of German courts. Once again the question raised for the French was: Could one trust the German judicial system with cases of crimes against humanity? They especially complained that the high court in Tübingen had a tendency to lift convictions based on crimes against humanity (in the first instance) and to cause acquittals by referring the cases anew to the district courts. Schraermayer's acquittal was seen as a particularly inauspicious indication that the trust the French had placed in the German courts was unjustified and had been abused disdainfully. It was considered particularly awkward that other courts would refer to the acquittal of Schraermayer in their adjudication of similar cases.[671] The French announced they were considering whether the case should undergo a "réformation" or "évocation" (i.e., transfer to a French military court).[672] The French were right in their assessment that the signal character of the case should not be underestimated. Members of the civil administration were, with the exception of two single cases, never again taken to court for a judicial reckoning of their role in the deportation of the German Jews.

---

669 Monthly Report Württemberg, August 1948, AOFAA, AJ 806, p. 618.
670 Monthly Report Württemberg, September 1948, AOFAA, AJ 806, p. 618.
671 Monthly Report Württemberg, August 1948, AOFAA, AJ 806, p. 618.
672 Monthly Report for the French Zone (and Saar), August 1948, AOFAA, AJ 3680, p. 22, Dossier 5.

Other Deportation Trials in the French Zone

One more time, a few years later, a member of civil government was put on trial. Once again, the trial took place in the French Zone, this time in Mainz. In November 1941 and March 1942, Dr. Philipp Hill – mayor of Alzey and SA staff sergeant – had requested the Gestapo (*Staatspolizei-Aussendienststelle*) Mainz and the Nazi Party of Alzey County deport Berta Frank, a woman originally from Berlin. The municipality of Alzey owed Mrs. Frank 4,800 RM due to the purchase of a house. To get rid of this liability the town administration initiated an expropriation. Miss Frank, who had countered with a lawsuit against the act of dispossession, was subsequently deported and since then had been missing.[673] The former mayor of Alzey was indicted in September 1948 for crimes against humanity, but acquitted in July 1949. His defense centered on the argument that although he had indeed signed the letter requesting the removal of the "impertinent Jew," he had neither dictated nor read the written communication. Due to overwork he had lacked the time to read the outgoing correspondence; furthermore he had always accorded a high autonomy to his subordinates. His acquittal met with criticism in the press.[674] The state prosecutor filed for revision. The high court overturned the acquittal and on October 11, 1950, Hill was sentenced to 10 months in imprison for crimes against humanity and deprivation of personal liberty resulting in death. The defendant appealed to the high court, where the case ended on March 4, 1953, with the court abandoning the case because of the amnesty of December 31, 1949. They did not consider the cause clearly proven, i.e., that the incitement for the deprivation of personal liberty (which resulted in the death of the victim) did indeed trigger the deportation. The court was of the opinion that Miss Frank would have been deported anyway in the course of the mass deportations without the mayor of Alzey being instrumental.

Not until 1961 would a sentence be passed against members of the civil administration, and then it was not in the territory of the former French Zone, but in Münster. The former mayor of Oelde had requested the Gestapo Münster to deport 12 Jews from Oelde; in a letter he also pointed to the provocative behavior of one Jewish couple. Though found guilty as an accessory to deprivation of liberty and sentenced to one year in jail, he did not have to serve the prison term as once again the amnesty law of December 1949 applied.[675]

---

[673] Mainz 3 Js 326/48 = Mainz 3 KLs 61/49, 3 Ks 3/52, AOFAA, AJ 3680, p. 25.
[674] See Otto Zahn: Warum herrscht noch Misstrauen gegen die Justiz? (Studio Koblenz: Manuscript of the broadcast "Rheinlandecho", August 8, 1949), AOFAA, AJ 3680, p. 25, Dossier 4.
[675] Münster 6 Js 989/52 = 6 Ks 1/55.

The remaining investigations and trials in the French Zone concerned members of the police and Gestapo. One notable case centered on the deportation of Jewish patients from the *Israelitische Kuranstalt* (Jewish medical institution) in Bendorf-Sayn. They were sent to the East in four transports: On March 22, 1942, 100 patients were taken to Izbica; another 100 patients were sent to Piaski near Lublin on April 30, 1942; 350 inmates of the institution were sent to Minsk on June 14, 1942; and about 20 were sent to Theresienstadt on July 27, 1942. One victim of the second transport was the expressionist German poet Jakob van Hoddis (aka Hans Davidsohn) who had suffered from schizophrenia since 1914. The transport lists had been compiled – on orders of the Gestapo – by the head of the medical institution, Paul Kochanek, and the senior physician, Dr. Rosenau. On November 11, 1942, the institution was dissolved altogether, with the last of the patients having been transferred to Berlin. The trial was initiated by a relative of a nurse who had been told by the doctor after the war that his sister had been deported.[676]

Heinrich R., the policeman in charge of the criminal police in Bendorf, was indicted in July 1947 for crimes against humanity, accessory to murder, deprivation of liberty and corruption, including the arrest of the Jewish nurse Hedwig Heymann in Bendorf-Sayn. As he had accepted bribes to exempt certain members from deportation, the initial indictment of crimes against humanity was dropped in September 1948 after consultation with the French Military Government because, as the state attorney argued, it was precisely the corruption of the former criminal police assistant Heinrich R. that showed that he did not act on racial or religious grounds in persecuting the Jews. Instead of crimes against humanity, he was accused of severe corruption as a civil servant (under § 332 StGB) according to German Penal Law, as he had accepted money to exempt Jews from impending deportation. However, for proof of venality as a civil servant, it was deemed necessary to show that he had not fulfilled his duties as a civil servant. Perhaps the Jews had been exempted according to other orders rather than because of bribery, e.g., because they did not fulfill the criteria set for each deportation or because the quota was already filled. On the other hand, from the point of natural justice he had acted correctly as he had alleviated the terrible fate of the Jews, and because all anti-Semitic laws and decrees were opposed to any natural law and could not form a law in a supralegal sense. An infringement against the anti-Semitic ordinances could thus not be considered contrary to duty and therefore did not fulfill the requirement for the application of Penal Code section 332. Heinrich R.'s action was thus deemed simple passive bribery in two cases according to § 331 StGB, since he accepted money for an official act. He was characterized as a

---

[676] Letter Erich Heymann, Johannesburg, South Africa to "Monsieur Le commandant de l'armée d'occupation Française," November 20, 1946, LHA Koblenz, Best. 584, 1, Nr. 1100-1101.

typically corrupt phenomenon of the Nazi state that had no compunction about accepting money from the very human beings who were constantly victimized by the Nazi system.

Still, the court could not bring itself to a sentence of more than six months, which again meant that the amnesty law applied. Thus no justice was meted out in the deportation of Hedwig Heymann and all the others.[677]

A few other trials took place in the French Zone. One concerned the Gestapo member, SS 1st Lieutenant Herbert Schubert and his participation in a deportation of elderly and mentally handicapped Jews from Koblenz on July 27, 1942. He was acquitted because he could not be identified as a perpetrator of violent acts and was not being prosecuted for participation in the deportation process alone because he had been under orders.[678] Arnold Uhlenhut, another member of the Gestapo Koblenz and the former secretary of the criminal investigation department, was sentenced to six months' imprisonment for crimes against humanity for mistreatment of a Jewish man who was not wearing the Star of David, but not for any of the deportations.[679] An inferior position and the acting under orders saved yet another police officer from having to account for his role in the deportations.[680]

Deportation Trials in the American Zone

The Würzburg and Nuremberg Cases

By far the most ambitious approach was taken by the Franconian state prosecutors in Würzburg and Nürnberg-Fürth.[681] On orders of the Reich Security Main Office, 4,754 Jews were deported from Franconia (northern Bavaria), 1,000 on November 29, 1941, to the Baltic Jungfernhof near Riga, 1,000 on March 24, 1942, and 955 on April 25, 1942, to the Lublin district, 1,000 Jews on September 10, 1942, and a further 680 Jews on September 23, 1942, to Theresienstadt, 36 to Theresienstadt and 73 to Auschwitz on June 17, 1943, and finally 10 Jews to Theresienstadt on January 17, 1944. The transit camp for the Jews from Franconia was located in Nürnberg-Langwasser; the Jewish orphanage in Fürth was used as collection

---

677 Koblenz 5 Js 288/47 = 9 KLs 2/49, LHA Koblenz, Best. 584, 1, Nr. 1100-1101.
678 Koblenz 9 Js 232/49 = 9 KLs 1/51, LHA Koblenz, Best. 584, 1, Nr. 1009.
679 Koblenz 9/5 Js 1214/48 = 9 KLs 12/49, LHA Koblenz, Best. 584, 1, Nr. 1815.
680 Koblenz 9 Js 205/49, LHA Koblenz, Best. 584, 1, Nr. 1011.
681 Würzburg 1 Js 1/48 = KLs 63/48, StA Würzburg, StAnw Würzburg 407/I-II; Nürnberg-Fürth KLs 230/48, Ks 6/51, StA Nürnberg, StAnw Nürnberg-Fürth 3070/I-XXV.

point for the later deportations. As is known from testimonies and documents, first the luggage was searched; forbidden items were removed and the suitcases then taken to a luggage collection point. Then the people had to hand in identity cards or passports, deliver valuable papers and pay 60 RM for the cost of travel and stay in the transit camp. After this, the strip search took place to locate any possible hidden money, jewelry, or other valuables. Furthermore, a bailiff informed the Jews of the confiscation and dispossession of their property; their identity cards were stamped with "Evacuated." Then they entered the transit camp proper (sometimes called a ghetto), an isolated part of the camp from which there was no exit before their journey to the East.

By a stroke of luck, the Gestapo files of Würzburg had – unlike many others – survived the end of the war, leaving a classic paper trail on the procedure of the deportations. The Franconian deportations were even mentioned in the American Justice Trial in Nuremberg.[682]

The Americans had seized the Würzburg Gestapo files, but soon formed the so-called Special Projects Division to transfer cases and files to German prosecution authorities. In 1946, a German state attorney working for the Special Projects Division compiled a list of more than 150 suspects, including Adolf Eichmann (here still erroneously presumed dead), as well as the cleaning ladies at the collection points. On November 27, 1947, nearly six years to the day after the first deportation from Franconia, the state prosecutor at the Special Projects Division of the Office of Chief of Council for War Crimes compiled a final report for the Bavarian Ministry of Justice, which was handed in a few days later: "On 9 December 1947 Mr. Lang, the acting director of this division, turned over to the Ministry of Justice an elaborate report concerning the mass evacuation from the Nürnberg-Würzburg area in 1942 and 1943 involving not less than 90 prospective defendants."[683] The proposed indictment listed 60 suspects from Würzburg, 24 from Nuremberg, three from Regensburg, and one person each in Bamberg, Coburg and Bayreuth. The investigation report turned in to the Bavarian Ministry of Justice was handed over to the prosecutor general at Nürnberg with the order to initiate prosecution. The prosecutor general in Nuremberg transferred the case with the report to the appropriate state prosecutors' offices, namely Nürnberg-Fürth, Würzburg, Regensburg, Bamberg, Coburg, and Bayreuth. The Americans continued to keep an eye on the trial:

---

[682] Lore Maria Peschel-Gutzeit, ed., *Das Nürnberger Juristen-Urteil von 1947: Historischer Zusammenhang und aktuelle Bezüge* (Baden-Baden: Nomos, 1996), 133.
[683] Monthly report, January 24, 1948, NARA, OMGBY 17/182 – 3/9; see also NARA, OMGBY 17/183 – 3/15.

It was found out that Nuremberg is far behind Bamberg [sic, Würzburg was part of the high court district Bamberg] as far as the status of investigation is concerned. The reason is chiefly that Nuremberg had no room available for the special prosecutor who had to conduct the investigation. It was decided at the meeting that one special prosecutor (not Untersuchungsrichter, but Spezialstaatsanwalt) should continue the investigations and that he will receive a room in Amtsgericht Erlangen. It was furthermore agreed upon that there will be no monster trial in one place but defendants will be tried locally whereby the different courts involved exchange their interrogation records. It should be avoided that the more insignificant defendants will be tried first. Defendants like former chief of police Nuremberg, Martin, have to be tried first if their guilt can be established.[684]

Though the Americans had advised against this course of events, the Würzburg trial (with subordinate defendants) took place before the trial in Nürnberg-Fürth. The outcome was to be less than satisfactory. The investigations of the mayors, district administrators and rural police chiefs who took part in the deportations in Lower Franconia were to be deferred until the two trials in Würzburg and Nürnberg-Fürth were concluded. In Upper Franconia the head of the Gestapo, Karl Bezold, was dead;[685] the investigations against the other two locally responsible suspects from Bayreuth and Coburg were terminated for unknown reasons.[686]

In the end, 19 members of the Gestapo, criminal investigation department and rural police (constabulary) were indicted on August 25, 1948, for accessory to deprivation of liberty and extortion in connection with the above-mentioned first six deportations to Riga-Jungfernhof, the Lublin district, Theresienstadt and Auschwitz. In April 1949, the main hearing resulted in six acquittals, while 13 defendants were sentenced for wrongful deprivation of personal liberty to temporary imprisonment, ranging from six months to one year and two months.[687] At nearly the same time, on September 11, 1948, seven members of Gestapo and criminal police were indicted in Nürnberg-Fürth, among them the former police president, Dr. Benno Martin. In May 1949, only two defendants were convicted for accessory to coercion and deprivation of personal freedom resulting in death to three years respectively 10 months' imprisonment. The other five had pleaded (successfully) that they were following superior orders or had not understood that an act was unlawful (which excluded liability) and were acquitted. The Americans found this mindboggling: "Contrary to Nuremberg where five persons were acquitted, Würzburg convicted defendants less guilty than those acquitted in Nuremberg. The prosecution of Nuremberg and Würzburg agrees that defendants acquitted

---

684 Monthly report, April 23, 1948, NARA, OMGBY 17/183 – 2/14.
685 Bamberg Js 517/48 (files destroyed).
686 Bayreuth 1a Js 2/48 (files destroyed); Coburg 1 Js 165/48 a, b (files destroyed).
687 Würzburg = KLs 63/48, StA Würzburg, StAnw Würzburg 407 I-II.

in Nuremberg were convicted in Würzburg although their crimes were not as serious as those of persons acquitted in Nuremberg who were found to have acted under duress."[688] In another report the subordinate character of the Würzburg defendants was mentioned: "It has to be considered that the Würzburg defendants were not the masters of the undertaking but the little men."[689] Neither the Würzburg nor the Nürnberg-Fürth judgment held up against the appeal before the Bavarian Supreme Court. Only a few weeks after the announcement of the judgment in Nürnberg-Fürth, it turned out that a member of the jury had a criminal record of no less than 13 offenses (among them recurring theft and fornication with children) and had done time in prison. The president of the district court was crestfallen. Considering his past life and prior convictions the juror should not have been included on the list of possible jury members.[690]

The former police president, Dr. Benno Martin, who had been sentenced in the first instance, mocked the judgment and refused to acknowledge its receipt by signing it. He stated that since the press had already found out about him, the criminal record of the jury member had been known to a broader public. It struck him as absurd that a jury member who had been arrested several times by members of the Nuremberg police had been placed in a position to adjudicate members of the former police force.[691]

It was thus an easy task for Martin's attorney to get the sentence quashed. Furthermore, the objectionable jury member had spread the rumor that the presiding judge had urged the jury to convict Martin in order to prevent Martin's extradition to Poland.

In June 1951, the district court of Nürnberg-Fürth was once again the setting of a renewed main hearing. While it involved the convicted Gestapo members from Würzburg, it also included the two Nuremberg members of the Gestapo, including Benno Martin. This time all of them were acquitted (one of the indicted benefitted from the amnesty, which led to a cessation of proceedings against him). The plea by the Gestapo members of Würzburg that they were following orders was accepted as justification. This, however, was not possible in the case of Dr. Benno Martin, who as a former superintendent of police in Nürnberg and higher SS and police chief had been very high-ranking himself. In his case, the

---

688 Monthly report, May 24, 1949, NARA, OMGBY 17/183 –2/14.
689 Monthly report, April 24, 1949, NARA, OMGBY 17/183 – 2/14.
690 Letter of President of district court Nürnberg-Fürth to President of high court Nürnberg, June 9, 1949, Dossier 1, Vol. 1: Announcement of the Bavarian Ministry of Justice and Ministry of the Interior concerning the selection of lay judges and members of the jury, July 26, 1949, General files 3221: members of the jury, Bavarian Ministry of Justice.
691 Letter Dr. Benno Martin to attorney Dr. Fritz Bergold, September 9, 1949, ibid.

sentence included the explanatory statement that while objectively he had acted as an accessory to the deprivation of personal liberty (resulting in death), subjectively, Martin – who had a doctorate in jurisprudence – had not deemed the illegal restraint as unlawful because he had lacked the knowledge to see the act as wrong. The state attorney in Nürnberg-Fürth appealed this sentence. For one last time Martin stood before the court and again the reasoning of the judges was similar to the above-mentioned rationale: Though the act as such was unlawful, Martin had not been in a position to understand and perceive the unlawfulness of the deportations. Due to the lack of criminal intent, he was once again acquitted. The state prosecutor in Nürnberg-Fürth considered filing an appeal, however an expert opinion from Federal Public Prosecutor Max Güde deemed an appeal futile, since even in the case of a renewed lifting of the sentence, Martin could count on an award of state of emergency (in keeping with Section 54 of the German Penal Code). Thus in 1954, despite serious reservations, the state attorney withdrew his formal objection.

As in Hechingen, public opinion was completely on the side of the accused. This went so far that the senior state prosecutor, Dr. Hans Meuschel, himself a victim of racial persecution,[692] was publicly ridiculed by an elderly woman who testified that "Chief Prosecutor Meuschel who has represented the case of the prosecution and who is well known in Nuremberg for this fact offered in a streetcar a seat to an elderly lady. She answered his offer saying: 'No, I surely do not want a seat from *you*.'"[693] Dr. Martin's ultimate acquittal in 1953 was greeted with cheers and applause in a packed courtroom.

Dr. Benno Martin, as superintendent and higher SS and police chief, had been the most high-ranking of all the defendants in all the Western German deportation trials. As it proved impossible to convict him, it seemed obvious that the prospects for convictions in other trials would be limited. In Würzburg, investigations against members of the civil administration and of police ceased without indictment. Among the dropped investigations were those of the district administrators of Würzburg, Ochsenfurt, Marktheidenfeld, Kitzingen, Karlstadt, Gemünden, and Brückenau; police in Kitzingen and Ochsenfurt[694] and security police in Würzburg; the concomitant unit (accompanying the transport/*Transportkommando*); the customs; the tax office and the *Reichsbahn* (railways); the director of the local court and the bailiff; the head of the local NSDAP group in

---

[692] Dr. Hans Meuschel had had to leave his office as a public prosecutor in 1933 due to his Jewish descent. Personal file Dr. Hans Meuschel, HStA München, MJu 25688.
[693] Monthly report, May 24, 1949, NARA, OMGBY 17/183-2/14.
[694] Würzburg 1 Js 111/48 (files destroyed).

Reichenberg (near Würzburg); and the director of the state archives in Würzburg (who had taken a confiscated Torah Scroll into his archival holdings).[695]

Five additional defendants were to be tried in Nürnberg-Fürth for their involvement in the proprietary aspects of deportation, i.e., the predation of Jewish property during the enforced transports. For three of the indicted, no main hearing was scheduled.[696] For the other two, the proprietary aspects – extortion and bribery – were admitted to the main hearing. In one case, however, the proof for extortion was not sufficient: a criminal investigator (*Kriminalsekretär*) of the Gestapo in Nürnberg supposedly had taken linens, groceries and perfume from a woman slated for deportation. In the case of the other culprit, the statute of limitation applied. Thus, despite an enormous effort of several courts in middle and lower Franconia, not a single valid conviction concerning deportations was achieved. Investigations in Regensburg (Upper Palatinate) referring to deportations to the Lublin district and the Theresienstadt ghetto (1942-1944) ended with the conclusion that the suspects had acted on superior orders; furthermore they did not know that their involvement was part of committing an offense.[697] It is likely that the only decision concerning deportations from Bavaria was the conviction in 1953 at Augsburg district court of a former member of the Gestapo for assault (in exercise of an office).[698]

Other Deportation Trials in the American Zone

The trials in Hesse were more successful – including one against two former members of the Gestapo Darmstadt.[699] The former head of the *Judenreferat* (Jewish Department), Georg Dengler, and former member of the department Bruno Böhm were indicted in 1949. In 1951, Böhm was – after several attempts – sentenced to two years and seven months in the penitentiary for accessory to the persecution of innocent people in conjunction with severe deprivation of liberty in exercise of office and bodily injury. In 1950, Dengler, his superior, had been sentenced to six years in the penitentiary for accessory to deprivation of liberty with fatal consequences, deprivation of liberty in exercise of an office, and persecution of inno-

---

[695] Würzburg 1 Js 113/48 (files destroyed).
[696] Nürnberg-Fürth 3d Js 902/48 = 162 Ks 7/49, 769 KLs 159/55, StA Nürnberg, StAnw Nürnberg-Fürth 3070/I-XXV.
[697] Regensburg I 1 Js 1044/53, StA Nürnberg GStA beim OLG Nürnberg 281.
[698] Augsburg 4 Js 197/50 = AK 207/51 (files destroyed).
[699] Darmstadt 2a Js 716/49 = 2a Ks 1/49. A further suspect was the head of the Gestapo Darmstadt, Robert Mohr, who had absconded and could not be traced until some time after the trial.

cent people. Both had been found guilty of persecuting Jews in so-called mixed marriages, having arrested them on false pretenses.

The only deportation trial in West Germany that ended in a life sentence took place in Frankfurt a few years after the end of the war. The investigation against the Frankfurt Gestapo concerned 14 suspects; eight additional suspects were not included in the investigation.[700]

The only person to be indicted in 1949 was Heinrich Baab, a somewhat lowly criminal investigator who in the final main hearing on April 3, 1950, would ask – rather peeved and with good cause – why he was the only member of the former Department II B (Frankfurt Gestapo) to be indicted. Similar to other deportation cases, the accusation here was not of assisting in the mass deportations (more than 10,000 Jews had been deported from Frankfurt am Main); rather, he was blamed for 55 individual cases of deportees who did not fall under the rules of action because they were deemed "half-Jewish" or were married to a non-Jew. In keeping with Gestapo policy, Baab had criminalized the victims in one way or another in order to include them in the deportations; offenses that resulted in deprivation of liberty and finally deportation were snide remarks made against the Nazi Party or Nazi executives, the omission of wearing the yellow star, or failure to use the imposed Jewish middle name. In the Nazi district of Hessen-Nassau, such "complaints" were probably made systematically to enable the Gestapo to step in and arrest the persons concerned.

One central point in the conviction of Heinrich Baab was that he knew about the fate of the deported Jews. He told Jews in no uncertain terms and most crudely that they would be killed. Another of his tasks was to inform people of the death of relatives in Auschwitz. In the post-war period, Baab was so annoyed, feeling that he had been made the only scape-goat for the whole Frankfurt Gestapo, that he wrote to the American Legal Division arguing that in Germany one would have to assume a collective guilt, not an individual guilt; the main culprits went scot-free while the man in the street had to atone.[701]

In 1949, two other members of the Gestapo in Frankfurt and its branch in Limburg were indicted for grievous bodily harm, extortion of evidence (in the case of Gestapo prisoners) and accessory to deprivation of liberty in cases of individual deportees. The sentence – two years and nine months' penitentiary for the higher-ranking defendant – however was based solely on the commission of

---

[700] Frankfurt 5 Js 1656/48 = 51 Ks 1/50, HStA Wiesbaden, Abt. 461, Nr. 37048/1-21.
[701] Summary of letter of Heinrich Baab dated April 17, 1950, NARA, OMGUS 17/199 – 1/22.

grievous bodily harm. The other defendant profited from the amnesty of December 31, 1949.[702]

Deportation Trials in the British Zone

If the trials we have looked at so far have proved a sorry affair, legal procedures in the British Zone were worse. Unlike in the French and American zones, there was no visible attempt to hold trials for several defendants in the British Zone, nor was there a systematic approach to investigating and adjudicating a complex of deportations from one particular region, although one crucial element here was the division of labor among different authorities. Instead, there were several trials against individual members of different Gestapo posts. Even so, if we look into the rate of convictions, the result isn't so bleak.

The state prosecutor of Düsseldorf initiated two separate trials against members of the *Judenreferat* at the Gestapo office in Düsseldorf. Police Investigator Hermann Waldbillig was indicted for crimes against humanity, murder, and grievous bodily harm, as well as deprivation of personal liberty. Once again, it was not the deportations of thousands of German Jews that was at issue (and the well-proven supervision of the Gestapo members in this procedure). Rather, it was individual offenses such as the arrest of one Jew or half-Jew that had been – by order of Nazi regulations – officially exempted from the enforced transport beyond the borders of the Reich. This applied to a Jew whose non-Jewish wife and child been killed in an air raid, thus leaving the victim without the legal protection of a mixed marriage; a "half-Jewish" woman who was simply included in a transport to fill a quota; or arrests of Jews to extort information on the whereabouts of other Jews in hiding. Waldbillig had, somewhat similarly to Heinrich Baab, frequently made anti-Semitic comments along the lines of: "If I could, I would cut the throats of all Jews. The Jew we have got, we never let go again." The indictment concerning crimes against humanity did open a broad spectrum of offenses including attempts to force Jews or "mixed Jewish-German" couples to move into other lodgings, insults against Jews, or pressure on non-Jewish partners to divorce. However, as these cases had not entailed grievous consequences for the victims – the Gestapo did try to force the people concerned to move or divorce and had insulted them, but these actions had not been followed by criminal acts of a greater dimension and thus did not classify as crimes against humanity, Waldbillig was sentenced to three years in prison. The question of whether he

---

[702] Frankfurt 54/52 Js 222/53 = Frankfurt 6 KMs 26/49, 13 KLs 1/54, HStA Wiesbaden, Abt 461, Nr. 31504.

knew what the deportees were facing was not examined. But since he had said at the time, "I need not say farewell to you as we will not see each other again," it was obvious that he had not expected the victims to return.[703]

In the case of Criminal Investigator Georg Pütz, the indictment was even more multifaceted. In addition to crimes against humanity, he was charged with embezzlement while in office, unjust enrichment, assault, deprivation of personal liberty, extortion of testimony, and murder.[704] Eventually, Pütz was convicted and sentenced to eight years in the penitentiary for crimes against humanity, together with assault in office and extortion of information. Pütz had admitted that he had considered the action against Jews as inhumane. The district court of Düsseldorf argued that activity on behalf of the Gestapo as such was a crime against humanity. Not only had Pütz fulfilled his official duties, he had also contributed to intensifying the anti-Semitic regulations through his personal behavior, i.e., by spiteful comments, petty insistence on regulations and imposition of unnecessary hardship.[705]

The first deportation trial in Cologne was directed against Criminal Investigator Heinrich Engels, a member of the *Judenreferat* of the Gestapo in Köln, but who again held a relatively low rank, being the most junior in office.[706] He had worked alongside a superintendent and three clerks who were also ranked as criminal investagors or assistant investigators. Their tasks were similar to those of other *Judenreferat* members in the Reich: They checked whether Jews were wearing the Star of David; whether Jews obeyed the prohibition on the use of public transportation, cinemas, or theatre; controlled the forced work of Jews as well as curfews and enforced transfers to *Judenhäuser* (Jews' houses) or collection points. The trial against Engels stemmed from a denazification procedure and led to an indictment for crimes against humanity, grievous bodily harm in office, and extortion of information.

To Engels' credit, it was assumed from the very beginning of the trial that he had only acted on orders. He was blamed, however, for the arrest and mistreatment of Jews including extortion of information in order to trace Jews who had

---

703 Düsseldorf 8 Js 114/46 = 8 Ks 19/49, HStA Düsseldorf – ZA Kalkum, Gerichte Rep. 372/82-85; "Skandalöses Urteil gegen Waldbillig. Drei Jahre Gefängnis, Internierungs- und Untersuchungshaft angerechnet," *Jüdisches Gemeindeblatt*, June 10, 1949.
704 "Judenmörder vor dem Schwurgericht. Exekutivbeamter Georg Pütz des Mordes an Juden angeklagt," *Jüdisches Gemeindeblatt*, May 20, 1949.
705 Düsseldorf 8 Js 127/48 = 8 Ks 21/49, HStA Düsseldorf – ZA Kalkum, Gerichte Rep. 372/86-92; see also: "Eine Mutter klagt an: 'Pütz ist der Mörder meines Kindes.' 'Ihre Kinder sind Bastarde und müssen vernichtet werden wie Vieh.'," *Jüdisches Gemeindeblatt*, May 27, 1949. The article contains an urgent plea for a death sentence against Pütz.
706 Köln 24 Js 753/48 = 24 Ks 3/49, HStA Düsseldorf – ZA Kalkum, Gerichte Rep. 231/217-219.

gone into hiding. He had also failed to restrain himself verbally and had insulted Jews and half-Jews on the occasion of arrests and deportations. Repeatedly he had advised non-Jews to divorce their Jewish partners, and had mistreated Jews whom he discovered without the obligatory yellow badge. Similar to the Düsseldorf deportation trial against Waldbillig, the indictment listed accusations for which there could be no atonement, since they were either too general – a witness had testified that the defendant Engels was dreaded in the Judenhaus because he read out deportation lists – or did not constitute a crime. Calling Jews beasts or Jew-dog were only misdemeanors under German penal law.

Reports of the death of deported Jews started to appear in 1942. Engels, as a member of the *Judenreferat*, received the death reports from the Reich Headquarters for Security (RSHA) and was required to pass them on to the Jewish community. It has been alleged that the Jewish community had to pay up to 15,000 RM for their cremations and inurnment. In at least three cases the Gestapo demanded several thousand RM. Due to the frequent issuing of death notices, Engels knew that deportation most certainly meant death. Still, he insisted in his defense that he had assumed that the Jews were to found a "Jewish state" in Poland or Russia and were thus being deported. He was sentenced to two-and-a-half years in prison for crimes against humanity in coincidence with deprivation of personal liberty (as a Gestapo official) and assault (also as a Gestapo official). The court was satisfied that Engels had participated in crimes in the execution of his official tasks and had also committed deeds that went beyond his orders. The press commented on the sentence vividly.[707]

In Lower Saxony, a member of the *Judenreferat* of the Gestapo in Hannover was sentenced to two and a half years of imprisonment for crimes against humanity in connection with extortion, assault in office, and constraint during the deportations.[708] Christian Heinrichsmeier, a former criminal investigation supervisor, had ordered the mistreatment of a Jew who had been put to work on preliminary preparations for the deportations. Heinrichsmeier had also forced Jews to make false confessions and hit them for these alleged crimes – usually racial

---

[707] "Im Kölner ELDE-Haus begann der Weg in den Tod." *Kölnische Rundschau*, October 11, 1949; "Schwurgericht: erster Tag," *Die Welt*, October 11, 1949; "Schwurgerichtsprozess gegen den Gestapobeamten Engels," *Rheinische Zeitung*, October 1, 1949; "Verbrechen gegen die Menschlichkeit?," *Westdeutsche Zeitung*, October 11, 1949: "2 1/2 Jahre Gefängnis für Gestapobeamten Engels," *Kölnische Rundschau*, October 12, 1949; "Zweieinhalb Jahre Gefängnis für den Gestapomann Engels," *Rheinische Zeitung*, October 12, 1949; "'Judenfänger' Engels vor Gericht," *Die Neue Zeitung*, October 12, 1949; "Zweieinhalb Jahre für Engels," *Westdeutsche Zeitung*, October 12, 1949; "Gefängnis für Gestapo-Agenten," *Die Welt*, October 12, 1949.

[708] Hannover 2 Js 425/47 = 2 Ks 1/49. Against three other suspects the investigations were terminated in 1948 without a trial.

defilement or forbidden economic enterprises. As far as the deportations were concerned, the court came to the opinion that Heinrichsmeier had not committed any excesses, but had kept strictly to his orders.

An additional trial referred indirectly to the deportations. Hans Bremer, a former criminal investigator, was sentenced to 10 years in prison for crimes against humanity involving extortion of information and assault while in an official capacity. These crimes had occurred most often during arrests of Jews and the enforced lodging of Jews in the so-called *Judenhäuser*.[709]

No trial involving former Gestapo members and their role in the deportations took place in Hamburg. The Gestapo man responsible, Claus Göttsche, had committed suicide in 1945. The victims' organization (VVN) reported their suspicions regarding an official of the Hamburg employment center. It turned out that at the beginning of 1943, this man – on Göttsche's orders – had compiled a list of 18 volunteers of the Jewish community and carefully picked the names of those who annoyed him from the card index. The victims were husbands of so-called privileged mixed marriages, who were normally exempt from deportations. The men were arrested by the Gestapo on February 27, 1943; 15 of them later died in Auschwitz. The member of the employment agency admitted that he had known of the high death rate among Jews deported to the East, but denied any more concrete knowledge although he had remarked to Mrs. Berendt (whose husband was Jewish), "Your husband is going to Auschwitz, you might as well think of yourself as a widow." As predicted, the husband did not survive. The former official of the Hamburg employment center was sentenced for crimes against humanity to three years and six months' in prison. A critical assessment of the trial, however, is impossible, as only Volume I of the main files has survived.[710]

Additional investigations from Hamburg concerned Hermann Kühn, an investigation supervisor in the *Judenreferat* of the Gestapo there. These investigations concerned deportations and mistreatment of Jews in the Gestapo building in Hamburg, but were terminated according to § 154 I German code of criminal procedure because Kühn had been sentenced for other offenses and a renewed trial would not lead to a greater penalty. Kühn had said that the Gestapo had adopted rough measures in depriving the deportees of objects that exceeded the allowed luggage weight of 50 kilograms.[711]

---

[709] Hannover 2 Js 299/47 = 2 Ks 4/48. Against three other suspects the investigations were terminated in 1948 without a trial.
[710] Hamburg 14 Js 278/48 = 14 Ks 56/50, StA Hamburg, Best. 213-11, Nr. 6370/53.
[711] Statement for Criminal Investigation Department, May 6, 1949, Hamburg 14 Js 829/48, StA Hamburg, Best. 213-11, Nr. 6669/64.

Kühn had already been sentenced in his denazification procedures to two years and six months in prison; furthermore he had also been sentenced to four years in the penitentiary for crimes against humanity for assault and extortion.⁷¹²

Other early investigation efforts concerning the deportations were all terminated without trial.⁷¹³

Summary and Outlook

Did investigations and trials of deportation crimes before West German judicial authorities improve after the Allied occupation ended? Alas, no. Records of attempts – and there were many – to maintain balance concerning the adjudication of these matters prove bleak indeed.

Forty-five members of the Gestapo, police, municipality, and fiscal authority in Stuttgart who had participated in the deportation of 2,462 Jews from Württemberg (to Riga, Izbica, Auschwitz, and Theresienstadt) between 1941 and 1945 were tracked down.⁷¹⁴ The head of the Gestapo in Stuttgart, Friedrich Mussgay, had died, but former members of the department responsible for Jews could still be indicted, among them the head of the department and his deputy. The indictment, drawn up in July 1950, included seven defendants (out of the original 45 suspects). At first, the Stuttgart District Court refused to schedule a main hearing because a conviction did not seem likely. After the state prosecutor protested and appealed to the high court in Stuttgart, the main hearing was scheduled accord-

---

712 Lüneburg 1 Js 99/47 = 1 Ks 1/48.
713 American Zone: Mannheim 1a Js 4996/50 (against a former member of Gestapo Mannheim re. deportation of Jews from Mannheim at the end of 1944/beginning of 1945). British Zone: Hannover 2 Js 155/48 (participation in deportation of Jews from Hennendorf and personal gain from Jewish property, files destroyed); Köln 24 Js 1007/48, HStA Düsseldorf – ZA Kalkum, Gerichte Rep. 231/180 (participation in the deportation of elderly Jews in 1944 by "evacuation" of the Jewish Home, Ottostrasse, Köln-Ehrenfeld by a member of the NSDAP-Ortsgruppe Köln-Ehrenfeld); Köln 24 Js 160/50, HStA Düsseldorf – ZA Kalkum, Gerichte Rep. 9/662 (against Kriminalkommissar Kurt Rose, head of the department IV B with the Gestapo Köln concerning the deportation of a Jew in a so-called mixed marriage to Auschwitz); Köln 24 Js 656/52, HStA Düsseldorf – ZA Kalkum, Gerichte Rep. 231/491 (against three former members of the Gestapo Köln who had arrested Jews for misdemeanours, the victims ended up in concentration camps). French Zone: Koblenz 9/2 Js 1062/48, AOFAA, AJ 1616, p. 802 (participation in deportation of Jews from Bad Kreuznach by the local police); Rottweil 4 Js 6948/47, StA Sigmaringen, Wü 29/2 T4, Nr. 676 (participation in the strip search of Jewish women during deportations from Rexingen); Rottweil 6 Js 6651-53/47, StA Sigmaringen, Wü 29/2 T4, Nr. 668 (enforced transfer of Jews from Mühringen to a Judenhaus and then move to Rexingen and Stuttgart.).
714 Stuttgart E Js 3803/48 = 3 KLs 117/50, 3 Ks 35/50.

ing to orders of the high court in 1951. The district court of Stuttgart terminated the trial in 1951 for lack of intent to commit the crime among the defendants. The court had seen a crime against humanity in the deportation but could not apply Control Council Law No. 10. The state prosecutor appealed this assessment to the Federal Supreme Court (founded in 1950), and in 1952 the reasons given for the judgment were vacated; the highest German court then acquitted the deputy head of the department for lack of proof of his participation in the deportations. Concerning the other defendants, the case was sent back to the district court. In 1952, five defendants were acquitted after successfully pleading that they had been following superior orders; the sixth defendant had died in the meantime.

Similarly, the state attorney in Munich capitulated in the prosecution of the perpetrators. From November 1941 to March 1943, at least 3,655 Jews from southern Bavaria had been deported from Munich towards the East (mainly to Kaunas, Auschwitz, and Theresienstadt); of those about 150 survived. While 16 former members of the Munich Gestapo (among them the former head, Oswald Schäfer) and the "Aryanization" authority could be traced, only seven were indicted in 1953. The indictment read: accessory to deprivation of liberty resulting in death and extortionate robbery (referring to the "Aryanization"). In 1954, proceedings ceased without a trial because the former Gestapo members had acted on superior orders according to Military Penal Code. Only the former head of the "Aryanization" authority in Munich, Hans Wegner, stood trial.[715] He was blamed for the deportation of the last head of the Munich Jewish Community, Julius Hechinger. Wegner claimed that Nazi Party functionary Adolf Wagner had ordered Hechinger's deportation because he suspected him of being a police informant for the Reich Security Main Office and Wagner was loath to tolerate a spy, let alone a Jewish one, in his jurisdiction. Hans Wegner claimed that he had simply transmitted Wagner's wish to the state police in Munich. As no proof of participation in the deprivation of Hechinger's liberty (transfer to the transit camp Milbertshofen and subsequent deportation) was possible, Wegner was acquitted.

The sad list of failure could go on. In 1952, two former members of the Gestapo branch in Offenbach who had participated in the deportation of Jews from "mixed marriages" were accused of accessory to severe deprivation of liberty with fatal consequences and accessory to the persecution of innocent people. The relevant district court of Darmstadt refused to admit the indictment to a main hearing, since the Offenbach Gestapo branch had solely obeyed orders from Darmstadt; it could not be proved beyond doubt that the two criminal investigators had been privy to the coordinated action against Jewish partners of "mixed marriages" and

---

715 München I 1 Js 224/53 = 3 KLs 2/54, StA München, StAnw 29499/1-7.

"half-Jews" that affected the Nazi Hessen-Nassau district in particular. Although the two had received 19 complaints against Jews in March and April 1943, they could not have deduced that it constituted a coordinated action aiming at the extermination of Jews. The Frankfurt High Court ordered the scheduling of the main hearing in June 1953, but when the trial took place in July 1953 before the district court in Frankfurt, both defendants were acquitted, partly for lack of proof, partly that they had believed they were in a state of emergency. Both had pleaded that they were conducting regular investigations in the course of which they had subpoenaed the victims, interrogated and arrested them, and subsequently transferred them to Darmstadt. It could not be proved that they had seen through the thinly masked action against Jews of "mixed marriages" and "half-Jews" as part of the general extermination of Jews; furthermore it was conceded that they may have acted under a state of emergency.[716]

Only in Cologne were leading members of the Gestapo convicted for their involvement in deportations. The trial against the former chief of the Köln Gestapo, Dr. Emanuel Schäfer, and two other Gestapo members, Franz Sprinz and Kurt Matschke, had a particularly bizarre origin. It sprang from a divorce procedure dating to 1950, which then led to a trial against Emanuel Schäfer as commander of the security police and the security service in Serbia. The husband of Schäfer's secretary had filed for divorce as his wife had entertained intimate relations with Schäfer, which had resulted in the birth of two children. Legal proceedings then directed against the husband, who was suspected of procuring. Allegations of the cuckolded husband centered first on the statement that Schäfer had started World War II (Schäfer had indeed partaken in the attack on the transmitter station in Gleiwitz in 1939). Schäfer's role in the deportation did not come to the fore until the spring of 1952. It also turned out that Schäfer had lived in Cologne for several years under the alias of Dr. Schleiffer.

The Cologne deportation investigations were first directed against 34 members of the former Cologne Gestapo. But aside from Schäfer, the 1952 indictment only involved two other individuals: Sprinz, his successor as head of the Gestapo, and Matschke, the head of the executive department. All three were convicted of accessory to severe deprivation of liberty with fatal consequences. Schäfer's sentence was one year in the penitentiary (he had already been sentenced in the Serbia case, so his full sentence added up to six years and nine months); Sprinz was sentenced to three years and Matschke to two years of imprisonment.[717]

Although by far the greatest number of German Jews had lived in Berlin of whom 42,000 had been deported, the immediate post-war years saw no trial there.

---

716 Darmstadt 2a Js 1065/50 = Frankfurt 4 Ks 2/53, HStA Wiesbaden, Abt. 461, Nr. 32710.
717 Köln 24 Js 266/52 = 24 Ks 3/53, HStA Düsseldorf – ZA Kalkum, Gerichte Rep. 231/512-521.

The first trial related – at least marginally – to the deportations from Berlin concerned the suspected participation of Dr. Walter Stock, a former criminal investigator and temporary head of the *Judenreferat* in the so-called "factory action" (the February 1943 arrest of Jewish men in "mixed marriages" at their jobs). The trial had been initiated, somewhat casually, in 1949 following a complaint lodged by an attorney from the state prosecutor's office at Oldenburg.[718] The deportations played a small role in the sentence because, the Berlin District Court explained, the deportations in Berlin had been carried out by a special command from the Reich Security Main Office, rather than by members of the Gestapo Berlin or by the defendant. Stock, however, was sentenced to nine months' imprisonment in 1952 for crimes against humanity – the arrest and transfer of a Jew to a work camp as well as the acquiescence to mistreatment of prisoners by the SS in the Gestapo headquarters at Burgstrasse 28 in Berlin. He could not be convicted for participation in the factory action for lack of proof.[719] Eight former members of the Berlin Gestapo were indicted in 1969; the main hearing was scheduled against only three of them.

Otto Bovensiepen, head of the Berlin Gestapo, the former civil service supervisor and SS major, became too ill to stand trial. Thus the proceedings were terminated in 1971 due to his ill health. The deputy head, Dr. Kurt Venter and a former criminal assistant were acquitted, despite continued serious suspicion.[720] Only one more trial took place in Berlin: In 1970, former SS Storm Troop Lieutenant Richard Hartmann was sentenced to six years' imprisonment for accessory to murder. The focus of the trial, however, was the deportation of Jews from Croatia.[721] Hartmann had belonged to the Department IV B 4 in the Reich Security Main Office, the notorious Eichmann department. In 1941/1942 Hartmann, then an SD Storm Trooper 2nd Lieutenant, was in charge of emigration affairs. His main task was to write negative administrative decisions concerning German Jews willing to emigrate to France, Belgium, or Denmark. In 1942, he was also charged with helping Franz Novak, the overburdened head of the transport division in the Reich Security Main Office. In this function he wrote on April 10, 1942, to the Düsseldorf Gestapo that the transport Da 52 from Düsseldorf was scheduled for April 22, 1942. The destination was first given as Trawniki, then as Izbica. The

---

718 Berlin 1 P Js 985/51 = 1 P KLs 3/52.
719 Aachen 2 Js 514/60, HStA Düsseldorf – ZA Kalkum, Gerichte Rep. 270/206; also ended in a termination without a trial.
720 Berlin 3 P (K) Js 9/71 = 3 P (K) Ks 1/71.
721 Berlin 1 Js 3/69 (RSHA) = 1 Ks 1/70 (RSHA). The case Berlin 1 Js 1/65 (RSHA) = (500) 1 Ks 1/71 (RSHA) against a further member of the department IV B 4, Friedrich Robert Bosshammer, did not concern deportations of German Jews, but deportations of Jews from Italy. Bosshammer was sentenced to life but died before the sentence became legally binding.

expected victims were 941 Jews, among them four so-called *Mischlinge* (of mixed Jewish and non-Jewish descent) whose relatives had tried to obtain an exemption through the Ministry of the Interior. Hartmann had the relatives of the intended deportees told by the Gestapo that they were banned from further petitioning for their family members. The so-called *Mischlinge* were thus deported and murdered. Hartmann's knowledge on the fate of the German Jews in the East was established beyond a doubt due to his affiliation with Department IV B 4, the office through which reports of SS task forces and task commandos, the contents of the Wannsee Conference protocol, and the constantly arriving death reports from concentration camps were readily available. Furthermore, he had been assigned the task of mail censorship in the department, where he must have gained insight into the prevailing conditions by reading postcards from Auschwitz.

The deportation of Jews from territories beyond western Germany became focus of a trial only once. In 1952, two former members of the Gestapo Erfurt and Gestapo Weimar were sentenced to one year's imprisonment for accessory to deprivation of liberty. After an appeal and an acquittal in 1954 – for mens rea – the defendant Waldemar Eissfeld was sentenced in 1957 to two and a half years in the penitentiary for accessory to severe deprivation of liberty in 12 cases. The sentence was confirmed in an appeal in 1960. Eissfeld's superior, however, a former departmental chief with the *Staatspolizei* (Gestapo) Weimar, was acquitted.

Eissfeld was convicted of having accompanied a few transports and of having arranged for the deportation of Jews whom a public health officer had deemed too ill for transport. One of the victims thus died in the collection zone. About this victim's wife he had said: "We'll take the old bag and chuck her out of the railway car."[722]

For some years now historians have tried to gauge the behavior of the non-Jewish German population in the face of the persecution of Jews. Though it is difficult to make general assertions, it is obvious that at least certain strata of the population – who hoped for gain – did support, maybe even welcomed the deportations, while others abhorred the brutality of the action against the Jews. Again, the records of the deportation trials, though scarce, can add further evidence. In Bruttig, a vintner cheered the "evacuation" route and voluntarily accompanied the march of the deportees to the ferry (across the river Mosel). He was sentenced to one year and three months' imprisonment for crimes against humanity.[723]

Altruistic help – and treason – were the motives behind one of the most moving stories that emerged from the judicial investigation of deportations. The Meyer family had run a shoe store in Langenfeld, Rhineland. One employee,

---

[722] Darmstadt 2 Js 420/51 = 2 Ks 1/52, Wiesbaden 7 Ks 1/57.
[723] Koblenz 9/2 Js 1620/48 = 9 KLs 2/50, LHA Koblenz, Best. 584, 1, Nr. 1274.

Heinrich Heinen (born in 1920 in Cologne), was engaged to be married to the shopkeeper's daughter, Edith Meyer (born in 1920 in Langenfeld).[724] On December 11, 1941, Edith was taken with a Gestapo transport of 1,010 Jews from Düsseldorf to the Riga ghetto. Heinrich, then a Wehrmacht soldier, followed her and arranged for her escape. Together they returned to the Reich and on April 30, 1942, reached the home of Paula Berntgen in Solingen-Ohligs, where some of of Edith's belongings were being stored. As the Berntgen family was not ready to help the escapees, the couple went to the flat of Paul and Helene Krebs – the latter being a relative of Edith Meyer. Paula Berntgen personally went to the Criminal Investigation Department in Wuppertal on May 11, 1942, to inform on the return of Edith Meyer from the ghetto of Riga. The Berntgens also refused to return Edith's trousseau of linens and china that had been given to them for safekeeping. Edith and her fiancé were arrested on June 22, 1942, while attempting to cross the border to Switzerland from Vorarlberg. On October 9, 1942, Edith Meyer was transferred from the police prison at Innsbruck to Auschwitz (confirmation of her death came in 1949). The Feldkirch district court in Tyrol initiated proceedings against Heinrich Heinen for "racial defilement" and desertion of his Wehrmacht duties.[725] When he tried to flee from prison, he was shot dead. Paul and Helene Krebs, who had sheltered the couple temporarily, were arrested on August 17, 1942. Paul Krebs was discharged from prison, having been deemed indispensable because of his work in an armament factory in Solingen. Helene Krebs, who was pregnant, admitted in an interrogation in September 1942 to having sheltered Edith Meyer and Heinrich Heinen. Paul Krebs pleaded in a heart-rending letter for the release of his wife: "I am willing to take any blame, but I cannot stand it that a human being to whom one has been married for years is being drawn into an uncertain misfortune without my being able to help."[726] On December 9, 1942, Helene Krebs was transferred from imprisonment on remand in Wuppertal to the Auschwitz Concentration Camp and on January 3, 1943, her husband was informed of her death. Paula and Willi Berntgen denied informing on Edith Meyer and embezzling the dowry. Edith Meyer's father, Max Meyer, who had survived, however, could rebut the claim that they had been given the objects as a present. The Gestapo file also proved that Paula Berntgen had indeed informed on Edith Meyer. Still, the investigation was terminated for lack of proof because

---

[724] The story is also told in detail in Holger Berschel, *Bürokratie und Terror: Das Judenreferat der Gestapo Düsseldorf 1935-1945* (Essen: Klartext, 2001), 415-422.
[725] Düsseldorf 8 I AR 18/65, HStA Düsseldorf – ZA Kalkum, Gerichte Rep. 372/1487, p. 302.
[726] Quoted in Berschel, *Bürokratie und Terror*, 422.

Edith Meyer's arrest (on the Austrian-Swiss border) and her subsequent fate had not necessarily been caused by the denunciation.[727]

In autumn 1941, there were about 300,000 Jews still living in the German Reich (including Austria and the protectorate of Bohemia and Moravia). Unless it was possible to go underground, which usually entailed countless preparations and reliance on helpers, the chances of survival for German Jews were slim. Most of those deported were murdered quite soon after their arrival in the camps; the few survivors suffered until the end of the war in ghettos and concentration camps.

In the face of fathomless suffering, even a most conscientious judicial reckoning would have left a lot to be desired. Alas, the overview shows that the German administration of justice was far from a systematic or exemplary preoccupation with the complex of deportations of German Jews from the Reich. As C.F. Rüter has already stated, the number of West German trials after 1945 was small.[728]

Why was this so? Especially in the early post-war years the administration of justice was subject to a particular haphazardness. The chaotic conditions did not facilitate any judicial enquiries, let alone difficult ones. Former Gestapo members had been issued false identities in the last months of the war. The head of the Frankfurt am Main Gestapo from 1941 to 1943, Civil Supervisor and SS Lieutenant Colonel Oswald Poche, assumed the alias "Koch" and lived until his death in 1962 in Salzwedel without ever having been called to account for his role. Others were missing, had committed suicide, and had been killed in action or otherwise died. Survivors and witnesses were occupied with the tasks of daily life; the Gestapo files, with only a few exceptions were destroyed. Thus several investigations and trials came about thanks to people whose relatives had been caught in the constant expansion of deportations to include people who had been considered protected by mixed marriages or by being of partial Jewish descent. However, the great majority of victims who had no non-Jewish relatives had nobody to press charges. The administration of justice was only rarely enacted of its own accord.

---

727 Wuppertal 5 Js 554/48, HStA Düsseldorf – ZA Kalkum, Gerichte Rep. 5/1275; Düsseldorf 8 Js 48/46, HStA Düsseldorf – ZA Kalkum, Gerichte Rep. 268/3.
728 Christiaan F. Rüter, "Ost- und westdeutsche Strafverfahren gegen die Verantwortlichen für die Deportation der Juden: Das Beispiel der Kölner Gestapo," in *NS-Unrecht vor Kölner Gerichten*, ed. Anne Klein and Jürgen Wilhelm (Köln: Greven, 2003). His listing, however, is incomplete as he did not trace all deportation trials. For a systematic, but necessarily also patchy description see also Christiaan F. Rüter and Dick W. de Mildt, *Die westdeutschen Strafverfahren wegen nationalsozialistischer Tötungsverbrechen 1945–1997: Eine systematische Verfahrensbeschreibung mit Karten und Registern* (Amsterdam: APA-Holland University Press, 1998). The early deportation trials were also analyzed by Henry Friedlander, "The Deportation of the German Jews: Post-War German Trials of Nazi Criminals," *Leo Baeck Institute Year Book* 29 (1984).

Although the deportations affected the whole Reich, investigations in the early post-war years are not spread evenly across western Germany. For Schleswig-Holstein and Bremen, no records of a single trial concerning the deportations could be located, despite the fact that 1,600 Jews from Schleswig-Holstein and about 550 from Bremen were deported to the East. For Bremen, there was only one investigation against an alleged Jewish informer, whose denouncements of other Jews meant their deportation.[729] For Baden and the Saar region no investigations or trials could be anticipated, as the more than 6,000 Jews from the Saarpfalz and Baden had been deported to the internment camp Gurs on orders of Regional Commanders Bürckel and Wagner in October 1940.[730] For Berlin and Hamburg, too, the investigation of deportations must be considered to have been a failure (at least in the early post-war years).

The dispossession of Jews by the fiscal authorities prior to deportation receives only rare mention; only the state prosecutors at Würzburg, Stuttgart, and Frankfurt included suspects from the Bureau of Internal Revenue. The expropriation of Jews by the "Aryanization authorities" was covered in the Munich trial and in one of the trials in Nürnberg-Fürth. The courts in Hechingen, Nürnberg-Fürth and Würzburg attempted one of the very few trials covering the total deportations from one region. Convictions did not usually concern the mass deportations of hundreds of victims, but rather excesses such as participation in the misteratment of one person or the selection of a particular person for transport.

The convictions concerning deportations of individuals took place mainly in the British Zone; additional convictions occurred in the American Zone, particularly in southern Hesse. The inclusion of the civil administrators into the circle of suspects – as favored in the French Zone – was doomed to failure, as was the particularly wide field of suspects as favored by the Franconian state attorneys in Würzburg and Nürnberg in the American Zone. The convicts were usually low-ranking former Gestapo members, while the sentencing of the higher Gestapo echelons was only achieved once – in Köln in the 1953 and 1955 trials against Schäfer, Sprinz, and Matschke. This trial could have served as a model for further legal procedures because it was not directed at the lower ranking members of the Gestapo in the *Judenreferate* but focused on the chiefs of the Gestapo or at least

---

729 Bremen 5 Js 2046/49. The investigation was terminated without trial as denunciations could not be followed up as Bremen as part of the American Zone could not apply Control Council Law No. 10.
730 Saarbrücken 11 Js 18/48; is an investigation which combines enquiry into crimes of the pogrom with the deportation of Jews from so-called privileged "mixed marriages" and "half-Jews" from Wiebelskirchen and Merchweiler in March 1945 to Theresienstadt ghetto.

the heads of the Gestapo department. It ended in convictions – if not for murder, then at least for accessory to deprivation of liberty with fatal consequences.

The crux of the matter when it came to acquittals or investigations concluded without trial was that the defendants or suspects flatly denied having had any knowledge of the mass murder of the Jews in "the East." State attorneys and courts accepted this line of argumentation uncritically, although simple common sense showed the absurdity of transporting elderly, infirm, mentally ill, babies, and toddlers over huge distances for the purposes of "work." The multitude of transports suggested moreover that the absorbing capacity of ghettoes was long exceeded and that in the overpopulated ghettos epidemics would rage. The courts proved unable to establish a personal connection between participants in the deportations from the Reich and the perpetrators of genocide in the East, although this link existed in several cases. I will just mention four Gestapo members who had been posted in the East before they were stationed with the *Staatspolizeistellen* in the Reich. Ernst Gramowski, chief of the Gestapo Würzburg, had belonged to a task commando (*Einsatzkommando* IX) during the war in Poland and had belonged to Department IV of the Secret Police (*Kommandeur der Sicherheitspolizei KdS*) in Lublin. From autumn 1941 to September 1942, Kurt Matschke, head of the Judenreferat of the Köln Gestapo, had belonged to *Sonderkommando* 7a of *Einsatzgruppe* B. Reinhard Breder headed *Einsatzkommando* 3 of *Einsatzgruppe* A and was deputy commander in Minsk before he became head of the state police in Frankfurt am Main at the end of August 1943. When confronted with the deportations of October 28–29, 1943, January 8, 1944, July 4, 1944, and February 14, 1945, he claimed to have no recollection.[731] Robert Mohr, registrar and SS lieutenant colonel, had belonged to the Gestapo, the Reich Security Main Office, and the SS task force C before finally becoming head of the Darmstadt Gestapo in October 1942. And yet, even though he had clearly been involved in the Nazi killing fields in Eastern Europe, an investigation into his role in the deportation of Jews from Hesse ended in 1975, as the state attorney could not prove that Mohr had been associated with the death or murder of those deported.[732] (Robert Mohr had, however, been sentenced in another Nazi crime case.[733])

Perhaps this connection between the perpetrators involved in deportations and the members of the SS task forces would have become obvious to the German

---

731 Frankfurt 4 Js 387/64, HStA Wiesbaden, Abt. 461, Nr. 30983/1-38.
732 Darmstadt 2 Js 135/73.
733 Robert Mohr was sentenced as former head of the Einsatzkommandos 6 for accessory to murder to eight years' penitentiary. Wuppertal 12 Js 220/61 = 12 Ks 1/62, HStA Düsseldorf – ZA Kalkum, Gerichte Rep. 240/105-138.

investigators had they had access – which was not yet the case in the occupation years – to such American military trials as the *Einsatzgruppen-Prozess*.

Was there no way for German state attorneys and courts to learn about the organization of mass murder so as to be in a better position to adjudicate the deportation crimes? Contrary to popular belief, there were indeed investigations and trials concerning the extermination proper. Trials concerning the fate of deportees in extermination camps were conducted at the same time or were at least in the offing. There were early trials concerning Auschwitz and its satellite camps, suspected participation in selections[734] and grievous bodily harm in Auschwitz,[735] Trzebinia,[736] and Jawischowitz.[737] The first of these early West German Auschwitz trials took place in 1948 in Berlin, where the defendant was sentenced to 10 years in the penitentiary for crimes against humanity.[738] The *Berliner Zeitung* noted: "One would have wished that the public would have been as interested in this first concentration camp trial before a German court in Berlin as they were in certain other trials, which clearly had the advantage of conveying a different atmosphere than that of a bleak concentration camp." In Munich Philomena M. was tried before a jury in 1949 for assault of female prisoners in Auschwitz-Birkenau.[739] The American observers noted: "This is the first instance in which a woman will be tried by a Bavarian court for atrocities committed during the war."[740] Displaced persons complained about the mild penalty: "That scum of humanity, after having caused the death and heavy bodily injuries to so many prisoners, was sentenced to only four years' imprisonment, however giving her full credit for her pre-trial detention covering a period of two and three quarters years. This is a striking case of a misjudgment that could only be made upon the subjective attitude of a considerable part of the jurymen."[741] Hermann J., another official at the Auschwitz satellite camp Fürstengrube, was tried for bodily harm first in Ansbach and later in Nürnberg-Fürth.[742] The chief executive manager of the

---

734 Regensburg – Zweigstelle Straubing I Js 1674/52 (previously München II Da 12 Js 1660/48), StA Nürnberg, GStA beim OLG Nürnberg 244.
735 München II Da 12 Js 1016/49 = Gen. KMs 20/50, StA München, StAnw 34452/1-2.
736 Augsburg 4 Js 470/49 = 4 KLs 23/51.
737 Bochum 2 Js 647/48 = 2 Ks 1/50, IfZ Gb 08.14/1-2.
738 Berlin 12 Js 195/46 = 1 P Ks 6/47.
739 München I 1 Js 1565/48 = 1 Ks 5/49; StA München, StAnw 17417.
740 Monthly report, March 3, 1949, NARA, OMGBY 17/184 – 2/4.
741 Letter J. Rywosh and E. Epstein (Legal Department, Central Committee of Liberated Jews in the American Occupied Zone in Germany) to Director, Legal Division, OMGUS, August 29, 1949, NARA, OMGUS 17/197 – 3/31.
742 Ansbach 5 Js 211/48 = Nürnberg-Fürth Ks 11/49; Ansbach 89/50 KMs 2/52, StA Nürnberg, StAnw Ansbach 1315-1324.

DEGESCH (*Deutsche Gesellschaft für Schädlingsbekämpfung*, German Company for Pest Control) which supplied the poison gas for Auschwitz, also stood trial.[743] Moreover, in 1950/1951 three trials concerning the extermination camps Sobibor and Treblinka took place in Berlin[744] and Frankfurt.[745]

While I cannot go into details of these trials, it is obvious that perpetrators who were more closely involved in the actual murder did run a higher risk of having to stand trial and be sentenced than those who had simply arranged for the transport into death.

Sometimes the parallelism of Allied and German prosecution hindered the German attempts at reckoning. Certain perpetrators had already been tried for other crimes by the Allies, and in some cases had already been executed. Dr. Walter Albath, head of the Düsseldorf Gestapo from 1941 to 1943 and chief commander of *Einsatzgruppe* V in the war against Poland, had been sentenced to 15 years' imprisonment by a British military court for the killing of Allied POWs. He was thus exempt from German prosecution. Heinz Hellenbroich, the former head of the *Judenreferat* and deputy chief of the Darmstadt Gestapo, criminal board, and SS lieutenant colonel had also been sentenced to death by an American military court for the killing of Allied POWs and had been executed in 1948, before he could be taken to task either for his role as a member of the SS task forces or as a participant in the deportations from Hesse. In addition to heading the Munich Gestapo and *Einsatzkommando* 8 of *Einsatzgruppe* B from December 1939 to November 1942, Senior Registrar Dr. Erich Isselhorst also served as *Einsatzkommando* 1 of *Einsatzgruppe* A before being appointed KdS in Minsk. He was first sentenced to death by a British, then by a French military court, for the killing of British POWs and Allied resistance fighters in his eventual position as BdS in Strassburg. His sentencing and execution took place without an investigation of his role in the deportations or in the SS task forces. SS Lieutenant Colonel Alfred Schimmel, Isselhorst's deputy at the Munich Gestapo, member of the BdS, and registrar in Strassburg, met a similar fate as he too had taken part in the killing of British POWs. The loss of these high-ranking potential witnesses – and potential defendants – hindered the German investigations concerning the fate of German Jews.

---

743 Frankfurt 4a Js 3/48 = 4 Ks 2/48, 4a Ks 1/55, Wiesbaden 3 Ks 3/51, HStA Wiesbaden, Abt. 461, Nr. 36342/1-12.
744 Berlin 1 P Js 137/49 (a) = 1 P Ks 3/50, IfZ Gb 06.08 (concerning Sobibor).
745 Frankfurt 8 Js 1055/49 = 52 Ks 3/50, HStA Wiesbaden, Abt. 461, Nr. 36346/1-130 (concerning Sobibor); Frankfurt 53/6 Js 3942/48 = 14/53 Ks 1/50, HStA Wiesbaden, Abt. 461, Nr. 35253-35257 (concerning Treblinka).

On the other hand, research in recent years has shown that rumors and knowledge from hearsay was much more widespread among the general public than previously assumed. Knowledge about the murder and genocide penetrated the police apparatus in the Reich and percolated to the lower echelons. Former female Gestapo secretaries testified that they had known since 1942 that the Jews in the East were being murdered. It was mentioned in the sentence against Schäfer, Sprinz, and Matschke that rumors about the liquidation of Jews were circulating and formed a frequent topic of conversation among Gestapo employees. The receptionists of Sprinz and Matschke said that at the Köln Gestapo it was common knowledge by late 1942/early 1943 that the deportees were going to be murdered. Police reports commented openly on the shootings and killings. Captain Salitter of the *Schutzpolizei*, who accompanied the transport from Düsseldorf on December 11, 1942 (with Edith Meyer) to Riga reported in his written account of the journey (dated December 26, 1941) on the shooting of Latvian Jews and the astonishment of the Latvians as to why Germany transported Jews to Latvia rather than exterminating them in their own country.[746]

Thus the judicial treatment of the matter of deportation from the Reich can only be seen as completely unsatisfactory. Although all sentences branded the deportations as a criminal offense according to the German Penal Code or Control Council Law No. 10, the courts were helpless when it came to attributing the crimes to specific persons. Perpetrators were generally not held to account if they had followed orders and had not committed deeds of excessive violence against their victims. Moreover, the courts were frequently inclined to accord the state of emergency to the perpetrators. The sentence against Schäfer, Sprinz, and Matschke mentioned that according to the Military Penal Code an order that was plainly violating the law was not to be obeyed. Whoever considered the deprivation of liberty of the Jews to be unjust – to which many defendants had conceded – could not rely on the protection of the Military Penal Code.

---

[746] Quoted according to Kurt Düwell, "'Riga ist städtebaulich eine sehr schöne Stadt...:' Die Düsseldorfer Judendeportationen vom Herbst 1941," *Augenblick: Berichte, Informationen und Dokumente der Mahn- und Gedenkstätte Düsseldorf* 20/21 (2002), 14.

Conclusion

In her book *Visit to Germany* (*Besuch in Deutschland*, 1949/1950), Hannah Arendt formulated two questions with which one is confronted when researching the history of occupied Germany: "What could be expected of a people after 12 years of totalitarian rule? And what could be expected of an occupation with the impossible task of resurrecting a people that had lost the ground under their feet?"[747]

As far as the German administration of justice, the Western Allies, and the German public are concerned, the conclusion is surprisingly positive – so that one can easily agree with Hannah Arendt's appraisal that "the dismal German post-war history is not a story of missed chances."[748]

This book has tried to show how complex the judicial struggle for coming to terms with the National Socialist past has been in the Western zones of Germany. The Allies had not only been forced to overpower National Socialism; in the Western zones they had also figured prominently as protagonists of the creation of a process for German post-war administration of justice and a system of law and order in a nascent democracy. The contribution of the Western Allies in choosing the first (unblemished) personnel and re-opening the courts was fundamental. Notwithstanding that some segments of justice remained an exclusively Allied affair, that German judicial personnel were being checked and were not immune to dismissal or suspension, that individual sentences could be lifted or altered – all factors incompatible with a truly democratic and independent justice system – occupation was, for the legal profession, a thoroughly benign affair in all three Western zones. Despite conflicts between German jurists and members of the legal divisions of the Western Allies, a fully benevolent attitude prevailed among the Western Allies regarding German legal authorities. Many prerogatives reserved for the Military Government were used little or not at all; sometimes simply the existence of control mechanisms and the possibility that the occupiers could intervene seemed to suffice. The Western Allies refrained from forcing their own legal systems onto the German judicial administration; similarly, they abstained from attempts at fundamental reform. Their main aim was to leave behind a functioning German justice administration that would serve a democratic state of law and order when their occupation was over. When the occupation aim of reconstruction of justice collided with the aim of denazification of the judicial staff, reconstruction took priority. Considering the changing, confusing, and inconsistent standards of denazification, this was a wise choice. The Western Allies defined the framework in which German judicature could develop.

---

747 Hannah Arendt, *Besuch in Deutschland* (Berlin: Rotbuch Verlag, 1993), 64.
748 Ibid.

They relied on loyal personnel in key positions and expected that former Nazi Party members (who received a small advance in trust) would be "seduced" and attracted by democracy. To quote a famous line: The German jurists did not act on their own accord in the reconstruction of the judicial system, but they acted for themselves. Though the occupation period was but a blink of an eye, permanent traces remain: The high courts of Bremen and Koblenz, as well as Saarbrücken owe their existence to these years.

It was one of the biggest challenges for the administration of justice: On the one hand they had to achieve the continuity of law (and not each single ordinance or administrative act dating from the Third Reich could be annulled, since major parts of the penal code had also applied during the National Socialist years), on the other hand they had to adjust to the rule of the Allies (with new laws and regulations) and the attempt to develop a new jurisdiction. The willy-nilly prosecution of Nazi crimes was experimental ground: Neither jurisprudence nor legal practice had any experience with occupation rule or with the atrocious adjudication of crimes during the Third Reich. That (West) Germany persevered with its Nazi criminal prosecution program long after the Allies had gone suggests that the Allies had successfully rammed their point home.

From early on, this punitive global project – which in the late 1940s not only applied to Germany and its European neighbors but also to the Far East, i.e. Japan and the Philippines – was deemed the "largest judicial enterprise recorded in the history of mankind."[749]

In each Western zone the influence of the respective Allies became visible, as the Western Allies each emphasized different aspects of prosecution. Just as the Allies dealt differently with their own trials, so did their approaches to German trials diverge. The British and French considered Control Council Law No. 10 (which was influenced by Anglo-Saxon legal thought) to be the lynchpin of the prosecution of Nazi crimes and could not relate to the objections of German jurists. The Americans saw CC Law No. 10 as an instrument to be used by international Military Tribunals and the Military Tribunals of the Allies, but not by the German legal system – either because they mistrusted the German jurists' ability to apply the law properly or because they took the qualms of the German higher legal personnel seriously. For the most part, German judges and lawyers rejected the application of Control Council Law No. 10. There were both good reasons for the law and good reasons to oppose it. For many Germans, denunciation had been their most direct experience of the arbitrariness of the Nazi state, thus the penalization of denunciation was an indicator of judicial success in coming to terms with the past. As soon became obvious in the American Zone, the prosecu-

---

[749] Koessler, "American War Crimes Trials in Europe," 21.

tion of this offense was particularly difficult by means of the German Penal Code. For German jurists, Control Council Law No. 10 was anathema due to its retroactive character. One may consider it absurd – or maybe admirable – to enforce the principle of legal certainty and the protection of the individual (usually against populist demands for punishment), and to insist on granting even perpetrators the benefit of the rule of law that they had denied their victims. In effect, the prosecution effort concerning denunciations and the principle of legal certainty were mutually exclusive. To paraphrase Shakespeare's *Merchant of Venice*: Should one stick to the letter of the law, or bend it for the sake of common sense?[750] The quandary tormented jurists, Allies, and the German population.

Jon Elster defined purges and reparations as attributes of transitional justice trials.[751] For a brief moment in history, when the Third Reich no longer existed and the Federal Republic of Germany had not yet come into being, these measures were all applied simultaneously in Germany: the trials by the International Military Tribunal; the Allied Military Tribunals and German penal courts; the purges by denazification commissions and denazification tribunals; reparations in the Soviet occupied zone and the French Zone; as well as the beginning of compensation and restitution.[752] This plethora of instruments for coping with the Nazi past applied only to Germany. Neighboring Austria had no International Military Tribunal. The Allies restricted themselves to a few court cases of prosecution of crimes against Allied POWs, while the Austrian People's Courts were responsible for both the political purge and the penal prosecution of Nazi crimes.[753] It is probably an irony of history that, of all these means for coping with the Nazi past, the German Nazi trials of the late 1940s are the ones that sank into oblivion.

Even the fact that there were so many penal procedures prior to the forming of the Federal Republic of Germany is astonishing. The material conditions for the administration of justice were never worse than in the immediate post-war period. Judges and state attorneys at all West German courts were controlled by the Western Allies and had to make their way through a complex (and ever-changing) network of legal competences alternating between Allied and German responsibilities. The processing of cases frequently had to be carried out without the files dating from the Nazi period, as they had been destroyed either in war action or

---

[750] William Shakespeare, *The Merchant of Venice*, Act 4, Scene 1.
[751] Jon Elster, *Die Akten schliessen: Recht und Gerechtigkeit nach dem Ende von Diktaturen* (Frankfurt am Main: Campus, 2005), 17.
[752] Ibid., 67.
[753] Winfried R. Garscha and Claudia Kuretsidis-Haider, "Die strafrechtliche Verfolgung nationalsozialistischer Verbrechen – eine Einführung," in *Holocaust und Kriegsverbrechen vor Gericht: Der Fall Österreich*, ed. Thomas Albrich, Winfried R. Garscha and Martin F. Polaschek (Innsbruck: StudienVerlag, 2006), 17, 19.

intentionally by the National Socialists towards the end of the war, or had been seized by the Allies. And yet, never again were so many investigations initiated as in the occupation years. Each of the state prosecutor's offices that existed at the time was occupied with research into National Socialist crimes, whereas in later years smaller prosecution offices delegated the often long-winded and complicated investigations to prosecution agencies specialized in Nazi crime investigation. The number of suspects and those indicted, and the number of investigations and trials was never higher than in the years 1945–1949. As the occupation period drew to a close, a first peak also ended. The first *Bundestag* (West German parliament) agreed on an amnesty (valid from December 31, 1949) and a further amnesty bill was ratified in 1954. As a result, research into Nazi crimes decreased substantially, although it never ceased completely.

"Justice starts at home." This maxim led Lion Feuchtwanger's heroine Johanna Krain in the novel *Erfolg* (Success), set in the 1920s, to fight for the rehabilitation of a victim of miscarriage of justice. This theme is fitting here, too. The Allies had assigned the Germans the task of examining local Nazi crimes against German victims. In the late 1940s these local crimes had – despite the wish of many Germans for oblivion – become part of a collective memory. Matters of arson, pillory marches with the aim of public shaming, arrests, bodily harm and murder could not be considered closed immediately.

Of the many crimes the Nazis committed in the Reich, the atrocities against Jews were the most harrowing. Furthermore, their prosecution was to be the most contentious and agonizing in the aftermath of the Nazi regime. While political opponents, religious dissenters, or women deemed guilty of forbidden sexual relations had still been considered members of the German state and following punishment in protective custody, prison, and even concentration camps, would be allowed to dwell at least on the fringes of the good graces of the Nazi society, the Jews (like gypsies) had been excluded due to their "racial" status. Not just the Nazi state and party, but German civil society as such had failed them by permitting their discrimination, exclusion, expulsion, deportation, and murder largely without protest. Thus, trying the crimes that had been committed against German Jews (as in the pogrom or deportation cases) meant putting German society as such on the moral proving ground: Why had so many Germans failed their Jewish neighbors, colleagues, and acquaintances when it came to basic human issues?

The perpetrators of these crimes were local dignitaries, colleagues, acquaintances, friends, neighbors, family. Storm troopers who stood guard in front of a Jewish store during the boycott; the neighbor or entrepreneur who pressured a Jewish proprietor into selling his house, shop, or firm; the Nazi Party functionary who arrested a Jewish family during the pogrom; the tax inspector who confiscated Jewish property; the auctioneer who sold the last belongings of deportees to bargain hunters; the district chief executive who ordered the implementation of Gestapo orders for the deportation of Jews; the innkeeper who used the Jewish cemetery as a chicken run; or the informer who let the police know of Jews in hiding – all these examples make painfully clear how many Germans had been participants in Nazi crime. To face all this and acknowledge guilt on a national level was an important step in the quest for rehabilitation – both for individual perpetrators and bystanders and for German society as a whole. Prosecution of individuals for Nazi crimes was necessary if Germany were to play a role among democratic nations. For German Jews driven into exile and for the victims murdered, the legal reckoning could be but a token gesture. The fact that, after all the mass murder and mayhem, at least one segment of German society – the legal service – to some extent understood and empathized and was compelled to deal with the suffering was an important step toward a society obeying the rule of law. Together with other instruments (denazification, reparation, indemnification payments, restitution), the trials – with all their shortcomings – constituted a not entirely futile attempt at rectifying at least some of the ills of the past.

The simple fact that a dreadful past was being reconstructed and that the perpetrators had to face a reckoning commands respect for the German administration of justice, which worked under tense conditions. The aims of the members of the judiciary were to stem the tide of forgetting and to set out on a search for justice despite the myriad material needs of post-war Germany. So far, the importance of these early trials in the process of democratization of West Germany has been thoroughly underestimated in comparison with the much better known Allied trials – a fact that I find quite ironic.

One shortcoming of these early investigations was that they remained isolated so that the investigators often lacked knowledge of the bigger picture of Nazi atrocities; often while looking at one particular episode in the career of a Nazi criminal, they overlooked other crimes committed by the same person at an earlier or later point. However, this criticism also applies to the prosecution activities of the Allies, who again covered merely portions of the vast pool of crimes committed. The failure of certain German trial programs – such as those involving deportation of German Jews or the investigation of mass atrocities – can be attributed to a lack of insight into the coercive powers of National Socialism and the organizations of perpetrators. It would, however, be unreasonable to compare the current amassed knowledge of decades of judicial and historical dealings regarding the Nazi past, with what was available at the beginning of prosecution in the late 1940s. On the other hand, crimes committed as part of the pogrom received exemplary treatment – both comprehensive and intensive – well before the founding of the Central Agency Ludwigsburg. Groundbreaking work was done for some categories of crime, such that no further trials were necessary.

However, crimes of the central authorities on the Reich level (as well as crimes in the occupied territories) had been reserved by the Allies for themselves and were thus beyond the scope of German judicial authorities.

In the Western Zones, assiduous and strenuous work by police, state attorneys, and courts went into the examination of the Nazi past, but soon the zeal faltered. Inexperienced police could not master the difficulties of investigation; the problems of simply tracing and transferring suspects from Allied internment camps into German prisons often proved too much for all concerned – not to mention that the overall condition of the German judicial authorities left a lot to be desired. Furthermore, the Western Allies criticized German personnel, the penal procedures as such, the investigations, and the trials, as well as sentences and enforcement of sentences. The German population bemoaned the sentences as too lenient; the German press sneered at the trials. But what punishment would have been adequate for the monstrosity of so many crimes? With which penalty could one have compensated for the injustice of the past in order to re-establish legal order? Retaliation (according to the absolute theory of punishment) would have been unworthy of a state of law and thus unsuitable for the German judicial authorities. From the standpoint of preventing a repetition of crimes that had been committed in connection with the Nazi state of lawlessness, which no longer exited, the courts could have refrained from punishment altogether because; the likelihood of recidivism under peaceful and democratic conditions was small. But for the purposes of general prevention (according to the relative theory of penalty) the sentences increased awareness that deeds have consequences, thus making prosecution reasonable. In this sense the penalties ultimately strengthened trust in the state of law.

However, the administration of justice in Germany seemed unable to please anybody. The high expectation of justice could only cause disappointment. Judicial personnel, Allies, population, and media would come to see that there are many forms of guilt and sin, but very few possibilities for atonement, as the German author Carl Zuckmayer put it. Or to repeat the words of P.D. James: "It is good for us to be reminded from time to time that our system of law is human and, therefore, fallible and that the most we can hope to achieve is a certain justice."[754]

One of the most important questions that arose in the course of my work on this book is this: Why were the unquestionable merits of the early judicial prosecution of Nazi crime so completely forgotten that even important works of reference fail to note them? While the Nazi trials of the 1960s enduringly shape our image of the crimes of the Third Reich, the trials of the 1940s did not exert a similar seminal influence. Trying to answer this question would go far beyond

---

754 Phyllis Dorothy James, *A Certain Justice* (London: Random House, 1998), 481.

our current observation, thus I can only offer conjectures. For one, the discussion about the method and modalities of denazification seems to have obscured the perception of activities of the regular German courts. Furthermore, the Allied trials won far more media coverage and thus dominated public perception of the occupation period.

German courts and their dealings with the Nazi crimes under Allied occupation were wrongly perceived as controlled by the Allies. This has much to do with the fact that Germany during the occupation period was commonly labeled as a society in collapse and capitulation, as well overwhelmed by ruin and rubble, leaving no room for recognition of the independent achievements of German administration of justice. In addition, a lack of personal continuity rendered the outcome inevitable. A massive change of generations took place in the administration of justice in 1949 and 1950: The often elderly jurists of the first post-war years were pensioned off and new personnel – often much more encumbered by Nazi affiliations – moved in, creating what can be rightfully called a re-nazification of the German administration of justice. More importantly, the Nazi crimes that concerned jurists in the early post-war years did not also play a role in the 1950s and in the following decades of coping with the Nazi past. Either the statute of limitations applied or Control Council Law No. 10 was no longer applicable. Starting points for West German jurists in the 1950s were mostly the Allied trials, which had dealt with concentration camps and mass atrocities abroad or the crimes committed at the Reich level. Were their activities thus misguided, as C.F. Rüter suggests?[755]

Resuming investigations concerning crimes against political opponents (usually grievous bodily harm or deprivation of liberty), crimes committed during the pogrom of 1938 (most often breach of domestic and public peace, wrongful arrests, arson), or killings (qualified as manslaughter) committed at the end of the war was out of the question due to the statute of limitations. Once the appropriate limitation period (specified in the German penal code) had expired, prosecution was no longer possible. Only few specific crimes – murder or accessory to murder, i.e., crimes such as mass executions at extermination sites, concentration camps or mental institutions – could still be investigated and prosecuted. Thus the German judiciary had acted – according to Allied requirements, due to the general conditions, and probably also unconsciously – in a most sensible way. The crimes for which the statute of limitations was looming dangerously close had been dealt with first. From an instructional point of view, the trials were thoroughly impressive. A certain portion of National Socialist crimes had not been committed in

---

[755] Christiaan F. Rüter, "Das Gleiche – aber anders: Die Strafverfolgung von Kriegsverbrechen im deutsch-deutschen Vergleich," *Deutschland-Archiv* 43 (2010), 214.

the far off occupied East, behind prison walls or concentration camp fences by crazed and dehumanized perpetrators in SS, Gestapo, or Wehrmacht uniforms, but rather amidst German society in ever increasing radicalization, often long before the war began. They had been committed by men and women with whom one had gone to school, by friends, by neighbors, and buddies from local associations and clubs. The public hearings that often took place in packed rooms in inns, gymnasiums, or town halls contributed significantly to the realization that dealing with the crimes of the past was not just a compulsory exercise for the judiciary, but a social necessity for the renascent German democracy and its citizens. Klaus Naumann described the mastering of the consequences of war as one of the most astonishing and yet most irritating achievements of German society after World War II.[756] One must add the judicial coping with the Nazi past during the occupation years to this success.

Was there a zero hour for the German judicial system? The ultimate, undeniable return of former Nazi members to their positions and functions (after a certain period of disgrace), along with the resumption of legal affairs mainly according to the status quo of the judicial system prior to January 30, 1933, could suggest that 1945 did not mean a new beginning for German justice. And yet new legal regulations (i.e., the introduction of Control Council Law No. 10 in the British and French zones and compensation for Nazi victims), denazification procedures for legal personnel, the commitment to account before Military Government authorities, the interaction of German and occupation law, the at least partial reception of foreign and international law, the agonizing over the unity of law and the struggle against legal uncertainty were all new challenges for the German judiciary. The prosecution of Nazi crimes surely was not an easy task for the German judges and state attorneys – and probably not one close to their hearts. But the Allies insisted that in order to build a stable democracy the judicial coping with the Nazi past was indispensable. The Western occupation powers did indeed view penalization of Nazi crimes as a litmus test for a functioning post-war judiciary. While the Western Allies had hoped the German judiciary would emulate the actions of the American and British War Crimes program to draw Nazi trials to an end and finish with the transitional justice, neither they nor the Germans had any idea that they were taking part in a historic process that would have to surmount many obstacles and would continue to this day.

Hans-Peter Schwarz points to the fact that the history of the Federal Republic of Germany can only be fully understood if one tries to view it from the perspec-

---

[756] Klaus Naumann, *Nachkrieg in Deutschland* (Hamburg: Hamburger Edition, 2001), 9.

tive of catastrophe as a reaction to physical, political, economic, and moral chaos from which the West German state and society worked its way up.[757]

Last but not least, the West German way of coping with the Nazi past cannot be fully comprehended without directing attention to the occupation period. West Germany has often been reproached for its belated judicial examination of National Socialist crimes. However, this criticism can only be raised by those who ignore the early post-war years. After a phase of intensive preoccupation with Nazi crimes on the part of both Allied and German courts in the late 1940s, a somewhat comprehensible slacking of investigation followed in the 1950s, when the topic seemed to recede from the public conscience. Exactly because there had been so many trials in the early post-war years, the (erroneous) notion took hold that all crimes already had been investigated by either the Allies or the Germans, when in fact the German Nazi trials that would galvanize the media and public attention on a major scale were still to come. In appraising the German judiciary's efforts in investigating Nazi crimes, one must consider the early investigations and trials as a pivotal period at the start of Germany's coming to terms with its Nazi past.

---

[757] Hans-Peter Schwarz, "Die ausgebliebene Katastrophe: eine Problemskizze zur Geschichte der Bundesrepublik," in *Den Staat denken: Theodor Eschenburg zum Fünfundachzigsten*, ed. Hermann Rudolph (Berlin: Siedler, 1990), 152.

Appendix

List of illustrations

Table 1. Number of investigations and dispensations by year
Table 2. Percentage of Nazi crimes by category
Table 3. Number of victims of murder, manslaughter, or grievous bodily harm resulting in death or suicide during the pogrom according to West-German judicial proceedings (1945-1949)

Abbreviations

Abg.	*Abgabe* (disposal)
Abt.	*Abteilung* (department)
AG	*Amtsgericht* (local court)
AJ	*Affaires Judiciaires* (legal affairs)
Akz.	*Akzession* (acquisition)
AMG	American Military Government
AOFAA	*Archives de l'Occupation Française en Allemagne et en Autriche*, Colmar (French Occupation Archives of Germany and Austria, Colmar)
BAK	*Bundesarchiv* Koblenz (German Federal Archives)
BAOR	British Army of the Rhine
BDC	Berlin Document Center
BDM	*Bund deutscher Mädel* (League of German Girls)
Best.	*Bestand* (holding)
BStU	*Bundesbeauftragter für die Unterlagen des Staatssicherheitsdienstes der ehemaligen Deutschen Demokratischen Republik* (Federal Commissioner for the former East German State Security Records)
CC	Allied Control Council
CCG (BE)	Control Commission for Germany (British Element)
CDU	*Christlich Demokratische Union* (Christian Democratic Union)
CIC	Counter Intelligence Corps
DAF	*Deutsche Arbeitsfront* (German Labour Front)
Det	Detachment
Diss.	Dissertation
Dr.	Doctor
DRiZ	*Deutsche Richter-Zeitung*
DRZ	*Deutsche Rechts-Zeitschrift*
EUCOM	United States European Command
FO	Foreign Office
Gerichte Rep.	*Gerichte-Repertorium* (finding aid concerning courts)
Gestapo	*Geheime Staatspolizei* (Secret State Police)
GMZFO	*Gouvernement Militaire de la Zone Française d'Occupation*
GStA	*Generalstaatsanwalt(schaft)* (solicitor general, attorney-generalship)

HJ	*Hitler-Jugend* (Hitler Youth)
HQ	headquarters
HStA	*Hauptstaatsarchiv* (Central State Archive)
IA & C Division	Internal Affairs and Communication Division
IfZ	*Institut für Zeitgeschichte*, München (Institute of Contemporary History)
IRO	International Refugee Organisation
JR	*Juristische Rundschau*
KPD	*Kommunistische Partei Deutschlands* (Communist Party of Germany)
KRG	*Kontrollratsgesetz* (Control Council Law)
KZ	*Konzentrationslager* (concentration camp)
LA	*Landesarchiv (state archive)*
LG	*Landgericht* (district court)
LHA	Landeshauptarchiv (Central State Archive)
L/R Det	*Länder-/Regierungsbezirk*-Detachment
LSO	Liaison and Security Office
MDR	*Monatsschrift für deutsches Recht*
MG	*Militärgericht* (military court)
Mil. Gov.	Military Government
Mil. Reg.	*Militärregierung* (Military Government)
MJu	*Akten des bayerischen Justizministeriums im Hauptstaatsarchiv München* (records of Bavarian Ministry of Justice, Main State Archive Munich)
MOJ	Ministry of Justice
NARA	National Archives and Records Administration (College Park, USA)
NJ	*Neue Justiz*
NJW	*Neue Juristische Wochenschrift*
Nr.	Number
NS	*nationalsozialistisch/Nationalsozialismus* (National Socialist/National Socialism)
NSDAP	*Nationalsozialistische Deutsche Arbeiterpartei* (National Socialist German Workers' Party)
NSFK	*Nationalsozialistisches Fliegerkorps* (National Socialist Flyers Corps)
NSKK	*Nationalsozialistisches Kraftfahrkorps* (National Socialist Motor Corps)
NSV	*Nationalsozialistische Volkswohlfahrt* (National Socialist Welfare)
OGHBZ	*Oberster Gerichtshof für die Britische Zone* (Supreme Court for the British Zone)
OMGBR	Office of Military Government, Bremen
OMGBY	Office of Military Government, Bavaria
OMGH	Office of Military Government, Hesse
OMGWB	Office of Military Government, Wurttemberg-Baden
OMGUS	Office of Military Government, United States
OLG	*Oberlandesgericht* (high court)
OSS	Office of Strategic Services
OStA	*Oberstaatsanwalt(schaft)* (senior prosecutor, senior public prosecution department)
P.	paquet (file bundle)
Pg.	*Parteigenosse* (Nazi Party member)
POW	prisoner of war

PRO	Public Record Office, London
RA	*Rechtsanwalt* (attorney at law)
RAD	*Reichsarbeitsdienst* (Reich Labor Service)
R/B Det	*Regierungsbezirk*-Detachment
Rep.	*Repertorium* (finding aid)
RGBl.	*Reichsgesetzblatt* (Reich Law Gazette)
RM	*Reichsmark*
RMG	Regional Military Government
RSHA	*Reichssicherheitshauptamt* (SS-Reich Main Security Office)
S.	*Seite* (page)
SA	*Sturmabteilung* (Brownshirts)
SAP	*Sozialistischer Arbeiterpartei Deutschlands* (Socialist Workers' Party of Germany)
SBZ	*Sowjetische Besatzungszone* (Soviet Occupation Zone)
SG	*Sondergericht* (special court)
SHAEF	Supreme Headquarters, Allied Expeditionary Forces
SJZ	*Süddeutsche Juristen-Zeitung*
SMAD	*Sowjetische Militäradministration* (Soviet Military Administration in Germany)
SPD	*Sozialdemokratische Partei Deutschlands* (Social Democratic Party of Germany)
SO	Senior Officer
SS	*Schutzstaffel* (Nazi Defence Corps)
StA	*Staatsanwalt(schaft)* (prosecutor, public prosecution department)
StA	*Staatsarchiv* (state archive)
StAnw	*Staatsanwaltschaft* (public prosecution department)
StGB	*Strafgesetzbuch* (German Penal Code)
StPO	*Strafprozessordnung* (Code of Penal Procedures)
TNA	The National Archives (Kew, United Kingdom)
USA	*Vereinigte Staaten von Amerika* (United States of America)
USGCC	United States Group, Control Council
USFET	United States Forces, European Theater
VfZ	*Vierteljahrshefte für Zeitgeschichte*
VGH	*Volksgerichtshof* (People's Court)
VO	*Verordnung* (statutory order)
ZAC	Zonal Advisory Council (*Zonenbeirat*)
ZECO	Zonal Executive Control Office
ZJA	*Zentral-Justizamt* (Central Legal Office, Central Judicial Authority for the British Zone)
ZStW	*Zeitschrift für die gesamte Strafrechtswissenschaft*

Archives

Archives de l'occupation française en Allemagne et en Autriche (AOFAA), Colmar
AJ: Affaires Judiciaires

National Archives and Records Administration (NARA), College Park
RG 260: OMGUS, Legal Division;
OMGBR, Legal Division
OMGBY, Legal Division
OMGH, Legal Division
OMGWB, Legal Division

The National Archives (TNA) (Public Record Office), Kew
FO 1060 Foreign Office, Legal Division

Federal Archives at Koblenz (Bundesarchiv Koblenz (BAK))
Z 1: Länderrat der amerikanisch besetzten Zone
Z 21: Zentral-Justizamt für die Britische Zone (Central Legal Office)
Z 34: Deutsche Rechtsabteilung bei der britischen Militärregierung
Z 38: Oberster Gerichtshof für die Britische Zone (Supreme Court for the British Zone)

Federal Commissioner for the Former East German State Security Records, Berlin (Bundesbeauftragter für die Stasi-Unterlagen (BStU), Berlin)
Branches: Berlin, Chemnitz, Cottbus, Dresden, Erfurt, Frankfurt/Oder, Gera, Halle, Leipzig, Magdeburg, Neubrandenburg, Potsdam, Rostock, Schwerin, Suhl

Main State Archive Düsseldorf; Branch Archive Schloss Kalkum
State Prosecutors Aachen, Bonn, Duisburg, Düsseldorf, Essen, Kleve, Köln, Krefeld, Mönchengladbach, Wuppertal; prosecutors general Düsseldorf and Köln; General files Ministry of Justice Northrhine-Westphalia

Main State Archive München
Ministry of Justice, Bavaria (MJu)

Main State Archive Wiesbaden
State prosecutors Frankfurt am Main, Hanau, Limburg, Wiesbaden; prosecutor general Frankfurt am Main

Ministry of Justice, Bavaria

Land Archive Schleswig-Holstein
State Prosecutors Flensburg, Itzehoe, Kiel, Lübeck; Prosecutor General Schleswig

Main Land Archive Koblenz
State Prosecutors Bad Kreuznach, Koblenz, Trier; Prosecutor General Koblenz

State Archive Augsburg
State Prosecutors Augsburg, Memmingen, Kempten

State Archive Aurich
State Prosecutor Aurich

State Archive Bamberg
State Prosecutors Bamberg, Bayreuth, Hof; Prosecutor General Bamberg; High Court Bamberg

State Archive Bückeburg
State Prosecutor Bückeburg

State Archive Coburg
State Prosecutor Coburg

State Archive Hamburg
State Prosecutor Hamburg; Prosecutor General Hamburg

State Archive München
State Prosecutors München I (city), München II (county), Traunstein; Prosecutor General München

State Archive Nürnberg
State Prosecutors Ansbach, Nürnberg-Fürth; Prosecutor General Nürnberg

State Archive Oldenburg
State Prosecutor Oldenburg; Prosecutor General Oldenburg

State Archive Osnabrück
State Prosecutor Osnabrück

State Archive Sigmaringen
State Prosecutors Hechingen, Ravensburg, Rottweil, Tübingen

State Archive Stade
State Prosecutors Stade, Verden

State Archive Wolfenbüttel
State Prosecutor Braunschweig; Prosecutor General Braunschweig

State Archive Würzburg
State Prosecutor Würzburg

Institute for Contemporary History (IfZ-Archiv)
Database "Die Verfolgung von NS-Verbrechen durch deutsche Justizbehörden seit 1945. Datenbank aller Strafverfahren und Inventar der Verfahrensakten," compiled on behalf of the Institute for Contemporary History Munich – Berlin by Andreas Eichmüller and Edith Raim.
Holding ED 120: Wilhelm Hoegner

Holding ED 125: Theodor Spitta
Holding G: Gerichtsakten
Holding MA 1304: OMGUS Opinion Surveys
Holding PA: Presseausschnitte

Joint Gazettes of the Occupation Authorities

Amtsblatt der Alliierten Hohen Kommission; Amtsblatt des Kontrollrats in Deutschland; Amtsblatt der Militärregierung Deutschland. Amerikanisches Kontrollgebiet; Amtsblatt der Militärregierung Deutschland. Britisches Kontrollgebiet; Amtsblatt des französischen Oberkommandos in Deutschland/Journal Officiel du Commandement en Chef Français en Allemagne – Gouvernment Militaire de la Zone Française d'Occupation

Sammlung der vom Alliierten Kontrollrat und der amerikanischen Militärregierung erlassenen Proklamationen, Gesetze, Verordnungen, Befehle

Legal Gazettes

American Zone
Amts-, Gesetz, Regierungs- und Verordnungsblätter (Bayern, Bremen, Hessen, Württemberg-Baden)

British Zone
Amts, Gesetz-, Justiz-, Mitteilungs- und Verordnungsblätter (Hamburg, Niedersachsen, Nordrhein-in-Westfalen, Schleswig-Holstein); Zentral-Justizblatt für die Britische Zone

French Zone

Amts-, Gesetz und Verordnungsblätter (Baden, Rheinland-Pfalz, Württemberg-Hohenzollern)

German legal periodicals

Deutsche Rechts-Zeitschrift (DRZ)
Deutsche Richterzeitung (DRiZ)
Juristische Rundschau (JR).
Monatsschrift für deutsches Recht (MDR)
Neue Juristische Wochenschrift (NJW)
Süddeutsche Juristen-Zeitung (SJZ)
Zeitschrift für die gesamte Strafrechtswissenschaft (ZStW)

Newspapers

Aufbau
Jüdisches Gemeindeblatt für die britische Zone – Allgemeine Wochenzeitung der Juden in Deutschland
Neue Zeitung
Rheinische Zeitung
Vorderpfälzer Tagblatt
Westdeutsche Zeitung
Wilhelmshavener Zeitung

Protocols of Regional Diets

Baden, Bayern, Gross-Berlin, Hessen, Niedersachsen, Nordrhein-Westfalen, Rheinland-Pfalz, Schleswig-Holstein, Württemberg-Baden, Württemberg-Hohenzollern

Bibliography

Albrich, Thomas, and Michael Guggenberger. "'Nur selten steht einer dieser November-verbrecher vor Gericht:' Die strafrechtliche Verfolgung der Täter der so genannten 'Reichskristallnacht' in Österreich." In *Holocaust und Kriegsverbrechen vor Gericht. Der Fall Österreich,* edited by Thomas Albrich, Winfried R. Garscha, and Martin F. Polaschek, 26-56. Innsbruck: StudienVerlag, 2006.

Arendt, Hannah. *Besuch in Deutschland*. Berlin: Rotbuch Verlag, 1993.

Bader, Karl S. "Rechtspflege und Verfassung. Zur Denkschrift des Zentral-Justizamts für die Britische Zone." *DRZ* (1949): 1-3.

Bader, Karl S. "Der Wiederaufbau: Tagebuch Juli 1945 bis Juni 1946." In *Gelb-rot-gelbe Regierungsjahre: Badische Politik nach 1945,* edited by Paul Ludwig Weinacht, 33-88. Sigmaringendorf: Regio, 1988.

Bahlmann, Peter. "Verbrechen gegen die Menschlichkeit? Wiederaufbau der Justiz und frühe NS-Prozesse im Nordwesten Deutschlands." PhD diss., University of Oldenburg, 2008.

Bamberger, Heinz Georg, and Johannes Kempf. "Zur Geschichte und Vorgeschichte des Oberlandesgericht Koblenz." In *50 Jahre Oberlandesgericht und Generalstaatsan-waltschaft Koblenz 1996,* 21-61. Frankfurt am Main: Peter Lang, 1996.

Becker, Erhard. "La Justice après 1945." In *L'Allemagne occupée 1945–1949,* edited by Henri Ménudier, 91-98. Paris: PIA, 1989.

Becker, Josef, Theo Stammen, and Peter Waldmann, eds. *Vorgeschichte der Bundesrepublik Deutschland: Zwischen Kapitulation und Grundgesetz*. München: Fink, 1979.

Benz, Wolfgang, ed. *Deutschland unter alliierter Besatzung 1945-1949/55: Ein Handbuch*. Berlin: Akademie Verlag, 1999.

Benz, Wolfgang. *Auftrag Demokratie: Die Gründungsgeschichte der Bundesrepublik und die Entstehung der DDR 1945-1949*. Berlin: Metropol Verlag, 2009.

Benz, Wolfgang. "Die Entnazifizierung der Richter: Justizalltag im Dritten Reich." In *Justizalltag im Dritten Reich*, edited by Bernhard Diestelkamp and Michael Stolleis, 112-130. Frankfurt am Main: Fischer Taschenbuch Verlag, 1988.

Benz, Wolfgang. *Die Gründung der Bundesrepublik: Von der Bizone zum souveränen Staat*. München: Deutscher Taschenbuch Verlag, 1999.

Benz, Wolfgang. *Potsdam 1945: Besatzungsherrschaft und Neuaufbau im Vier-Zonen-Deutschland*. München: Deutscher Taschenbuch Verlag, 2005.

Benz, Wolfgang. *Von der Besatzungsherrschaft zur Bundesrepublik: Stationen einer Staatsgründung 1946-1949*. Frankfurt am Main: Fischer Taschenbuch Verlag, 1984.

Berschel, Holger. *Bürokratie und Terror: Das Judenreferat der Gestapo Düsseldorf 1935-1945*. Essen: Klartext, 2001.

Birke, Adolf M., Almut Bues, and Ulrike Jordan, eds. *Akten der britischen Militärregierung in Deutschland: Sachinventar 1945-1955*. München: K.G. Saur, 1993.

Birke, Adolf M.. *Nation ohne Haus: Deutschland 1945-1961*. Berlin: Siedler, 1989.

Boberach, Heinz. "Die Verfolgung von Verbrechen gegen die Menschlichkeit durch deutsche Gerichte in Nordrhein-Westfalen 1946 bis 1949." In *Themen juristischer Zeitgeschichte: Schwerpunktthema: Recht und Nationalsozialismus,* edited by Franz Josef Düwell and Thomas Vormbaum, 212-231. Baden-Baden: Nomos, 1998.

Broszat, Martin. "Siegerjustiz oder strafrechtliche 'Selbstreinigung': Aspekte der Vergangenheitsbewältigung der deutschen Justiz während der Besatzungszeit 1945-1949." In *Vierteljahrshefte für Zeitgeschichte* 29 (1981): 477-544.

Cobb, Richard. *A Second Identity: Essays on France and French History*. London: Oxford University Press, 1969.

Deuerlein, Ernst. *Deutschland nach dem Zweiten Weltkrieg 1945-1955*. Konstanz: Akademische Verlagsgesellschaft Athenaion Dr. Albert Hachfeld, 1964.

Diestelkamp, Bernhard, and Susanne Jung. "Die Justiz in den Westzonen und der frühen Bundesrepublik." *Aus Politik und Zeitgeschichte* 13 (1989): 19-29.

Diestelkamp, Bernhard. "Die Justiz nach 1945 und ihr Umgang mit der eigenen Vergangenheit." *Rechtshistorisches Journal* 5 (1986): 153-174.

Diestelkamp, Bernhard. "Die Justiz nach 1945 und ihr Umgang mit der eigenen Vergangenheit." In *Justizalltag im Dritten Reich,* edited by Bernhard Diestelkamp and Michael Stolleis, 131-150. Frankfurt am Main: Fischer Taschenbuch Verlag, 1988.

Dördelmann, Katrin. "Denunziationen und Denunziationsopfer – Auseinandersetzungen in der Nachkriegszeit." In *Versteckte Vergangenheit: Über den Umgang mit der NS-Zeit in Köln*, edited by Horst Matzerath, Harald Buhlan, and Barbara Becker-Jákli, 195-231. Cologne: Emons, 1994.

Dorn, Walter L. *Inspektionsreisen in der US-Zone. Notizen, Denkschriften und Erinnerungen aus dem Nachlass*. Stuttgart: Deutsche Verlags-Anstalt, 1973.

Düwell, Kurt. "'Riga ist städtebaulich eine sehr schöne Stadt...:' Die Düsseldorfer Judendeportationen vom Herbst 1941." *Augenblick. Berichte, Informationen und Dokumente der Mahn- und Gedenkstätte Düsseldorf* 20/21 (2002): 13-15.

Düx, Heinz. *Die Beschützer der willigen Vollstrecker: Persönliche Innenansichten der bundesdeutschen Justiz*. Bonn: Pahl-Rugenstein, 2004.

Eberhardt, Albert. "Die Denunziation im Spiegel des Kontrollratsgesetzes Nr. 10 als Verbrechen gegen die Menschlichkeit." Law diss., Ludwig Maximilians University Munich, 1950.

Eichmüller, Andreas. "'Es ist ganz unmöglich, diese Milde zu vertreten:' Die strafrechtliche Verfolgung von NS-Verbrechen im Saarland 1945-1955." In *Last aus tausend Jahren:*

NS-Vergangenheit und demokratischer Aufbruch im Saarstaat, edited by Ludwig Linsmayer, 24-79. Saarbrücken: Saarland Landesarchiv, 2013.

Eichmüller, Andreas. *Keine Generalamnestie: Die strafrechtliche Verfolgung von NS-Verbrechen in der frühen Bundesrepublik*. München: Oldenbourg Wissenschaftsverlag, 2012.

Eichmüller, Andreas. "Die Datenbank des Instituts für Zeitgeschichte München-Berlin zu allen westdeutschen Strafverfahren wegen NS-Verbrechen." In *Vom Recht zur Geschichte: Akten aus NS-Prozessen als Quellen der Zeitgeschichte*, edited by Jürgen Finger, Sven Keller, and Andreas Wirsching, 231-237. Göttingen: Vandenhoeck & Ruprecht, 2009.

Eichmüller, Andreas. "Die Strafverfolgung von NS-Verbrechen durch westdeutsche Justizbehörden seit 1945 – Eine Zahlenbilanz." *Vierteljahrshefte für Zeitgeschichte* 56 (2008): 621-640.

Eichmüller, Andreas. "Die Verfolgung von NS-Verbrechen durch westdeutsche Justizbehörden seit 1945 – Inventarisierung und Teilverfilmung der Verfahrensakten: Ein neues Projekt des Institut für Zeitgeschichte." *Vierteljahrshefte für Zeitgeschichte* 50 (2002): 508-516.

Eitz, Thorsten, and Georg Stötzel. *Wörterbuch der 'Vergangenheitsbewältigung': Die NS-Vergangenheit im öffentlichen Sprachgebrauch*. Hildesheim: Olms, 2007.

Elster, Jon. *Die Akten schliessen. Recht und Gerechtigkeit nach dem Ende von Diktaturen*. Frankfurt am Main: Campus, 2005.

Erdmann, Karl Dietrich. *Das Ende des Reiches und die Entstehung der Republik Österreich, der Bundesrepublik Deutschland und der Deutschen Demokratischen Republik*. München: Deutscher Taschenbuch Verlag, 1999.

Erdsiek, Gerhard. "Strafrecht." *SJZ* (1948): column 35-42.

Eschenburg, Theodor. *Jahre der Besatzung 1945-1949*. Stuttgart: Deutsche Verlagsanstalt, 1983.

Etzel, Matthias. *Die Aufhebung von nationalsozialistischen Gesetzen durch den Alliierten Kontrollrat (1945-1948)*. Tübingen: Mohr Siebeck, 1992.

Felbick, Dieter. *Schlagwörter der Nachkriegszeit 1945-1949*. Berlin: de Gruyter, 2003.

Festschrift zum 275-jährigen Bestehen des Oberlandesgerichts Celle. Celle: Eigenverlag, 1986.

50 Jahre Oberlandesgericht und Generalstaatsanwaltschaft Koblenz 1996, Frankfurt am Main: Peter Lang, 1996

Fischer, Torben, and Matthias N. Lorenz, eds. *Lexikon der 'Vergangenheitsbewältigung' in Deutschland: Debatten- und Diskursgeschichte des Nationalsozialismus nach 1945*. Bielefeld: transcript Verlag, 2007.

Frei, Norbert, ed. *Transnationale Vergangenheitspolitik: Der Umgang mit deutschen Kriegsverbrechen in Europa nach dem Zweiten Weltkrieg*. Göttingen: Wallstein Verlag, 2006.

Frei, Norbert. *Vergangenheitspolitik: Die Anfänge der Bundesrepublik und die NS-Vergangenheit*. München: C.H. Beck, 1996.

Frenzel, Björn Carsten. *Das Selbstverständnis der Justiz nach 1945: Analyse der Rolle der Justiz unter Berücksichtigung der Reden zur Wiedereröffnung der Bundes- und Oberlandesgerichte*. Frankfurt am Main: Peter Lang, 2003.

Freudiger, Kerstin. *Die juristische Aufarbeitung von NS-Verbrechen*. Tübingen: Mohr Siebeck, 2002.

Friedlander, Henry. "Across the Stunde Null: the Continuity of German Law." In *Staatsverbrechen vor Gericht: Festschrift für Christiaan Frederik Rüter zum 65. Geburtstag*, edited by Dick de Mildt, 48-60. Amsterdam: Amsterdam University Press, 2003.

Friedlander, Henry. "The Deportation of German Jews: Post-War German Trials of Nazi Criminals." *Leo Baeck Institute Year Book* 29 (1984): 201-226.

Friedlander, Henry. "The Judiciary and Nazi Criminals in Postwar Germany." *Simon Wiesenthal Center Annual* 1 (1984): 27-44.

Gaab, Jeffery Scott. *"Zusammenbruch und Wiederaufbau:" The Restoration of Justice in Bavaria, 1945-1949*. Stony Brook: State University of New York at Stony Brook, 1992.

Gaab, Jeffery. *Justice Delayed: The Restoration of Justice in Bavaria under American Occupation, 1945-1949*. New York: Peter Lang, 1999.

Garscha, Winfried R., and Claudia Kuretsidis-Haider. "Die strafrechtliche Verfolgung national-sozialistischer Verbrechen – eine Einführung. " In *Holocaust und Kriegsverbrechen vor Gericht. Der Fall Österreich*, edited by Thomas Albrich, Winfried R. Garscha, and Martin F. Polaschek, 11-25. Innsbruck: StudienVerlag, 2006.

Gebhardt, Cord. *Der Fall des Erzberger-Mörders Heinrich Tillessen: Ein Beitrag zur Justizgeschichte nach 1945*. Tübingen: Mohr Siebeck, 1995.

Gilsdorf, Wilhelm. "Franzosenzeit eines Justizministers." In *Das Land Württemberg-Hohenzollern 1945-1952: Darstellungen und Erinnerungen*, edited by Max Gögler and Gregor Richter, 275-278. Sigmaringen: Thorbecke, 1982.

Godau-Schüttke, Klaus-Detlev. *Ich habe nur dem Recht gedient: Die "Renazifizierung" der schleswig-holsteinischen Justiz nach 1945*. Baden-Baden: Nomos, 1993.

Goldberg, Bettina. *Abseits der Metropolen: Die jüdische Minderheit in Schleswig-Holstein*. Neumünster: Wachholtz, 2011.

Grabitz, Helge. *Täter und Gehilfen des Endlösungswahns: Hamburger Verfahren wegen NS-Gewaltverbrechen 1946-1996*. Edited by Justizbehörde Hamburg. Hamburg: Ergebnisse Verlag, 1999.

Graveson, Ronald Harry. "Der Grundsatz 'nulla poena sine lege' und Kontrollratsgesetz Nr. 10." In *MDR* (1947): 278-281.

Greim, Gerhard. "Der Tatbestand des Verbrechens gegen die Menschlichkeit in der Rechtsprechung der Nürnberger Gerichtshöfe unter Hinweis auf die hiervon abweichende Rechtsprechung deutscher Gerichte." Law diss., Munich, 1951.

Greve, Michael. *Der justitielle und rechtspolitische Umgang mit den NS-Gewaltverbrechen in den sechziger Jahren*. Frankfurt am Main: Peter Lang, 2001.

Gross, Joachim. *Die deutsche Justiz unter französischer Besatzung 1945-1949: Der Einfluss der französischen Militärregierung auf die Wiedererrichtung der deutschen Justiz in der französischen Besatzungszone*. Baden-Baden: Nomos, 2007.

Gruchmann, Lothar. "'Reichskristallnacht' und Justiz im 'Dritten Reich.'" *NJW* (1988): 2856-2861.

Güde, Max. "Die Anwendung des Kontrollratsgesetzes Nr. 10 durch die deutschen Gerichte." *DRZ* (1947): 111-118.

Haehling von Lanzenauer, Reiner. "Das Oberlandesgericht Karlsruhe und sein Präsident Max Silberstein," *Zeitschrift für die Geschichte des Oberrheins* 151 (2003): 479-492.

Haensel, Carl. "Zur Auslegung des Kontrollratsgesetzes Nr. 10." *NJW* (1947/1948): 55-57.

Hauschildt, Dietrich. "Vom Judenboykott zum Judenmord: Der 1. April 1933 in Kiel." In *"Wir bauen das Reich": Aufstieg und erste Herrschaft des Nationalsozialismus in Schleswig-Holstein*, edited by Erich Hoffmann and Peter Wulf, 335-360. Neumünster: Wachholtz Verlag, 1983.

Haverkamp, Alfred and Friedrich Prinz, eds. *Gebhardt: Handbuch der deutschen Geschichte, vol. 1*. Stuttgart: Klett-Cotta Verlag, 2004.

Heike, Irmtraud. "Ehemalige KZ-Aufseherinnen in westdeutschen Strafverfahren." In *Schuldig: NS-Verbrechen vor deutschen Gerichten: Beiträge zur Geschichte der nationalsozialis-*

tischen Verfolgung in Norddeutschland, edited by KZ-Gedenkstätte Neuengamme, 89-101. Bremen: Edition Temmen, 2005.

Heilbronn, Wolfgang. "Der Aufbau der nordrhein-westfälischen Justiz in der Zeit von 1945 bis 1948/9." In *50 Jahre Justiz in Nordrhein-Westfalen*, edited by Justizministerium des Landes NRW, 1-59. Düsseldorf: Justizministerium des Landes NRW, 1996.

Hodenberg, Hodo Freiherr von. "Zur Anwendung des Kontrollratsgesetzes Nr. 10 durch deutsche Gerichte." *SJZ* (1947): column 113-122.

Hoffmann, Dierk. *Nachkriegszeit: Deutschland 1945-1949.* Darmstadt: Wissenschaftliche Buchgesellschaft, 2012.

Hoffmann, Friedrich. *Die Verfolgung der nationalsozialistischen Gewaltverbrechen in Hessen.* Baden-Baden: Nomos, 2001.

Hottes, Christiane. *Zum Aufbau der Justiz in den Oberlandesgerichtsbezirken Düsseldorf, Hamm und Köln in der frühen Nachkriegszeit.* Edited by Justizakademie des Landes Nordrhein-Westfalen. Recklinghausen: Justizministerium des Landes NRW, 1995.

Hurwitz, Harold. "Die Pressepolitik der Alliierten." In *Deutsche Presse seit 1945,* edited by Harry Pross, 27-55. Bern: Scherz, 1965.

Ihonor, Daniel. *Herbert Ruscheweyh: Verantwortung in schwierigen Zeiten.* Baden-Baden: Nomos, 2006.

Isermann, Edgar and Michael Schlüter, eds. *Justiz und Anwaltschaft in Braunschweig 1879-2004: 125 Jahre Oberlandesgericht und Rechtsanwaltskammer Braunschweig.* Braunschweig: Joh. Heinr. Meyer, 2004.

Jagusch, Heinrich. "Das Verbrechen gegen die Menschlichkeit in der Rechtsprechung des Obersten Gerichtshofs für die Britische Zone." *SJZ* (1949): column 620-624.

Jakobczyk, Mandy. "'Das Verfahren ist einzustellen:' Staatsanwaltschaftliche Ermittlungsverfahren wegen nationalsozialistischer Gewaltverbrechen in Schleswig-Holstein bis 1965: Überblick auf der Basis eines empirisch-quantifizieren Ansatzes". In *Demokratische Geschichte* 15 (2003): 239-290.

Johannsen, Uwe. "Zum Problem der Strafbarkeit von Denunziationen nach dem Kontrollratsgesetz 10." Law diss., University of Hamburg, 1948.

Kewer, L. "Aus der Geschichte des Oberlandesgerichts Hamm." In *Rechtspflege zwischen Rhein und Weser: Festschrift zum 150-jährigen Bestehen des Oberlandesgerichts Hamm*, edited by Verein für Rechtgeschichte im Gebiet des Oberlandesgerichts Hamm, 37-120. Hamm: Verein für Rechtgeschichte im Gebiet des Oberlandesgerichts Hamm, 1970.

Kiesselbach, Wilhelm. "Zwei Probleme aus dem Gesetz Nr. 10 des Kontrollrats." *MDR* (1947): 2-6.

Klefisch, Theodor. "Die NS-Denunziation in der Rechtsprechung des Obersten Gerichtshofes für die britische Zone." *MDR* (1949): 324-329.

Klessmann, Christoph. *Die doppelte Staatsgründung: Deutsche Geschichte 1945-1955.* Göttingen: Vandenhoeck & Ruprecht, 1982.

Koessler, Maximilian. "American War Crimes Trials in Europe." *The Georgetown Law Journal* 39 (1950/1951): 18-112.

Korden, Ralf. "Wiederaufbau der Justiz im Landgerichtsbezirk Koblenz." *Jahrbuch für westdeutsche Landesgeschichte* 31 (2005): 437-508.

Kulka, Otto D., and Eberhard Jäckel, eds. *Die Juden in den geheimen NS-Stimmungsberichten 1933-1945.* Düsseldorf: Droste Verlag, 2004.

Lachmann, Werner. "Die Denunziation unter besonderer Berücksichtigung des Kontrollratsgesetzes Nr. 10." Law diss., Ludwig Maximilians University Munich, 1951.

Lange, Richard. "Das Kontrollratsgesetz Nr. 10 in Theorie und Praxis." *DRZ* (1948): 155-161.
Lange, Richard. "Das Kontrollratsgesetz Nr. 10 und deutsches Recht." *DRZ* (1948): 185-193.
Lange, Richard. "Zum Denunziantenproblem." *SJZ* (1948): column 302-311.
Lasker-Wallfisch, Anita. *Ihr sollt die Wahrheit erben: Die Cellistin von Auschwitz: Erinnerungen*. Reinbek bei Hamburg: rororo, 2000.
Laurien, Ingrid. *Politisch-kulturelle Zeitschriften in den Westzonen 1945-1949: Ein Beitrag zur politischen Kultur der Nachkriegszeit*. Frankfurt am Main: Peter Lang, 1991.
Lechleitner, Hubert. "Das Verbrechen gegen die Menschlichkeit in Theorie und Praxis." Law diss., University of Marburg, 1951.
Loewenberg, Peter. "The Kristallnacht as a Public Degradation Ritual." *Leo Baeck Institute Year-book* 32 (1987): 309-323.
Loewenstein, Karl. "Justice." In *Governing Postwar Germany*, edited by Edward H. Litchfield, 236-262. Ithaca: Cornell University Press, 1953.
Loewenstein, Karl. "Reconstruction of the Administration of Justice in American-Occupied Germany." *Harvard Law Review* 61 (1948): 419-467.
Löhnig, Martin, ed. *Zwischenzeit: Rechtsgeschichte der Besatzungsjahre*. Regenstauf: Gietl Verlag, 2011.
Maier, Regina. *NS-Kriminalität vor Gericht: Strafverfahren vor den Landgerichten Marburg und Kassel 1945-1955*. Darmstadt: Hessische Historische Kommission Darmstadt, 2009.
Meisenberg, Michael, ed. *200 Jahre Appellationsgericht/Oberlandesgericht Bamberg: Festschrift*. München: C.H. Beck, 2009.
Meyer, [no first name given]. "Das Kontrollratsgesetz" Nr. 10 in der Praxis der deutschen Strafgerichte." *MDR* (1947): 110-112.
Meyer, Paul. "'Die Gleichschaltung kann weitergehen!:' Das Kriegsende in den nördlichen Emslandlagern und der falsche Hauptmann Willi Herold im Spiegel britischer und deutscher Gerichts- und Ermittlungsakten." In *Die frühen Nachkriegsprozesse: Beiträge zur Geschichte der nationalsozialistischen Verfolgung in Norddeutschland, vol. 3*, edited by Kurt Buck, 209-213. Bremen: Edition Temmen, 1997.
Meyrowitz, Henri. *La répression par les tribunaux allemands des crimes contre l'humanité et de l'appartenance à une organisation criminelle en application de la loi no. 10 du Conseil de Contrôle Allié*. Paris: Librairie générale et de jurisprudence, 1960.
Miquel, Marc von. *Ahnden oder amnestieren?: Westdeutsche Justiz und Vergangenheitspolitik in den sechziger Jahren*. Göttingen: Wallstein Verlag, 2004.
Müller, Ingo. *Furchtbare Juristen: Die unbewältigte Vergangenheit unserer Justiz*. München: Kindler Verlag, 1987.
Müller, Walter. "Die Verfolgung von NS-Strafsachen im OLG-Bezirk Oldenburg." In *175 Jahre Oberlandesgericht Oldenburg: 1814 Oberappellationsgericht, Oberlandesgericht 1989: Festschrift*, 373-385. Köln: Heymanns, 1989.
Münchbach, Werner, ed. *Festschrift 200 Jahre Badisches Oberhofgericht – Oberlandesgericht Karlsruhe*. Heidelberg: C.F. Müller, 2003.
Nachama, Andreas, Uwe Neumärker, and Hermann Simon, eds. *Fire!: Anti-Jewish Terror on "Kristallnacht" in November 1938*. Berlin: Topography of Terror Foundation, 2008.
Nadler, Ekhard. "Deutsches Recht vor dem Court of Appeal in Herford." *MDR* (1949): 17-18.
1948-1998. 50 Jahre Schleswig-Holsteinisches Oberlandesgericht in Schleswig. Aufsätze und Erinnerungen, Schleswig: Schleswiger Gesellschaft Justiz + Kultur e.V., 1998.
Napoli, Joseph F. "Denazification from an American's Viewpoint." *Annals of the American Academy of Political and Social Science* 264 (1949): 115-123.

Naumann, Klaus, ed. *Nachkrieg in Deutschland*. Hamburg: Hamburger Edition, 2001.
Niermann, Hans-Eckhard. "Zwischen Amnestie und Anpassung: Die Entnazifizierung der Richter und Staatsanwälte des Oberlandesgerichtsbezirks Hamm 1945 bis 1950." In *50 Jahre Justiz in Nordrhein-Westfalen,* edited by Justizministerium des Landes NRW, 61-94. Düsseldorf: Justizministerium des Landes NRW, 1996.
Nobleman, Eli E. "The Administration of Justice in the United States Zone of Germany," *Federal Bar Journal* 8 (1946): 70-97.
Obst, Dieter. *"Reichskristallnacht": Ursachen und Verlauf des antisemitischen Pogroms vom November 1938*. Frankfurt am Main: Peter Lang, 1991.
Olenhusen, Peter Götz von, ed. *300 Jahre Oberlandesgericht Celle*. Göttingen: Vandenhoeck & Ruprecht, 2011.
100 Jahre Oberlandesgericht Frankfurt am Main; 1879-1979. Frankfurt am Main: Eigenverlag, 1979.
Parisius, Bernhard, and Astrid Parisius. "'Rassenschande' in Norden: Zur Geschichte von zwei Fotos, die das Bild Jugendlicher von der NS-Zeit prägen." *Ostfreesland: Kalender für Ostfriesland, Norden* (2003): 129-137.
Paulsen, Sven, ed. *175 Jahre pfälzisches Oberlandesgericht: 1815 Appellationshof, Oberlandesgericht 1990: Festschrift*. Neustadt an der Weinstrasse: Meininger, 1990.
Pendaries, Yveline. *Les Procés de Rastatt 1946-1954: Le jugement des crimes de guerre en zone française d'occupation en Allemagne*. Bern: Peter Lang, 1995.
Pendas, Devin. "Retroactive Law and Proactive Justice: Debating Crimes against Humanity in Germany, 1945-1950." *Central European History* 43 (2010): 438-463.
Peschel-Gutzeit, Lore Maria, ed. *Das Nürnberger Juristen-Urteil von 1947: Historischer Zusammenhang und aktuelle Bezüge*. Baden-Baden: Nomos, 1996.
Potthoff, Heinrich and Rüdiger Wenzel, eds. *Handbuch politischer Institutionen und Organisationen 1945-1949*. Düsseldorf: Droste Verlag, 1983.
Radbruch, Gustav. "Gesetzliches Unrecht und übergesetzliches Recht." *SJZ* (1946): column 105-108.
Radbruch, Gustav. "Zur Diskussion über die Verbrechen gegen die Menschlichkeit." *SJZ Sondernummer* (1947): column 131-136.
Raim, Edith. *Justiz zwischen Diktatur und Demokratie: Wiederaufbau und Ahndung von NS-Verbrechen in Westdeutschland 1945-1949*. München: Oldenbourg Wissenschaftsverlag, 2013.
Raim, Edith. "'So that everyone... gets the punishment he or she deserves.': The legal prosecution of 'Reichskristallnacht' crimes by the West German judiciary after 1945." In *Fire!: Anti-Jewish Terror on "Kristallnacht" in November 1938*, edited by Andreas Nachama, Uwe Neumärker, and Hermann Simon, 146-153. Berlin: Topography of Terror Foundation, 2008.
Rechtspflege zwischen Rhein und Weser. Festschrift zum 150-jährigen Bestehen des Oberlandesgerichts Hamm, Hamm: Verein für Rechtsgeschichte im Gebiet des Oberlandesgerichts Hamm e.V. in Hamm, 1970.
Reuss, Ernst. *Berliner Justizgeschichte: Eine rechtstatsächliche Untersuchung zum strafrechtlichen Justizalltag in Berlin von 1945-1952, dargestellt anhand der Strafgerichtsbarkeit des Amtsgerichts Berlin-Mitte*. Berlin: Berliner Wissenschafts-Verlag, 2000.
Reuss, Ernst. *Vier Sektoren – eine Justiz: Berliner Justiz in der Nachkriegszeit*. Berlin: Berliner Wissenschafts-Verlag, 2003.

Richter, Walther. "Die Errichtung des Hanseatischen Oberlandesgerichts in Bremen." *Zeitschrift für Sozialreform: Festschrift für Harry Rohwer-Kahlmannn* 29 (1983): 573-590.

Richter, Walther. *Die Organisation der ordentlichen Gerichte in der Enklave Bremen 1945-1947*. Bremen: Senator für Justiz und Verfassung, 1990.

Rothenberger, Curt, ed. *Das Hanseatische Oberlandesgericht: Gedenkschrift zu seinem 60jährigen Bestehen*. Hamburg: Hanseatische Verlagsanstalt, 1939.

Rottleuthner, Hubert. *Karrieren und Kontinuitäten deutscher Justizjuristen vor und nach 1945*. Berlin: Berliner Wissenschafts-Verlag, 2010.

Rüping, Hinrich. *Staatsanwälte und Parteigenossen: Haltungen der Justiz zur nationalsozialistischen Vergangenheit zwischen 1945 und 1949 im Bezirk Celle*. Baden-Baden: Nomos, 1994.

Ruscheweyh, Herbert. "Die Entwicklung der hanseatischen Justiz nach der Kapitulation bis zur Errichtung des Zentral-Justizamtes." *Festschrift für Wilhelm Kiesselbach zu seinem 80. Geburtstag*, edited by Zentral-Justizamt für die Britische Zone, 37-71. Hamburg: Gesetz und Recht Verlag, 1947.

Rüter, Christiaan F. and Adelheid L. Rüter-Ehlermann. *Justiz und NS-Verbrechen: Sammlung deutscher Strafurteile wegen nationalsozialistischer Tötungsverbrechen 1945-1966*. Amsterdam: University Press Amsterdam, 1968.

Rüter, Christiaan F. and Dirk W. de Mildt, eds. *Die westdeutschen Strafverfahren wegen nationalsozialistischer Tötungsverbrechen 1945-1997: Eine systematische Verfahrensbeschreibung mit Karten und Registern*. Amsterdam: APA-Holland University Press, 1998.

Rüter, Christiaan F. "Das Gleiche – aber anders: Die Strafverfolgung von Kriegsverbrechen im deutsch-deutschen Vergleich," *Deutschland-Archiv* 43 (2010): 213-222.

Rüter, Christiaan F. "Ost- und westdeutsche Prozesse gegen die Verantwortlichen für die Deportation der Juden: Das Beispiel der Kölner Gestapo." In *NS-Unrecht vor Kölner Gerichten*, edited by Anne Klein and Jürgen Wilhem, 45-56, 225-228. Köln: Greven, 2003.

Scholz, Friedrich. *Berlin und seine Justiz: Geschichte des Kammergerichtsbezirks 1945-1980*. Berlin: de Gruyter, 1982.

Schönke, Adolf. "Grundsätzliche strafrechtliche Fragen des KRG 10 im ausländischen Schrifttum." *NJW* (1947/1948): 673-675.

Schütz, Hans. *Justitia kehrt zurück: Der Aufbau einer rechtsstaatlichen Justiz nach dem Zusammenbruch 1945*. Bamberg: Fränkischer Tag, 1987.

Schwarz, Hans-Peter: "Die ausgebliebene Katastrophe. Eine Problemskizze zur Geschichte der Bundesrepublik." In *Den Staat denken. Theodor Eschenburg zum Fünfundachtzigsten*, edited by Hermann Rudolph, 151-174. Berlin: Siedler, 1990.

Seibert, Claus. "Abschied vom KRG 10." *NJW* (1952): 251-252.

Spender, Stephen. *Deutschland in Ruinen: Ein Bericht*. Frankfurt am Main: Suhrkamp, 1998.

Spitta, Theodor. *Neuanfang auf Trümmern: Die Tagebücher des Bremer Bürgermeisters Theodor Spitta 1945-1947: Biographische Quellen zur deutschen Geschichte nach 1945*. Edited by Ursula Büttner and Angelika Voss-Louis. München: Oldenbourg Wissenschaftsverlag, 1992.

Steininger, Rolf. *Deutsche Geschichte: Darstellung und Dokumente in vier Bänden*. Frankfurt am Main: Fischer Taschenbuch Verlag, 2002.

Stein-Stegemann, Hans Konrad. "Das Problem der 'Nazi-Juristen' in der Hamburger Nachkriegsjustiz 1945-1965." In *Karrieren und Kontinuitäten deutscher Justizjuristen vor und nach 1945*, edited by Hubert Rottleuthner, 309-380. Berlin: Berliner Wissenschafts-Verlag, 2010.

Steinweis, Alan E. *Kristallnacht 1938*. Cambridge: Harvard University Press, 2009.
Stilz, Eberhard, ed. *Das Oberlandesgericht Stuttgart, 125 Jahre, 1879-2004*. Villingen-Schwenningen: Neckar-Verlag, 2004.
Stolleis, Michael. "Rechtsordnung und Justizpolitik 1945-1949." In *Europäisches Rechtsdenken in Geschichte und Gegenwart: Festschrift für Helmut Coing zum 70. Geburtstag*, edited by Norbert Horn, 383-407. München: C.H. Beck, 1982.
Strucksberg, Georg. "Zur Anwendung des Kontrollratsgesetzes Nr. 10." *DRZ* (1947): 277-280.
Szanajda, Andrew. "The Restoration of Justice in Hesse, 1945-1949." PhD diss., McGill University Montreal, 1997.
Szanajda, Andrew. *The Restoration of Justice in Postwar Hesse, 1945-1949*. Lanham: Lexington Books, 2007.
Tausch, Volker. *Max Güde (1902-1984): Generalbundesanwalt und Rechtspolitiker*. Baden-Baden: Nomos, 2002.
Turner, Ian. "Research on the British Occupation of Germany." In *Reconstruction in Post-War Germany: British Occupation Policy and the Western Zones, 1945-55*, edited by Ian D. Turner, 327-358. Oxford: Berg, 1989.
250 Jahre Oberlandesgericht Celle 1711-1961, Celle: Pohl, 1961.
Ueberschär, Gerd R., ed. *Der Nationalsozialismus vor Gericht: Die alliierten Prozesse gegen Kriegsverbrecher und Soldaten 1943-1952*. Frankfurt am Main: Fischer Taschenbuch Verlag, 1999.
Ueberschär, Gerd R. and Rolf-Dieter Müller. *1945. Das Endes des Krieges*. Darmstadt: Primus Verlag, 2005.
Vogel, Walter. "Organisatorische Bemühungen um die Rechtseinheit in den westlichen Besatzungszonen 1945-1948." In *Aus der Arbeit des Bundesarchivs: Beiträge zum Archivwesen, zur Quellenkunde und Zeitgeschichte*, edited by Heinz Boberach and Hans Booms, 456-479. Boppard: Boldt, 1977.
Vogel, Walter. *Westdeutschland 1945-1950: Der Aufbau von Verfassungs- und Verwaltungseinrichtungen über den Ländern der drei westlichen Besatzungszonen*. Vol. 1, *Geschichtlicher Überblick: oberste beratende Stellen und Einrichtungen für Gesetzgebung, Verwaltung und Rechtsprechung; einzelne Verwaltungszweige: Ernährung, Landwirtschaft und Forsten*. Koblenz: Bundesarchiv, 1956.
Vogel, Walter. *Westdeutschland 1945-1950: Der Aufbau von Verfassungs- und Verwaltungseinrichtungen über den Ländern der drei westlichen Besatzungszonen*. Vol. 2, *Einzelne Verwaltungszweige: Wirtschaft, Marshallplan, Statistik*. Boppard am Rhein: Harald Boldt Verlag, 1964.
Warmbrunn, Paul. "Wiederaufbau der Justiz nach Kriegsende." In *Beiträge zu 50 Jahren Geschichte des Landes Rheinland-Pfalz*, edited by Heinz-Günther Borck, 201-218. Koblenz: Verlag der Landesarchivverwaltung Rheinland, 1997.
Wassermann, Rudolf, ed. *Justiz im Wandel der Zeit: Festschrift des Oberlandesgerichts Braunschweig*. Braunschweig: Joh. Heinr. Meyer, 1989.
Weber, Hellmuth von. "Das Verbrechen gegen die Menschlichkeit in der Rechtsprechung." *MDR* (1949): 261-266.
Wehler, Hans-Ulrich. *Deutsche Gesellschaftsgeschichte, vol. 4: Vom Beginn des Ersten Weltkriegs bis zur Gründung der beiden deutschen Staaten 1914-1949*. München: C.H. Beck, 2003.

Weinke, Annette. *Die Verfolgung von NS-Tätern im geteilten Deutschland: Vergangenheitsbewältigung 1949-1969 oder: Eine deutsch-deutsche Beziehungsgeschichte im Kalten Krieg.* Paderborn: Ferdinand Schöningh Verlag, 2002.

Weisz, Christoph, ed. *OMGUS-Handbuch: Die amerikanische Militärregierung in Deutschland 1945-1949.* München: Oldenbourg Wissenschaftsverlag, 1994.

Wengst, Udo. *Thomas Dehler, 1897-1967: Eine politische Biographie.* München: Oldenbourg Wissenschaftsverlag, 1997.

Wenzlau, Joachim Reinhold. *Der Wiederaufbau der Justiz in Nordwestdeutschland 1945-1949.* Königstein: Athenäum, 1979.

Werkentin, Falco. *Die Restauration der deutschen Polizei: Innere Rüstung von 1945 bis zur Notstandsgesetzgebung.* Frankfurt am Main: Campus Verlag, 1984.

Werner, Wolfhart. "Die ersten Entscheidungen des OGH zum Kontrollratsgesetz 10." *NJW Heft* 5 (1949): 170-174.

Wiesen, Heinrich, ed. *Fünfundsiebzig Jahre Oberlandesgericht Düsseldorf: Festschrift.* Köln: Heymanns, 1981.

Wiesen, Heinrich. "Das Oberlandesgericht von 1945 bis zur Gegenwart." In *Fünfundsiebzig Jahre Oberlandesgericht Düsseldorf: Festschrift*, edited by Heinrich Wiesen, 85-116. Köln: Heymanns, 1981.

Wildt, Michael. *Volksgemeinschaft als Selbstermächtigung: Gewalt gegen Juden in der deutschen Provinz 1919 bis 1939.* Hamburg: Hamburger Edition, 2007.

Wimmer, August. "Die Bestrafung von Humanitätsverbrechen und der Grundsatz 'nullum crimen sine lege'." *SJZ Sondernummer* (1947): column 123-132.

Winkler, Heinrich August. *Der lange Weg nach Westen, vol. 2: Deutsche Geschichte vom "Dritten Reich" bis zur Wiedervereinigung.* München: C.H. Beck, 2000.

Wirsching, Andreas. "Jüdische Friedhöfe in Deutschland 1933-1957." *Vierteljahrshefte für Zeitgeschichte* 50 (2002): 1-40.

Wolffram, Josef, and Adolf Klein, eds. *Recht und Rechtspflege in den Rheinlanden.* Köln: Wienand, 1969.

Wrobel, Hans. *Verurteilt zur Demokratie: Justiz und Justizpolitik in Deutschland 1945-1949.* Heidelberg: Decker & Müller, 1989.

Wrobel, Hans. "Wie die Täter nach 1945 zur Verantwortung gezogen wurden." In *"Reichskristallnacht" in Bremen: Vorgeschichte, Hergang und gerichtliche Bewältigung des Pogroms vom 9. /10. November 1938*, edited by Der Senator für Justiz und Verfassung der Freien Hansestadt Bremen, 72-92. Bremen: Steintor, 1988.

Zimmer, Erhard. *Die Geschichte des Oberlandesgerichts in Frankfurt am Main.* Frankfurt am Main: Waldemar Kramer, 1976.

Zimmermann, Volker. *NS-Täter vor Gericht: Düsseldorf und die Strafprozesse wegen nationalsozialistischer Gewaltverbrechen.* Düsseldorf: Justizministerium des Landes NRW, 2001.

Index of Names

Adenauer, Konrad 142
Albath, Walter 300
Asthalter, Wilhelm 159

Baab, Heinrich 285, 286
Bader, Karl Siegfried 1, 7, 233, 317
Beyerle, Josef 31, 32, 34, 71, 77, 83
Bezold, Karl 281
Bock, Gerhart 168
Boeckmann, Eugen 103
Böhm, Bruno 284
Bollinger, Heino 54
Boulton, W.W. 38, 88, 92, 125, 140, 141, 142, 147, 148, 151
Bovensiepen, Otto 293
Breder, Reinhard 298
Bremer, Hans 289
Bürckel, Josef 168, 266, 297

Carstens, Karl 80
Clay, Lucius D. 144, 145

Dehler, Thomas 69, 74, 84, 252, 326
Dengler, Georg 284
Dörmann, Karl 89

Ebert, Jean 270
Ehard, Hans 84, 145
Eichholz, Max 163
Eichmann, Adolf 280, 293
Ellenbogen, Julius 102
Ellinghaus, Wilhelm 1, 53
Engels, Heinrich 287, 288

Fahy, Charles 21, 71
Fechenbach, Felix 158
Fecht, Hermann 102
Filbinger, Hans 107
Furby, Charles 23, 103, 106

Goebbels, Joseph 93
Goerdeler, Carl 124
Gog, Franz 270, 271, 272, 273
Göttsche, Claus 289

Gramowski, Ernst 298
Güde, Max 6, 126, 135, 283, 320, 325
Gustloff, Wilhelm 165, 196

Harbough, J. L. 143, 144, 145
Hartmann, Richard 293, 294
Heinen, Heinrich 295
Heinrich, Hans 69, 70
Heinrichsmeier, Christian 288, 289
Hellenbroich, Heinz 300
Henderson, Christopher Mayhew 146
Hermsen, Ernst 91, 92, 93
Hill, Philipp 277
Hinselmann, Hans 122
Hodenberg, Hodo von 89, 93, 94, 97, 98, 135, 136, 137, 321
Hoegner, Wilhelm 50, 72, 76, 152, 226, 315
Holz, Karl 70, 169

Ilkow, Johann 253
Isselhorst, Erich 300

Jackson, Richard J. 78, 82, 128
Johnson, Robert W. 54, 80, 81, 129
Juncker, Raymond 149

Kaisen, Wilhelm 62, 63, 80
Kiesselbach, Wilhelm 37, 43, 44, 87, 88, 89, 108, 119, 135, 138, 321, 324
Kirkpatrick, Ivone, Sir 142
Klaas, Walter 92
Koch, Ekhard 43, 44, 95, 144, 145, 191, 296
Konrad, Anton 50, 51, 121, 142, 324
Koppel, Oscar 227
Krapp, Lorenz 67, 68, 69, 74
Kremer, Eduard 7, 41, 42
Kühnast, Wilhelm 89
Kühn, Hermann 289, 290
Kuhnt, Gottfried 88, 89

Laffon, Émile 269, 270
Lebègue, Henri 23
Levi, Albert 102, 165, 172
Lingemann, Heinrich 43, 88, 92

Littman, Edward H. 29, 53, 82, 256
Lobmiller, Hans 67, 74, 252
Löser, Friedrich 188

Mansfeld, Wilhelm 88
Manstein, Erich von 146
Martin, Benno 164281, 282, 283
Matschke, Kurt 292, 297, 298, 301
Maydell, Paul von 67
McLendon, Ernest L. 105, 128
Mettgenberg, Wolfgang 43
Meyer, Friedrich Wilhelm 93
Mohr, Robert 284, 298
Moller, Nils 85, 149
Müller, Josef 53, 73, 78, 230
Mussgay, Friedrich 290

Nellmann, Erich 275
Neuberger, Alois 250, 253
Niethammer, Emil 83, 102
Normann, Alexander von 270, 271, 272, 273, 274, 275
Novak, Franz 293

Odenheimer, Emil 102

Priess, Friedrich 43
Pütz, Georg 287

Quabbe, Georg 72, 266

Radbruch, Gustav 135, 136, 323
Rathbone, J. F. W. 22, 23, 26, 36, 37, 41, 43, 44, 50, 51, 80, 87, 89, 92, 93, 94, 95, 97, 98, 99, 100, 121, 124, 132, 133, 134, 139, 146, 147
Raymond, John M. 21, 50, 81, 84, 133, 134, 135, 143, 149, 251, 252
Ritterspacher, Ludwig 107
Rockwell, Alvin J. 21, 51, 61, 64, 71, 72, 131, 132, 143, 252
Rosenwald, Henry M. 72, 130
Rothenberger, Curt 6, 43, 324
Röver, Carl 242
Rudhardt, Alfred 269, 270
Ruscheweyh, Herbert 6, 43, 163, 321, 324

Sachs, Camille 70, 232, 233
Schäfer, Emanuel 291, 292, 297, 301
Schimmel, Alfred 300
Schmid, Richard 70
Schraermayer, Paul 270, 271, 272, 273, 274, 275, 276
Schubert, Herbert 279
Schumm, Friedrich 159
Seither, Karl 78
Silberstein, Max 70, 320
Sölling, Kurt 169
Speidel, Hans 271
Spiegel, Wilhelm 158
Spitta, Theodor 6, 36, 80, 108, 316, 324
Sprinz, Franz 292, 297, 301
Staff, Curt 44, 88, 92, 97, 119, 143
Ständer, Josef 185
Stark, Edmund 255
Stock, Walter 293
Sträter, Artur 99, 230
Suhren, Fritz 150

Thierack, Otto 93
Tuteur, Paul 102

Uhlenhut, Arnold 279

Valentin, Fritz 255
Vates, Heinrich 250, 253
Venter, Kurt 293
Völker, Franz 250, 253

Wagner 266, 291, 297
Wagoner, Murray D. Van 84
Waldbillig, Hermann 286, 287, 288
Weigert, Hans W. 38, 55, 71, 85, 132, 133, 251, 252
Weinkauff, Hermann 253
Wimmer, August 135, 137, 326
Wolf, Richard A. 145, 190, 192, 252, 253

Zinn, Georg August 71, 85
Zürcher, Paul 34, 46, 52

Index of Places

Aachen (Aix-la-Chapelle) 8, 33, 47, 51, 52, 57, 63, 99, 123, 124, 204, 206, 228, 247, 258, 293, 314
Alzenau 233
Amberg 76, 219, 254, 261
Ansbach 68, 69, 78, 164, 165, 166, 167, 180, 184, 190, 194, 215, 216, 242, 254, 299, 315
Aschaffenburg 75, 180, 184, 193, 216, 233, 250
Aurich 11, 123, 160, 162, 180, 181, 189, 195, 196, 198, 199, 217, 220, 225, 244, 245, 258, 315

Bad Ems 100, 177, 178, 202, 213, 233
Baden 4, 6, 8, 11, 22, 23, 31, 32, 34, 40, 46, 50, 52, 56, 61, 65, 66, 70, 71, 76, 77, 78, 79, 82, 83, 84, 85, 100, 101, 102, 104, 105, 107, 108, 109, 116, 126, 127, 128, 130, 134, 144, 149, 150, 152, 207, 226, 248, 257, 262, 266, 280, 297, 312, 316, 317, 318, 320, 321, 323, 324, 325
Baden-Baden 4, 6, 11, 23, 34, 52, 102, 104, 126, 149, 150, 280, 318, 320, 321, 323, 324, 325
Baden-Württemberg 66, 107, 262
Bamberg 5, 31, 40, 46, 47, 55, 58, 67, 68, 69, 70, 73, 74, 83, 84, 152, 161, 180, 183, 189, 190, 193, 203, 223, 224, 226, 246, 250, 251, 252, 253, 264, 265, 280, 281, 315, 322, 324
Bavaria 4, 22, 26, 29, 34, 35, 40, 46, 57, 60, 66, 68, 69, 70, 72, 74, 76, 78, 83, 101, 110, 116, 117, 128, 134, 135, 145, 150, 151, 152, 160, 251, 254, 256, 262, 266, 279, 284, 291, 312, 314, 320
Bayern 8, 180, 316, 317
Bayreuth 46, 161, 182, 183, 193, 280, 281, 315
Berlin 4, 1, 2, 3, 5, 6, 9, 10, 12, 13, 14, 22, 23, 24, 26, 35, 36, 37, 38, 40, 41, 43, 44, 48, 50, 51, 52, 56, 60, 63, 73, 77, 80, 81, 83, 85, 89, 94, 97, 98, 99, 100, 106, 121, 124, 128, 129, 130, 131, 132, 133, 134, 139, 141, 142, 146, 147, 148, 149, 164, 168, 169, 174, 175, 176, 179, 262, 263, 267, 277, 278, 292, 293, 297, 299, 300, 302, 310, 311, 314, 316, 317, 318, 319, 322, 323, 324, 325
Bonn 6, 47, 51, 52, 99, 189, 195, 204, 208, 212, 215, 222, 227, 247, 314, 318
Braunschweig (Brunswick) 5, 8, 13, 14, 16, 39, 41, 44, 51, 59, 88, 89, 90, 92, 94, 95, 97, 119, 139, 315, 321, 325
Bremen 4, 7, 8, 22, 35, 36, 37, 38, 40, 49, 50, 51, 53, 54, 62, 63, 70, 71, 79, 80, 81, 83, 108, 118, 122, 128, 129, 133, 151, 195, 250, 262, 297, 303, 312, 316, 321, 322, 324, 326
Bremerhaven 38, 63, 71, 133
Burgsteinfurt 46

Celle 5, 6, 36, 39, 41, 89, 90, 94, 95, 96, 97, 136, 137, 264, 319, 323, 324, 325

Dachau vi, 44, 102, 115, 116, 143, 161, 162, 166, 169, 176, 206, 244, 249, 250, 255
Darmstadt 3, 11, 40, 47, 49, 57, 151, 225, 245, 246, 250, 255, 267, 284, 291, 292, 294, 298, 300, 321, 322, 325
Deggendorf 132, 151, 189
Düsseldorf 1, 2, 4, 5, 7, 11, 25, 39, 41, 42, 43, 46, 47, 49, 51, 52, 56, 64, 85, 88, 90, 92, 95, 96, 99, 121, 123, 124, 125, 126, 137, 138, 148, 158, 164, 168, 170, 173, 174, 175, 176, 180, 187, 189, 191, 192, 195, 199, 203, 204, 205, 206, 208, 210, 212, 213, 215, 216, 217, 218, 219, 220, 222, 227, 228, 232, 233, 235, 239, 240, 244, 246, 247, 250, 258, 263, 266, 267, 286, 287, 288, 290, 292, 293, 294, 295, 296, 298, 300, 301, 314, 318, 321, 323, 326

Ellwangen 50, 54, 159, 171
Erlangen 48, 281
Esens 181, 258
Essen 47, 49, 50, 51, 52, 62, 90, 91, 99, 217, 220, 227, 266, 295, 314, 318

Flensburg 53, 88, 206, 228, 314
Forchheim 67, 224, 264, 265
Franken (Franconia) 31, 56, 67, 68, 69, 144, 169, 279, 280, 281, 284
Frankenthal 46, 168, 176, 180, 182, 189, 192, 203, 206, 208, 218, 232, 234, 235, 237, 247
Frankfurt am Main 3, 4, 5, 6, 9, 10, 11, 40, 47, 57, 162, 177, 194, 218, 250, 263, 267, 285, 296, 298, 304, 314, 317, 318, 319, 320, 322, 323, 324, 325, 326
Freiburg 1, 29, 34, 40, 55, 57, 102, 190, 233, 272, 273
Fulda 53, 62
Fürth 16, 48, 70, 144, 161, 165, 167, 169, 170, 172, 188, 189, 190, 193, 195, 200, 206, 211, 212, 213, 214, 218, 219, 220, 232, 233, 243, 245, 267, 279, 280, 281, 282, 283, 284, 297, 299, 315

Geisenheim 166, 215, 258
Gelsenkirchen 51, 62, 220, 227
Giessen 49, 57, 60, 64, 81, 164, 179, 180, 182, 183, 189, 236, 254, 255
Gunzenhausen 164

Hadamar 116, 177, 178
Hamburg 5, 6, 7, 11, 13, 16, 25, 29, 33, 36, 37, 38, 39, 41, 42, 43, 44, 50, 53, 54, 55, 65, 71, 79, 88, 89, 92, 95, 96, 108, 117, 121, 122, 123, 124, 126, 133, 138, 140, 147, 150, 161, 163, 197, 204, 248, 255, 259, 262, 263, 266, 289, 297, 309, 315, 316, 320, 321, 322, 323, 324, 326
Hamm 4, 5, 6, 7, 33, 39, 40, 41, 46, 49, 51, 85, 88, 90, 91, 92, 93, 125, 219, 321, 323
Hanau 70, 164, 182, 188, 203, 218, 223, 227, 228, 229, 231, 232, 246, 247, 250, 314
Hannover 13, 25, 33, 59, 65, 89, 90, 92, 93, 94, 96, 97, 121, 124, 139, 174, 179, 232, 288, 289, 290
Hassloch 191, 203
Hechingen 34, 165, 171, 172, 182, 183, 237, 247, 257, 267, 268, 269, 270, 271, 272, 273, 274, 275, 283, 297, 315
Heidenheim 58, 190
Heilbronn 4, 42, 48, 159, 231, 321

Herford 22, 27, 29, 37, 38, 40, 41, 43, 54, 56, 63, 80, 88, 92, 93, 95, 99, 121, 132, 133, 134, 140, 141, 142, 146, 147, 148, 149, 151, 322
Hesse 4, 8, 11, 13, 22, 29, 40, 46, 49, 70, 71, 72, 83, 116, 128, 144, 187, 225, 227, 254, 256, 262, 284, 297, 298, 300, 312, 325
Hettenleidelheim 181

Kaiserslautern 102, 117, 165, 169, 207, 208, 210, 211, 217, 219, 223, 228, 245, 250
Kamp 188, 234
Karlsruhe 5, 40, 70, 105, 162, 207, 208, 250, 320, 322
Kassel 11, 40, 53, 61, 62, 70, 71, 72, 89, 159, 162, 223, 322
Kempten 35, 84, 103, 105, 315
Kiel 39, 52, 53, 55, 88, 89, 94, 117, 158, 159, 174, 247, 314, 320
Kitzingen 56, 250, 283
Koblenz 4, 5, 7, 39, 40, 45, 58, 101, 141, 165, 167, 170, 171, 173, 174, 178, 183, 184, 187, 188, 189, 192, 193, 194, 196, 197, 198, 199, 200, 201, 202, 203, 204, 205, 208, 209, 210, 211, 212, 213, 215, 216, 218, 220, 227, 229, 230, 231, 232, 233, 234, 235, 236, 237, 239, 240, 241, 246, 248, 260, 261, 263, 277, 278, 279, 290, 294, 303, 311, 314, 315, 317, 319, 321, 325
Köln (Cologne) 4, 5, 7, 8, 11, 33, 35, 39, 40, 41, 46, 47, 49, 51, 52, 57, 61, 64, 86, 90, 95, 96, 98, 99, 123, 168, 175, 227, 247, 250, 267, 287, 290, 292, 295, 296, 297, 298, 301, 314, 318, 321, 322, 324, 326
Konstanz (Constance) 2, 34, 46, 54, 56, 126, 318
Kronach 68
Krumbach 197, 203

Laasphe 62
Lampertheim 47
Landau 46, 167, 168, 180, 189, 191, 198, 200, 203, 204, 206, 207, 208, 211, 238, 244, 247, 250, 259
Landstuhl 186, 240
Leer 59, 198

Index of Places — **331**

Limburg 71, 116, 181, 190, 191, 215, 224, 225, 229, 239, 242, 245, 285, 314
Lindau 34, 35, 103, 104, 105
Lübeck 175, 314

Magdeburg 178, 179, 314
Mainz (Mayence) 8, 160, 161, 166, 173, 190, 191, 200, 202, 203, 208, 217, 267, 277
Mannheim 70, 79, 165, 179, 180, 201, 207, 217, 245, 290
Mauthausen 93, 115
Miehlen 186
Mönchengladbach 45, 125, 172, 173, 205, 217, 218, 240, 314
Mosbach 171, 210, 248
München (Munich) vi, 2, 3, 4, 5, 6, 7, 8, 10, 12, 13, 40, 53, 57, 60, 69, 70, 74, 78, 83, 116, 117, 152, 176, 226, 242, 250, 253, 263, 266, 267, 283, 291, 297, 299, 300, 312, 314, 315, 317, 318, 319, 320, 321, 322, 323, 324, 325, 326
Münster 46, 123, 198, 208, 226, 267, 277

Neuss 175
Neustadt 8, 40, 101, 102, 165, 168, 184, 207, 217, 232, 234, 237, 240, 242, 250, 323
Neustift 117
Niedersachsen (Lower Saxony) 1, 13, 29, 33, 39, 41, 53, 59, 90, 110, 123, 124, 126, 139, 140, 147, 262, 288, 316, 317
Nordrhein-Westfalen (North Rhine-Westphalia) 4, 7, 11, 13, 41, 42, 52, 55, 90, 121, 123, 124, 230, 258, 262, 316, 317, 318, 321, 323
Nürnberg (Nuremberg) 2, 5, 14, 16, 40, 43, 47, 48, 69, 70, 73, 78, 83, 84, 115, 117, 119, 129, 142, 143, 144, 152, 157, 158, 160, 161, 162, 163, 164, 165, 166, 167, 169, 170, 172, 176, 178, 180, 188, 189, 190, 193, 194, 195, 196, 200, 206, 210, 211, 212, 213, 214, 215, 216, 218, 219, 220, 226, 227, 232, 233, 239, 242, 243, 245, 250, 254, 255, 256, 261, 263, 267, 279, 280, 281, 282, 283, 284, 297, 299, 300, 315

Oelde 277

Offenbach 209, 225, 291
Offenburg 34, 55, 56, 64, 102, 197, 209, 246
Oldenburg 5, 11, 13, 27, 36, 39, 41, 43, 44, 60, 89, 90, 95, 122, 123, 162, 180, 194, 195, 198, 199, 202, 225, 226, 232, 234, 242, 244, 293, 315, 317, 322
Osann 170, 209, 258
Osnabrück 47, 54, 122, 171, 181, 185, 196, 197, 199, 201, 203, 204, 208, 211, 217, 225, 228, 231, 241, 242, 247, 315

Paderborn 10, 47, 51, 52, 99, 158, 171, 226, 253, 254, 262, 264, 326
Passau 117, 151, 159
Pfalz (Palatinate) 4, 8, 13, 23, 35, 40, 46, 57, 58, 59, 100, 101, 107, 152, 154, 168, 189, 206, 207, 214, 236, 245, 250, 262, 284, 316, 317, 325

Rastatt 117, 149, 150, 323
Ravensbrück 115, 150
Ravensburg 34, 174, 195, 196, 255, 257, 261, 315
Regensburg 16, 78, 176, 184, 196, 227, 250, 280, 284, 299
Rheinland-Pfalz (Rhineland-Palatinate) 4, 316, 317, 325
Rheinland (Rhineland) 4, 8, 13, 23, 35, 57, 58, 59, 65, 74, 100, 154, 198, 227, 236, 262, 294, 316, 317, 325
Rheydt 45, 217
Rottweil 34, 49, 166, 172, 174, 180, 204, 209, 210, 217, 218, 260, 268, 290, 315

Saarbrücken 14, 35, 162, 163, 184, 196, 197, 208, 217, 226, 228, 297, 303, 319
Saarpfalz 168, 266, 297
Saar (Sarre) 13, 14, 26, 35, 36, 59, 100, 101, 107, 127, 152, 168, 184, 206, 207, 228, 257, 269, 276, 297
Sachsenhausen 115, 206, 212, 249, 258
Schleswig-Holstein 11, 25, 29, 33, 39, 41, 52, 57, 65, 88, 90, 94, 96, 108, 117, 121, 124, 126, 140, 147, 148, 154, 158, 159, 174, 175, 206, 228, 247, 262, 297, 314, 316, 317, 320, 321
Schlüchtern 182, 226, 232

Solingen 173, 180, 191, 203, 216, 239, 250, 295
Sprendlingen 173
Stuttgart 3, 5, 30, 31, 32, 34, 40, 70, 79, 83, 103, 116, 171, 174, 267, 268, 269, 290, 291, 297, 318, 319, 320, 325
Tauberbischofsheim 171
Trier (Trèves) 8, 35, 39, 164, 165, 170, 173, 183, 192, 196, 197, 203, 205, 208, 209, 211, 216, 218, 232, 234, 238, 239, 240, 248, 314
Tübingen 10, 31, 34, 40, 47, 48, 55, 102, 103, 104, 183, 209, 210, 257, 261, 269, 272, 275, 276, 315, 319, 320
Ulm 31, 50, 180, 205, 226
Vilshofen 117
Wachenbuchen 187
Waldshut 34, 46
Westphalia 4, 7, 11, 13, 22, 25, 29, 33, 39, 41, 42, 52, 54, 55, 65, 85, 88, 90, 93, 96, 99, 121, 123, 124, 125, 140, 142, 147, 219, 230, 232, 258, 262, 314
Wiesbaden 46, 48, 52, 61, 70, 93, 159, 162, 164, 166, 177, 181, 182, 184, 188, 190, 191, 193, 194, 202, 203, 205, 214, 215, 216, 218, 219, 223, 224, 225, 227, 228, 229, 231, 232, 235, 236, 238, 239, 242, 245, 246, 247, 264, 265, 285, 286, 292, 294, 298, 300, 314
Wuppertal 47, 51, 52, 99, 158, 173, 176, 179, 180, 191, 192, 203, 213, 216, 239, 240, 247, 295, 296, 298, 314
Württemberg 8, 22, 23, 31, 32, 34, 35, 40, 46, 49, 50, 52, 53, 55, 57, 60, 61, 64, 65, 66, 70, 71, 76, 77, 78, 79, 82, 83, 84, 85, 100, 101, 103, 104, 105, 106, 107, 108, 109, 116, 127, 128, 130, 134, 144, 152, 159, 226, 248, 257, 262, 267, 268, 269, 270, 273, 275, 276, 290, 316, 317, 320
Württemberg-Baden 8, 22, 31, 32, 40, 50, 61, 70, 71, 76, 77, 78, 79, 82, 83, 84, 85, 105, 108, 109, 116, 128, 130, 134, 144, 226, 248, 316, 317
Württemberg-Hohenzollern 23, 52, 55, 57, 101, 107, 276, 316, 317, 320
Würzburg 64, 67, 68, 69, 74, 75, 164, 208, 220, 250, 251, 252, 253, 267, 279, 280, 281, 282, 283, 284, 297, 298, 315
Zweibrücken 8, 35, 40, 46, 102, 186, 207, 240

www.ingramcontent.com/pod-product-compliance
Lightning Source LLC
Chambersburg PA
CBHW050851160426
43194CB00011B/2117